P9-DWP-772

100 Years of Anne

Imagining Anne

The Island Scrapbooks of L.M. Montgomery

Elizabeth Rollins Epperly

Foreword by Adrienne Clarkson

Afterword by Dr. Francis W.P. Bolger, CM

PENGUIN
CANADA

PENGUIN CANADA

Published by the Penguin Group

Penguin Group (Canada), 90 Eglinton Avenue East, Suite 700,
Toronto, Ontario, Canada M4P 2Y3 (a division of Pearson Canada Inc.)

Penguin Group (USA) Inc., 375 Hudson Street, New York, New York 10014, U.S.A.
Penguin Books Ltd, 80 Strand, London WC2R 0RL, England
Penguin Ireland, 25 St Stephen's Green, Dublin 2, Ireland (a division of Penguin Books Ltd)
Penguin Group (Australia), 250 Camberwell Road, Camberwell, Victoria 3124, Australia
(a division of Pearson Australia Group Pty Ltd)
Penguin Books India Pvt Ltd, 11 Community Centre, Panchsheel Park, New Delhi – 110 017, India
Penguin Group (NZ), 67 Apollo Drive, Rosedale, North Shore 0745, Auckland, New Zealand
(a division of Pearson New Zealand Ltd)
Penguin Books (South Africa) (Pty) Ltd, 24 Sturdee Avenue, Rosebank, Johannesburg 2196,
South Africa

Penguin Books Ltd, Registered Offices: 80 Strand, London WC2R 0 RL, England

First published 2008

1 2 3 4 5 6 7 8 9 10

Manufactured in Asia. GCC/01

ISBN-13: 978-0-670-06687-2
ISBN-10: 0-670-06687-7

Library and Archives Canada Cataloguing in Publication data available upon request.

Visit the Penguin Group (Canada) website at **www.penguin.ca**

Special and corporate bulk purchase rates available; please see **www.penguin.ca/corporatesales**
or call 1-800-810-3104, ext. 477 or 474

Air Castles

When I am tired of toil and strife
And wearied of pursuing care,
I turn aside from real life
And build a castle in the air.

A wondrous mansion fair and tall,
Where fadeless roses ever bloom,
And sunlit court and stately hall
Are steeped in Araby's perfume.

There music rings its sweetest strain
And endless summer lingers there,
And I am queen and chatelaine
In this, my castle in the air.

Laughter and youth their glamor weave
And Love's an ever welcome guest,
No fears delude, no hopes deceive,
And there is time to dream and rest.

When things go wrong and skies are gray,
Enchantment-led I wander there,
And doff this world of workaday
In my fair castle of the air.

— published in *The Story Paper,* September 24, 1904,
under the pseudonym Joyce Cavendish

L. M. Montgomery.

Timeline of Important Dates for L.M. Montgomery

1874	Born on November 30 to Clara Woolner Macneill and Hugh John Montgomery. Young Maud's mother contracts tuberculosis and dies in 1876; the baby remains with her maternal grandparents in Cavendish.
1890–91	Travels with Grandfather Montgomery to Prince Albert, Saskatchewan, to visit her father and stepmother. First poem published in the Charlottetown *Patriot.*
1893–94	Attends Prince of Wales College in Charlottetown and earns a First Class teaching certificate and license. Poem accepted by *Ladies World* journal.
1894–95	Teaches in Bideford, P.E.I.
1895–96	Takes one-year course in English literature at Dalhousie University in Halifax, Nova Scotia; lives in Halifax Ladies' College (now Armbrae Academy).
1896–97	Teaches in Belmont, P.E.I.
1897–98	Teaches in Lower Bedeque, P.E.I. Grandfather Macneill dies in March 1898. Montgomery returns to Cavendish.
1901–02	From September to June, works in Halifax on the newspaper *The Daily Echo.*
1905	In June she begins to write *Anne of Green Gables* (it is rejected several times before being accepted in 1907 by the L.C. Page Company in Boston).
1906	Becomes secretly engaged to the Rev. Ewan Macdonald.
1908	*Anne of Green Gables* published in the spring to immediate acclaim.
1909–11	Publishes *Anne of Avonlea* (1909), *Kilmeny of the Orchard* (1910), *The Story Girl* (1911); Grandmother Macneill dies. Marries the Rev. Ewan Macdonald in Park Corner on July 5, 1911. The Macdonalds move to Leaskdale, Ontario.
1912–21	Maud and Ewan's son Chester Cameron is born on July 7, 1912; Hugh Alexander is stillborn on August 13, 1914; and Ewan Stuart is born on October 7, 1915. Publishes *Chronicles of Avonlea* (1912), *The Golden Road* (1913), *Anne of the Island* (1915), *The Watchman and Other Poems* (1916), *Anne's House of Dreams* (1917), *Rainbow Valley* (1919), *Further Chronicles of Avonlea* (1920), and *Rilla of Ingleside* (1921).
1923	Montgomery is made a Fellow of the Royal Society of Arts in Great Britain, the first Canadian woman to be so honoured. Publishes *Emily of New Moon.*
1925	Publishes *Emily Climbs.*
1926–33	The Macdonalds move to Norval, Ontario, near Toronto. Publishes *The Blue Castle* (1926), *Emily's Quest* (1927), *Magic for Marigold* (1929), *A Tangled Web* (1931), and *Pat of Silver Bush* (1933).
1935	Montgomery is made an Officer of the Order of the British Empire. Publishes *Mistress Pat.* The Macdonalds retire to Toronto, Ontario.
1936–39	Publishes *Anne of Windy Poplars* (1936), *Jane of Lantern Hill* (1937), and *Anne of Ingleside* (1939).
1942	Montgomery dies on April 24 and lies in state in Green Gables in Cavendish. She is buried in the Cavendish cemetery.

Foreword

By The Right Honourable Adrienne Clarkson, PC, CC, CMM, CD
26th Governor-General of Canada

When I was about eight, we moved to another apartment in Ottawa and became the neighbours of a young family with a beautiful baby boy who I went to worship on a daily basis. His name was Jamie and he was the blondest, most blue-eyed creature that could possibly exist. Luckily, I did not babysit him because I knew that my mother would not allow this, as she distrusted my approach to the outside world. She felt that I always looked at things through the lenses of all the books I was reading and had been reading since I was five. She was certain that reality in the form of a baby would not bring out the best in me.

But the greatest benefit of living close to Jamie was that his mother gave me for my ninth birthday *Anne of Green Gables,* by L.M. Montgomery. I plunged into that book and subsequently was given all the Anne books. The world that opened up before me was the world of Canada, my adopted country. As an immigrant family, we had no prior knowledge or attachments to the history and culture of the country that had allowed us to find refuge here. But through the writing of L.M. Montgomery, I became a Canadian. Yes, it was about a certain part of Canada – Prince Edward Island – but the particularity of it was wonderfully comforting to absorb.

Through L.M. Montgomery's perceptions about family feuds, the difference between Tories and Grits, and the beauty of puffed sleeves, I was able to situate myself in a world and a past that I was determined to make my own.

All great literature does this for its reader. When you read *War and Peace,* you realize that you understand what a battlefield is and why wars are fought; the world that opens to you is not one that you could have described for yourself even if you might have had some of the experience that it describes. The larger world of understanding, perception, and compassion is what emerges from great writing. L.M. Montgomery did this, and more, for all her readers through the century.

That she was undoubtedly talented and driven as a personality goes without saying. But the depth of her understanding of why a small rural community could come to represent all of Canada is nothing short of phenomenal.

From the last in the Anne series, *Rilla of Ingleside,* I first learned about Canada's role in the First World War. I understood the sacrifices that had been made by the story of Anne's two sons, Jem and Walter. I understood what people at home felt about this war fought on foreign territory with unpronounceable names from the reactions of Susan, Anne's devoted housekeeper.

I absorbed all of these things as my own history, and for that I have always been enormously grateful. Everything L.M. Montgomery taught me was more valuable than any of the history lessons I learned later, and for me she is the writer who understands more than anyone what it is to come out of a country that was basically rural and become a player on the world stage because of circumstances. I understand the continuing appeal of her work because I have never forgotten it. I have never considered it to be a "childish thing." I have never put away L.M. Montgomery. I love her to this day.

L.M. Montgomery and Anne of Green Gables

LUCY MAUD MONTGOMERY's novel *Anne of Green Gables* has become a much-loved classic, selling over fifty million copies worldwide and remaining constantly in print for one hundred years. Perhaps the key to its enduring success is that Montgomery wrote it from her heart. Already a successful author, having published in periodicals almost three hundred short stories and more than two hundred poems, Montgomery decided to take a chance at realizing her lifelong dream to write a novel, filling it with the images and intimate drama she loved. After being repeatedly rejected, the novel was finally published by the L.C. Page Company of Boston in 1908, to immediate acclaim.

L.M. Montgomery (1874–1942) was born on Prince Edward Island in a tiny rural community now called New London. Her mother, Clara Woolner Macneill, died of tuberculosis when Maud was a baby of twenty-one months, and she remained with her maternal grandparents in Cavendish, P.E.I., while her father, Hugh John Montgomery, moved out west to start a new life. Prince Edward Island was her home for thirty-six years while she studied, wrote, taught school, and took care of her grandmother; during her last thirty-one years, she and her Presbyterian minister husband, Ewan Macdonald, lived in Ontario, bringing up two sons and burying a third. P.E.I. inspired the setting for nineteen of her twenty novels and for the majority of her five hundred short stories and five hundred poems. She achieved international fame with *Anne of Green Gables* and was a celebrity during her lifetime in the United States, Canada, and Britain. One hundred years later, her works have been translated into dozens of languages.

All her life, Montgomery, known to her friends as Maud, revelled in colour; *Anne of Green Gables* is brimming with it. Many of her passions – for kindred spirits, natural beauty, romance, poetry, words, and fashion – became her heroine Anne Shirley's. Montgomery experienced the everyday world as a vivid place – full of humour as well as pathos. She was firmly anchored in the real world even though she could also travel freely in worlds of her own imagination. Similarly, Anne Shirley imagines that she should pine to be the heroine of a romance story, but actually she is enraptured with daily life, stricken dumb by the beauty of sunsets and apple boughs.

Montgomery set *Anne of Green Gables* on her own beloved north shore of Prince Edward Island, and she gave to Anne two of her most significant dreaming places: a private bedroom with a view of trees and fields, and Lover's Lane, a curving, red woodland path with green arches formed by tree branches. The novel's poetic descriptions of nature were drawn from Montgomery's years of looking through her window and walking under those arches. Montgomery also gave to Anne her own love for friends, parties, pretty clothes, and secrets. The novel dances with energy, an energy found in Montgomery's early letters and diaries, and in the mixed-media collages of souvenirs and memorabilia on the pages of her scrapbooks.

Montgomery consulted her early scrapbooks while writing *Anne of Green Gables* in 1905. Puffed sleeves are here and so are "the bend in the road" (one of Montgomery's favourite images and expressions), remnants of formal and woodland bouquets, Queen's Academy hilarity (inspired by Montgomery's own happy times at Prince of Wales College), girlhood secrets, sentimental poems, and jokes. Scenes, dialogues, drama, stories – the arranged items speak to each other, suggesting ways of seeing, being, and imagining. Amid the fragments of daily life, lifetime patterns and narrative lines emerge. The scrapbooks stored memories that could be revisited and reshaped into new life; to imagine *Anne,* Montgomery immersed herself in her own past.

George Gibbs's portrait on the cover of the January 1905 edition of *Delineator* became the illustration for the cover of the first edition of *Anne of Green Gables.*

The Island Scrapbooks

ONE OF THE MOST BEAUTIFUL and satisfying sights Montgomery ever beheld, she said, was a rainbow dance, where coloured lights were flashed on a white-clad, dancing figure. The vibrant colours and artistic freedom she enjoyed in that dance may also have attracted her to scrapbooking. In scrapbooks she could preserve and celebrate special moments, and also explore and map ideas through images and colour. In mixed-media collages, chronology was not a restraint, and bright fragments could suggest metaphors and layers of story and feeling. The personal scrapbooks – especially these two Island scrapbooks that she created as a young woman and struggling artist – reveal Montgomery enjoying memories and images, reshaping events in collages that become richer, with drama and irony, over time. Here she could also create among the pages an audience for her own writing life.

Montgomery kept two kinds of scrapbooks. She preserved clippings of her (and sometimes other people's) published stories, poems, and articles – and, later, reviews of her novels. She also kept personal scrapbooks filled with souvenirs, her own and other people's photographs, postcards, cats' fur, swatches of fabric, magazine pictures, and pressed flowers. There are six of these personal scrapbooks – two from her P.E.I. years and four from her married life in Ontario. From comments in her diary we know she kept earlier scrapbooks, but she destroyed them, just as she destroyed her earliest journals. All her life she kept boxes and small trunks of treasures and secrets, and periodically she would sort through them to create scrapbook pages, sometimes burning what she did not use.

The two Island scrapbooks are the most colourful and vibrant of the six personal scrapbooks. They reflect Montgomery's youth and optimism, and she lavished time on arranging the items. The scrapbooks are filled with meaningful markers that very likely prompted Montgomery to recall what Wordsworth referred to as "spots of time" – pictured moments whose details carry more power than words may be able to capture.

Reading over Montgomery's shoulder, we find nineteenth-century and early-twentieth-century rural Canadian life come alive. Church and school are social centres for the community, whether that community is on Prince Edward Island or in Prince Albert, Saskatchewan. Teachers and ministers are respected leaders; a whole community turns out to pay tribute to a minister or a teacher who has done good work and is moving away.

Local literary societies and school concerts are highlights for all ages. Religious revivals are much-anticipated social events. Magazines and newspapers are treats to read, and they bring pictures from the wide world, with images of fashions and hobbies and news of faraway conflicts and debates. Newspapers also carry intimate news of neighbours' comings and goings. Trains connect villages and provinces. Montgomery sighed over ball gowns and expensive satins and lace; she and her friends had their own codes for elegance: fancy name cards, where, as she described years later in her journal, "the name of the owner was concealed under a gorgeous cluster of flowers held in a slender hand cut off at the wrist. . . . Anybody who at all aspired to be fashionable sent for a packet of these cards and exchanged them with her mates." Barn dances, sleigh rides, basket auctions, church picnics: Montgomery's youth was recaptured in the scrapbooks and later was re-created in Anne's life.

The scrapbooks are living records – Montgomery edited them over the years and borrowed from them to illustrate her handwritten journals. She treated her diaries this way as well, rewriting events to conform to a larger story of her life. An intensely private person, Maud protected from casual view what was most painful and what was most vulnerable. Perhaps this is why there is now no clear evidence in the scrapbooks of several key events in her life, including her engagement to Ewan Macdonald and her writing of *Anne of Green Gables.* There are also no images of the Boer War (1899–1902), though she shared much of Canada's fascination with the war when it began and she cut other images from the wartime magazines that carried pictures of P.E.I. soldiers and P.E.I. streets festooned with Union Jacks. It is possible to uncover clues about Montgomery's private life and the larger world around her as you begin to spot markers and patterns over many pages. The scrapbooks reward close reading.

Montgomery wrote two long diary entries about the scrapbooks, on July 30, 1905, and on November 22, 1926. In the summer of 1905, she was happily writing *Anne of Green Gables* and she looked at the Blue Scrapbook with nostalgic affection: "I had many a laugh over it – and many a sigh!" In late 1926, she was a world-famous author but was sorely pressed with worries over lawsuits and recurrences of her husband's mental illness. She had forgotten many of the old jokes of the Blue and Red Scrapbooks and lamented that "my latest scrapbook of today is filled with the weddings of the children of those gay brides and bridegrooms!" Yet "the ghostly charm of the old books seized hold of me and I stayed longer than I should."

Similarly, readers today may be charmed by the scrapbooks – for the revealing details they preserve, for the flavour of the times, and for the experience of feeling an artist's passion for the vivid rainbow dance of life she creates and imagines.

Editing the Scrapbooks

THIS BOOK CONTAINS A SELECTION of pages and images from Montgomery's two Island scrapbooks: the Blue Scrapbook and the Red Scrapbook. The scrapbooks are owned by the Lucy Maud Montgomery Birthplace Trust and are preserved by the Confederation Centre Art Gallery and Museum. Each summer, a few of the scrapbook pages are on view at Montgomery's birthplace in New London, P.E.I. My notes and annotations here aim to put these pages in the context of Montgomery's life and the society of the time. For these details, I have ransacked published and unpublished materials, contemporary periodicals and books, and the scholarship of several generous researchers.

Montgomery was never very interested in the precise spelling of names or exact dates, and pages in the scrapbooks do not follow strict chronology. She used old calendars to commemorate more recent events and liked to preserve souvenirs on small white cards, often adding a date, quotations from poetry, or bits of dialogue from the event, but sometimes misdating the event itself. She pointedly mixed together images from decades apart. Souvenir photographs from the 1930s are pasted amid memorabilia of the 1890s. The alterations and deletions that cannot now be explained make the remaining stories all the more interesting. It is now impossible to tell when she assembled certain pages since glue marks and torn edges suggest she removed items and pasted others in to replace them.

Montgomery edited her journals all her adult life, jotting down notes hurriedly and writing them up later when she had leisure to balance words and expressions. Perhaps she did the same with the scrapbooks, removing items later when their presence became irksome or, as is the case with Laura Pritchard Agnew's wedding souvenirs, when she wanted to store them elsewhere for safekeeping.

This habit of editing the scrapbooks and moving items from one place to another leads to an intriguing question: Had Montgomery originally stored in her scrapbook the photograph she later said reflected her conception of Anne? Years after the fact, Montgomery wrote in her diary that while she was writing *Anne of Green Gables,* she kept by her side a photograph of an unidentified girl from an American magazine. We now know that this girl was copper-haired model Evelyn Nesbit (1884–1967), who became famous in the 1906 celebrity trial of her millionaire husband, Harry Thaw, for the murder of wealthy

Magazine photograph of Evelyn Nesbit that inspired Montgomery's image of Anne.

Stanford White, her former lover. The beautiful, youthful Nesbit had posed for many artists at the turn of the nineteenth century. Most famously, she had inspired U.S. artist Charles Dana Gibson, originator of the Gibson Girl look that dominated women's fashion from the late 1890s up until the First World War: an hourglass figure, masses of glossy hair in pompadour or bouffant style, a hint of mischief or independence, and unmistakable femininity and elegance. The Gibson Girl was suggested to be well educated but was no suffragist. This look was reproduced throughout the Western fashion world, and it was the inspiration for what would become the cover portrait for the 1908 edition of *Anne of Green Gables*. Illustrator George Gibbs's "Anne" portrait had actually appeared as the cover image of *Delineator* magazine in January 1905 (see p. 2), at the same time that Montgomery was mapping out her novel. How ironic that the photograph of Nesbit, who would later be tarnished with scandal, inspired Montgomery's image of Anne and that the same Gibson Girl style inspired the artist's illustration that was to become Anne on the cover of the first edition. Had Montgomery preserved in one of her scrapbooks the magazine photograph of Nesbit, removing it to keep by her as she wrote? Certainly many of the fashion-plate images she left in the scrapbooks (such as that of the Kodak Girl, the model pictured in the Eastman Kodak advertisements of the time) reflect the influence of the Gibson Girl.

Even in her lifetime, Montgomery was worried that the scrapbooks were crumbling. Since then, they have been opened and displayed repeatedly, and now almost each time the cover is disturbed an item is lost or damaged. Even during the creation of this book, dried flowers and leaves broke apart and fancy name tabs caught in the brittle hand-stitched edges of pages. The scrapbook pages are now digitally displayed and conservators search for ways to restore and preserve the items that have survived years of handling. It is my hope that by making this record of the scrapbook pages in their current state we can preserve the scrapbooks while sharing with Montgomery's many fans the daily intrigues of her life on her beloved Prince Edward Island.

The Blue Scrapbook roughly covers the years 1893 to 1897, though the very last page includes clippings from the 1920s and photographs from the 1930s. The Red Scrapbook seems to begin in 1896 (with the image of Sally Ward) but then flips almost immediately to 1902–03 and the comic doings of Maud and schoolteacher Nora Lefurgey, who boarded at the Macneills' for the first half of 1903. The last page of the Red Scrapbook belongs to the early months of 1910, and the first pages of the Ontario scrapbooks begin with the fall of 1910, when Montgomery met the Governor General of Canada, Earl Grey, a great fan of *Anne of Green Gables.*

Together the Blue and Red Scrapbooks tell a story about Montgomery's life and imagination in the years that she went to school and then taught, struggled as a writer, and achieved fame with *Anne of Green Gables.*

— Elizabeth Rollins Epperly

All quotations from the published diaries or journals of L.M. Montgomery are from the five volumes of *The Selected Journals of L.M. Montgomery,* edited by Mary Rubio and Elizabeth Waterston (Oxford University Press). Unpublished diary entries are from the University of Guelph Archives; and the "secret" diary, jointly composed by Montgomery and Nora Lefurgey, has been edited by Irene Gammel and published in *The Intimate Life of L.M. Montgomery* (University of Toronto Press). We preserve the order of Montgomery's scrapbook pages and number them accordingly, beginning with the inside front cover and page 1 for the Blue and then the Red Scrapbooks.

The Blue Scrapbook roughly covers the years 1893 to 1897, when Montgomery was from eighteen to twenty-two years old. During those years, she earned a First Class Teacher's License at Prince of Wales College in Charlottetown, received her first payments for published poems and short stories, taught in three P.E.I. schools, attended Dalhousie University in Halifax for one year, flirted, fell in love, fell out of love, and focused her writing ambitions. Frequently, images in this scrapbook refer to her school year in Saskatchewan (1890–91), when she was visiting her father. Indeed, some clippings and souvenirs belong to her childhood, while others, after she had edited the scrapbooks over the years, extend into the 1930s, when Maud was in her fifties.

The Blue Scrapbook is filled with girlhood and young adult exuberance, experimentation, and nostalgia, with cats and comic capers, beaux and beauty. Montgomery used her diaries for grumbles, but in the early scrapbooks she hid sorrows and disappointments within layers of colourful collage, creating a code to baffle prying eyes.

One fascinating theme that runs through the Blue Scrapbook, as well as the Red Scrapbook, and is especially compelling for fans of the outspoken Anne Shirley is womanhood itself and what it meant to be a young woman of fashion and sensibility at the turn of the nineteenth century. Young Maud collected images of beautiful women from history and put them alongside fabrics and fashion plates from advertisements of the 1890s. The pompadour and bouffant hairstyles, the wasp-waisted and puffed-sleeve gowns, and the graceful leisure suggested were surrounded in Montgomery's time by debates about the New Woman, the Gibson Girl, and the Kodak Girl. As a young woman in love with natural beauty and also with fashion, Montgomery had much to intrigue her in small Cavendish and also in magazines from the wide world, brought to her via the Cavendish post office housed in the Macneill kitchen.

Reading the Blue Scrapbook is like catching a glimpse of Montgomery in full, creative play. Every image is laden with memory and meaning. Uncovering some of the stories connecting the images is like deciphering clues in a mystery; sleuthing is rewarded by a new appreciation for the lively, gifted imagination of an author who has given the world the classic *Anne of Green Gables* and more than a century of reading pleasure.

The Blue Scrapbook

1893 to 1897

The inside front cover of the first Island scrapbook marked a triumph in eighteen-year-old Maud Montgomery's life – one she enhanced and gave to Anne Shirley in *Anne of Green Gables*. On July 18, 1893, Montgomery passed the rigorous provincial examinations, achieving fifth place out of 264 candidates. This success meant she could go to Prince of Wales College in Charlottetown to study to be a teacher.

Shoe buckle: Cavendish schoolteacher Selena Robinson helped young Maud prepare for the college entrance exams. Close in age, they were friends and began scrapbooks at the same time. Selena gave Maud a tiny horseshoe shoe buckle as a mascot. "Perhaps it may turn out a song / Perhaps turn out a sermon" was borrowed from Maud's favourite Robert Burns's "Epistle to a Young Friend," in which an older friend gives advice to a younger one going out into the world.

Glove: The glove opens to reveal a calendar marked with the initials W.G.P. Willie G. Pritchard and his sister Laura befriended Maud while she was visiting her father and new stepmother in Saskatchewan during the 1890–91 school year. Red-haired, grey-green-eyed, laughing Willie wore Maud's ring until he died unexpectedly in 1897; Laura, possibly a model for Anne Shirley's best friend, Diana Barry, was a lifelong "bosom friend." Montgomery marked seventy-six jolly "rackets" on the calendar to commemorate happy days (see also Blue Scrapbook, p. 39). On the very last page of this scrapbook, Willie and his sister Laura are remembered with flowers, photos, and clippings.

Dainty calendar: This calendar, too, was marked with dots, though neither calendar marked Montgomery's birthday, November 30, as a special day. *Youth's Companion* was considered a good magazine, and Montgomery was thrilled to receive twelve dollars from it for her poem "Fisher Lassies" in 1896.

Inside front cover from the Blue Scrapbook

L. M. Montgomery compressed a two-year teachers' program at Prince of Wales College (PWC) into one year, opting for First Class study and passing the necessary exams to enter the program. Anne Shirley would do the same. PWC, located in the Island capital city of Charlottetown, served as a model for Anne's Queen's Academy. Montgomery's love for her PWC studies and "rackets" was reflected in her scrapbooks and reproduced in Anne's story. At the PWC graduation ceremony, Montgomery read an essay on Portia, heroine of Shakespeare's *Merchant of Venice,* which received high praise in the Charlottetown *Guardian.* Sitting on the stage of the Opera House, Montgomery had the pleasure of hearing Jim Stevenson give the valedictory address she had written for him. Prince of Wales College and Saint Dunstan's University amalgamated in 1969 to create the present-day University of Prince Edward Island.

Clipping: On June 9, 1894, the *Guardian* called Montgomery's essay on Portia a literary gem. With "phrases of almost perfect art" it was the "*pièce de résistance* of the evening."

Program: Montgomery glued the PWC colours, red and blue, onto the program.

Flowers: Montgomery preserved the pansies she wore at graduation. The words beneath the ribbon read "We part but not forever."

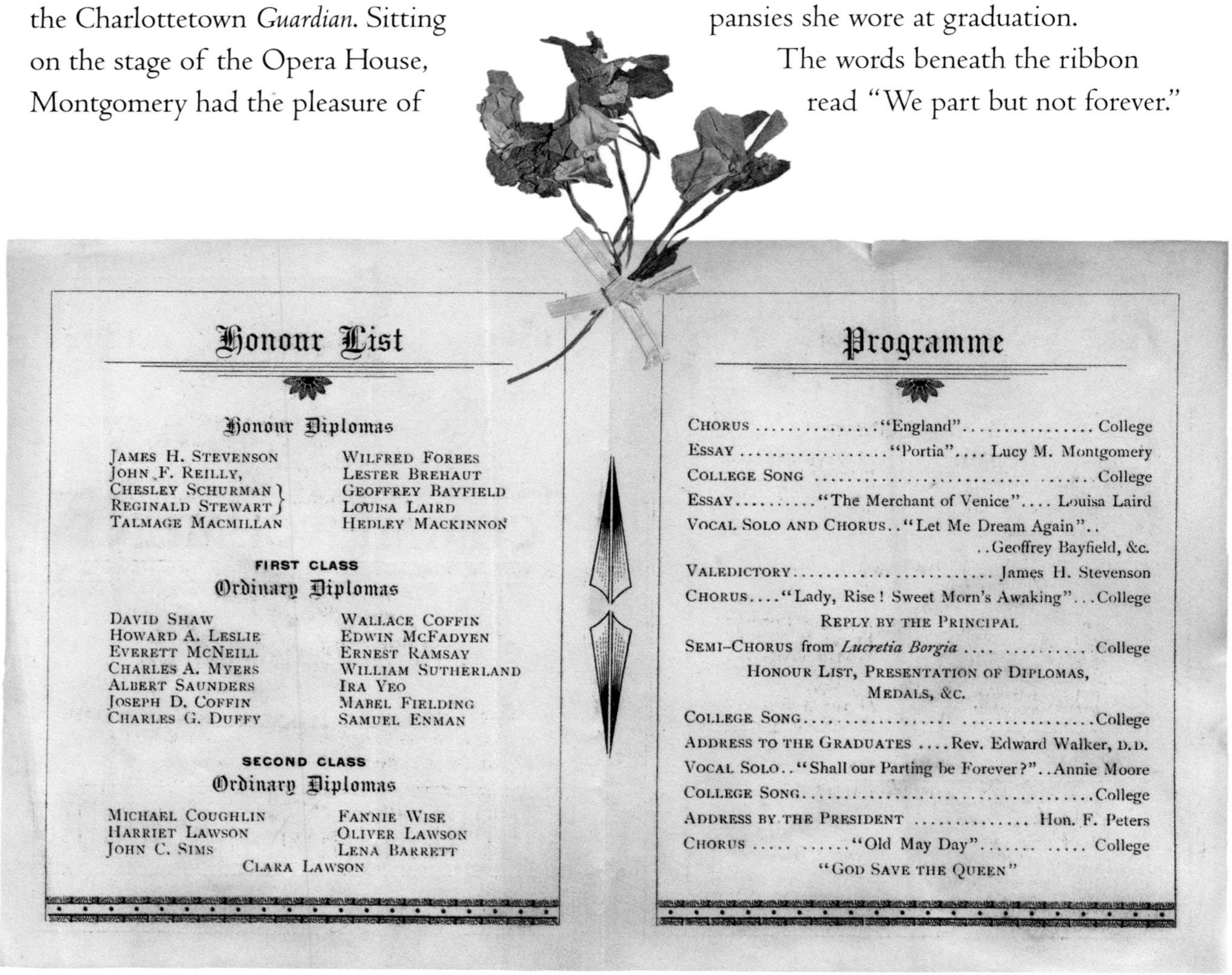

Honour List

Honour Diplomas

James H. Stevenson
John F. Reilly,
Chesley Schurman }
Reginald Stewart }
Talmage MacMillan
Wilfred Forbes
Lester Brehaut
Geoffrey Bayfield
Louisa Laird
Hedley MacKinnon

FIRST CLASS

Ordinary Diplomas

David Shaw
Howard A. Leslie
Everett McNeill
Charles A. Myers
Albert Saunders
Joseph D. Coffin
Charles G. Duffy
Wallace Coffin
Edwin McFadyen
Ernest Ramsay
William Sutherland
Ira Yeo
Mabel Fielding
Samuel Enman

SECOND CLASS

Ordinary Diplomas

Michael Coughlin
Harriet Lawson
John C. Sims
Fannie Wise
Oliver Lawson
Lena Barrett
Clara Lawson

Programme

Chorus ....“England”............... College
Essay ....“Portia”.... Lucy M. Montgomery
College Song .... College
Essay.........."The Merchant of Venice".... Louisa Laird
Vocal Solo and Chorus.."Let Me Dream Again"..
..Geoffrey Bayfield, &c.
Valedictory......................... James H. Stevenson
Chorus...."Lady, Rise! Sweet Morn's Awaking"...College
Reply by the Principal
Semi-Chorus from *Lucretia Borgia* .... College
Honour List, Presentation of Diplomas,
Medals, &c.
College Song.................. ....College
Address to the Graduates ....Rev. Edward Walker, D.D.
Vocal Solo.."Shall our Parting be Forever?"..Annie Moore
College Song...............................College
Address by the President .... Hon. F. Peters
Chorus ...."Old May Day"...... ..... College
"God Save the Queen"

OF W. CONVOCATION

Pleasant Evening of Speech and Song.

mier Petors Announces That a w College Worthy of the Province Will be Built.

vernor Howlan certainly spoke with-e mark when he said that the sight e assembled Prince of Wales stud- —"maidens fair and manly youths" hey appeared on the platform e Temple Opera House last evening sight the sister provinces of the should have seen. It was the Col-onvocation night; and the students in the garb and mood of a high al.

e program was unique among the f fare served at functions such as True, it followed the hoary, ortho-custom of reserving the greatest s for the finale, but it placed the best most attractive features first. There is m to doubt that the *piece de resistance* evening was Miss Lucy Montgomery's on "Portia." It was a character-h such as might have come from ge Eliott in her 'teens. It was not a subtle, analytical study; it was a ry gem. Miss Montgomery began with rl Portia in maiden meditation but ree; bound by the mystery of the s of lead and silver and gold, "the y, graceful heiress of a long past

phrases of almost perfect art, Miss gomery praised the beauty of the an type of hear and mind and soul. cially heart; for that was where the anity lay, was it not? And Portia, a little touch of human frailty now hen endeared herself to every heart." ne, this sweet, strong heroine of espeare's greatest thought was, to-the suitor of her choice, "a perfect el of maidenly delicacy and womanly ." But it was in her capacity as the ssessor of a magnificent intellect" Portia won the young essayist's most usiastic words of praise. To say that Montgomery in this analysis did ce to Portia's intellectual worth seem a strong statement and undue e; but it is simple truth.

ss Louisa Laird, too, proved beyond her mastery of the sense and her ap-iation of the dramatic power of the popular of Shakespeare's plots if not greatest of his plays. Her essay on "Merchant of Venice" was a resume he plot rather than a study of the . I was necessarily, therefore, less nal than that of Miss Montgomery, it showed none the less that power of rpretation which Shakespearean clubs e the *sine qua non* of admission to charmed and charming circles.

he valedictory by Mr. J. H. Steven-began as most of its predecessors ties have done, by uttering the nt of the parting class But before it hed, it made practical suggestions and ex ssed other thoughts of such value as won praise of the principal of the P of W the Premier of the Province. It said example, that the students of the C l were "cribbed, cabined and confined" lack of sufficient elbow room, or words that effect, vigorous yet not inelegant. en it recounted the glories of the otball Club, the *Times* and the Debat, g Society, the professors one and all, and ch of the other institutions which the "boys" hold in deep and, as it were, pro prietary love. Whereat the aforesaid boys filled the house with loud and lusty cheers. And when the valedictorian closed with the conventional but intensely earnest appeal to the class, girls as well as boys, to remember their Alma Mater in the days of their youth and forever, the male members of the class cheered again and in chorus inquired as the nature of the ailment of Mr. Stevenson to which came the stentorion reply, "he's all right, oh, yes you bet."

Prof. Anderson made a very characteristic, which is to say, a very happy, wholesome response. He was proud of the graduates of the Prince of Wales "University." The word "University" was prophetic. He had a right to be proud of the Prince of Wales students.

He likened their diligence and energy to the radii of a circle, representing the extent of human knowledge. As the radii increased the circumference length ened, the area grew and the infinity of the unexplored darkness outside the circle became, if that were possible, less infinite. At all events the area of knowledge grew and the world was brighter and better

Nor should the search for knowledge cease with college life, even with these alumni who entered upon careers of "business." It were apostacy for them to turn away from the goddess of truth, to sell themselves to the hideous god of mammon. That was the gist of the Principal's speech, emphasized by grace-ful gestures peculiarly his own, and punctuated by the plaudits of the boys.

Rev. Dr. Edward Walker gave a practical and a really valuable address. He urged particularly a more systematic and assiduous study of English literature. Grammar was not enough. The power to express one's own thought was by far a greater desideratum than the power to analyze the sentences of others.

Mr. Stevenson's eloquent suggestion as to the need of more room in the "Alma Mater" was its text. Mr. Peters thanked Mr. Stevenson for that happy utterance. The overcrowding of the college *was* a disgrace. It was an outrageous disgrace. It endangered the bloom of health that made the beauty of the young ladies of that class.

Premier Peters' speech was more than a mere congratulatory address. It was some what of a political pronouncement.

Education, he said, had the most important bearing on the social and political welfare of the people. While he had any charge of the conduct of public affairs in this province, popular education would never be neglected. It was hardly possible to waste public money for this purpose so long as the results were commensurate with the expenditure, however great it be. And what he had heard this evening proved the adequacy of the results. Therefore, he hoped that in the near future the College, as it now stood, would be swept away and a building worthy of the pro-vince erected in its stead. ment was regarded as worthy of more than the common kind of applause. Three cheers and a tiger was its meed.

Governor Howlan's speech was greeted with equal enthusiasm. His Honor reviewed the History of the school. He knew it when it was the Central Academy, then as the Prince of Wales College and he hoped before his term of office as Governor expired to know it as the University of the Province. The class of 94 should be worthy of their Alma Mater; but he impressed upon them that only by persistent effort could they reach positions that would maintain the reputation of the Prince of Wales as students as they were now known in almost every land. Then, as true men and women they must be true to each other, and they would find as he had found, that they would never lack a friend as long as their classmates lived.

"Old May Day", the last of a goodly list of choruses and songs, and the national hymn closed the convocation.

Following is a list of the winners of diplomas and prizes:

HONOR DIPLOMAS.

James H. Stevenson, New Glasgow, 95.
John F. Reilly, Summerside, 94.
Chesley Schurman, Summerside, 90.
Reginald Stewart, Charlottetown, 90.
Talmage Macmillan, New Haven, 88.
Wilfred Forbes, Vernon River, 86
Lester Brehaut, Murray Harbor, 86
Geoffrey Bayfield, Charlottetown, 83
Louise Laird, Charlottetown, 81.
Hedley Mackinnon, Charlottetown, 78.

FIRST-CLASS ORDINARY DIPLOMAS.

David Shaw, Covehead, 94.
Howard A. Leslie, Souris, 93.
Everett Macneill, Lower Montague, 92
Charles A. Myers, Charlottetown, 89.
Albert Saunders, Summerside, 88.
Joseph D Coffin, Charlottetown, 87.
Charles G. Duffy, Shamrock, 86.
Wallace Coffin, Mount Stewart, 86
Edwin McFadyen, Tignish, 83.
Ernest Ramsay, Hamilton, 81.
William Sutherland, Sea View, 81.
Ira J. Yeo, Charlottetown, 78.
Samuel Enman, Pownal, 76.
Mabel Fielding, Alberton, 75.

SECOND-CLASS ORDINARY DIPLOMAS.

Michael Coughlan, Hope River, 72.
Harriet Lawson, Charlottetown, 70
John C. Sims, French River, 68.
Fannie Wise, Milton, 68
Oliver Lawson, Charlottetown, 65
Lena Barrett, Charlottetown, 63.
Clara Lawson, Charlottetown, 61.

MEDAL WINNERS.

Governor-General's Silver Medal—Jas. H. Stevenson.

Governor-General's Bronze Medal, for Teaching and School Management—Ethel Conners, North Bedeque.

Medal awarded by Mr. Miller for the best kept set of books in the class of Book-keeping—John A. McPhee.

The judges of bookkeeping were John S. Lewis, R. H. Jenkins and John Connolly. In awarding the medal they desired honorable mention to be made of the work of Kenneth Graham, Ella J. Stavert and Jessie Stavert.

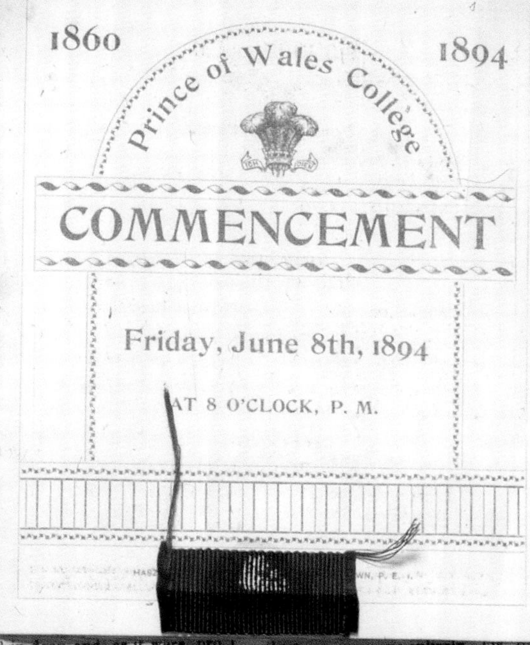

1860 1894

Prince of Wales College

COMMENCEMENT

Friday, June 8th, 1894

AT 8 O'CLOCK, P. M.

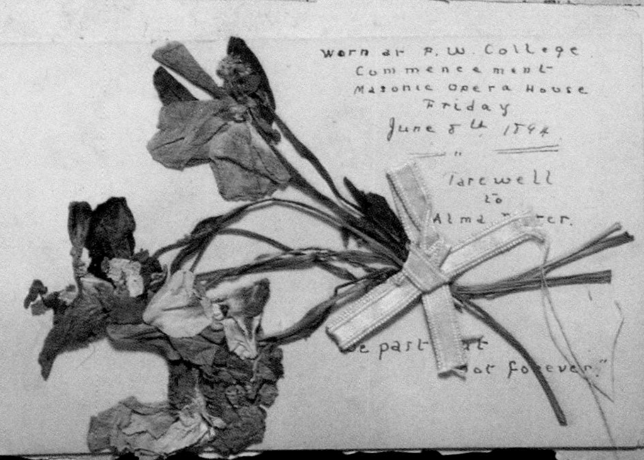

Basket Ball match on Thursday Come one! Come all!! and shout for College.

We notice that the barque "Maud M." is now being towed into Shaw's wharf.—Prince Street School Times.

We are pleased to learn that one of our young lady students has just recovered from a severe attack of inflammat and is now able to attend concerts u

Schoolgirl high spirits and camaraderie are woven into a light-hearted collage, suggesting the tenor of Maud's days at PWC and in Prince Albert.

Souvenirs from 1890 to 1894 form a border for an illustration of a starry-eyed young woman encircled by lilies and crowned with a jewel. Montgomery pasted onto this picture a calling-card cover bearing the image of a ship and the words "Many Pleasures," perhaps to link the picture with the poem beneath it.

The four corners of the page reflect happy times.

Top left: Montgomery spent an enjoyable Easter holiday with PWC friend Mary Campbell in 1894. She recited "The Old Settler's Story" at a church concert in Hunter River, P.E.I., on March 29, 1894.

Top right: The McGregor and Jones cards belong to Prince Albert school days, as do the prairie flowers beside them.

Bottom right: Maud and Mary often passed the "famous lamppost" on Prince Street during their evening strolls through downtown Charlottetown. Beneath the splinter the text reads "The prince of good fellows" and then "Oh whistle and I'll come to you my lad" – Burns's line that Montgomery's Emily Byrd Starr would quote about Teddy Kent in the Emily series. On April 7, 1894, Maud and Mary met Stuart Simpson and Jim Stevenson at this corner by the lamppost and later learned that the two boys were coming to board with them at the MacMillans' at 187 Fitzroy Street. "Spondee and Dactyl" could refer to the rhythmic pronunciation of Simp-son and Ste-ven-son.

Bottom left: Friday, June 15, 1894, was a "landmark of freedom": the end of examinations. The burnt match, now lost, came from a ritual burning of school papers with Mary. The "quartette" consisted of Mary Campbell, Ida McEachern, Nell McGrath, and Montgomery.

Centre right: The bit of white wool with the mysterious line "I'll dye it black tomorrow" was from the white square shawl Montgomery wore the first night she was formally escorted home.

Hunter River
March 29th 1894
Easter Holidays

"Providence"
"the pink of perfection"
Chap: I. "The Creaking Floor".

Startling the Division
"The Old Settler's Story"

Saskatchewan Prairie

Miss Kate McGregor.

Mr. and Mrs. T. S. J

H PRICE WEBBER had a splendid audience at the Masonic Opera House last night. It was a crowded house. "Jessie Brown or the Relief of Lucknow" was presented. The play is a spirited one and the acting was excellent. Frequent bursts of applause were heard. Edwina Grey as Jessie Brown was of course the star and all the others did their parts well. The audience was much pleased with the play. This afternoon at 2 o'clock a matinee performance will be given, viz. Tobin's Comedy of "The Honeymoon." The windows will be darkened and the hall will be lighted by electricity during this performance. Price to all parts of the hall 25 cents. Tonight "Arrah-na-Pogue" will be presented and this will be the last appearance here of the Company.

We may assume that X equals Y multiplying both sides by Y, XY Y²; and of course -XY equa Then adding X² to both sides, X equals X²—Y². Using X—Y as X(X—Y) equals (X+Y) (X— cancelling out X—Y we have equals X+Y equals 2X, since X e Dividing both sides by X, one equ

Four Happy Hearts.

TWO MARRIAGES—CONTRACTING PARTIES WELL KNOWN IN CHARLOTTETOWN.

[WHEAR—MURCHIESON.]

(Daily Sept 5.)

This morning, as the GUARDIAN goes to press, Mr. John F Whear, Attorney-at-Law, of this city, leads to Hymen's Alter, Miss Florrie Murchison, formerly of Point Prim, but now one of the most popular young ladies of Charlottetown. The happy event takes place at the residence of Capt. Alex. Cameron, uncle of the bride, the officiating Clergyman being the Rev. T. F. Fullerton. The fair bride is attired in navy blue broad cloth, trimmed with blue and gold surah silk, blue hat to match, and carrying a beautiful white bouquet. She is attended by Miss Matilda Wyatt, and Miss Whear, sister of the groom. The bridesmaids wear pearl grey crepon with silver irridescent trimmings, hats to match, and carrying pink bouquets. The groom is supported by his brother, Mr. Louis G. Whear. The wedding presents are both numerous and costly—that of Messrs James Paton & Co, being a handsome mahogany case, containing half a dozen silver fish knives and forks, while her fellow employes presented a very beautiful mirror. After partaking of a sumptous breakfast the happy couple will take the morning express for St. John and other Maritime centres, not omitting the historical Blomidon and other points of interest in the Land of Evangeline. The GUARDIAN extends congratulations.

"I'll dye it black to-morrow"

How She Heeded His Wor
"...member dear," said the father as he sent his youn most pitied daughter away to school, "that all my hopes centered on you. Remembe your struggles for intellectual acy, your triumphs, your defe your temptations, that a good rather to be chosen than great
"I will, father," replied the w girl, and the train bore her awa
Will it be believed that thre later that girl married a man wi the vilainous name of Gandersh

Friday 1894
June 15th
"Landmark of freedom!"
"In memory of "the quartette"
"Caramels."
"Stars"

"No matter where o'er the world we roam
We'll remember each other for aye and aye"

MY SHIP.

One day I watched a white-winged ship
Sweep out beyond the harbor-bar;
She bore from me my dearest hope,
And sailed toward the evening star.

Long months have passed; but ne'er again
In evening's hush, or morning's glow,
Her gleaming sails mine eyes have seen—
The ship I love, and long for so.

I think she drifted on, and on,
And far beyond the evening star,
And through the happy "Golden Gate";
And furled her sails within the bar.

LILLIAN GRE

"That famous lamp-post Cat Concert"
"Corner Corner Corner"
"The Fatal Spot"
"The grand rallying-place"
"My heart is in Prince Street
my heart is not here"
"Beauties"
Evening strolls.
"The Prince of Wales..."
Spondees & Dactyl

Calling card: John A. Mustard was Montgomery's teacher in Prince Albert. He annoyed her with his attentions and proposed to her. The flowers behind his name may be an allusion to the time he gave her a bouquet of roses and, instead of wearing them, she pointedly tore them apart and scattered them as she and Mustard walked.

Birch bark: The bark, with Longfellow's line "Give me thy bark, oh birch tree," commemorated a golden outing in Lover's Lane in June 1893 with friend and teacher Selena Robinson.

Cards with dried flowers: The lilacs and the unidentifiable flower on the June 1894 card belong to PWC adventures. The initials A.F.I.M.L.M.M. may stand for PWC friends Annie Moore, Fanny Wise, Ida McEachern, Mary Campbell, and Lucy Maud Montgomery.

"Mock trial" clipping: This mentions a "gross breach of discipline" in Mr. Harcourt's class, referring to March 8, 1894, when students disrupted class by throwing peanuts at each other. Montgomery worked the incident into a comic story for PWC's magazine, *The College Record*: "Selections from the Diary of a Second-Class Mouse."

Woman in the moon: The new moon was always a favourite image. When Montgomery was writing *Anne of Green Gables*, she wrote to Scottish pen pal George Boyd MacMillan in a letter dated August 23, 1905:

I saw a poem the other night. I was out for a solitary walk. It was an August night, calm, golden, dewless. On the crest of a hill I turned and glanced over my shoulder and saw what I shall carry in my remembrance all through eternity. Two spruces were clasping dark hands over an arch of silvery twilight sky; and right in the arch was the new moon like a shallop of red gold. I looked at it – and thanked God for life in a world where such a sight could be seen. Will there be no new moon in heaven? No twilight? Oh, yes, there must be!

White lilacs.
Charlottetown.
"In lilac time
The noons are still
At night we hear
The whipoorwill"
P.W. College.
June 1894
"Remember me when far away
And I'll remember you.
most extraordinary
Scrap of desk
Dr. Anderson's room
P.W.C.
1893 - 94.
"The path of learning is no royal road."
J. A. Mustard
While this short greeting I indite I pray God grant you prospects bright

—As will be seen in another column, ome of our mathematicians have proved conclusively that one equals two. One of our students recently made a practical pplication of this grand truth. He owed fellow-student two cents, and paid him n full with one.

IN THE PORTRAIT GALLERY

By May Lennox

Grandfather looks from the paneled wall
At grandmother hanging across the hall,
In the ripened glow of her stately grace;
And a frown comes over his shadowed face
As he says: "The world has grown askew,
My dear, since we were young—we two.

"Nothing that was is the same to-day;
Old-time fancies are cast away;
All our scruples are laughed to scorn;
All our customs are quite out-worn;
Each is seeking for something new—
We were content with the old—we two."

Into the shade of the grim old room,
Steal two forms through the twilight's gloom.
Grandfather's eyes are sharp to see,
And a deep voice utters tenderly:
"For aye will I love, and love but you,
And we'll follow love to the end—we two."

Grandfather's face has lost its frown,
And his eyes grown softer gaze gently down
On the pair who naught of his watching know,
And grandmother smiles and whispers low:
"One thing goes on as it used to do—
In the days when we were young—we two."

The Mock Trial is degenerating into a farce. The evidence for the prosecution has been entirely too long; and much valuable time is consumed, without an practical benefit to the average student, except, perhaps, in developing his natur talent for noise and disorder. In the language of Byron, "we feel the fulness of satiety." Give the defence a chance.

Undoubtedly a gross breach of discipline has been committed in Mr. Harcourt's room. Many of the students are justly indignant at the base manner in which several of the most guilty sneaked out of the affair, leaving the innocent to pay for the damage.

PERSONALS.

It is with sorrow that we hear of the death of Mrs. Ramsay of Hamilton, the mother of Mr. E. H. Ramsay '95. We are sure we speak the sentiments of his college mates when we say that Mr. Ramsay has our deepest sympathy.

Island students abroad have, as usual, been very successful. Mr. W. S. Ferguson, of P. W. C. '93, took best general standing in arts for the Maritime Provinces at McGill. The other Island men at McGill, among whom may be mentioned Messrs. Geo. D. Mckinnon, Charlottetown; Geo. McLeod, Uigg; R. H. Rogers, Alberton, acquitted themselves very creditably. At Dalhousie, Brehaut of Murray Harbour is a tie with Logan of Pictou for the medal. In the Freshman Class Mr. R. L. Coffin, Charlottetown, leads in Latin, and takes high place in other subjects.

Montgomery celebrated good times and academic triumphs with mementoes from Prince of Wales days. Cards and annotations suggest how intensely dramatic she found everyday life.

PAGE 4: In 1905, while writing *Anne of Green Gables,* Montgomery noted in her diary that this playbill was from her first "opera"; she saw the play twice, with Hedley Buntain, at the Opera House in December 1894. On October 22, 1893 (misdated 1894), Montgomery's landlady, Mrs. MacMillan, proposed an outing to Southport, P.E.I., by ferry, but made the girls board a ferry named *Southport* that took them instead across the harbour to Rocky Point. Typically, Montgomery made a joke and a story from the mistake and saved moss to remember the occasion. The card at the bottom of the page turned a Saturday-night antic with Mary Campbell in "Hotel de McMillan" into notes for a story in four chapters after they broke a bed slat and hid the pieces. The high-flown sentiments of the poem "Sir Hugo's Choice" would have appealed to young Anne Shirley.

PAGE 5: This clipping shows the pass list for the provincial matriculation examination, where Montgomery came fifth out of 264. Mary Campbell and Montgomery's cousin Stella Campbell placed considerably lower. Fashion pictures were more than just pretty markers: They suggest Montgomery analyzing "woman" and her place in the world.

PAGE 7: Here Montgomery said farewell to Dr. Anderson of PWC with a souvenir flower, preserved the teachers' licensing examination program for 1894 (candidates graduated and then took the teachers' license exams), and pasted the P.E.I. emblems and motto "Parva sub ingenti" (the small under the protection of the great). The fashionable woman at the top right is reminiscent of the photograph of Evelyn Nesbit that would inspire Montgomery's image of Anne (see Editing the Scrapbooks, p. 5; and p. 84).

PAGE 8: Between the 1893 examination notice and the annotated examination timetable, Montgomery preserved a little card suggesting some comedy probably involving Selena Robinson and the examinations. The porthole and ship recall the earlier ship images (Blue Scrapbook, p. 2).

PAGE 9: On this long clipping, Montgomery proudly underlined four firsts (highlighted here) – in English, English Literature, Agriculture, and School Management – while, in comic contrast, a demure maiden averts her eyes. (The School Management first is noted on page 10 of the scrapbook, where the newspaper article continues.) The program at the beginning of the article also mentions Montgomery's reading of her essay on Portia (Blue Scrapbook, p. 1).

Mary J. Campbell

Alex. Mac Neill Esq
Cavendis

October 22nd 1894
"Did you ever get left?"
Moss from old French fort Rocky Point P.E. Island

"What's in a name?"

SIR HUGO'S CHOICE.

BY JAMES JEFFREY ROCHE.

It is better to die, since death comes surely,
In the full noontide of an honored name,
Than to lie at the end of years obscurely,
A handful of dust in a shroud of shame.

Sir Hugo lived in the ages golden,
Warder of Aisne and Picardy:
He lived and died, and his deeds are told in
The Book immortal of Chivalrie;

How he won the love of a prince's daughter—
A poor knight he with a stainless sword—
Whereat Count Rolf, who had vainly sought her,
Swore death should sit at the bridal board.

'A braggart's threat, for a brave man's scorning!'
And Hugo laughed at his rival's ire.
But couriers twain, on the bridal morning,
To his castle gate came with tidings dire.

'The first a-faint and with armor riven:
In peril sore have I left thy bride,—
False Rolf waylaid us. For love and Heaven!
Sir Hugo, quick to the rescue ride!'

Stout Hugo muttered a word unholy;
He sprang to horse and he flashed his brand,
But a hand was laid on his bridle slowly,
And a herald spoke: 'By the king's command

'This to Picardy's trusty warder:—
France calls first for his loyal sword,
The Flemish spears are across the border,
And all is lost if they win the ford.'

Sir Hugo paused, and his face was ashen,
His white lips trembled in silent prayer—

God's pity soften the spirit's passion
When the crucifixion of Love is there!

What need to tell of the message spoken?
Of the hand that shook as he poised his lance?
And the look that told of his brave heart broken,
As he bade them follow, 'For God and France!'

On Cambray's field next morn they found him,
'Mid a mighty swath of foemen dead;
Her snow-white scarf he had bound around him
With his loyal blood was baptized red.

It is all writ down in the book of Glory,
On crimson pages of blood and strife,
With scanty thought for the simple story
Of duty dearer than love or life.

Only a note obscure, appended
By warrior scribe or monk perchance,
Saith: 'The good knight's ladye was sore offended
That he would not die for her but France.'

Did the ladye live to lament her lover?
Or did roystering Rolf prove a better mate?
I have searched the records over and over,
But nought discover to tell her fate.

And I read the moral.—A brave endeavor
To do thy duty, whate'er its worth,
Is better than life with love forever—
And love is the sweetest thing on earth.

LOVE IS REALLY BLIND, AFTER ALL.

SHE—"How I love to sit in your lap and have your big manly arms about me!"
HE—"My little darling!"

THE ORGAN.

Oh that ancient College Organ
With its yellow-tinted keys,
With no tone at all to speak of
Getting lesser by degrees.
Ten successive generations
Patiently have thumped away,
Hoping ever,—always vainly—
They at last would make it play.
How they practise with their fingers.
Then they try it with a thumb;
And at last they never mind it,
For the poor old thing is dumb.

—*Ulysses Webster.*

THIS EVENING

For the first time here by this Company, the Beautiful Irish Comedy Drama, by Dion Boucicault, entitled;

ARRAH-NA-POGUE

—— OR ——

The Wicklow Wedding

ARRAH-MEELISH, (Arrah-na-Pogue)	**EDWINA GREY**
Shaun, the post, a Wicklow Carman	C. H. STEVENS
Michael Feeney, a process-server	W. H. BEDELL
Major Coffin, commanding the detachment of troops at Wicklow	J. McMILLAN
Hon. Ailsa Craigg, chief secretary of State for Ireland	J. INGRAHAM
Beamish McGoul, an outlawed patriot	W. R. NOBLE
Oiney Farrell, a friend of Shaun's	F. H. HILL
Col. Bagnal O'Grady, the O'Grady	H. PRICE WEBBER
Lanty Louchlin	ROSE LILLEY
Nora McTaggerty	ISABEL CLIFTON
Fanny Powers, of Cabinteely, in love with Beamish	LOTTIE CARMEN
Katie Welsh	LOUISE CLIFTON

ACT I. The Wicklow Wedding. The Arrest.
ACT II. The Trial. The Sentence.
ACT III. The Escape. The Denouement.

PRICES TO SUIT THE TIMES.

Admission 25 cts., Reserved Seats, 35 cts.

Doors Open at 7.15. Commences at 8 o'clock.

RESERVED SEATS ON SALE AT USUAL PLACES

Positively Last Night.

JOHN COOMBS, Steam Printer, Queen Street, Charlottetown.

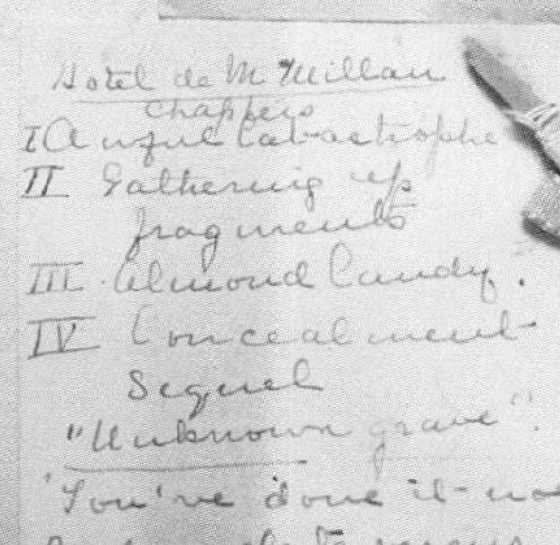

Hotel de McMillan
Chappers
I Awful catastrophe
II Gathering up fragments
III Almond Candy.
IV Concealment
Sequel
"Unknown grave".
"You've done it now Mary".
Broken slats versus irate landladies
Saturday Night April 14 1894
A fatal secret

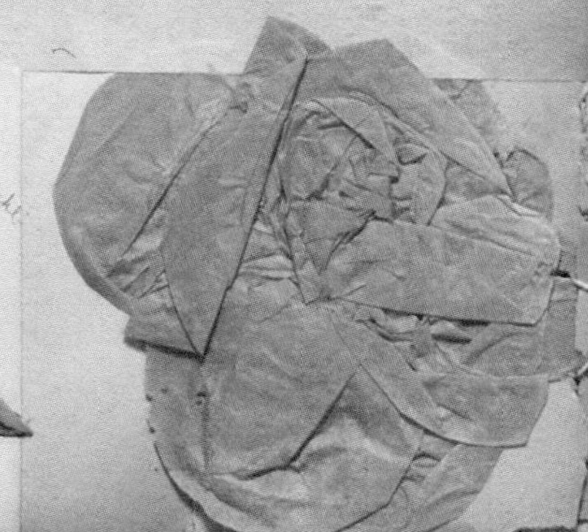

nce of Wales College and Normal School.

ATRICULATION EXAMINATION, JULY, 1893.

The result of the recent examination r entrance to the Prince of Wales Col- ge and Normal School will be found elow. The number of marks attainable was 650; necessary to pass, 325. Of the 264 candidates who presented themselves for examination 118 were successful, as ollows:

Annie Moore, Crapaud, 491.
J Samuel Willis, Kingston, 490.
E N M Hunter, Alberton, 477.
Innis Fraser, Miscouche, 471.
Lucy Maud Montgomery, Cavendish, 470.
Nellie McGrath, Tignish, 465.
W S Lea, Victoria, 460.
Lawrence J Curran, Victoria Cross, 451.
Faustina McIver, Kinkora, 450.
Edward Laird, North Bedeque, 441.
Allen Matthews, Alberton, 437.
yrus McMillan, Wood Islands West, 437.
P S Duffy, Emerald, 435.
William J Haberline, Murray Harbor South, 431.
innie McKay, Clifton, 430.
atrick Campbell, Souris, 429.
ames A Campbell, Montague, 426.
ary J O'Connor, Tignish, 426.
illiam McCheyne Robertson, Marshfield, 422.
Ethel Dutcher, Orwell, 415.
ussie Bentley, Kensington, 418.
eginald P Smith, Emerald, 413.
hos L LeClerc, Wellington Station, 410.
llen Taylor, Ch'town, 409.
nnie J McLean, New Dominion, 408.
da McLeod, Eldon, 407.
essie Haslam, Springfield, 403.
Vinfield Matheson, Ch'town, 402.
helbert McDuff, Kingston, 402.
wen L Horne, Milton, 399.
zzie Kirwin, Tignish, 394.
liza Rodgerson, Pisquid, 390.
lice B Kelly, Kinkora, 390.
gnes McWilliams, Hope River, 389.
thur Campbell, Souris, 389.
ary Campbell, Darlington, 386.
a B Scott, Warren Grove, 382.
irdie Leard, Victoria, 377.
nnie Hennessy, Kensington, 376.
thur Trainor, Ch'town, 372.
Clara Fleming, North Rustico, 369.
olin C Ferguson, Marshfield, 367.
ellie Hodgson, Ch'town, 366.
Joseph S DesRoches, Wheatley River, 366.
atie McFarlane, Sea Cow Head, 363.
arles C Richards, Ch'town, 363.
rin Gallant, New Glasgow, 362.
ennie Leard, North Carleton, 362.
eorge Cameron, West Royalty, 357.
aggie C McDonald, Kinkora, 354.
osephine E Dwan, Fortune Road, 353.
y Cameron, Souris, 352.
eo H Jardine, Mt Stewart, 351.
ucetta McInnis, St Peters Bay, 351.
lora McPhee, Gray's Road, 350.
rtle McGregor, Ch'town, 368
lla Campbell, Park Corner, 346.
James, Ch'town, 345.
s A Todd, Bradalbane, 345.
as McLeod, Georgetown, 344.
Cowan, Murray Harbor South, 342.
Stevenson, Warren Grove, 341.
am E Campbell, Union Road, 341.
min L Mellish, Victoria Cross, 338.
Beers, Ch'town, 336.
McKenna, Rennie's Road, 334.
Pigott, Mt. Stewart, 332.
tavert, Kensington, 332.
Stavert, Kensington, 329.
B Connors, North Bedeque, 329.
a Read, Summerside, 328.
ose Stewart, Ch'town, 326.
McKenzie, Ch'town, 325.
phy, Emyvale, 325.

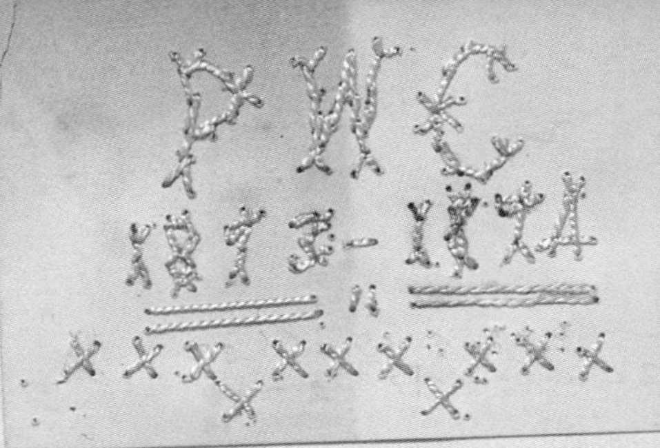

Albert Lynch

The following ...

metic, a vital subject, will be study in the college, but not fo te the license:

Stuart Simpson, Bay View, 382.
Esther Oxenham, Brookfield, 370.
Annie Fraser, Kensington, 351.
Agnes B Sharkey, Corraville, 341.
Wal Curtis, Milton, 336.
Ella atthew, Souris, 335.

Th following candidates, unsuccessful in th senior examination, passed the junior:

Nora Reid, Ch'town, 261.
Emmanuel Arsenault, Abram's Village, 247.
A D McArthur, New Dominion, 246.
Katie Monaghan, Treugh, 244.
Wallace Ellis, Mill Cove, 243.
Willie Coombs, Ch'town, 242.
Fenten T. Aitken, Lower Montague, 242.
Alma Robertson, Ch'town, 242.
Charles Kennedy, Bradalbane, 241.
Bessie McKinnon, Souris, 240
John Callaghan, Emyvale, 233
Cecil Stewart, Ch'town, 232
J Stewart McNeill, Rocky Point, 230
Katie B McLean, Culloden, 2
Maggie McDonald, Souris, 229
Norman Campbell, Darlington, 228
Donald M C H Crawford, Wood Is North, 226
Edith Finlayson, Ch'town, 226
Percy Crosby, Marshfied, 225
Hugh McEachern, Rock Barra, 225

Junior examination—Number of marks attainable, 450; necessary to pass, 225:

Jemima McPhail, Argyle Shore, 281
Alexander Martin, Eldon, 278
Marianne Cummings, Hunter River, 257.
A J Myers, Ch'town, 257
Louis H Douglas, Mt Stewart, 252
Maurice McDonald, Kelly's Cross, 2
Adeline Arsenault, Tignish, 246
Agnes Arsenault, Abram's Village, 2
Clement F Flood, Kelly's Cross, 237
Oscar W Roberts, Murray Harbor N 227
Peter Morrison, Georgetown, 227
James A Rodd, Brackley, 226.

The following having previously pass the junior examination have been succes ful in the senior:

Enoch Mugford, Ch'town, 144
Minnie Shea, Kensington, 137
Katie McMurdo, Kensington, 133

PARENT AND OFFSPRING.

Mamma—What are you playing with Essie?

Essie—A caterpillar an' two little kittenpillars.

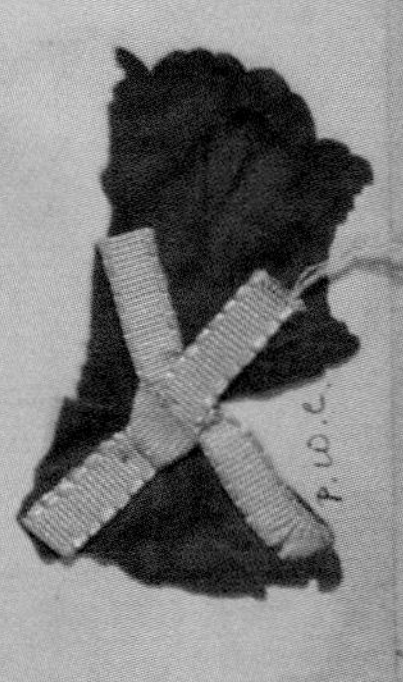

GRANDFATHE OCK.

"Yes, my boy, it's over a hundred years old, and goes for eight days without winding."

"And how long does it

Page 5 from the Blue Scrapbook

Nor do we often find any thing more genuinely, passionately tender than this from "Interludes:"

"Good night! I have to say good night
To such a host of peerless things!
Good night unto that fragile hand
All queenly with its weight of rings;
Good night to fond, uplifted eyes,
Good night to chestnut braids of hair,
Good night unto the perfect mouth,
And all the sweetness nestled there—
The snowy hand detains me, then
I'll have to say good night again!

But there will come a time, my love,
When, if I read our stars aright,
I shall not linger by this porch
With my adieus. Till then good night!
You wish the time were now? And I—
You do not blush to wish it so?
You would have blushed yourself to death
To own so much a year ago—
What, both these snowy hands! ah, then
I'll have to say good night again."

THE WEAKER SEX.

She'd been a belle all winter long—the queen, in fact, of all,
She'd been to all the coaching meets; had danced at every ball.
No function of society had this fair maiden missed,
Her name was certain to be found on every social list.

When summer came she went away to get a needed rest,
And to the hills she hied herself, because they pleased her best,
And this is how she took her ease, this lovely city belle,
And this is how she 'rested' in that little mountain dell:

She walked each day a dozen miles 'twixt breakfast-time and one;
She bowled five games of tenpins ere the lunch-hour was begun;
She played five sets of tennis, and she took a horseback ride,
And then a row upon the lake this worn-out maiden tried.

She dressed for dinner after six; and when the meal was o'er
She promenaded up and down the hotel corridor,
Until at nine the orchestra began its evening task,
And then she danced the hours through with any one who'd ask.

She danced the waltz with Billy Jones; she danced the York with me:
She tripped the polka with a boy whose age was ten and three;
And when the men were all worn out and ready for repose,
This lovely belle was just as fresh as any budding rose.

And as I watched this maiden when the day at last was done,
I deemed her the most wonderful of wonders 'neath the sun.
Her kind of 'rest' would take a man—the strongest man I know—
And but a single week of it would surely lay him low.

And so I asked this question, which this maid brought to my mind,
As I sat wrapped in wonderment at her and all her kind;
Why is it that these girls can do the things that make men wrecks,
And yet be called by all mankind at large 'The Weaker Sex?'

COURTSHIP IN CHURCH.

A YOUNG gentleman happening to sit in church in a pew adjoining one in which sat a young lady, for whom he conceived a sudden and violent passion, was desirous of entering into a courtship on the spot; but the place not suiting a formal declaration, the exigency of the case suggested the following plan: He politely handed his fair neighbor a Bible (open) with a pin stuck in the following text: Second Epistle of John, verse fifth—"And now I beseech thee, lady, not as though I wrote a new commandment unto thee, but that which we had from the beginning, that we love one another." She returned it, pointing to the second chapter of Ruth, verse tenth—"Then she fell on her face, and bowed herself to the ground, and said unto him, "Why have I found grace in thine eyes, that thou shouldst take knowledge of me, seeing that I am a stranger?'" He returned the book, pointing to the thirteenth verse of the Third Epistle of John—"Having many things to write unto you, I would not write with paper and ink, but I trust to come unto you, and speak face to face, that our joy may be full." From the above interview a marriage took place the ensuing week.

HARVARD
BRONCHIAL
SYRUP

PROVINCIAL EXAMINATIONS

JUNIOR EXAMINATION

FOR

ENTRANCE TO THE NORMAL SCHOOL

COMMENCING ON THE

FIRST TUESDAY IN JULY

1894

This examination will be held at the following local centres:—Charlottetown, Summerside, Montague, Souris, and Alberton.

Subjects for Examination:

ENGLISH—Parsing and Analysis from Goldsmith's Traveller, Reading, Composition, and Literature from page 1 of the Sixth Reader to page 200. (The candidates' papers on this subject will be examined as an exercise in dictation). 85

HISTORY.—British and Canadian History, as in Schmitz' History of England, and Calkin's History of British America. British, from the beginning of the Tudor Period to the end of the Brunswick. Canadian History from Chapter 17 to the end. 78

Souvenir of Dr. Anderson's Room. P. W. College 1893–94

"Professors who led us thro' learning's dark maze
Who crammed us with classical knowledge"!

Page 7 from the Blue Scrapbook

Education office
Charlottetown June 1893

On July 4th you will be expected to present yourself at Charlottetown for the Senior & Junior Examination
your number will be 32

D. J. McLeod
Chief Supt. of Educatn

California Grass.

In Memoriam
of
"The Saturdayite".

"A friend in need is a friend indeed"
"Man was made to mourn".

Prince of Wales College.
July 5. 4
/93

Time - Table
of
Matriculation Examination into
Prince of Wales College and Normal School _
July 1893.

Tuesday July 4th.
10 - 1 - - - - English done
2.30 - 5 - - - - History done

Wednesday July 5th.
9 - 12 - - - - - Arithmetic done
2 - 4.30 - - - Geography & Agriculture done

Thursday July 6th.
9 - 12 - - - Geometry & Algebra done
2 - 4.30 - - Latin. done

Hurrah! Hurrah!! Hurrah!!!

ON THE ROAD.

We were out on the road that moonlight night,
Willie and I sitting side by side:
The little bay mare stepped gayly and light,
It was such a beautiful night for a ride.

We passed Nell Howe in the phæton with Paul
(She madly loved Willie, and that I knew);
Sweet lover-like words in my ear he let fall,
And vowed we would ever, yes, ever be true.

The little bay mare would be mine, he said,
And I would reign queen of his heart for aye;
Then he kissed me good night, while the stars overhead
Shone bright, and the full moon flooded the sky.

. . . .

'Tis a whole year ago, oh alas and alack!
We quarreled and parted—a sorry affair;
Paul and I, best of friends, in the phæton lean back,
While Nell, Willie's wife, drives the little bay mare.

PRINCE OF WALES COLLEGE

Commencement Exercises This Evening at the Masonic Opera House.

Programme of Exercises---Honor List of the Year---Names of Those Who Won Prizes.

Prince of Wales College "Commencement" will be held this evening at the Masonic Opera House, beginning at 8 o'clock. Premier Peters will occupy the chair. The programme prepared for the occasion is as follows:

PROGRAMME.

Chorus—"England"..................College
Essay—"Portia"....Lucy M. Montgomery
College Song............................College
Essay—"The Merchant of Venice"...
.............................Louise Laird
Vocal Solo and Chorus—"Let Me Dream Again"..Geoffrey Bayfield, etc
Valedictory.............James H. Stevenson
Chorus—"Lady, Rise! Sweet Morn's Awaking".........................College
Reply by the Principal.
Semi Chorus from Lucretia Borgia....
....College
Honor List, Presentation of Diplomas, Medals, &c.
College Song............................College
Address to the Graduates.................
............Rev. Edward Walker, D. D.
Vocal Solo—"Shall Our Parting be Forever?"..................Annie Moore
College Song............................College
Address by the President...Hon. F. Peters
Chorus—"Old May Day"...........College
"God Save the Queen."

The diplomas and prizes of the year have been awarded to the following young ladies and young gentlemen:

GRADUATING DIPLOMAS.

HONOR DIPLOMAS.

James H Stevenson, New Glasgow, 95.
John F Reilly, Summerside, 94.
Chesley Schurman, Summerside, 90.
Reginald Stewart, Charlottetown, 90.
Talmage McMillan, New Haven, 88.
Wilfred Forbes, Vernon River, 86.
Lester Brehaut, Murray Harbor, 86.
Geoffrey Bayfield, Charlottetown, 83.
Louise Laird, Charlottetown, 81.
Hedley McKinnon, Charlottetown, 78.

FIRST-CLASS ORDINARY DIPLOMAS.

David Shaw, Covehead, 94.
Howard A Leslie, Souris, 93.
Everett McNeill, Lower Montague, 92.
Charles A Myers, Charlottetown, 89.
Albert Saunders, Summerside, 88.
Joseph D Coffin, Charlottetown, 87.
Charles G Duffy, Shamrock, 86.
Wallace Coffin, Mount Stewart, 86.
Edwin McFadyen, Tignish, 83.
Ernest Ramsay, Hamilton, 81.
William Sutherland, Sea View, 81.
Ira J Yeo, Charlottetown, 78.
Samuel Enman, Pownal, 76.
Mabel Fielding, Alberton, 75.

SECOND-CLASS ORDINARY DIPLOMAS.

Michael Coughlan, Hope River, 72.
Harriet Lawson, Charlottetown, 70.
John C Sims, French River, 68.
Fannie Wise, Milton, 68.
Oliver Lawson, Charlottetown, 65.
Lena Barrett, Charlottetown, 63.
Clara Lawson, Charlottetown, 61.

MEDALS.

Governor-General's Silver Medal—James H Stevenson.

Governor-General's Bronze Medal, for Teaching and School Management—Ethel Connors, North Bedeque.

Medal awarded by Mr. Miller for the best-kept set of books in the class of Bookkeeping John A. McPhee.

The judges of bookkeeping were John S. Lewis, R. H. Jenkins and John Connolly. In awarding the medal, they desired honorable mention to be made of the work of Kenneth Graham, Ella J. Stavert and Jessie Stavert.

THIRD YEAR.

Note.—Those students who have gained 75 per cent., or over, of the attainable number of marks are placed in the first rank; those from 60 to 74 in the second rank.

Latin, Horace and Livy—first rank: J H Stevenson and Chesley Schurman, equal; L MacMillan, J Reilly and Reginald Stewart, equal; W Forbes, L Brehau[t] H McKinnon, Louise Laird and Norm[an] Hunter, Alberton, equal; Geoffrey Bayfi[eld]

Latin Composition—first rank: J

Stevenson, J Reilly, T K MacMillan and C Schurman, equal; R Stewart, W Forbes; second rank: L Brehaut, H McKinnon, G Bayfield, Louise Laird.

Greek, Homer and Herodotus—first rank: J H Stevenson, R Stewart, J F Reilly, C Schurman, L R McMillan, W Forbes, L Brehaut, equal; second rank: H McKinnon.

Greek Composition—first rank: J H Stevenson, W Forbes, R Stewart, J F Rielly, C Schurman, L Brehaut; second rank: L R McMillan, H McKinnon.

Higher Algebra—first rank: J F Reilly, R Stewart, C Schurman, equal; J Stevenson, L McMillan, equal; L Brehaut, W Forbes, G Bayfield, equal; second rank: H McKinnon.

Geometry, conic sections, &c—first rank: J H Stevenson, R Stewart, J F Rielly, equal; C Schurman, L Brehaut, L R McMillan, W Forbes, equal; Louisa Laird; second rank: H McKinnon, G Bayfield.

English, Childe Harold, &c—first rank: J F Reilly, R Stewart, H McKinnon, equal; J Stevenson, W Forbes, equal; Louise Laird, L McMillan, G Bayfield, equal; L Brehaut.

English Literature—first rank: Louisa Laird, R Stewart, equal; J H Stevenson, J Reilly, L Brehaut, H McKinnon, G Bayfield, equal; W Forbes.

French, Chateaubriand, "Aventures du dernier Abencerage," &c—first rank: J Stevenson, C Schurman, R Stewart, equal; Louise Laird, W Forbes, L Brehaut, L McMillan, equal; H McKinnon, J Rielly, equal; G Bayfield.

Chemistry—first rank: J Rielly, J H Stevenson, W Forbes, C Schurman, L Brehaut, equal; L. McMillan, Louise Laird, R. Stewart, G. Bayfield; second rank: H. McKinnon.

History of Rome, first rank—J. H. Stevenson, J. F. Reilly, C. Schurman, L. McMillan, G. Bayfield, R. Stewart, L. Brehaut, W. Forbes, H. McKinnon; second rank: Louise Laird.

SECOND YEAR.

Latin, Virgil & Cicero—1, David Shaw; 2, Howard Leslie, Albert Saunders and Norman Hunter, equal; 3, Everett McNeil; 4, Charles Myers; 5, Edwin McFadyen a[nd] ... equal.

Latin Composition—1, Howard Leslie; 2, David Shaw; 3, Samuel Willis, Kingston; 4, Everett McNeill; 5, Joseph Coffin ... Albert Saund[ers]

Greek Gr[ammar] and Xenophon—1, David Shaw; 2, Howard Leslie; 3, S Willis; 4, Stuart Simpson, Bay View; 5, Edwin McFadyen; 6, William Sutherland.

Greek Composition—1, N Hunter; 2, S Willis, E. McFadyen and Ernest Ramsay, equal; 3, D Shaw and H. Leslie, equal; 4, Matthias Smith, Kelly's Cross, and Ethelbert McDuff, Kingston.

English, "The Merchant of Venice," &c—1, Lucy M Montgomery; 2, Charles Myers, David Shaw and Charles Duffy, equal; 3, Everett McNeill and Michael Coughlan, equal; 4, Annie Moore, Crapaud, and Wallace Coffin, equal; 5, Nellie McGrath.

English Literature—1, Lucy Maud Montgomery; 2, Samuel Willis and Albert Saunders, equal; 3, Charles Duffy and David Shaw, equal; 4, Howard Leslie, Charles Myers and Everett McNeill, equal.

French, "Racine's Iphigenie," etc—1, David Shaw; 2, Charles Duffy; 3, Everett McNeil and Jos Coffin, equal; 4, Wallace Coffin; 5, Chas Myers and Howard Leslie, equal.

Geometery—1, Chas Myers, 2, H Leslie, Matthias Smith and C Duffy, equal; 3, Stuart Simpson, Chester Houston, Wallace Coffin and Everett McNeill, equal; 4, W Sutherland; 5, E McFayden.

Algebra—1, D Shaw, C Myers and N Hunter, equal; 2, S Willis; 3, H Leslie and E Ramsay, equal; 4, Annie Moore; 5, Oliver Beck and Everett McNeil, equal.

Trigonometry—1, Matthias Smith; 2, D Shaw, C Duffy, S Willis and E McDuff, equal; 3, C Myers; 4, C Schurman; 5, A Saunders, F Dougherty and Wallace Coffin; 6, Everett McNeill and H Leslie, equal.

Chemistry—1, C Myers; 2, E McNeill; 3, D Shaw and Joseph Coffin, equal; 4, C Duffy; 5, H Leslie and E Ramsay, equal.

Physiology—1, C Duffy; 2, D Shaw; 3, M Smith; 4, O Lawson; 5, S Willis.

Horticulture—1, D Shaw, E McNeill, C Duffy and J Fraser; 2, E Ramsay; 3, J Sims; 4, H Leslie and J Howatt.

History of Rome—1, H Leslie and E McNeil; 2, N Hunter and T Willis, equal; 3, S Simpson, D Shaw and C Myers, equal; 4, A Saunders.

Agriculture—1, Lucy M Montgomery; 2, Matthias Smith; 3, Bessie ... [Spr]ingfield.

FIRST Y[EAR]

...—1, Lilian Robertson, Ch'town, Flora McPhee, Gray's Road; 2, Grace Dutcher, Souris, Mary McGregor, Gray's Road, equal; 4, Ellen Taylor, Ch'town; 5, Owen Horne, Milton.

Latin Composition—1, Ellen Taylor; 2, Edna Laird, North Bedeque; 3, Lilian Robertson; 4, Flora McPhee, Grace Dutcher, equal.

English, Milton's Paradise Lost, etc—1, Ellen Taylor; 2, Lillian Robertson, 3, Flora McPhee; 4, Thomas Driscoll, Mount Herbert, Edna Laird, Ethel Connors, North Bedeque.

French—1, Nellie Hodgson, Ch'town; 2, Flora McPhee; 3, Mary Jost, Ch'town; 4, Blanche Smallwood, Ch'town; 5, Ellen Taylor, Walter Curtis, Milton.

Bookkeeping—1, Katie McMurdo; 2, L B Mellish, Thomas Driscoll, Jenny Laird, equal.

Geometry—1, Grace Dutcher; 2, Lester Mellish, Union Road, George McLeod, Milton; 3, W. Curtis; 4, T. Driscoll, O. Horne equal; 5, James Todd, Bradalbane.

Algebra—1, Hattie McFarlane, Sea Cow Head; 2, L. Mellish; 3, T. Driscoll; 4. James Todd, George McLeod equal.

Arithmetic—1, Grace Dutcher, Patrick Campbell, Souris, T. Driscoll, L. Mellish equal; 2, O. Horne, Kenneth Graham, Bradalbane; 3, Hattie McFarlane; 4, W. Curtis.

Chemistry—1, Lillian Robertson; 2, Flora McPhee: 3, O Horne, Mary McGregor equel; 4, Peter L. Duffy, Emerald; 5, Edna Laird; 6, Ella Stavert, N. Bedeque.

Physiology—1, Peter Duffy; 2, Lilian Robertson, T. Driscoll, John McPhee, Bayfield, equal; 3, Charles C. Richards, Charlottetown; 4, O. Horne; 5, Edna Laird.

Physical Geography—1, James Campbell, Montague; 2, Lillian Robertson; 3, O. Horne; 4, Patrick Campbell; 5, W. Curtis, Hattie McFarlane equal.

Physics—1, Hattie McFarlane, P. Campbell equel; 2, Mary McGregor; 3, Katie McMurdo, Elytha Reid, S'Side, Annie McLean, New Dominion equal.

Agriculture—1, Katie McMurdo, Wilmot Valley; 2, L Driscoll, Elytha Reid and John McPhee, equal; 3, J Campbell; 4, Flora McPhee; 5, Grace Dutcher and G McLeod, equal.

History of England—1, P Campbell; 2, O Horne; 3, W Matheson, Ch'town; 4, Peter Duffy and J. McPhee, equal; 5, John Campbell and Lillian Robertson.

SECOND DIVISION.

Latin—1, William Robertson, Marshfield, and Cora White, North River, equal; 2, Annie McMillan, Wood Islands, and Colin Ferguson, Tulloch, equal; 3, Ellen Rodgerson, Pisquid; 4, Lawrence Curran, Victoria Cross.

Latin Composition—1, W Robertson and Josephine Dwan, equal; 2, Faustina McIver, Kinkora; 3, Esther Oxenham, Brookfield, and Annie McMillan, equal; 4, Agnes Sharkey, Corraville and Ellen Rodgerson, equal.

English—1, W Robertson; 2, Annie McMillan and Cora White, equal; 3, Esther Oxenham and Ellen Rodgerson, equal; 4, Maggie James and Willie Myers, Ch'town, equal.

French—1, Lizzie Kirwan, Tignish; 2, Esther Oxenham; 3, Clara Flemming, North Rustico; 4; Mary Campbell, Darlington; Ida B. Scott, Warren Grove; Annie Hennessey and Annie McMillan.

Geometry—1, W Robertson; 2, Ellen Rogerson, Lawrence Curran, Cora White, equal; 3, Colin Ferguson; 4, Esther Oxenham.

Algebra—1, W Robertson; 2, Ellen Rogerson; 3, Ida McEachern, Summerside; 4, Mary Campbell; 5, Colin Ferguson.

Arithmetic—1, W Robertson; 2, Annie McMillan, Colin Ferguson, Esther Oxenham, equal; 3, Ellen Rogerson, Percy Crosby, Marshfield, equal; 4, Cora White, Mary Campbell, equal.

Chemistry—1, Annie McMillan; 2, Cora White, Esther Oxenham, equal; 3, Ellen Rogerson, L Curran, equal; 4, W Robertson.

Physiology—1, Thomas Trainor, Kingston; 2, Annie McMillan, L Curran, equal; 3, Ellen Rogerson; 4, Cora White; 5, Bessie McKinnon, Souris; 6, W Robertssn, W Myers, equal.

Physical Geography—1, Cora White; 2, Ellen Rogerson; 3, Percy Crosby, Wallace Ellis, Millcove, equal; 4, W Myers; 5, Colin Ferguson.

Physics—1, Annie McMillan, Josephine Dwan, equal; 2, Regina Smith, Emerald; 3, Esther Oxenham; 4, Thomas Trainor; 5, W Robertson.

Agriculture—1, Esther Oxenham; 2, Cora White, Ellen Rogerson, equal; [3,] Annie Macmillan; 4, W. Roberts[on]

Page 9 from the Blue Scrapbook

On these pages, Montgomery brings Prince Albert and Prince of Wales days together, keeping "kindred spirits" interacting in imaginative play with events.

PAGE 10: Flowers were a part of the language Montgomery enjoyed with Laura and Willie Pritchard in Prince Albert. Bordered by flower cut-outs, a program from the Prince Albert St. John's Dramatic Club bears a white card on which someone has written "See his little eye" and attached the same dried grasses found on the inside front cover close to Willie's calendar. The program is for the play *Our Boys,* in which Willie had the part of Kempster, a footman. On this page, Montgomery brought Willie into contact with Jim Stevenson (who may have been a model for Anne Shirley's beau, Gilbert), whose valedictory address she wrote.

PAGE 12: The small clipping on the right-hand side appeared in Prince Albert, no doubt to the satisfaction of Maud's father and her Prince Albert friends. The almond flowers were from Portland, Oregon, possibly from Hattie Gordon, her former teacher in Cavendish. Montgomery put a radiant angel next to her gleeful annotation on the June 15 completion of exams.

PAGE 13: Montgomery probably collected souvenir railway photographs such as the one here when she made the trip to Saskatchewan in 1930 to visit Laura Pritchard Agnew and used them in the scrapbooks to replace items she may have removed to share with Laura. She collected clippings about her public recitations; she also kept the tissue flower from the January 8, 1894, concert at Winsloe Hall. Several sassy poems and jokes accompany a dyed feather and a ticket to a revival meeting she attended with Mary Campbell. Montgomery wrote in her diary: "B. Faye Mills, a noted evangelist, is at present holding meetings here and the place seems wild with excitement. . . . Mr. Mills did not impress me as being much of a speaker but there is something very magnetic about him. Ida 'got converted', as they say – how I hate the expression! – and I imagine Mary C. was pretty hard hit." The PWC magazine, *The College Record,* published Maud's playlet "The Usual Way" in April (Red Scrapbook, p. 42).

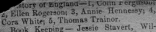

…story of England—1, Colin Ferguson; 2, Ellen Rogerson; 3, Annie Hennessy; 4, Cora White; 5, Thomas Trainor.

Book Keeping— Jessie Stavert, Wilmont Valley; Lester Mellish, Jennie Leard, North Carleton; Annie McLean; Hattie McFarlane; Ella Stavert, Kelvin Grove; Katie McMurdo, T. Driscoll.

Essays—Louise Leard and Lucy M. Montgomery.

School Management—1, Lucy M. Montgomery, David Shaw, equal; 2, Ida McEachern, Stuart Simpson, Nellie McGrath, Tignish, equal; 3, Howard Leslie, Lawrence Curran, Thomas Trainor, equal; 4, A[illegible] Robertson, Annie McMillan, equal;

Teaching—Ethel Connors; Annie Clark, Bay View; Mary Smith, Roseneath; Ellen Taylor; Lucy M. Montgomery; Edward Ryan, Johnston's River; Walter Curtis.

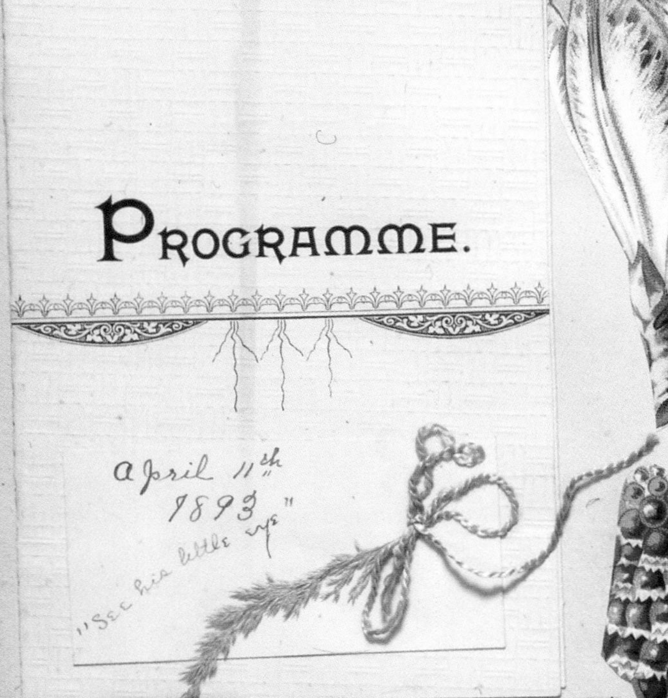

PRINCE OF WALES COLLEGE.

Commencement Exercises Last Evening.

The Valedictory and Dr. Anderson's Reply.

Music and Essays by the Pupils.

The Important Address of Rev. Dr. Walker, D. D.

Speeches by His Honor the Lieutenant-Governor and the Premier.

A New College Building Promised.

The Prince of Wales College commencement exercises in the Opera House last evening were well attended, and the greatest interest was taken in the proceedings. The programme prepared for the occasion was carried out in a manner which reflect[ed c]redit on all concerned.

The Hon. Fred. Peters, President of the Board of Education, presided. There were also on the platform His Honor the Lieutenant-Governor, the Superintendent of Education, Rev. Dr. Walker, Hon. Donald Farquharson, Hon. Angus McMillan, and Dr. Anderson and the teaching staff of the College. The pupils occupied seats on the stage, and a more intelligent-looking company of young ladies and gentlemen it would be hard to find anywhere.

Professor Earle presided at the piano and led the musical exercises, the different numbers being well executed considering the short period in which the pupils have been under the instruction of the Professor. Mr. James Hyndman assisted with his violin, playing with his usual skill.

Miss Annie Moore appeared for the first time as a soloist. She possesses a fine voice, which she will do well to cultivate fully.

The essay on "Portia," by Miss Montgomery, was well written and clearly and distinctly read. Miss Laird's subject was "The Merchant of Venice." Her paper was also well written, and it [was] capita[lly] read by Dr. Anderson. We regret [that] space will not admit of their publication in full to-day. But we shall try to find room for them in a future issue. T[he] valedictorian was Mr. James H. Steven[son,] "the best scholar in the school." …

Prince of Wales College Commencement.

BRILLIANT GATHERING

IN THE OPERA HOUSE.

THE CLOSING EXERCISES.

Graduation Day of the most important educational institution, (not yet university), in this province is numbered with the past, but joyous recollections will linger in the memories of the staff and students throughout a life time. It is a good thing to be a P E Islander.

Never has a more animated, more intellectual or more inspiring picture been seen on any stage in this Island, than that beheld by the large and select audience assembled last night. Lieut Governor, Premier, Judge and Mayor, all were there honoring and being honored.

On the platform, besides the chairman, Premier Peters, were Lieut Governor Howlan, who gracefully awarded the diplomas, the Hons. Angus McMillan, Donald Farquharson, Prof D J MacLeod, Chief Superintendent of Education, Dr. Anderson, the famed Principal of the Prince of Wales College, and its staff of Professors as follows, namely:—Messrs. Caven, Harcourt, Robertson Shaw and Miller. The students were arranged on the stage, the young ladies in the front row and centre, while the young men were grouped on either side.

The numbers on the pretty souvenir programme were rendered in true college style under the skilful direction of Prof. Earle, who presided at the piano and was publicly and warmly thanked at the conclusion of the exercises by Dr. Anderson.

The two essays read we hoped to have published in full to day, but owing to the length of Rev Dr Walker's excellent address to the graduates, we will have to defer their publication until Monday. Miss Lucy Maud Montgomery's analysis of Portia was of a high order. In well rounded periods she described the noble characteristics of mind and heart which make this heroine of Shakespeare one of the most admired of all the creations of his genius. We must add also that the essay was read with good effect

Miss Louisa Laird's resume of the plot in the Merchant of Venice showed a good deal of power of condensation. The chief points were seized, and spiritedly epitomized.

When the Valedictory number on the programme was announced, Mr. James H. Stevenson, the winner of the medal stepped forward, and after the loud and prolonged cheering had ceased, read in excellent form and with suggestive emphasis the following

VALEDICTORY.

Another year in the annals of the Prince of Wales College has rolled by and once again its students assemble here to welcome with pleasure those who have so kindly come to witness our commencement exercises. This is an hour when joy and happiness and and kindly feeling should pervade every heart, when every petty annoyance or disappointment of the past year should be forgotten, and everyone clasp hands in friendly affection, for to-night many of us must part to meet no more [as] fellow students and classmates.

Some in higher colleges will steadily strive to reach that far off shining goal where fame holds out her laurel crown; while some will bid farewell to college life to-night, and plunge at once into the busy w[orld] … thereto … wrest from the hands of fate the influence and fortune ever to be won by industry and perseverance. But whatever part we may pursue, whatever pleasures await us in after life, no memory will be so dear to our hearts as that of our college course. A tie of common fellowship will forever bind those who have wandered together through classic mazes or wrestled with mathematical mysteries at P. W. College.

A larger number of students than ever before have attended our college this session, and lack of accommodation has been the greatest drawback to satisfactory work. It is earnestly to be hoped that the powers that be will see fit at no distant day to provide us with a more commodious building. But notwithstanding this, the past year has been one of steady progress. All the various branches of the curriculum have been well sustained, and drawing has been added under the the able instruction of Prof Shaw.

But the College year has not been one of wholly unrelieved toil. Pleasant, and we also hope profitable, recreation was afforded by the Debating Society, where our budding orators displayed their powers, and by the football contests where strength and activity of body as well as of mind were promoted. A new departure has been witnessed by the publication of a monthly newspaper by some enterprising students. This bright little periodical is devoted to the interests of the College and has formed a pleasurable feature in the history of the year.

And as regards our Professors, what can we say but what has been said again and again by students who have gone out from this our college, encouraged and strengthened by their hearty assistance and sympathy. None of us will ever forget the instruction and advice of our energetic and esteemed Principal, Dr. Anderson. The recollection of Prof. Caven's genial humor will ever bring a smile to our faces and a hearty remembrance to our hearts. Prof. Harcourt, our teacher of science, has interested all and opened to our view many of the wonders of the natural world. Profs. Shaw and Robertson have taken the chairs formerly occupied by Profs. Robinson and West. It is superfluous to speak of the splendid work they have accomplished in their various departments; suffice it to say, that deserved success has crowned their efforts. Among the athletes of the college, Prof. Shaw will be gratefully remembered for the interest he has displayed in their sports. Prof. Miller and Arsenault have officiated in their several branches to the satisfaction of the students and all concerned. Owing to Mr Lloyd's departure from the province we had no instructor in music until late in the term, when Prof Earle commenced an enthusiastic and successful course of instruction, and the hours spent with him have been enjoyed, and will long be remembered by us all. We take this opportunity of extending our heartiest thanks to our friends in Ch'town, who have done so much to make our sojourn among them pleasant.

And now, dear fellow students, we turn to each other for a last farewell. Let each and all of us take this as a sacred trust through life to keep the reputation of our *Alma Mater* unsullied, to reflect honor on the teachers to whom we owe so much, and to help our fellow men to higher planes of thought and action. Let us take the sublime yet simple motto as our own: "*Ich Dien*—I serve." And let us serve—not ignoble ends, petty factions and the darker passions of human nature, but rather acknowledge as our masters only the noblest thoughts and motives, the highest aspirations and the kindliest feelings between man and man. Such a servitude would be glorious indeed. Once more, friends, professors, classmates, we bid you all farewell, and yet to the end of time we will be students, for what is the world, but one great college, where we must all learn the deepest lessons of human life. Let us then,

"Go forth prepared in every clime
To love and help each other,
And know that they who counsel strife,
Would bid us strike—a brother."

Page 10 from the Blue Scrapbook

Portland Oregon
Edmund Moscoun
The ties of love and friendship true no power on earth can sever
Greeting

Examinations For Teachers Certificates.

18 FIRST CLASS—31 SECOND CLASS.

FIRST CLASS.

Total number of marks 1400—necessary to obtain a license 840.

avid Shaw, Covehead, 1,083.
harles Myers, Charlottetown, 1,064.
verett McNeill, Lower Montague, 1,059.
harles Duffy, Shamrock, 1,044.
muel Willis, Kingston, 1,040.
aud Montgomery, Cavendish, 1,034.
allace Coffin, Mt Stewart, 1,031.
atthias Smith, Kelly's Cross, 1,028.
oward Leslie, Souris, 983.
oseph Coffin, Charlottetown, 964.
rnest Ramsay, Hamilton, 924.
William Grant, Mill View, 915.
Mabel Fielding, Alberton, 909.
Nellie McGrath, Tignish, 890.
nnis Fraser, Miscouche, 882.
Samuel Enman, Pownal, 877.
ra Yeo, Charlottetown, 846.
Mary V Connor, Tignish, 844.

Candidates for First Class License who have obtained Second Class.

Fannie Wise, Milton, 818.
Annie Moore, Crapaud, 805.
Bessie Haslam, Springfield, 794
Allan Matthews, Alberton, 765.
Frank Dogherty, Charlottetown, 752.
Oliver Lawson, Charlottetown, 751.
Michael Coughlan, Hope River, 746.
Ethelbert McDuff, Kingston, 742.
Oliver Beck, Murray Harbor South, 741.
Lena Barrett, Chalottetown, 742.
Winnie McKay, Clifton, 723.
Edward Ryan, Johnson's River, 680.
Rex Cameron, Souris East, 653.

SECOND CLASS—(Regular).

Total number of marks 1400—necessary to obtain a license 840.

Annie McMillan, Wood Islands, 1,004.
Esther Oxenham, Brookfield, 981.
Eliza Rogerson, Pisquid, 973.
Filias LeClerc, St Dunstan's, 971.
Mary Campbell Darlington, 947.
J F McDonald, Morell, 912.
Katie McMurdo, Wilmot Valley, 906.
Eliza McKinnon, Lot 14, 905.
Tillie O'Keefe, Avondale, 898.
Josie Dwan, Fortune Road, 891.
Ida McEachern, Summerville, 878.
Cora White, North River, 875.
Owen Horne, Milton, 856.
Grace Dutcher, Souris, 855.
Flora McPhee, Gray's Road, 852.
Laurence Curran, New Perth, 849.
Annie McLean, New Dominion, 838.
Regina Smith, Emerald, 838.

A Happy New Year

No 8 Lucy Maud Montgomery
P. W. College
1893-94.
September 6th – June 8th
Monday. June 11th
Begun!

At a teachers examination in Charlotteton, P. E. I., Miss Maud Montgomery, eldest daughter of Mr. H. J. Montgomery, succeeded in passing with high honers; standing fifth in a list of one hundred and thirty candidates. Miss Montgomery formerly resided in Prince Albert.

Time Table of Examination for Teachers' Licenses, June 1894.

Monday June 11th

	Class I		Class II
9 - 12	English	done all.	English
1.30 - 3.30	History	done all.	History
3.45 - 5.45	Agriculture	Done some	Agriculture

One day over

Tuesday. June 12th

9 - 12	Geometry	Done. 6 out of 8.	Geometry
1.30 - 3.30	French	done some.	French
3.45 - 5.45	Scientific Temperance	done	Scientific Tempe.

One step nearer freedom

Wednesday, June 13th

9 - 11.30	Latin	done all.	Latin
1.30 - 3.30	English Literature	done most.	Physics
3.45 - 5.45	School Management	done all	School Management

Light ahead.

Thursday, June 14th

9 - 11.30	Greek	done all	Geography
1.30 - 3.30	Chemistry	done some	Chemistry.
3.45 - 5.45	Algebra	done some.	Algebra

Almost there.

Friday. June 15th

9 - 11.30	Trigonometry		Arithmetic
	Optional English	done.	

At last.

"Hail, Freedom hail! Sweet Liberty!"
All finished.
20 minutes to twelve.
Friday Morning

10

Concert
&
Basket Social
Winsloe Hall
Jan 8th/94.

"Let him have it then".

"And it was cold
Oh it was cold!
$5.20. Amen!

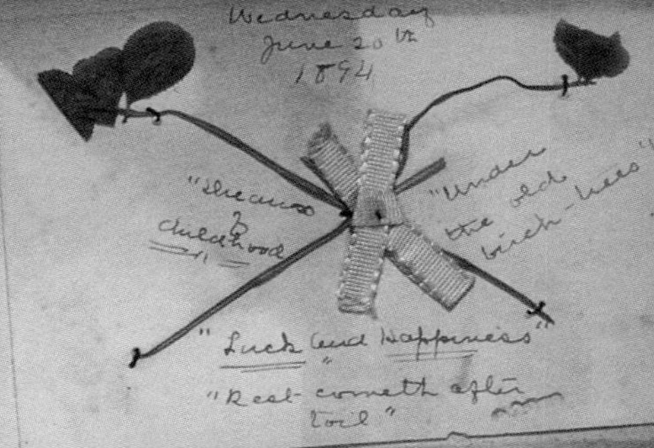

CONCERT AND BASKET SOCIAL.—Quite a number of people from the city drove up to Winsloe yesterday afternoon to "take in" the concert and basket social for the benefit of the hall at that place. The Choir of the First Methodist Church, assisted by some of our local talent rendered a programme of choruses and songs in a most pleasing manner. The songs were received with much applause by those present. Particularly good were the recitations by Miss Montgomery and the vocal selections by Messrs. Bremner and F. deC. Davies and Master Chas. Earle. In his selection, "The Cork Leg," Mr. Bremner fairly "brought down the house," as also did Master "Tod," by his capital rendition of "Sarah Jane." Both were encored. The second part of the entertainment consisted of the sale of baskets, which were rapidly bought up by the young men, some thirty being disposed of, bringing from $1 to $4 per basket. Messrs. L. E. Prowse, E. H. Norton and Sheriff Horne were the auctioneers. This brought the proceeding to a close. All were well pleased with the capital manner in which the entire proceedings were carried out.

Concert at Winsloe.

A very large audience assembled in the Winsloe Hall last night to listen to a concert given by the Choir of the First Methodist Church and their friends. The programme was a good one and faithfully carried out. The selections by the choir were fine. Messrs. Cooke, Lewis, and Davies' solos were well rendered. Master Charles Earle's "Good Bye Susan Jane," and Mr. Bremner's "Cork Leg," brought down the house. Miss Montgomery's Recitations were splendidly given. The good people of Winsloe are to be congratulated upon being the owners of such a beautiful Hall capable of seating we understand 300 people. The choir and friends are loud in their praise of the kindness shown them by the committee, and thoroughly appreciate their kindness. The baskets, which realized good prices, were auctioned off by Messrs L E Prowse, Sheriff Horne and E H Norton,—each of whom seemed to know his business thoroughly. Mr John T Holman's beautiful residence was open to receive the guests. It looked splendid—lit up from top to bottom. The Charlottetonians say "Long live Mr and Mrs J T Holman." They will not forget their kindness for some time to come.

Leading Clothier—D. A. BRUCE.

The College Record

"Non Collegio sed vitæ discimus."

VOL. I. P. W. COLLEGE, CHARLOTTETOWN, APRIL, 1894. NO. 3.

The College Record.

THE RECORD will be published monthly during the remainder of the term.

Subscription price 25 cents, in advance. Single copies 10 cents.

EDITORS—E. N. M. Hunter, H. McKinnon.

BUSINESS MANAGER—T. R. MacMillan.

☞ Address all communications to

BUSINESS MANAGER,
P. W. College,
Charlottetown.

DOROTHY: A DISAPPOINTMENT

BY CHARLES B. GOING

Her hair is soft—the brown that glows
With sudden little glints of gold;
Her rounded cheek, faint flushing shows,
Like apple buds that half unfold.

Her throat is full and round and white—
The sweet head poised so daintily;
She reads a note; I wish I might
Address her, too, "Dear Dorothy."

Ah, Dorothy, so very dear!
With clear sweet eyes of tender brown
And, close above the small pink ear,
The dark hair rippling gently down.

Dear Dorothy, so very fair!
My thoughts outrace the rushing train
To build strange castles in the air,
With Dorothy for chatelaine.

How sad when pleasures born of hope
Are born so late so soon to die!
She drops her letter's envelope
Addressed to—Mrs. Arthur Why!

MOUSTACHE EXAMINATION.

Passed—
Daniel Chowen.

Honorable Mention—
Thomas James.
Howard Leslie.

POMPADOUR EXAMINATION.

First Class—
Reginald Stewart.
Frederick Miller.

Passed—
Hedley McKinnon.
Charles Myers.

Honorable Mention—
Wallace Coffin.
Samuel Willis.

COMPLIMENTS OF
W. B. ROBERTSON,
Dealer in FARM SEEDS AND IMPLEMENTS.

1892

Jan.	1	2	3	4	5	6	7
	8	9	10	11	12	13	14
	15	16	17	18	19	20	21
	22	23	24	25	26	27	28
	29	30	31	...	...	...	...
Feb.	...	...	...	1	2	3	4
	5	6	7	8	9	10	11
	12	13	14	15	16	17	18
	19	20	21	22	23	24	25
	26	27	28	29	...	...	...
March	...	...	...	...	1	2	3
	4	5	6	7	8	9	10
	11	12	13	14	15	16	17
	18	19	20	21	22	23	24
	25	26	27	28	29	30	31
April	...	...	...	...	...	...	...
	1	2	3	4	5	6	7
	8	9	10	11	12	13	14
	15	16	17	18	19	20	21
	22	23	24	25	26	27	28
	29	30	...	...	...	...	...
May	...	...	1	2	3	4	5
	6	7	8	9	10	11	12
	13	14	15	16	17	18	19
	20	21	22	23	24	25	26
	27	28	29	30	31	...	...
June	...	...	...	...	...	1	2
	3	4	5	6	7	8	9
	10	11	12	13	14	15	16
	17	18	19	20	21	22	23
	24	25	26	27	28	29	30
July	1	2	3	4	5	6	7
	8	9	10	11	12	13	14
	15	16	17	18	19	20	21
	22	23	24	25	26	27	28
	29	30	31	...	...	...	...
Aug.	...	...	...	1	2	3	4
	5	6	7	8	9	10	11
	12	13	14	15	16	17	18
	19	20	21	22	23	24	25
	26	27	28	29	30	31	...
Sept.	...	...	...	...	...	...	1
	2	3	4	5	6	7	8
	9	10	11	12	13	14	15
	16	17	18	19	20	21	22
	23	24	25	26	27	28	29
	30	...	...	...	...	...	...
Oct.	...	1	2	3	4	5	6
	7	8	9	10	11	12	13
	14	15	16	17	18	19	20
	21	22	23	24	25	26	27
	28	29	30	31	...	...	...
Nov.	...	...	...	...	1	2	3
	4	5	6	7	8	9	10
	11	12	13	14	15	16	17
	18	19	20	21	22	23	24
	25	26	27	28	29	30	...
Dec.	...	...	...	...	...	...	1
	2	3	4	5	6	7	8
	9	10	11	12	13	14	15
	16	17	18	19	20	21	22
	23	24	25	26	27	28	29
	30	31	...	...	...	...	...

GOOD REASON FOR CRYING.

Among the early lawyers of Missouri were Judge James C—— and Gen. John C——, brothers, both excellent lawyers and splendid advocates. Gen. John, when occasion required, closed his argument to the jury bathed in tears himself, with most of the jury and audience weeping, too.

One day he and Judge James were trying a case, James prosecuting and John defending. James made his speech, a strong one for his side of the case, and ended with telling the jury:

"Gentlemen, my brother John will next address you on the other side of the case; and I want to caution you, he will cry and try to make you cry. He does it in all his cases."

Gen. John then spoke to the jury, making one of the very best of his pathetic appeals, causing jury and audience to forget James' admonition; and as tears were freely flowing, John, with great drops rolling down his cheeks, said to the jury:

"My brother Jim told you I would cry; I am crying; and, gentlemen of the jury, if you had such a darned mean brother as Jim, you would cry, too."

John's client was acquitted.

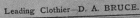

May 6th. New hats.

ADMIT TWO
DOORS OP N 3 00 P M

THE LAST DAY, SUNDAY, 3.30, P. M.

REV. B. FAY MILLS

AT FIRST METHODIST CHURCH

Owing to the crowds, this ticket must not be used by any church member, unless accompanied by one who is not.

Page 13 from the Blue Scrapbook

At the top of the page, the names printed beneath the flower tabs are (left) Selena Robinson, (centre) L.M. Montgomery, and (right) Lucie MacNeill, her cousin. The writing space shown in the magazine picture is very like Montgomery's own writing space in the Macneill homestead in Cavendish (below).

On June 30, 1891, Maud and Mary Stovel drove from Prince Albert to Lindsay to help a former schoolmate put on a concert at the Native school there. In her journal, Montgomery remarked on the flowers she saw en route: "The prairies are just one blush with wild roses now and we had a charming drive. We ... drove down to the log schoolhouse. It was in a state of glorious confusion, with loads of poplar boughs, wild roses, and orange lilies heaped about." As yet, Montgomery had no camera to take a picture of the place.

"LET THERE BE KITTENS."—"Who makes the kittens, Jackie?" "Why, God makes them, Ethel. He doesn't make them as he does babies, one by one, but He just says, 'Let there be kittens,' and there are kittens."

A TOUCH OF NATURE

BY MADELINE S. BRIDGES

FATHER (winding the clock): "Time to lock up now. It's nearly ten o'clock."

Mother: "Oh, don't hurry, father."

Father: "Don't hurry? We ought to be asleep by this time, considering we've got to be at the haying by sun-up to-morrow. Are the boys in bed?"

Mother: "They've gone up-stairs."

Father: "Well then, I'll close the——"

Mother: "Ida hain't come in yet."

Father: "Hain't come in? Why?"

Mother: "Oh, she's at the gate. She's been down to singing-class."

Father: "Well, why doesn't she——"

Mother: "Sh—sh—they'll hear you. There's a young man with her."

Father: A young man? Who?"

Mother: "Isaac Penn came up with her."

Father: "I should think her brothers would be company enough."

Mother (dryly): "Should you?"

Father: "And if a young man does walk up with her he needn't stand three hours at the gate."

Mother: "He hasn't been there ten minutes."

Father (severely): "He has no business to be there any minutes. Why doesn't he know enough to say good-night and go?"

Mother: "Ephram, wasn't there ever a young fellow that used to walk home with me from singing, and hang over the gate till all hours, especially a night like this?"

Father: "That was different. You were woman big."

Mother: "Ida's woman big. She's nineteen past."

Father: "Ida's nothing but a child."

Mother: "Well, she's a whole year older than I was, when you——"

Father (hastily): And, besides, er—ah—I was dead in love."

Mother (quietly): "How do you know that Isaac hain't?"

Father: "Isaac Penn in love with Ida? Sho! The boy hasn't a vote yet."

Mother: "He's got a heart, though. You had your first vote the year we were married—just remember that."

Father: "Mother, I'm surprised at you putting up with such nonsense about Ida. Time enough for her to keep company five years from now."

Mother (approvingly): "Of course it is, and it's time enough now, if the right one comes along. Isaac is good and steady."

Father (firmly): "Well, I won't have it, that's all. Call her in. It's bedtime."

Mother: "Ephram, you don't suppose I would do such a thing as that?"

Father (with sternness): "Neelie, it's your duty."

Mother (with spirit): "It isn't my duty to insult my daughter. My mother never did it to me."

Father (half smiling): "She never had to; you wouldn't let me stay so long."

Mother: "Oh, I wouldn't let you stay——"

Father: "And no sensible fellow would want to stay."

Mother: "You were a sensible fellow, Ephram."

Father: "Now, mother."

Mother (with decision): "But you were; every one said so."

Father: "I couldn't be sensible with Neelie; you just turned my head."

Mother (softly): "Well, they were pleasant times. I love to remember them."

Father: "Ye-es. I don't know as any one ever had a pleasanter courtship."

Mother: "But you were mighty jealous."

Father (musingly): "Was I? I suppose I was. I know there seemed to be always some one trying to cut me out."

Mother: "Do you remember the night at Lucy Crumm's wedding, when you sat and sulked all evening in a corner."

Father: "And that big student fellow from New Haven was shinning up to you? But I walked home with you, after all."

Mother: "I guess you did! And how you scolded. We stood at the gate till the moon rose—the little silver half moon."

Father: "And you cried, and we made it all up."

Mother: "And the next day you wrote me a letter"—(the gate clicks)—"oh, there comes Ida."

(Enter Ida, smiling, radiant.)

Ida: "It's the loveliest night! Just a sin to go to bed."

Father (smiling, also): "Well, Ida, dismissed your company, have you?"

Ida (demurely): "Isaac? Oh, yes."

Father: "What a shame to send him off so early."

Mother: "Ida knows what to do."

Father: "But Isaac don't. I'm blest if any girl could hustle me like that when I was Isaac's age!"

Forget Not the Old Folks at Home

BY LOUISE S. UPHAM.

Afar from the scenes your young hearts loved
Afar from the homestead's shade
O, active women and busy men,
Your toiling feet have strayed.
But whether you strive in the public mart,
Or by firesides of your own,
O, never forget the home of your youth,
And the couple who wait alone.

Their cups are *not* brimming o'er with joys,
Their hands are *not* full of flowers;
They live in life's silvering, autumn years,
And dwell in life's solemn hours.
When, together, they struggled up life's fair hill,
Child-voices made music sweet
In their happy home, while their hearts kept time
To the patter of little feet.

But now, adown the shadowy side
They wearily move, and slow;
And their eyes grow dim, when, with faltering tones,
They speak of the "long ago."
They gave their youth, they gave their strength,
That their children might attain
To station, or wealth, or heights of fame,
That never were theirs, to gain.

And now by the lonely hearth *they* wait,
Whose years are almost done,
Like shocks of corn that are whitening fast
In the mellow, autumn sun;
And the Benjamin-cup, in their burdened sacks,
The joy of all priceless joys,
Is the clasping hand and the yearning heart
And the love of their "girls and boys."

So, never forget the dear "old folks,"
And the blessings far away;
Far, farther off from their peace and rest,
Your feet each year will stray;
And, by and by, when the turf is pressed
O'er their graves, you will long, in vain,
For the loving smile and the welcoming kiss
That will never be yours again.

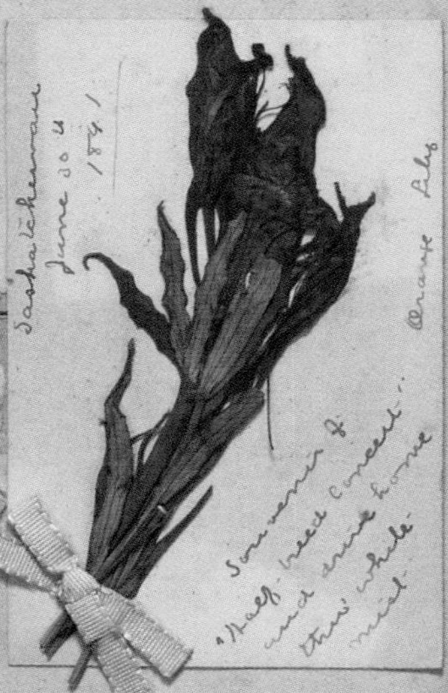

Wednesday
June 21st 1893

"Is that Mid. Easy?
"No it's not Mid. Easy
"Is that you Mid. Easy.

'Twas a beautiful
night
And the moonlight
bright
O'er the sparkling
waters played.

KISSES.

There's a great deal of bliss in a lingering kiss,
And oceans of solid rapture;
There are lots of fun in a stolen one—
If you're clever about the capture.

The cutest trick in a kiss that's quick
Is to put it where it belongs;
To see that it goes below the nose
And knocks at the gate of songs.

A kiss that is cold may do for the old,
Or pass with a near relation;
But one like that is a work—that's flat—
Of supererogation.

If your'e going to kiss, be sure of this—
That the girl has got some heart in her;
I wouldn't give a darn for the full of a barn
Of kisses without a partner.

The point of this rhyme is to take your time
Kiss slowly, and do it neatly;
If you do the thing right, and are halfway keen
You can win her sweet heart completely.

In one page, Montgomery created a playful overview of her happy first months in her first teaching post, in Bideford, P.E.I., which she held from 1894 to 1895. Three of the clippings in the corners are wedding announcements and the fourth (bottom right) is a notice about Lou Dystant, a local young man who fell in love with her. The central souvenir is a farewell to Cavendish, the village which Montgomery later fictionalized as Anne's Avonlea. Flowers signify exuberance, and cards sketching small dramas were arranged like small nosegays around a central bouquet.

On Thursday, July 26, 1894, Maud received word in Cavendish that she had been accepted as teacher for the Bideford school (card bottom right). On the same day, she had a letter from Laura Pritchard out west hinting that she would soon be engaged to Andrew Agnew. Maud celebrated her new life and old friendships, especially with her cousins Pensie and Lucie Macneill, the "trio."

On July 28 (card centre), Pensie and Lucie drove Maud to the Hunter River train station at five in the morning.

Maud was met at the Ellerslie train station, which serviced Bideford, by Bayfield Williams (card top centre) and his fiancée, Edith England, both of whom would remain her friends and would appear in scrapbooks decades later.

Maud enjoyed a series of parties and dances held in August in honour of Bayfield Williams and his brother Arthur, who were home on holidays (August 9 and August 16, 1894, cards left and right of centre). She adored dancing.

On October 19, 1894 (card top right), she danced the night away at Charley McKenzie's party in Cavendish. "After the Ball Is Over," a sentimental song by Charles K. Harris, was the Tin Pan Alley platinum hit of the 1890s.

On Guy Fawkes' Night, November 5, 1894 (card top centre), Maud met Lewis Dystant (she spelled his name Lew and Lou) at an Ellerslie social and he invited her out. He escorted her and his sister Sadie to the November 15 (card bottom left) Tyne Valley Social. He would continue to send her poetry even after she refused him.

On December 28, 1894 (card top left; the year is mistakenly written as 1895), Maud celebrated her first successful school examination with flowers. School (oral) examinations were open to the public and were big community events, complete with speeches and tributes.

Maud finished the year with another triumph. At the Tyne Valley Concert (card bottom centre) on December 29, she played in two dramatized dialogues and had the pleasure of finding that her basket, decorated with the apricot-coloured crepe paper preserved here, claimed the highest price of any when it was bought by the smitten Lou Dystant. Decorated baskets of food, often pies, were auctioned off to raise money for community projects, this time for a new hall in Bideford.

Page 15 from the Blue Scrapbook

Several stories revealed on this page comment on courtship and marriage. Beneath the comic poem "A Duet" Montgomery placed the announcement of her Uncle Leander's engagement to the woman who was to be his third wife. The title of the more melancholy poem "After the Ball" may deliberately echo the popular song "After the Ball Is Over," which Maud quoted on the preceding page. A bouquet of flowers picked in 1890, when young Maud was on her way to Prince Albert with Grandfather Montgomery, marks an especially happy surprise: In Regina, her father joined them to travel on to Prince Albert.

Suitors

It is ironic that a woman who received more than a dozen marriage proposals and even more declarations of passion should end up marrying a man she did not love intensely. Having secretly accepted the Rev. Ewan Macdonald's proposal in October of 1906, the almost thirty-two-year-old Montgomery wrote that same day in her journal: "Perfect and rapturous happiness, such as marriage with a man I loved intensely would give me, I have ceased to hope for." She had felt rapturous happiness with Herman Leard when she was twenty-three, but they were both engaged to other people, and she did not consider him her equal in either intellect or ambition. The unfulfilled romance with Herman was to be the touchstone for passion for the rest of her life, and against which she would measure her physical attraction to Oliver Macneill in 1909.

Maud's first declaration of love came in her early teens, and Nate Lockhart continued to write to her well into his Acadia University years. When she was sixteen, visiting her father in Prince Albert, she was sent an anonymous Christmas present by one boy; welcomed the attentions of her best friend's brother, Willie Pritchard; and deflected the proposal of her teacher, John A. Mustard. At least three Cavendish youths – Jack Laird, Henry McLure, and Alec Macneill – pursued her; and while she was teaching, Lem McLeod and Lou Dystant proposed, as did Edwin Simpson, to whom she was so miserably engaged while she was trysting with Herman. Imagine the havoc in the Belmont Simpson family: She rejected, then accepted, then rejected Ed; his brother Fulton became obsessed with her; and she drove about with another brother, Alf.

By the time Ewan Macdonald came to Cavendish in 1903, perhaps Montgomery was tired of the struggle she had identified between "the passionate Montgomery blood and the Puritan Macneill conscience" and had opted optimistically for a comfortable match of backgrounds and ambitions.

With the Christmas greetings of the Editor

Picked on prairies between Regina and Prince Albert — souvenir of ride in a "caboose"

A DUET.

BARITONE—Now we're engaged, if you have brothers.
By that I mean the men whom you've refused.
They must be on a footing with the others;
I won't have any mild endearments used.
Now we're engaged.

SOPRANO—If you had any sister and I knew it,
I mean a girl who said she'd be your sister,
She should be taught how not to do it,
And comprehend that you can quite resist her.
Now we're engaged.

BARITONE—As if I wished to look at other beauties,
Now you are mine.
SOPRANO— As though I cared for men
Compared to you! I hope I know my duties;
Of course we used to flirt, but that was then:
Now we're engaged.

BARITONE—Who was the man with topcoat lined with sable?
SOPRANO— Who was the girl with bonnet trimmed with pink?
BARITONE—I would inform you, but I am unable.
SOPRANO— I'd tell his name, but really I can't think.
Now we're engaged.

BARITONE—Now no more lingering in conservatories,
Under dim colored lights and tropic bowers.
SOPRANO— Now no more reading sentimental stories
To girls and giving them bonbons and flowers;
Now we're engaged.

BARITONE—I shall not tolerate the least flirtation,
I warn you fairly.
SOPRANO— Please don't be enraged;
But might we sometimes take a brief vacation,
Now we're engaged!
—*Yankee Blade.*

The engagement is announced of the Rev. L. G. Macneill, the eloquent and able pastor of St. Andrew's church, to Miss Mary Kennedy, daughter of Ald. James Kennedy of Summer street.

After the Ball.

They sat and combed their beautiful hair,
Their long, bright tresses, one by one,
As they laughed and talked in the chamber there,
After the revel was done.

Idly they talked of waltz and quadrille;
Idly they talked, like other girls,
Who over the fire, when all is still,
Comb out their braids and curls.

Robe of satin and Brussels lace,
Knots of flowers and ribbons, too,
Scattered about in every place,
For the revel is through.

And Maud and Madge in robes of white,
The prettiest nightgowns under the sun,
Stockingless, slipperless, sit in the night,
For the revel is done.

Sit and comb their beautiful hair,
Those wonderful waves of brown and gold,
Till the fire is out in the chamber there
And the little bare feet are cold.

Then out of the gathering winter chill,
All out of the bitter St. Agnes weather,
While the fire is out and the house is still,
Maud and Madge together—

Maud and Madge in robes of white,
The prettiest nightgowns under the sun,
Curtained away from the chilly night,
After the revel is done,

Float along in a splendid dream
To a golden gittern's tinkling tune,
While a thousand lusters shimmering stream
In a palace's grand saloon.

...hing of jewels and flutter of laces,
...al odors sweeter than musk,

Men and women with beautiful faces
And eyes of tropical dusk—

And one face shining out like a star,
One face haunting the dreams of each,
And one voice sweeter than others are,
Breaking into silvery speech—

Telling, through lips of bearded bloom,
An old, old story over again,
As down the royal bannered room,
To the golden gittern's strain,

Two and two they dreamily walk,
While an unseen spirit walks beside,
And, all unheard in the lover's talk,
He claimeth one for a bride.

O Maud and Madge, dream on together,
With never a pang of jealous fear!
For, ere the bitter St. Agnes weather
Shall whiten another year—

Robed for the bridal and robed for the tomb,
Braided brown hair a... ...lden tress,
There'll be only one of yo... left for the bloom
Of the bearded lips to press—

Only one for the bridal pearls,
The robe of satin and Brussels lace,
Only one to blush through her curls
At the sight of a lover's face.

O beautiful Madge in your bridal white
For you the revel has just begun,
But for her who sleeps in your arms tonight
The revel of life is done.

But, robed and crowned with your saintly bliss,
Queen of heaven and bride of the sun,
O beautiful Maud, you'l... ...ver miss
The kisses another ha... ...n.
—Nora Perry.

Page 16 from the Blue Scrapbook

PAGE 18: Two bouquets of flowers, almost exactly three years apart, celebrate Montgomery's progress from high school student to teacher. August 26, 1891, was her last day in Prince Albert. Maud and Laura tearfully picked bouquets of petunias, mignonette, and sweet peas in the garden outside Eglinton Villa (the name her father chose to emphasize his family's link with the Earls of Eglinton) to exchange as keepsakes. On August 8, 1894, Maud was enjoying a lively social life in Bideford. An outing to Indian Island was one of a series of parties the Williams put on for their vacationing sons, Bayfield and Arthur. The clipping headed Ellerslie Notes gratified Montgomery by saying she was "proving herself a good teacher."

PAGE 19: A writer plays with the idea of romance. Marie Duplessis (1824–47), the famous French courtesan sometimes called Camille, was celebrated for her beauty and wit. Her tragic early death inspired novels, plays, opera (Verdi's *La Traviata*), and films; the poignancy of Duplessis's story would have thrilled Anne Shirley. The memory of a comic drama is preserved with the daisy: On the evening of June 16, 1893, in the last days before Maud took the entrance exams for Prince of Wales College, Maud, Selena Robinson, and Jack Laird forced entrance into the locked schoolhouse as a lark, accidentally breaking a window.

PAGE 20: Here, Montgomery assembled mementoes from each of the years from 1891 to 1895. In 1895, she left her happy post in Bideford to take a year-long special course in English at Dalhousie. She would give Anne Shirley the same cheerful teaching experiences and expand her own one year at the Halifax university into Anne's four-year B.A. program at the fictitious Redmond College of Kingsport. Pasted above a magazine cut-out of the Saskatchewan River (a prominent part of her Saskatchewan life) is an invitation for the April 8, 1891, wedding of Maud's stepmother's aunt, Mary McKenzie, to Cyrus Stovel. The **burnt match** on the white card at the bottom left is from December 19, 1892, when Montgomery was back in Cavendish at her old school preparing for the entrance examinations for Prince of Wales. The verse reads: "When half-smiling, half sighing you're musing / Over pleasures you've had in the past / Oh say if you still had the choosing / Would you choose that such pleasures could last?" In the centre of the page is a February 1895 obituary for her Uncle John Montgomery, of whom she was fond. The horseshoe of flowers, like the 1893 horseshoe mascot celebrating the prospect of Prince of Wales life that opened the scrapbook, embraces Dalhousie school colours.

Eglinton Villa
Prince Albert
Saskatchewan
Lennox Island,
Wednesday,
Picnic
My thoughts are with you this Christmastide
Thought with thought is fondly meeting,
While our hearts with love are beating.

THE FIRST SONG-SPARROW.

Sunshine set to music!
  Hear the sparrow sing!
In his note is freshness
  Of the new-born Spring:
In his trill delicious
  Summer overflows—
Whiteness of the lily,
  Sweetness of the rose.

Splendor of the sunrise,
  Fragrance of the breeze,
Crystal of the brooklet
  Trickling under trees,
Over moss and pebbles,
  Hark! you have them all
Prophesied and chanted
  In the sparrow's call.

Pilgrim of the tree-tops,
  Burdened with a song
That he drops among us
  As he flies along,
Promises and blessings
  Scattering at our feet,
Till we sing together,
  "Oh, but life is sweet!"

Listen! the song-sparrow!
  Spirit! or a bird
Simple joy of singing
  In his song is heard.
Somewhere, far in glory,
  Love our life has kissed;
He resounds the rapture,—
  Heavenly optimist!

Resurrection-singer!
  Gladness of the year!
In thine Easter-carol
  Bringing heavens so near
That we scarcely know it
  From the earth apart;—
Sing immortal summer
  To the wintry heart!

Waft us down faith's message
  From behind the sky,
Till our aspirations
  With thee sing and fly!
"God is good forever!
  Nothing shall go wrong!"
Sunshine set to music—
  'Tis the sparrow's song!—*Lucy Larcom.*
[Written in 1889.]

BASHFUL.

JOHN—"Sallie, ef I was to ask you if you'd marry me, do you think yo[u] yes?"

SALLIE—"I—er—I guess so."

JOHN—"Wa-al, ef I ever git over this 'ere darn bashfulness I'll ask y[ou] o' these times."

Ellerslie Notes.

[We]lcome Division is in a flourishing condition. [Br]other Williams, our Worthy Patriarch, is [a youn]g man of push and ability and under his [able] direction we prophecy success for our

[Som]e of our young people have not lost their [love] for the old fashioned dance. Quite a num[ber of] select ones met at the house of James [...], at Bideford, a few nights ago and were [ca]ptivated by the sweet strains of music from the [fi]ddle of Angus Currie until the "wee sma' 'ours."

The people of Bideford have decided to build [a]n English Church. It will be built upon the [ol]d site adjoining the beautiful grounds of the [M]ethodist parsonage, and the frame, which was [buil]t about four years ago, will be used.

The trustees of the Bideford School have at [la]st succeeded in getting a teacher. Miss M. [M]ontgomery is the one selected and is proving [he]rself a good teacher.

A large congregation assembled at the Meth[odi]st Church on Sunday evening, the 12th inst., [to] hear Rev. J. Dystant, a former resident of the [pla]ce, preach. His text was Luke 17: 14. The [ser]mon was well delivered, very impressive and [wa]s listened to with rapt attention.

OBSERVER.

ABOUT twenty guests assembled at the residence of Mr Alexander McLeod, Valleyfield Dec 5, 1893 to witness the marriage of his second daughter Margaret Anna Bella, to Mr William Ramsay of Park Corner. The ceremony was performed by Rev D B McLeod M A of Orwell, assisted by the Rev J M McLeod M A of Kensington, brother of the bride. The contracting parties were supported by Dr J Martin of Montague, and Miss Lizzie P McLeod sister of the bride. Both bride and bridesmaid were simply and beautifully dressed in white. An elegant supper was served and all did ample justice to the good things prepared. The remainder of the evening was very pleasantly spent in conversation and singing. Mr Charles R McLeod of Orwell presided at the organ in his usual happy manner. At a late hour—or rather an early hour—the delighted guests returned to their homes. The happy couple will make their home at Park Corner.—COM

Page 18 from the Blue Scrapbook

NOT ROMANTIC.

STORY OF A SPRAINED ANKLE.

It is Not so Easy to Carry a Young Woman Home as it Looks in a Novel.

"Some things are romantic in novels," said little Miss Drusilla, pensively, "that somehow don't turn out that way in real life. For instance, in a story, when there has been a sprained ankle, or a faint, the young man 'supports the heroine's fainting form,' and 'chafes her delicate hand,' and 'bathes her lily temples,' or something of that sort, but he never drops water on her gown, or spoils her best bonnet ribbons. If she sprains her ankle, why, he 'cuts the lacing of a fairy shoe,' and does not seem to find it any particular trouble to carry her home a mile or two. But in real life—well! —did I ever tell you how Marthy Gates and I went to ride with the two Hicks boys when we were young? That was a case in point. It ought to have been romantic, but it wasn't "They took us to ride, Marthy and me. The roan colt that drew us in our two seated waggon was as frisky as a kitten, and Jake, who was driving, was too much taken up with Marthy (she wore a pink bonnet and gray gown, and looked as pretty as a rose) to be attending to the spirited animal properly. So when a hare jumped up under the colt's nose, it bolted, took the bit between its teeth, and tore along at a furious rate before we hardly knew what was happening. There wasn't anything to do but sit still and hold on. The

ROAD WAS FAIRLY LEVEL

till we got to Stony Brook Hill. There we hoped the colt would get over his fright. But he didn't. He started down the hill with the sparks flying under his heels, and the stones rolling, and Jake pulling back and shouting, 'Whoa!' like a wild Indian. Just as we reached the bridge at the bottom he stumbled, pitched forward in a heap, and out we all went into the road. Neither of the boys was hurt. But when I came to myself Tom was wringing his hands and [illegible] me [illegible] tell him if I was dead, and [illegible]

Jake was on his knees by Marth[illegible] get her boot off. She was squirming like an eel, shrieking and declaring that he shouldn't touch her; her leg was broken, she knew it was, and he was a brute to hurt her so, instead of going for a doctor. Well, it didn't take me long to tell Tom I was alive, and then I staggered over to Marthy and sat down beside her, and tried to help Jake get off her boot. We did it at last, and found she had a sprained ankle and

NO BONES WERE BROKEN,

and the question was how to get her home. The colt was lamed, and the carriage wrecked. Jake was a big fellow, and said he would carry her; and Tom said he'd spell him if he gave out. They tried it. She screamed so when Jake picked her up that he nearly dropped her. She said it hurt her ankle so to let it hang she couldn't endure it, and he must put her down at once. He didn't do it on the instant, and she seized his hair with one hand, and pulled till she shook his head so he must have been dizzy. She was wild with pain, and too hysterical to know what she was doing. But he put her down after the hair-pulling, you may be sure, and then she sat on a heap of stones with the tears rolling down the side of her nose, while we stood round

AND SHE SCOLDED US

like so many primary-school children, declaring that we were cruel, and did not know anything. Then suddenly she cried out: "'Look there! Here you've been murdering me, when, if you'd had a spark of sense you might have got me most home by this time!' She pointed to an old wheel barrow that had been left by the side of the road. Tom went and got it, and Jake put her in—and they wheeled her home. She cried all the way. The rusty old barrow squeaked like a pig being killed, and whenever there was a jounce she screamed in unison with it. I walked behind on Tom's arm, white and trembling, and thoroughly wet from the water he had flung over me when I fainted, and with my skirt half out of the gathers, and my hat mussed, and scratches all over my face. That was the way we went down the village street, and I never was so mortified in my life. But there was a runaway, and a faint, and a sprained ankle all together—and it ought to have been romantic!"

Friday:
"Sleeves to the dimpled elbow".
"Just look at the window"!
"Nevermind the window!"

1893.

June 16th
"Go out and circumnavigate the premises".
"Is it fate or foreordination or —what?"
" "
Good night. So be it.

MORE POTATO.

RENAN had a great contempt for mere words, however eloquent. One evening he met, at a sort of literary dinner, Caro, the philosopher beloved of fine ladies. His eloquent assertions did not seem to interest the sage. In the midst of one of his most sonorous periods Renan attempted to make himself heard. But all the ladies were intensely interested; they would not have their pleasure spoiled. "In a moment, M. Renan; we will listen to you in your turn." He bowed submissively. Toward the end of dinner, Caro, out of breath, stopped with a rhetorical emphasis. At once everyone turned toward the illustrious scholar, hoping that he would enter the lists, and the hostess, with an encouraging smile, said: "Now, M. Renan" — "I am afraid, dear lady, that I am now a little behindhand." "No, no!" "I wanted to ask for a little more potato."

With best Christmas Wishes.

I have nothing so much at heart as your happiness both in this world and the next

"MARIE DUPLESSIS"

[From the only portrait known to exist.]

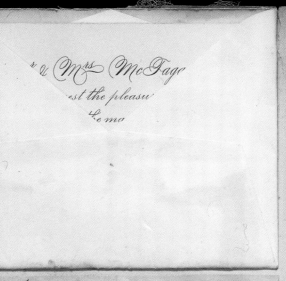

VIEW ON THE SASKATCHEWAN.

Gathered to their Fathers.

THE subject of this notice was born at the family home on the 4th day of January, A.D., 1843, and was the third son of the late James T. Montgomery, and one of a family of ten, four sons and six daughters, all of whom survive him—he was nephew of the late Senator Montgomery of Park Corner, and grandson of the Hon. Donald Montgomery, a native of Argyleshire, Scotland, who emigrated to this Island and settled with his parents in Malpeque about the year 1770—and who was the leading magistrate and a representative of Prince County in the House of Assembly for over a quarter of a century and up till the time of his death, when he was succeeded by his son Donald, the late senator. He was married to Miss Perman of New England, by whom he had a family of sixteen, nine sons and seven daughters. The homestead descended to James T., the fifth son and father, who was born in March 1800 and died in June 1871, leaving a widow and 10 children, the homestead again descending to John M. It now descends to the fifth generation in uninterrupted succession. John married in March 1882, Mary Emily, youngest daughter of Alexander McNeill, Esq., of Cavendish, who survives him with a family of five small children. He was a man of robust constitution, and enjoyed almost perfect health all through his life—until about the middle of November last when he had a attack of paralysis which slightly affected his speech and some time afterwards his right hand. Notwithstanding the close attention of the family physician, Dr. Kier, who visited him nearly every day, and by his well-known skill and long experience, supplemented by several of the most prominent physicians Drs. Taylor and McLeod of Charlottetown, Carruthers of Alberton, and McNeill of Kensington, who held consultations on his case on the different occasions—all their efforts proved unavailing as the slow but steady march of the disease manifested that death had marked him for its own. During a long illness under the most excruciating suffering he retained all his faculties to a most surprising degree—he bore it all with the most Christian fortitude and patience that surprised all who saw him—he seemed to rally on Friday and to continue better on Saturday and Sabbath and peacefully passed away at 5 o'clock on Monday, the 18th inst., so composed that the immediate attendants could hardly tell what moment the spirit fled. Mr. Montgomery was a member of the Presbyterian Church at Malpeque—a prominent and useful citizen and an ardent temperance worker and reformer. He was for a term of years usher of the black rod. For four years he represented the 3rd district of Prince County in the House of Assembly. He made an excellent representative and was a great favorite with the masses of the people. Every year it was his custom to hold meetings through the district to meet his constituents and to attend to the local wants. He was an honest and faithful and sagacious public servant. More than that he had a firmness and determination that would not stoop to promote party purposes when he felt his party was in the wrong. This was specially manifested when biennial sessions were proposed as a means of curtailing expenditure. He and one or two others on that occasion took strong grounds against the party and proposed and insisted upon the amalgamation bill instead of biennial sessions. The result proved the soundness of his judgment and the wisdom of his choice. To John M. Montgomery above all other men this province owes a permanent debt of gratitude. Notwithstanding the state of the roads there were over 100 sleighs in the funeral procession. The pall-bearers were Hon. John Yeo, M.P., George Ramsay, Esq., William McN. Simpson, Esq., Robt. Crozier, Esq., Robt. Stewart, Esq., and Geo. Beairsto, Esq. The funeral services at the house and grave were conducted by Rev. W. P. Archibald of Cavendish. The floral tributes contributed by lady friends in the settlement were artistic and beautiful. No man in recent years in this province has passed away more highly respected or more deeply and widely mourned.

Friday. June 23rd 1893

"Who is it!"

"We're going to Rocky Point too."

"I'll be after you. I'll pay you back."

A FASHIONABLE PRAYER.

Give me an eye to others' failings blind—
Miss Smith's new bonnet's quite a fright be
hind!

Wake in me charity for the suffering poor—
There comes that contribution plate once more!

Take from my soul all feelings covetous—
I'll have a shawl like that, or make a fuss!

Let love for all my kind my spirit stir—
Save Mrs. Jones—I'll never speak to her!

Let me in truth's fair pages take delight—
I'll read that other novel through to-night.

Make me contented with my earthly state—
I wish I'd married rich. But it's too late!

Give me a heart of faith in all my kind—
Miss Brown's as big a hypocrite as you'll find!

Help me to see myself as others see—
This dress is quite becoming unto me!

Let me act out no falsehood, I appeal—
I wonder if they think these curls are real!

Make my heart of humility the fount—
How glad I am our pew's so near the front!

Fill me with patience and strength to wait—
I know he'll preach until our dinner's late!

Take from my heart each grain of self-conceit—
I'm sure the gentleman must think me sweet!

Let saintly wisdom be my daily food—
I wonder what we'll have for dinner good!

Let not my feet ache in the road to light—
Nobody kno s how these shoes pinch and bite.

In this world teach me to deserve the next—
Church out! Charles, do you recollect the text!

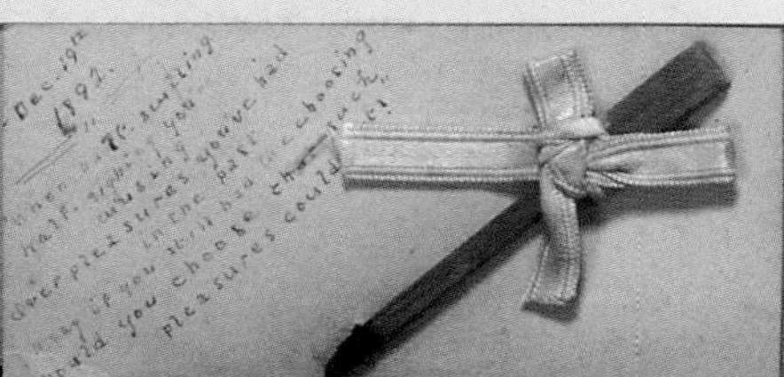

Bideford Breathings.

The Debating Society of East Bideford is a rapidly growing institution, and deserves credit for its great progress. The young people take a very active interest in the meetings, which are well attended every Saturday night, in spite of blizzards and snow banks. The meeting of Feb. 9th was specially interesting, the subject for discussion being, "Which could we do without with the less inconvenience, wood or iron?" It was hotly contested and resulted in a majority of six for those that upheld that iron is more useful than wood. After the debate was closed, Mr. Preston Ellis favored the meeting with an amusing song of his own composition which was loudly applauded. Mr. Bruce Hayes, ambitious of emulating the proceeding production, then sang an extempore song, in which he made so many personal illusions that he was frequently interrupted by storms of applause. The subject of debate next night is, "Which is the most benefit ... a family of boys or a family of girls?"

In celebrating adventures and romances, Montgomery preserved items she could draw on later in her fiction.

At least three travel stories are recalled on this page. The pressed carnation commemorated a marvellous day, August 11, 1890, when Montgomery and her grandfather began their long train trip to visit Hugh John Montgomery in Prince Albert, Saskatchewan. When the old senator heard that his long-time political crony, Sir John A. Macdonald, was travelling on the Island by train, he telegraphed ahead and asked his friend to make an unscheduled stop to pick them up. Thus it was that the fifteen-year-old aspiring writer, who would create a classic synonymous with Canada itself, had her first train ride and began her cross-Canada trip in the company of Canada's first prime minister and his wife. Montgomery described their meeting in her diary:

I assure you I was quite excited over the prospect of seeing the Premier of Canada. When the special came I followed grandpa on board and the next moment was in the presence of the great man himself. He was very genial and motioned me to a seat between himself and Lady M. where I sat demurely and scrutinized them both out of the tail of my eye.

Sir John is a spry-looking old man – not handsome but pleasant-faced. Lady M. is quite stately and imposing, with very beautiful silver hair, but not at all good looking and dressed, as I thought, very dowdily.

I never was on a train before but I enjoyed this, my first ride, very much.

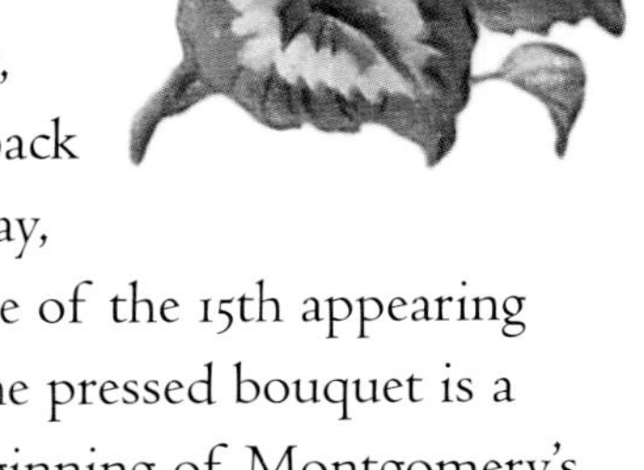

Frank K. Rochester (calling card) was among those who saw Maud off on the return train trip, a year later, from Prince Albert back to Cavendish. Monday, June 17, 1895 (the date of the 15th appearing on the page beside the pressed bouquet is a mistake), was the beginning of Montgomery's last week of teaching in Bideford.

Gazing steadily at the viewer is Henriette Ronner-Knip's "Banjo," reprinted in an 1891 review of her art. The Dutch painter (1821–1909) is famous for her cats, quiet interiors, and landscapes. Montgomery loved cats and used many of Ronner-Knip's images to illustrate her scrapbook pages, for example, page 35 of the Red Scrapbook. This Banjo may have inspired the name of one of the cats in Montgomery's novel *The Blue Castle* (1926).

IN PRAISE OF CATS.

Cat-fancying and the cult of the cat have made rapid and popular progress during the last few years. We have cat shows, cat societies, and cat clubs (which have nothing to do with "The Kitcat"), and lastly we have Mrs. Graham R. Tomson's dainty little Anthology of Cats† and Mr. Spielmann's gorgeous volume in praise of Madame Ronner and her cat pictures.‡ All these phenomena would seem to suggest that long ages of neglect, ill-treatment, and absolute cruelty have passed and are done with, and that Shylock's "harmless, necessary cat" is gaining general favour, not merely as a creature given to us by Providence for the destruction of rats and mice and the consumption of kitchen scraps, but as an animal fitted by beauty and intelligence, devotion and courage to be the companion and pet of mankind.

Mrs. Tomson very properly says in her preface or "foreword" that her anthology "needs neither excuse nor justification." In these days of anthologies it was inevitable, considering the fresh vogue of the cat, that it should occur to some one to ask, "Why should not a selection be made of what poets have said and sung concerning the mysterious and suspected beast?" It is fortunate for the cat and for the reader that Mrs. Tomson should have been prompted to make the selection: she has the necessary sympathy with cats, and she has herself written graceful verses on her favourites. It is no reproach to her that, in spite of her industry in research and her taste in selection, the result should be comparatively disappointing. For, though the poets have written a tolerable deal about cats, very few of them have set down aught of consequence. It must be sorrowfully admitted that in the past not even poets have fully understood and appreciated the cat: they have usually dwelt on her common or garden characteristics—her irresponsible grace and playfulness as a kitten, the secrecy of her ways, the mystery of her look when grown up, and the persecuted life she leads in maturity. Even Mrs. Tomson

MADAME RONNER'S "BANJO."

seems mainly fascinated with her "sombre, sea-green g[illegible] inscrutable"; and though Cowper (in his "Colubriad"), the neglected Joanna Baillie (who in her heyday was compared to Shakspere's self), and Wordsworth have written with a certain charm about kittens, they have but expressed at tedious length — Wordsworth has even made the kitten minister to his moral improvement! — what the schoolboy more successfully said in a few words of prose: "A kitten is an animal that is remarkable for rushing like mad at nothing whatever, and generally stopping before it gets there." Mrs. Tomson gives Gray's delightful "Elegy on the Death of a Favourite Cat drowned in a Tub of Gold Fishes," Calverley's "Sad Memories," Dr. Garnett's pretty little "Marigold," and (in her preface) Matthew Arnold's admirable elegy on "Poor Mathias"; yet, on the whole, one is compelled to the conclusion that our English poets have not sufficiently studied the cat before writing about her. Besides the Scots "Auld Bawthren's Song" (which, with its burden of "Three threads and a thrum," is perfect of its kind), the best home productions are those in the section called "Children's Cats"—a section which Mrs. Tomson might have made a little more of. We miss, for instance, "I love little pussy, her coat is so warm," "Three little kittens, one stormy night," and "The old black cat." It is to the French, however, that we must go for the most sympathetic verses about the cat, and especially to the Romanticists of 1830 and their successors. From these—from Baudelaire, from Joseph Boulmier, and (to be quite up to date) from Paul Verlaine—Mrs. Tomson has culled choice examples.

It is remarkable that where the poets have mostly failed the painters have failed too. Where the great masters (as Mr. Spielmann says in his excellent monograph on Madame Ronner) have attempted the painting of a cat, "they have [illegible]regiously." The cat's great friend [illegible] truly declares: "The lines [illegible] one must be feline one's self." But to be feline is not enough, for the cat will surrender her secret to no one, painter nor poet, who does not love her much and who does not study her with unremitting attention. The artists who have succeeded in rendering the cat may be counted on the fingers of one hand—the Japanese Hokusai, the Swiss Mind, the English Burbank, the French Lambert, and the Dutch Madame Ronner—and the greatest of these, the one who has succeeded absolutely and all round, is the last, the lady. Has not Champfleury well said "one must be feline one's self"? The pictures of the industrious Madame Ronner are more than a liberal education in cat life and character—they must be to many a revelation of these. Moreover, the technique, the manipulation of the paint, is a superb achievement, and thus Madame Ronner's work gives the supremest delight both to those who are ignorant of art and to those who know what art should be. She represents for preference the most pleasing sides of cat life and character—the simple and amazed gamesomeness of the kitten and the demure satisfaction and anxiety of the cat; the frank mischief infusing the splendid orbs of "Banjo" and the elegant sentiment suffusing the liquid eyes of "Sans Souci"; but, however she sets her cats before us, whether asleep or awake, at rest or in action, all are graceful with the singular feline grace, and all are true—how delightfully true one only perceives by comparing them with the *felidæ* of other artists who have essayed to compass the portrayal of the cat. Mr. Spielmann, in his monograph, has much to say of both critical and biographical interest concerning Madame Ronner, but to artists no item will be of more interest than that about her method of work. "She does not stay to draw her outlines and then proceed to fill them in; she adopts the higher method of regarding in the first instance the object to be painted purely as masses of light and shade." The result is that both the form and the fur of cats and kittens (Madame Ronner prefers the long-haired varieties) are rendered in the most masterly manner, as may be judged from the numerous photogravures with which the work is adorned. The volume is published simultaneously in England, France, and Holland in celebration of Madame Ronner's seventieth birthday, and many a lover of cats would give untold wealth to possess it.

J. MacLaren Cobban.

Wishing you a very happy Christmas.

At what season should I send, this true wish of mine?
"May all happiness attend ever thee and thine!"
Let me send it when I will - when the year is new
When the year is ended - still it is always true!

Given me ~~[illegible]~~ by Lady McDonald

Monday Aug. 11th 1890

"My native land Good-night!"

Souvenir of my first ride on a train.

Good-bye to all!

Monday. June 15th 1885.

Frank A. Rochester

This page is a good example of how Montgomery used her scrapbooks to store gems she would use later in her fiction. So struck was she by C. Lauron Hooper's "When Kissing Came into the World" that she borrowed it for her March 31, 1902, Halifax *Daily Echo* newspaper column (published under the pseudonym "Cynthia," the column featured articles Montgomery clipped from other papers, along with her own fictive observations on the passing scene), and later still she adapted it for her fourth novel, *The Story Girl* (1911), the last novel she would write on the Island while still compiling the Blue and Red Scrapbooks. In Chapter 18 of the novel, Montgomery has the Story Girl introduce the Hooper story (changing details and the characters' names) this way: "But talking of kissing makes me think of a story I found in Aunt Olivia's scrapbook the other day. Would you like to hear it? It is called, 'How Kissing Was Discovered.'"

Two relatives' wedding notices and a wedding invitation (the small clipping at the top left is on the back of the handwritten invitation for the Montgomery-Johnstone wedding) flank the story. The card from July 17, 1894, preserving a bit of white satin, some dialogue, and quotations suggests a romance that did not happen. On its right side Maud wrote: "'Mr. L. this is Miss M.' 'I know it is.' Alas!!!" At this time, Montgomery had finished her PWC program and was home in Cavendish writing feverishly to find a teaching post. She had gone driving with Maggie and Chesley Clark on that evening, and she had heard during the day that her story "A Baking of Gingersnaps" (under the pen name Maud Cavendish) had been accepted by the Toronto *Ladies' Journal*. The quotation at the bottom of the card is from her own poem "The Wreck of the Marco Polo, 1883," published in 1892.

MARRIED.

At the home of the bride, on the 8th inst., by Rev J M McLeod, James T Montgomery, Park Corner, to Mrs Eliza R Johnstone, Clifton.

WHEN KISSING CAME INTO THE WORLD

By C. Lauron Hooper

NO one has ever been able to improve the wheelbarrow. It was perfect when first invented. Since the days of Aristotle the science of logic has remained practically unchanged, for that eminent Greek established it in its perfection at the outset. The first epoch is still better than all that have followed it, nor can any one ever learn to write such poetry better than did Homer, for he reached the utmost perfection of the art at a bound. So, also, those who discovered—or invented—kissing did their work so well that no one has been able to improve it to this day. It may seem strange that there was ever a time when kissing was unknown among men and women, but such is the case. For many thousands of years our ancestors lived in profound ignorance of the blissful, kissful art, and it was only after the process of evolution had gone so far as to rid man entirely of the characteristics of his tailed ancestors, and there grew in him those higher sentiments and emotions which the poets have been singing to us since the days of Sappho, that kissing came into vogue. I have delved deeply for many years into the ancient writings of Oriental peoples and have at last discovered the exact manner and place—though the time is somewhat doubtful—in which kissing began.

MOST things began in Greece. At least many of the best things of life did, and kissing is among the number. The account of its beginning is carefully and accurately narrated in the old writings which I have mentioned, and I will endeavor to repeat it as best I can, knowing that I cannot, with our strong and vigorous English speech, reproduce the soft and tuneful flow of the Greek tongue. It would be well if I could, for much of the charm of the account is in the very musical sound of the language in which it was first told, and indeed the account needs this charm, for it is not a story in the true meaning of that word, a story with an unexpected and surprising end, but only a little incident which terminated just as any one would expect. So wholly unremarkable was it that only one man in all Greece thought it worthy to be written down and preserved. But thanks to him and his posterity, who carefully kept it, it has at last come into my possession. And as I shall now tell it to you in good faith you must know that every word of it is true.

KISTHENES was a shepherd in that part of Greece known as Bœotia. He lived with his father in a little village named Thebes, which in after years became a great walled city, the most powerful one in all Greece, about and in which occurred some of the events that have been handed down to us in the tragedies of Sophocles. Here lived Kisthenes until he grew to be a young man—a very handsome one, too, the writing says—when home life became wearisome ... burden on his back and his shepherd's crook in his hand, he turned his face to the north. After many days he came into Thessaly, another province of Greece. Here he entered into the employ of a man named Dryades, who had many sheep to pasture. Each day Kisthenes led the sheep up the slopes of Mt. Pelion, and let them graze while he played on a pipe. In the distance he could see the Ægean glistening in the sun, the same Ægean upon which the baby Perseus was sent adrift, the same Ægean upon which Agamemnon's fleets sailed to Troy, the same Ægean (to speak of more authentic events) which Xerxes caused to be whipped because its waves broke his bridge of boats. Now Dryades had a daughter named Eurybia, beautiful in form and face, gentle in nature, and skilled in all the accomplishments known to young ladies at that time. Very naturally she and Kisthenes became acquainted, and as she was just as high as his heart and seemed to think very much of him, and as he thought equally as much of her, he hoped some time to have flocks of his own and a little cottage for her to live in with him. Sometimes Eurybia in her rambles over the mountain slopes would meet Kisthenes—by chance of course—with his flock. On such occasions they would talk together with such pleasure that the sun would sink behind them and stretch old Pelion's shadow to the Ægean before they knew that it was time to lead the sheep home. At other times Eurybia, filled with maidenly shyness, would loiter just out of sight among the rocks or in the groves near where her lover pastured his flocks, and listen to the melodies that floated dreamily from his pipe.

And he, knowing in some mysterious way that she was near, would pour forth such dulcet strains that even the sheep would raise their heads to listen.

BUT Kisthenes at length persuaded Eurybia to be less coy and to come out on the mountain every day. They soon became so well acquainted and addressed each other so often that they really hadn't time to pronounce their long names, so Eurybia came to call Kisthenes merely Kiss, and Kisthenes called Eurybia merely Rib. This latter fact is of peculiar significance; for though Kisthenes and Eurybia, young heathens that they were, had never heard that Eve, their first mother was made from a rib of Adam, their first father, yet he—Kisthenes, not Adam—called his sweetheart by the name of the very thing of which the first of her sex was made. Let this carry what proof it may. One day, in wandering over old Pelion within sound of her lover's mellow pipe, Eurybia found a very beautiful little stone in the edge of a mountain stream. She sat down on a rock to examine it. It was scarcely as large as a pea and had very ragged edges. As she turned it round and round in the sunlight she was surprised and delighted to see it flash every color she knew. "The rainbow, the rainbow," she exclaimed, and was about to carry it to Kisthenes when she heard a clatter of hoofs and a snort behind her. Turning she saw a being whom all her life she had prayed the gods she might never meet. It was the great god Pan. There he stood, horns, coarse, hairy face, goat legs and all. Eurybia had often heard the sound of his ... woods, but thought the notes discordant, enamored as she was by the music of her lover's pipe, and now she trembled as she looked at the terrible creature before her.

"Give me the stone," said Pan, holding out his hand.

"But," faltered the quaking Eurybia, "I want it for Kisthenes."

"Bah! Who's Kisthenes? I want it for one of my wood nymphs," said the god, advancing with a menacing step; but before he could reach the girl she was running screaming up the mountain.

SHE heard the clatter of the god's cloven hoofs behind her, heard his hoarse, angry bellowing, and was so terrified that only the thought that Kisthenes would be her protector prevented her from fainting on the spot. In less than a minute she rushed into her lover's arms. Her sudden coming, followed by the terrible roaring god, set the sheep flying, and Kisthenes, brave as he was, trembled like the young lamb in his flock.

Nevertheless he addressed the god ... humble language, beseeching him to ... away, and promising that on the next s... rificial day he should receive a double of... ing. Grunting and muttering to hims... Pan clattered away over the mountain, ... he always granted the fervent praye... honest shepherds.

"Now, Rib, tell me what all this is abo..." said Kisthenes, and Eurybia told him ... simple tale of her meeting with Pan.

"But," said he, when she had finis... "where is the stone thou wast going ... bring to me? By Jupiter, I fear that in ... fright thou hast thrown it away."

Kisthenes, however, was mistaken, ... Eurybia had put the jewel in her mo... and she now thrust it out between her ... where it glistened and flashed every c... of the sunlight.

"Take it," she whispered.

Now Kisthenes had both his arms aro... Eurybia, and both Eurybia's arms ... held close to her side by the strong ... brace of Kisthenes, so how could e... have a hand to remove the stone from ... maiden's lips?

Kisthenes solved the problem. O... genius could have conceived the idea ... came into his head at that moment. ... curred to him to take the stone from ... rybia's lips with his own.

Bending over, his face came near ... Nearer and nearer until their lips tou... and then—well, Kisthenes forgot all a... the stone, for such a series of thrills and tremors scampered and scurried over his frame that he not only forgot the stone, but the sheep, the pipe, the mountain, the sea, the sky, the earth, everything in fact but the bliss of that one moment. And Eurybia. She had forgotten the stone, the sheep, the pipe, the mountain, the sea, the sky, the earth, even Pan himself in the bliss of that one moment. And not that one moment alone was this new ecstasy enjoyed, for in fulfillment of Kisthenes' desire and the tender yearning in Eurybia's limpid eyes, again and again their lips met in blissful osculation.

It was something new. Never before had anything like this been discovered by mortal man. Kisthenes and Eurybia, feeling themselves the originators of the delight, and thinking on that account they should have the exclusive right to it, and further, as there was no patent office in those days where inventors could be assured no one would trespass on their rights, these two selfish lovers, I say, determined to keep their secret to themselves.

BUT alas! alas! the secret got out, as secrets are said to when entrusted to women. Forgetting her agreement, Eurybia told a friend of hers, a little Miss Leda, who lived down by the sea. Little Miss Leda, being somewhat coquettish, had two lovers, Magon and Nesides, both of whom she taught this new thing which Eurybia, in honor of her lover, called a "kiss." Now Magon had another sweetheart in a town in Epirus, and on his first visit to her he taught her this new thing called a kiss. Nesides had two other sweethearts west of old Pelion, and to them the secret, as well as its practical workings, was soon confided. One of these young ladies soon jilted Nesides, and as he wearied of the other shortly after this, they both found other lovers to whom they communicated the blissful discovery. From that time it spread, until kissing was not onl... known in Epirus and Thessaly, but ... Thebes, where Kisthenes had spent his b... hood, and in all Greece, and in all th... world. It is told of an Athenian statesma... that, learning of the art of kissing while i... the market-place, he kissed fourteen shop girls on the way home that he might be i... practice to show his wife just how it wa... done. At least kissing has become uni... versal, having spread from earth to th... heavens, for who does not know how ofte... our novelists say the sun was kissing th... ... or the ... and roots of some city, or even ... hair of some fair girl? Now when th... the old rascal whom we have looked up to and even worshiped in the centuries gone by, is up to such tricks, how can you know, ladies, whom to trust?

Be it known, finally, that Kisthenes and Eurybia were afterward married, and in all their long life Kiss never kissed any woman but his "own dear Rib," as he called her, for he was as true-hearted a fellow as ever bore a shepherd's crook. Their bodies have these many hundred years reposed in old Pelion's side and their names are known to but a few, but their discovery is known wherever men and women have gone over the great earth, and it is still sweetening the joys of life, lessening its sorrows, increasing its love, decreasing its hate, as I hope it may until the day after the end of time.

WEDDING BELLS.

Rev. Mr. Macneill and Miss Kennedy Married—Robertson-Holly.

A quiet but none the less interesting event took place at 12.30 on Thursday at the residence of Ald. James Kennedy on Summer street, when his only daughter, Mary Gray Kennedy, was united in marriage to Rev. L. G. Macneill, pastor of St. Andrew's Presbyterian church. Only the near relatives of the bride and groom were present. Rev. Dr. Bruce tied the nuptial knot. The bride was charmingly attired in a handsome bluish grey travelling costume of Avon cloth, with a jacket to match, and a brown straw hat, daintily trimmed with forget-me-nots. She carried a large bouquet of bridal roses. She was attended by little Miss Flo. Bullock as a maid of honor. She looked very pretty in a dress of cream-colored surah and a large white leghorn hat. Immediately after the ceremony the bridal party and guests partook of a sumptuous repast, after which Mr. and Mrs. Macneill took the C. P. R. train for Halifax. A large number of friends were at the station to bid them good bye. From Halifax they will take the steamer Vancouver for England. They will go direct from there to Paris and travel as far as Vienna. They will be absent until August. The bride received many beautiful presents. Her father's gift was a substantial cheque and a silver tea service. Her mother's gift was an elegant Japanese tea service. The Boys' Association of St. Andrew's church presented their pastor with a fine engraving. The groom presented the maid of honor with a gold link bracelet.

Tuesday
July 17
1894

"Is the post-office shut"?

"alas!"

Montgomery created dialogues among scenes and people from her past and present. Later she would give Anne Shirley a similar passion for the past.

PAGE 25: Montgomery pasted a cut-out of a horseshoe around an old-fashioned magazine illustration above an article about her late beloved Grandfather Montgomery, who died shortly before she entered PWC in 1893. The misspelled name card at the bottom may also be misdated: Maud was in Halifax, not Bideford, in 1895. The pressed rose seems to belong to her school exam and concert triumphs in Bideford (Blue Scrapbook, p. 15), and that impression is reinforced by the name under the fancy card cover, Hattie L. Gordon, her favourite Cavendish teacher. The poem illustrations of the two little girls are certainly appropriate for Montgomery, who suffered acutely from the lack of light in winter.

PAGE 26: France's last empress, Eugenie (1826–1920), spent decades exiled in England building a memorial to the Second Empire of France and to her late husband and son. The haloed figure and Empress Eugenie form the centre for a triangle of cards commemorating social outings and flirtations. Willie Pritchard pinned daisies and sweet clover, which he characterized as "innocence and beauty," on Maud's dress at a picnic in Saskatchewan in July 1891. The daisy at the bottom left belonged to times of hilarity with the Clarks and Jack Laird in Cavendish during fall break from Bideford school, just two days after Lem McLeod had proposed to Maud in Park Corner (Blue Scrapbook, p. 33). Maud met Lou Dystant in November of 1894, and the card on the right suggests he was already in love with her by December. The initials stand for Sadie Dystant, Lucy Maud Montgomery, Lou Dystant, East Bideford Concert, Prince Edward Island. On the left, the death notice and the sentimental poem about the grandfather companion the preceding page's notice about her Grandfather Montgomery.

PAGE 27: The dramatic flower-wreathed woman in a toga makes a visual connection between the bonnet poem and the Cleopatra "literary curiosity." Wellington Nelson, who – together with his brother David – boarded with the Macneills for three years and attended the Cavendish school with Maud, is the name under the fancy cover. The Cavendish keepsake, now lost, may also have been connected in Maud's imagination with June of 1892, for it was then that she and Pensie exchanged secrets outside the schoolhouse, only to discover that Miss Gordon was inside alone in the dark, overhearing every word. On June 1, 1892, Maud was visiting in Park Corner, P.E.I., and she and her cousin Stella Campbell searched for four-leaf clovers in the orchard. It was during this trip that she first met Edwin Simpson; he and Lem McLeod competed for her attention.

"Better be born lucky than rich."
Friday Aug 16th 1894
"Three is company in this case"
the circle. Bideford

They Did Not Try.

Three men-of-war ships, Dutch, French, and English, while anchored in port, were contending with each other for the best display of seamanship, so the captain of each vessel determined to send aloft an active sailor to perform some deed of grace and daring. The Dutch captain sent a Dutchman, the French a Frenchman and the English an Irishman. The Dutchman stood on the top of the mainmast with his arm extended. The Frenchman then went aloft and extended both arms.

Now, the Irishman thought if he could stand on the top of the mainmast with a leg and an arm extended he would be declared the most daring sailor. Nimbly he clambered aloft untill he reached the highest point. Thence he carefully balanced himself upon both feet, extending his right hand with a graceful motion. Then he threw out his left leg untill in a line with his right arm. In doing this he ingloriously lost his balance and fell from the masthead, crashing through the rigging toward the deck.

The various ropes against which his body came in contact broke his fall, and his velocity was not too great to prevent his grasping a rope attached to the mainyard To this he hung for two seconds, then dropped lightly to the deck, landing safely on his feet. Folding his arms triumphantly, as if fall and all were in the programme, he glanced toward the rival ships and joyously exclaimed, "There, ye frog ating and sausage-stuffed furriners, bate that if you can!"

THE SHADOW.

The sun's in a cloud,
The morning is dreary,
The way is too long,
The feet are too weary.
The friend is not kind,
And smiles are not shining,
The roses and robins
Are paling and pining.
That hour is the saddest
From May day to Yule
When little Dolores
Is going to school.

What is the reason? She turns from the light,
And walks in her shadow from morning till night.

WHERE IS IT?

The sun is the brightest,
The morn is the clearest,
The burden is lightest,
The friend is the dearest,
The flowers are all waking,
The way is not long,
The birds are all breaking
At once into song.
That hour is the gladdest
From May day to Yule,
When little Allegra
Is going to school.

What is the secret? Wherever you find her,
The shadow of little Allegra's behind her.

MARY A. LATHBURY.

Reminiscences of the Late Senator Montgomery.

The Ottawa Citizen contains a letter signed P.E.I., who is evidently resident at the capital, giving some interesting reminiscences of the late Senator Montgomery. Among other things he says:

It is not absolutely correct to speak of the late Senator's "continuous service" as a parliamentarian. There was one General Assembly or parliament of Prince Edward Island of which he was not a member. I refer to the 21st, which was convened in Charlottetown on 17th February, 1859, prorogued two days later and followed immediately by dissolution. There had been a general election in the summer of 1858, at which Mr. Montgomery was defeated by Mr. John Ramsay. When the Legislature met, Mr. Ramsay declined to take the oath of qualification, while parties were so equally divided that it was found impossible to elect a speaker. After waiting two days, the Lieut. Governor, Sir Dominick Daly, prorogued the Legislature, and forthwith dissolved the House. At the new general election Mr. Montgomery was successful, and upon the opening of the session, on 12th April, 1859, was elected Speaker of the House Assembly. Thus, although he missed one parliament, he was yet a representative of the people in every year from the time he was first elected in 1838.

One other reminiscence: In company with a friend, I was talking to Senator Montgomery during the session of 1892, when he showed us a photograph of a venerable lady, living in London, England. Said he. "I have just received this photograph—she is a cousin of mine. Last year I sent her my photograph and she has sent me hers in exchange. I have not seen her for 80 years." And the old gentleman spoke as unconcernedly as though it had been only ten years instead of four score.

"SUMMER."—JOHN SCOTT, R.I.

"In the heart of a rose"

Lucie M. Montgomery
Bideford
P.E.I.

Dec. 28th
1895.

Page 25 from the Blue Scrapbook

RISING STAR DIVISION,
French River, Feb. 21st, '95.

At a meeting of this Society held on the above date the following resolution was unanimously adopted :—

Whereas, It hath pleased God in His Providence to remove from our midst by death our late sister, Mary J. Cameron;

Therefore Resolved, That we, the members of Rising Star Division, do hereby place on record our appreciation of her worth as a member of our Society; and further, we would desire to convey to the bereaved parents and surviving brothers and sisters our sincere and heartfelt sorrow with them in the loss of a dutiful daughter and loving and affectionate sister, and as we erase her name from the roll of our Society on earth, we would sincerely cherish the hope that it may be recorded in the Lamb's Book of Life;

It was further resolved, that we drape our charter in mourning for thirty days.

Signed on behalf of the Division: Newton McLeod, W. P.; Louisa Crosby, R. S.; Emma J. Smith, Florence Orr, A. Simpson.

Friday July 24th 1891

"Innocence and Beauty"

"Hair as a summer's day ... purple hills O'ergrown with daisies sweet"

Madeira Lake Picnic Saskatchewan.

A MODEL HUSBAND.

Most wives will end their story with :
"Ah well, men are but human,"
I long to tell the secret of
A truly happy woman.

Through all the sunshine-lighted years,
Lived now in retrospection,
My husband's words brought never tears,
Nor caused a sad reflection.

Whate'er the burdens of the day,
Unflinching, calm and steady,
To bear his part—the larger half—
I always find him ready.

House-cleaning season brings no frown,
No sarcasm, pointed keenly ;
Through carpets up, and tacks head down
He makes his way serenely.

Our evenings pass in converse sweet,
Or quiet contemplation,
We never disagree except
To "keep up conversation."

And dewy morn of radiant June,
Fair moonlight of September,
April with bird and brook atune,
Stern, pitiless December—

Each seems to my adoring eyes
Some new grace to discover,
For he unchanging through the years,
Is still my tender lover.

So life no shadows holds, though we
Have reached the side that's shady ;
My husband ? Oh ! a dream is he,
And I'm a maiden lady.

ELEANOR M. DENNY, in the *Ladies' Home Journal*.

WHEN GRANDPA WAS A LITTLE BOY.

BY MALCOLM DOUGLAS.

"When grandpa was a little boy about your age," said he,
To the curly-headed youngster who had climbed upon his knee,
"So studious was he at school, he never failed to pass;
And out of three he always stood the second in his class—"
"But if no more were in it, you were next to foot, like me!"
"Why, bless you, grandpa never thought of that before!" said he.

"When grandpa was a little boy about your age," said he,
"He very seldom spent his pretty pennies foolishly;
No toy or candy store was there for miles and miles about,
And, with his books, straight home he'd go the moment school was out—"
"But if there had been one, you might have spent them all, like me!" said he.
"Why, bless you, grandpa never thought of that before!" said he.

"When grandpa was a little boy about your age," said he,
"He never stayed up later than an hour after tea;
It wasn't good for little boys at all, his mother said;
And so, when it was early, she would march him off to bed—"
"But if she hadn't, maybe you'd have stayed up late, like me!"
"Why, bless you, grandpa never thought of that before!" said he.

"When grandpa was a little boy about your age," said he,
"In summer he went barefoot, and was happy as could be;
And all the neighbors round about agreed he was a lad
Who was as good as he could be except when he was bad—"
"But, 'ceptin' going barefoot, you were very much like me."
"Why, bless you, grandpa's often thought of that before!" said he.

—*St. Nicholas.*

Milking-time.

"I TELL you, Kate, that Lovejoy cow
Is worth her weight in gold;
She gives a good eight quarts o' milk,
And isn't yet five year old.

"I see young White a-comin' now;
He wants her, I know that.
Be careful, girl, you're spillin' it!
An' save some for the cat.

"Good evenin', Richard, step right in;"
"I guess I couldn't, sir,
I've just come down"—"I know it, Dick,
You've took a shine to her.

"She's kind an' gentle as a lamb,
Jest where I go she follers;
And though it's cheap I'll let her go;
She's your'n for thirty dollars.

"You'll know her clear across the farm,
By them two milk white stars;
You needn't drive her home at night,
But jest le' down the bars.

"Then, when you've own'd her, say a month,
And learnt her, as it were,
I'll bet,—why, what's the matter, Dick?"
"'Taint her I want,—it's—*her!*"

"What? not the girl! well, I'll be bless'd!—
There, Kate, don't drop that pan.
You've took me mightily aback,
But then a man's a man.

"She's your'n, my boy, but one word more;
Kate's gentle as a dove;
She'll foller you the whole world round,
For nothin' else but love.

"But never try to drive the lass;
Her natur's like her ma's.
I've allus found it worked the best,
To jest le' down the bars."

PHILIP MORSE.

"Procrastination is the thief of time."
Banks of seaweed
fortunate youths.
"Two is company three is a crowd"
"Two school-teachers are too many for a crowd of six"
A sulky companion
Wednesday October 24th 1894
Good-night

EUGENIE, EMPRESS OF FRANCE

"Jingle bells, jingle bells
Jingle all the way"

"Gaily over the moonlit snow"

"That's to be continued".

"Distance lends enchantment to the view".

Lover's Lane

S. D. L. M. M. L. D.
E. B. C. P. E. S.

East Bideford Concert Tuesday Dec. 11th 1894

Page 26 from the Blue Scrapbook

"What is it?"

A fair exchange is no robbery.

"There's no time like the old time."

Cavendish School 1890

1.

HER BONNET.

BY MARY E. WILKINS.

When meeting bells began to toll,
When pious folks began to pass,
She deftly tied her bonnet on,
The little sober meeting lass,
All in her neat, white-curtained room, before her tiny looking-glass.

So nicely round her lady cheeks
She smoothed her bands of glossy hair,
And innocently wondered if
Her bonnet did not make her fair;
Then sternly chid her foolish heart for harboring such fancies there.

So square she tied the satin strings,
And set the bows beneath her chin;
Then smiled to see how sweet she looked;
Then thought her vanity a sin,
And she must put such thoughts away before the sermon should begin.

But, sitting 'neath the preached word,
Demurely, in her father's pew,
She thought about her bonnet still,
Yes, all the parson's sermon thro',
About its pretty bows and buds, which better than the text she knew.

Yet, sitting there with peaceful face,
The reflex of her simple soul,
She looked to be a very saint—
And maybe was one on the whole—
Only that her pretty bonnet kept away the aureole.

A LITERARY CURIOSITY.

The two following poems, either of which might have inspired the other, have long been favorites with the lovers of poety of both continents. We have no knowledge when the one by Thomas S. Collins was written, but that by General William Lytle was written on the eve of the battle of Chickamauga, where General Lytle was killed. The late Colonel Realf, poet, author and soldier, has placed upon record the peculiar circumstances under which the poem was written, which briefly amount to the fact that on the night preceding the battle referred to, General Lytle read the poem, which was then in an unfinished state, to Col. Realf, at the same time telling him that he had a premonition that he would never live to finish it. Col. Realf laughed at his friend, and rallied him upon his superstition, but acknowledged afterward that he himself became so thrilled with unnatural fear that he begged the general to finish the piece before he slept, that such a fine work might not be lost to the world. When Col. Realf next saw his friend he lay cold in death among the heaps of slain. Then he thought of the poem, and searching the pocket where he had seen him place it, he drew it forth and forwarded it to General Lytle's friends.

The lines by Thomas S. Collins were written first and are probably the best, but readers can judge for themselves.

CLEOPATRA DYING.

Sinks the sun below the desert,
Golden glows the sluggish Nile;
Purple flame crowns Sphynx and temple.
Lights up every ancient pile,
Where the old gods now are sleeping;
Isis and Osiris great!
Guard me, help me, give me courage
Like a queen to meet my fate.
"I am dying, Egypt, dying!"
Let the Caesar's army come—
I will cheat him of his glory,
Though beyond the Styx I roam.
Shall he drag this beauty with him,
While the crowd his triumph sings?
No, no, never! I will show him
What lies in the blood of kings.
Though he hold the golden sceptre,
Rule the Pharaoh's sunny land,
Where old Nilus rolls resistless,
Through the sweeps of silvery sand,
He shall never say I met him
Fawning abject like a slave—
I will foil him, though to do it
I must cross the Stygian wave.
Oh, my hero, sleeping, sleeping—
Shall I meet you on the shore
Of Plutonian shadows? Shall we
In death meet, and love once more?
See, I follow in your footsteps—
Scorn the Caesar and his might;
For your love, I will leap boldly
Into the realms of death and night.
Down below the desert sinking,
Fades Apollo's brilliant car,
And from out the distant azure
Breaks the bright gleam of a star;
Venus, Queen of Love and Beauty,
Welcomes me to death's embrace,
Dying free, proud and triumphant!
The last sovereign of my race.
Dying! dying! I am coming,
Oh, my hero, to your arms;
You will welcome me, I know it—
Guard me from all rude alarms.
Hark, I hear the legions coming,
Hear their cries of triumph swell;
But, proud Caesar, dead, I scorn you,
Egypt—Antony—farewell!
—Thomas S. Collins.

ANTHONY AND CLEOPATRA.

I am dying, Egypt, dying!
Ebbs the crimson life tide fast,
And the dark Plutonian shadows
Gather on the evening blast.
Let thine arm, O, Queen, support me,
Hush thy sobs and bow thine ear,
Listen to the great heart secrets
Thou, and thou alone, must hear.
Though my scarred and veteran legions
Bear their eagles high no more,
And my wrecked and scattered galleys
Strew dark Actium's fatal shore;
Though no glittering guards surround me,
Prompt to do their master's will,
I must perish like a Roman—
Die the great Triumvir still!
Let not Caesar's servile minions
Mock the lion thus laid low;
'Twas no foeman's arm that struck him
'Twas his own that dealt the blow—
His, who pillowed on thy bosom
Turned aside from glory's ray—
His, who drunk with thy caresses,
Madly threw a world away.
Should the base plebeian rabble
Dare assail my fame at Rome,
Where the noble spouse, Octavia,
Weeps within her widowed home,
Seek her! Say the Gods have told me—
Altars, augurs, circling wings—
That her blood with mine commingled,
Yet shall mount the throne of kings!
As for thee, star-eyed Egyptian!
Glorious sorceress of the Nile!
Light the path to Stygian horrors
With the splendor of thy smile.
Give to Caesar crowns and arches,
Let his brow the laurel twine;
I can scorn the Senate's triumphs,
Triumphing in love like thine.
I am dying, Egypt, dying!
Hark! the insulting foeman's cry!
They are coming! Quick, my falchion!
Let me front them ere I die.
Ah! no more amid the battle
Shall my heart exulting swell;
Isis and Osiris guard thee—
Cleopatra—Rome—farewell!
Gen. Wm. H. Lytle.

Linkletter Road Notes.

The Literary Society of this place is a rapidly growing institution. The members take quite a lively interest in the meetings, which are well attended every Friday evening. There is always a well filled programme consisting of readings, recitations and dialogues, after which a debate is brought on.

Our school is doing good work under the management of our efficient teacher Miss Fyfe.

Miss Lulu M. Gamble arrived home on Saturday from Bideford where she has been attending school during the fall and winter.

Mr. and Mrs. Ed. Bell, who have been visiting their many friends on Linkletter Road, returned to their home in Cape Traverse on Friday last.

Messrs. J. W. Everett and Edwin Clark are having large quantities of hay pressed.

Page 27 from the Blue Scrapbook

Mr & Mrs Wm. McKenzie

request the pleasure of your company at the Marriage of their neice

Mary McRae

to

Hugh J. Montgomery

On Tuesday morning, April 5th, 1887.

Ceremony in Presbyterian Church at 10.30.

DETAIL FROM PAGE 28: The invitation is for the wedding of Maud's father, Hugh John Montgomery, to Mary McRae. Montgomery pasted the invitation above a short story entitled "A Mistake," no doubt intending the title to comment on her father's choice. She was not happy with her stepmother.

DETAIL FROM PAGE 29: The difficult-to-read date on the card seems to be June 28, 1893 (though that was a Wednesday, not a Tuesday). The dried flowers and lines of poetry mark one of the numerous farewells at the end of Cavendish school days and before the entrance examinations for Prince of Wales. The rose here echoes the roses on mementoes of farewell to Cavendish (e.g., Blue Scrapbook, p. 15), when Montgomery was leaving to teach in Bideford.

DETAIL FROM PAGE 30: In 1890–91, when Montgomery was a student in Prince Albert, Saskatchewan, high school classes were held in the building that had formerly been the Royal Hotel.

Dreams and dramas connect Prince Albert, Cavendish, Prince of Wales, and Bideford days. The scrapbooks highlight the good times and erase or temper sorrows.

PAGE 33: Using an old moon mislabelled a new moon at the centre of the page may be a marker for romance gone awry. Beside the reversed moon, Montgomery commemorated the Sunday evening in 1894 when Lem McLeod proposed to her and was rejected. A small woollen rose decorated the sofa cushion where Maud sat that night. The lines by Whittier are from the poem "Maud Muller," in which an older man and woman separately look back to lament that they did not marry each other. Complementing the woollen rose is a square of plaid from a Bideford party Maud enjoyed hugely (Blue Scrapbook, p. 15). Perhaps the prairie sunflower, from her 1890 trip out west, was yet another reminder of good times in other places.

PAGE 34: The romantic story of Zara takes place in old Grenada, Spain, a location Montgomery loved because of Washington Irving's colourful romance, *The Alhambra.* The string of mysterious initials (L.D.M.C.M.S.M.H.R.M.C.) on the card at the bottom right includes the long name that Frederica Campbell and Maud gave to Frede's black-and-yellow spotted kitten, Carissima, in 1892: Mignonette Carissima Montgomery Campbell. Avoiding Alec Macneill (and an unwelcome romance), Maud drove home with Chesley Clark from a prayer meeting on July 20, 1893, and something happened involving a broken window, Euclid, and moonlight; she may have been reminded of the other broken-window evening of June 16 (Blue Scrapbook, p. 19). A Bideford column in a local newspaper mentions the August 8, 1894, Lennox Island outing referred to on a card on the previous page, as well as Maud's "grand work" as a teacher.

PAGE 35: In the centre of this page, Montgomery placed a joke article on heroism at Prince of Wales College, followed by a picture of Halifax Ladies' College, where she would board in 1895–96 while attending Dalhousie. Flanking these two college pieces are two poems about grandmothers, one in which the grandmother explains to her grandchildren how "life is a stocking" they knit all their lives, and the other in which a young boy complains of all he does for his grandmother and ends by remembering how much love and support she has given him. Grandmother Macneill was (and Grandfather Macneill was not) supportive of both Maud's two educational ventures, to PWC and to Dalhousie. Montgomery was pleased to be mentioned as "our popular teacher" in "Bideford Notes." The 1892 British portrait of the Hon. Mrs. Devereux was painted by Frederick Goodall (1822–1904). Montgomery enjoyed collecting pictures of famous or conspicuously fashionable women whose clothes and bearing were distinctive. Would young Anne Shirley's ideal of beauty have looked like this?

A Skating Lesson

We spoke in sentences condensed,
Yet said enough.
Sometimes I wildly bumped against
Her furry muff.

Sometimes her lovely weight half hurled
Me from my feet,
Nor would I miss for all the world
This onslaught sweet.

Sometimes with both dear hands she clung
In dire alarm;
Again, quite calm, she merely hung
Upon my arm.

Oh, moonlight night! oh, silvery ring
Of skaters' steel!
With fingers locked we glide and swing,
We carol and reel.

I feel her skirt that flutters warm
Against my knees,
I turn and twist her pliant form
With graceful ease.

Last—kneeling, draw the straps apart
From ankle neat;
My gloves are in her lap—my heart
Is at her feet.

. . . .

A half-forgotten memory—
Yet, at a word
How clearly it comes back to me!
Just now I heard

My eldest-born, my handsome Claude,
(Oh, smile of fate!)
Coaxing her lovely daughter Maud
To learn to skate!

M. S. Bridges.

FARCE

'My Turn Next.'

DRAMATIS PERSONÆ.

"Taraxicum Twitters" (Apothecary) T. N. Campbell.

"Tim Bolus," (Apothecary's Assistant) Mr. Gray.

"Tom Trap," (Commercial Traveller) J. F. Betts, M.L.A.

"Farmer Wheatear" (Farmer) Mr. Pavier.

"Lydia," (Mrs. Taraxicum Twitters) Miss Pritchard.

"Cicely," (Mrs. Twitters Sister) Miss F. A. Reid.

"Peggy," (Housekeeper to Mr. Twitters) Miss Clarke.

A Schoolroom Idyl.

How plainly I remember all!
The desks, deep-scored and blackened,
The row of blackboards 'round the wall,
The hum that never slackened;
And, framed about by map and chart,
And casts of dusty plaster,
That wisest head and warmest heart,
The kindly old schoolmaster!

I see the sunny corner nook
His blue-eyed daughter sat in,
A rosy, fair-haired girl, who took
With us her French and Latin.
How longingly I watched the hours
For Ollendorf and Cæsar!
And how I fought with Tony Powers
The day he tried to tease her!

And when, one day, it took the "Next!"
To stay some Gallic slaughter,
Because I quite forgot the text
In smiling at his daughter,
And she and I were "kept till four
To study, after closing,"
We stopped the clock an hour or more
While he, poor man, was dozing!

And there he sits, with bended head,
O'er some old volume poring
Or so he thinks; if truth be said
He's fast asleep and snoring),
And where the shaded lamplight plays
Across the cradle's rocking,
My schoolmate of the olden days
Sits, mending baby's stocking.

Charles B. Going, in the *Ladies' Home Journal.*

THE NEW MOON.

"Of all sad words of tongue or pen
The saddest are, 'it might have been'" Whittier
"Here there was laughing of old." Swinburne.
"Compliment."

AN ODE TO SPRING.

"Oh, beautiful, budding, verdant Spring,"
So sang a poet of renown;
But he, himself, alone was *green*,
For the snow lay deep on the ground.

"All hail!" he cried, "thou beautiful Spring,"
And it did just as he said;
And the hail came down from the Heavenly King,
And hit him and knocked him dead.

We give this warning to 'poets of Spring,'
Who write when the snow's on the ground,
Be careful about the words you use,
Or when Spring comes you won't be found.

U. G. H——e

Gathered Sunday Aug. 17th
Prairie Sunflower
Winnipeg Manitoba Can.

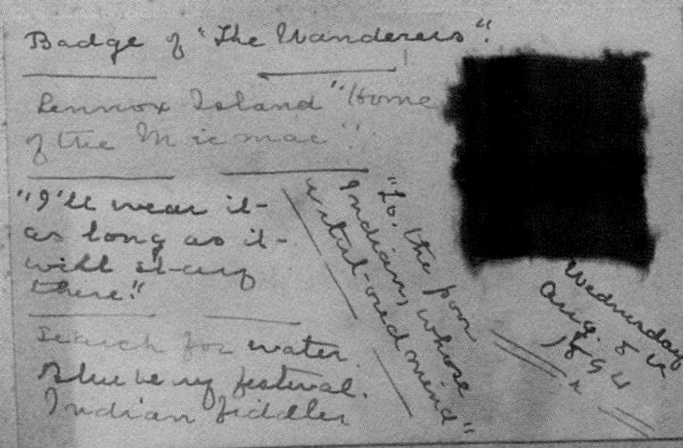

Badge of 'The Wanderers'.
Lennox Island "Home of the Micmac"
"I'll wear it as long as it will stay there!"
"Lo, the poor Indian, whose untutored mind"
Search for water
Indian fiddler
Wednesday

Page 33 from the Blue Scrapbook

f murmuring sound,
er face."

ZARA.

"A silvery veil of pure moonlight
Is glancing over the quiet water,
And oh! 'tis beautiful and bright
As the soft smile of Selim's daughter.

"Sleep, moonlight! sleep upon the wave,
And hush to rest each rising billow,
Then dwell within the mountain cave,
Where this fond breast is Zara's pillow.

"Shine on, thou blessed moon! brighter still,
Oh, shine thus ever night and morrow;
For day-break mantling o'er the hill,
But wakes my love to fear and sorrow."

'Twas thus the Spanish youth beguiled
The rising fears of Selim's daughter;
And on their loves the pale moon smiled,
Unweeting of the morrow's slaughter.

Alas! too early rose that morn,
On harnessed knight and fierce soldada—
Alas! too soon the Moorish horn
And tambour rang in Old Grenada.

The dew yet bathes the dreaming flower,
The mist yet lingers in the valley,
When Selim and his Zegris' power
From port and postern sternly sally.

Marry! it was a gallant sight
To see the plain with armour glancing,
As on to Alpuxara's height
Proud Selim's chivalry were prancing.

The knights dismount; on foot they climb
The rugged steeps of Alpuxara;
In fateful and unhappy time,
Proud Selim found his long-lost Zara.

They sleep—in sleep they smile and dream
Of happy days they ne'er shall number;
Their lips breath sounds—their spirits seem
To hold communion while they slumber.

A moment gazed the stern old Moor,
A scant tear in his eye did gather,
For as he gazed, she muttered o'er
A blessing on her cruel father.

The hand that grasped the crooked blade,
Relaxed its gripe, then clutched it stronger;
The tear that that dark eye hath shed
On the swart cheek is seen no longer.

'Tis past!—the bloody deed is done,
A father's hand had sealed the slaughter!
Yet in Grenada many a one
Bewails the fate of Selim's daughter.

And many a Moorish damsel hath
Made pilgrimage to Alpuxara;
And breathed her vows, where Selim's wrath
O'ertook the Spanish youth and Zara.

—o—

Joy and
all good things attend your Christmastide.

Bideford Notes.

On Wednesday last a small party of our young folk paid a visit to Lennox Island, the home of the Micmacs. They sailed from Bideford wharf in the pleasure boat "Discipline" and after landing and enjoying an excellent lunch they repaired to Mr. Thomas Abram's house and indulged in a rustic dance in which both Micmac and pale-face enjoyed themselves. The music furnished by Messrs Abram and Prospere was excellent and showed that those gentlemen are masters of the violin.

Harvesting has been begun here, and although the the oats are only fair, the wheat crop is good.

A new Episcopal church is about being started here and when completed will add greatly to the beauty of our already beautiful village.

Our young friend, Mr. John Dystant, preached an excellent sermon in the Methodist church on Sunday last. We are glad to note the success of this estimable young man and hope for its continuance.

Our school is doing grand work under the guiding hand of Miss Lucy M. Montgomery, who, although only a few weeks in charge, is fast becoming very popular with both scholars and ratepayers.

COM.

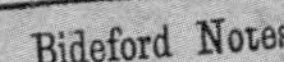

Thursday,
July 20th
1893

"Have you got any veils down there?"
"Who broke that window?"
"You couldn't prove that by Euclid."
"He couldn't prove it either on a moonlight night."

Carissima
"Park Corner".
1892

L. D. M. C. M[illegible] M. H. R. M. C.

THE HON. MRS. DEVEREUX.—F. GOODALL, R.A.

courage of Horatius. His assailants have got the advantage; they surround him on all sides. Overpowered with numbers he is forced to give up the contest and is driven from the field, yet not till he had shown by his valour that some of the blood of the knights of Arthur's Round Table still courses in the veins of the Celt. Although we can only mourn for his defeat, it is no more than we could have expected from the unequal contest, and let us hope that his name may be inscribed by worthier hands than ours among the Great Ones of History.

N. O. T.

CLEMATIS.

WHAT ONE BOY THINKS

A stitch is always dropping in the everlasting knitting,
And the needles that I threaded, no, you couldn't count to-day;
And I've hunted for the glasses till I thought my head was splitting,
When there upon her forehead as calm as clocks they lay.

I've read to her till I was hoarse the Psalms and the Epistles,
When the other boys were burning tar-barrels down the street;
And I've stayed and learned my verses when I heard their willow whistles,
And I've stayed and said my chapter with fire in both my feet.

And I've had to walk beside her when she went to evening meeting,
When I wanted to be racing, to be kicking, to be off;
And I've waited while she gave the folks a word or two of greeting,
First on one foot and the other and 'most strangled with a cough.

"You can talk of Young America," I say, "till you are scarlet,
It's Old America that has the inside of the track!"
Then she raps me with her thimble and calls me a young varlet,
And then she looks so woe-begone I have to take it back.

But! There always is a peppermint or a penny in her pocket—
There never was a pocket that was half so big and deep—
And she lets the candle in my room burn 'way down to the socket,
While she stews and putters round about till I am sound asleep.

There's always somebody at home when every one is scattering;
She spreads the jam upon your bread in a way to make you grow;
She always take's a fellow's side when every one is battering;
And when I tear my jacket, I know just where to go!

And when I've been in swimming after father said I shouldn't,
And mother has her slipper off according to the rule,
It sounds as sweet as silver, the voice that says "I would'nt;
The boy that won't go swimming such a day would be a fool!"

Sometimes there's something in her voice as if she gave a blessing,
And I look at her a moment and I keep still as a mouse—
And who is she by this time there is no need of guessing;
For there's nothing like a grandmother to have about the house!

—*Harriet Prescott Spofford.*

Bideford Notes.

The beautiful waters of Goodwood river are now dotted with boats whose occupants are obtaining for the markets the bivalves for which the place is noted. The oysters are very scarce and the price consequently very high.

The talk of the day in society circles, is the prospective entrance into the ranks of matrimony of some of our *sage* young folk. We hope the summer villas of Bideford will all be occupied by them next season.

The people of this place of every denomination hear with pleasure that the term of residence of the Methodist ministers has been extended by the General Conference, as the work on the new church would be greatly retarded by the removal of our present pastor.

Our sportsmen are mercilessly slaughtering the partridge since the season began and judging by the numbers bagged they must be exceedingly plentiful.

Social gatherings are now the order of the day, or rather of the evening, and many enjoyable evenings are thus passed by our young folk.

Our popular teacher, Miss Montgomery is at present spending her vacation at her home in Cavendish.

We are glad to see again among us our old friend, Mr. Thomas McDougall, who has just returned from his sojourn in the land of Uncle Sam.

LIFE A STOCKING.

The supper is over, the hearth is swept,
And in the wood-fire's glow
The children cluster to hear a tale
Of that time so long ago,

When grandma's hair was golden brown,
And the warm blood came and went
O'er the face that was scarcely sweeter then
Than now in its rich content.

The face is wrinkled and careworn now,
And the golden hair is gray,
But the light that shone in the young girl's eye
Has never gone away,

And her needles catch the fire's bright light
As in and out they go,
With the clicking music that grandma loves,
Shaping the stocking-toe.

And the waiting children love it too,
For they know the stocking's song
Brings many a tale to grandma's mind,
Which they shall hear ere long.

But it brings no story of olden time
To grandma's heart to night;
Only a sermon, quaint and short,
Is sung by the needles bright.

"Life is a stocking," grandma says,
"And yours is just begun;
But I am knitting the toe of mine,
And my work is almost done.

"With merry hearts we begin to knit,
And the ribbing is almost play;
Some are gay-colored, and some are white,
And some are ashen-gray;

"But most are made of many a hue,
With many a stitch set wrong,
And many a row to be sadly ripped
Ere the whole is fair and strong.

"There are long plain spaces without a break,
That in youth are hard to bear,
And many a weary tear is dropped
As we fashion the heel with care.

"But the saddest, happiest time is that
Which we court, and yet would shun,
When our heavenly Father breaks the thread
And says that our work is done."

The children come to say "Good-night"
With tears in their bright young eyes,
While in grandma's lap with a broken thread,
The finished stocking lies.

HEROISM.

Peace has so long reigned supreme throughout the world that we sometimes come to doubt the authenticity of history that treats of startling conflicts, heroic deeds and such like seemingly fabulous performances. But these events were localized in the recent collision witnessed on the campus of the Prince of Wales College, when one individual was seen to contend against a multitude of "the most cruel of animals." While we are moved by his heroic conduct, we cannot but reprimand the action of the number of young men who witnessed the scene and with that wanton spirit, which forms such a marked feature of students everywhere, exhausted themselves with laughter at the perilous situation of their fellow-being. No voice was raised to urge them on, no one was found to lead the band. Alas! "the day of chivalry is past." Meanwhile the battle thickens; the multitude rush on "with the prodigal exuberance of early youth," but retreat with the instability of savages. Step by step he is driven back; now he gains some advantage, but it is only momentary. The attack is renewed again and again. Still he fights with the

Page 35 from the Blue Scrapbook

PAGE 37: The Thomas Lawrence 1827 portrait of Lady Peel, like the Goodall portrait of the Hon. Mrs. Devereux, presents a beautiful woman of fashion and aristocratic bearing. Perhaps Lady Peel reminded Montgomery of the Lady in the fictional political scene from *Punch*. Montgomery's autobiographical Emily would often imagine herself as an articulate, politically astute Lady Trevanion in savoured daydreams. According to an unpublished diary entry, Montgomery and Lucie walked to the Clark family's home on the evening of May 29, 1895. There, they may have indulged in ghost stories and games. Certainly, they would have walked through a world transformed by wild cherry and apple blossoms. Lou Dystant's calling card, tellingly, rests among relics. Note the fur from three of Montgomery's cats: Topsy (one of the oldest dated items in these scrapbooks), Mephistopheles, and Lady Katherine (comically placed beside the picture of Lady Peel).

PAGE 38: Above the Bideford parsonage souvenir chips of wood from the door, step, walls, and bench is another strip of wood commemorating "'Black Night' Easter Sunday, April 14, 1895." Easter night was rainy and dark, and Mrs. Estey insisted Lou Dystant stay the night after he had escorted her and Maud home from the evening service. Local boys, thinking to give Lou an embarrassingly hard time getting out of the house, blocked the doorways with logs.

PAGE 39: The numerous jolly "rackets" marked on the 1890 calendar may have reflected how Maud felt about her crowded social calendar in Bideford. On Wednesday, June 26, 1895, a final dance followed a half-holiday when she and friend Maud Hayes sold lemonade and candy at a Sewing Circle bazaar.

Lady Katherine

POLITICS AND POLITENESS.

(Punch.)

Dear Mr. Punch,—I see that the Duke of Argyll, when he received the freedom of the Burgh of Paisley, the other day, told the following interesting story:—

'I was going once to call on a lady in London, and when the door was opened and the servant announced my name, I saw the lady advancing to the door with a look of absolute consternation on her face. I could not conceive what had happened, and thought I had entered her room at some inconvenient moment, but, on looking over her shoulder, I perceived Mr. and Mrs. Gladstone sitting at the tea-table, and she evidently thought that there would be some great explosion when we met. She was greatly gratified when nothing of the kind occurred, and we enjoyed a cup of tea as greatly as we had ever done in our lives.'

Now, my dear Mr. Punch, I have great sympathy with 'the Lady,' and think (with her) the meeting, as described by his Grace of Argyll, was mild in the extreme. If something out of the common had taken place, it would have been far more satisfactory. To make my meaning plainer, I give roughly (in dramatic form) what should have happened to have made the action worthy of the occasion.

Scene—A drawing-room. Lady entertaining Mr. and Mrs. G. at tea. A loud knock heard without.

Mrs. G. (greatly agitated.)—Oh dear, I am sure it is he!

Mr. G. (with calm dignity.)—Do not fear—if he appears, I shall know how to deal with him.

Lady (pale, but calm.)—Nay, my good, kind friends, believe me, you shall not suffer from the indiscretion of the servant.

Mrs. G. (pushing her husband into a cupboard.) Nay, William, for my sake! And now to conceal myself, so that he may not suspect his presence by my proximity. [Hides behind the curtains.

The Duke of Argyll (breaking open the door, and entering hurriedly)—And now, madam, where is my hated foe? I have tracked him to this house. It is useless to attempt to conceal him

The Lady (laughing uneasily)—Nay, your Grace, you are too facetious! Trace the Premier here! Next you will be saying that he and his good lady were taking tea with me.

The Duke (suspiciously)—And, no doubt, so they were! This empty cup, that half-devoured muffin—to whom do they belong?

The Lady (with forced gaiety)—Might I not have entertained Mr. and Mrs. Joseph Chamberlain, my Lord Duke?

The Duke (aside)—Can I believe her? (Aloud.) But if it is as you say, I will send away my clansmen who throng the street without. (Opens window and calls.)—Gang a waddy Caller Herring! They will now depart. (A sneeze heard off) What was that?

The Lady (terrified)—I fancy it was the wind—the cold wind—and now, believe me, Mr. Gladstone will abandon home rule.

Mr. G. (suddenly appearing)—Never! I tell you to your face that you are a traitor! [Sneezes, and hurriedly closes the window.

The Duke (savagely)—That sneeze shall be your last! [Takes up a knife lying on the table.

Mr. G. (repeating the action)—I am ready, Sir!

Mrs. G. (rushing between them)—Oh, William! Do not fight!

The Lady (falling on her knees)—I prithee stay!

Mr. G.—Never! May the better man win!

The Duke—So be it! [The scene closes in upon a desperate duel. Curtain.

There, Mr. Punch!—What do you think of that? Still, perhaps, under the circumstances of the case, it is better as it is.

Yours most truly,

ONE WHO NEVER PAID TWOPENCE FOR MANNERS.

By permission of Messrs. Graves, Pall Mall.

JULIA, LADY PEEL.

From the Picture by Sir Thomas Lawrence, in the Victorian Exhibition.

1890.

Mephistopheles
"Eglinton Villa" R.A.

Wednesday
May 29th
1895

"Which gate
is the terminus"

Ghostly rooms
vs.
Haunting ghosts.

"The orchards hung out their sweet
white screen
In the time of blossoming"

1887

Topsy
"Clovernook Farm."

Ld. Kyslant.

TWILIGHT.

COURTSHIP AT THE CHURN

BY S. K. BOURNE

HE—O leave that hateful churning!
For your company I'm yearning!
How reluctantly I'm turning
To the woods and fields away!

SHE—Pray do not stand and tease, sir!
Go as quickly as you please, sir!
Do not wait at all for me, sir,
I must stay and churn to-day.
Hark! I have begun already,
And the cream says "Flap a-tap,"
And my arm is strong and steady,
"Flap a-tap, a-tap, a-tap."

HE—Will it take you all the day, dear?
Can I help you if I stay, dear?
Come and welcome back the May, dear,
Welcome back the lovely spring!

SHE—Oh, I fear 'twill be too late, sir,
And too long for you to wait, sir,
Better seek some other mate, sir.
I've no time to laugh and sing!
See! how rapidly I'm turning!
And the cream says "Flop a-top;"
Oh, I love the work of churning!
"Flop a-top, a-top, a-top!"

HE—Dear, you know how I adore you;
How my heart is longing for you,
Since the time when first I saw you
Full of girlish life and joy!

SHE—Do not speak of trifles now, sir;
Say good-bye, and make your bow, sir.
Sentiment I can't allow, sir,
Work must all my mind employ.
Hark! I do believe I hear it!
For the cream says "Flump a-tump,"
And the butter sure is near it!
"Flump a-tump, a-tump, a-tump!"

HE—Your indifference is killing!
And your answers, hard and chilling,
Show too well a heart unwilling;
I will leave you to your churn!

SHE—Really now, 'twas all in fun, dear;
See, my work is almost done, dear;
And my heart is fairly won, dear,
Take it for your own!
Yes, my heart is in a flutter!
For the cream says "Swish a-wish!"
And—Hurra! there comes the butter!
"Swish a-wish, a-wish, a-wish!"

cy—The lines which you refer to are as follows:
farried in white, you have chosen all right.
farried in gray, you will go far away.
farried in black, you will wish yourself back.
arried in red, you will wish yourself dead.
rried in green, ashamed to be seen.
rried in blue, he will always be true.
ried in yellow, ashamed of your fellow.
ried in brown, you will live out of town.
rried in pink, your spirits will sink.

STARTLING HISTORICAL FACTS.

The following examples of schoolgirl erudition are not from the recent great examinations, but from some papers at a girls' school of some standing in the Eastern districts. The funny thing about them is the complete mastery of isolated facts, with the ability to mate them properly. It reminds one of the yokel who said he knew his letters all right, but 'never could put them together.' Here are the extracts:—

The cotton famine was when the grass was so scarce that the sheep had nowhere to go for food, and there was no wool for the people to make clothes with.

The Indian Mutiny was when the people all had to be mutinied, and all the husbands and wives and children had to be mutinied, because the Indians were very cross if one was left out.

The American war was a very civil war, the people had hardly anything to eat. The war lasted for seven years, there was scarcely a shoe in the camp. People were all starved to death, the king escaped to England, then he went to France.

The battle of Waterloo was fought because the Americans did not want the tea and they threw it into the water. Then they said they did not want to be taxicated so they fought the battle of Waterloo.

The Jacobites were people who lived in huts and they took 300 men and those who lapped like a dog were taken.

[French translation].—Sickness is a strange thing in the interior of a peasant.

Walpole was the man who fought the battle of Waterloo. Having beaten the French he died in the moment of victory.—'Cape Mercury.'

Page 38 from the Blue Scrapbook

Now August brings the holidays
To gladden us once more,
And tempt us to her wooded hills
And rugged, rock-bound shore;
While scented breeze from field and lane
Steals softly through the air,
And low, sweet notes the happy birds
Are piping everywhere.

Now all of us may freely choose
The way we love the best,
Of all that nature offers us,
In these long days of rest.
The river gaily beckons us
To float adown the stream
And drift away the idle hours
Along a fairy dream.

Or on a mossy bank we lean
With fishing-rod held fast,
In hope that some unwary trout
Will take the bait at last;
Or in the surf we boldly plunge
When waves are rolling high,
Or drowse beside the lapping tide
To hear its lullaby;

Or wander by the winding shore
In nooks we love so well,
To search for gleaming ocean weed
Or gaily tinted shell.
For young and old in childish mood
These simple sports enjoy,
Which August brings with lavish hand
To every girl and boy.

The Masens of Port Hill.

THE brethren of Alexandra Lodge of A.F. and A.M. met at their Lodge Room, Port Hill, on the 27th ult., being St. John's Day, and installed the following officers for the ensuing year: Hugh Montgomery, W.M.; J. W. Brown, S.W.; Harry Williams, J.W.; John Maynard, sr., Treas.; Rev. H. Harper, Sec'y; Past Grand Master Yeo, Chaplain; Hugh A. McDonald, S. D.; Robert Hayes, J. D.; Wm. Woolridge, I. G.; Edward Gorrill, S. S.; W. W. McDonald J. S.; Dr. McLaughlin, Marshall; Norman McPhail, Tyler. After the installation an excellent supper followed. It is needless to say the repast was prepared in splendid style and did grand credit to the committee who had the affair in charge. The gentlemen who composed the committee are experienced hands at such work, but on this occasion they more than surpassed themselves, for the tables fairly groaned under the weight of the good things provided. Several toasts (drunk in cold water) were happily proposed and felicitously responded to. A most interesting address appropriate to the occasion was given by the Rev. Henry Harper. It was listened to with keen attention and at its close the appreciation of the audience was manifested by enthusiastic applause. We must not forget to mention that the festive board was graced by the presence of a number of ladies, and this was one of the pleasing features of the entertainment. During the evening some of them favored the company with recitations and songs all of which were heartily enjoyed. Where all did so well it may seem invidious to particularize, but the recitations given by Miss Montgomery, teacher at Bideford school, were so well rendered as to deserve special mention. Miss Bennett of Port Hill, also recited very nicely. After spending a most enjoyable evening the proceedings were closed by singing "God Save the Queen." The unfavorable weather prevented many members of the Mystic Tie residing at a long distance from Port Hill, from being present. Their company was greatly missed, but they were not forgotten for the toast "Absent Brethren" was duly honored both in words and song. Long may Alexandria Lodge live to give such pleasant entertainments as was the one of last Thursday evening.—[Com.

1890

January.

S	M	T	W	T	F	S
			1	2	3	4
5	6	7	8	9	10	11
12	13	14	15	16	17	18
19	20	21	22	23	24	25
26	27	28	29	30	31	

February.

S	M	T	W	T	F	S
						1
2	3	4	5	6	7	8
9	10	11	12	13	14	15
16	17	18	19	20	21	22
23	24	25	26	27	28	

March.

S	M	T	W	T	F	S
						1
2	3	4	5	6	7	8
9	10	11	12	13	14	15
16	17	18	19	20	21	22
23	24	25	26	27	28	29
30	31					

April.

S	M	T	W	T	F	S
		1	2	3	4	5
6	7	8	9	10	11	12
13	14	15	16	17	18	19
20	21	22	23	24	25	26
27	28	29	30			

May.

S	M	T	W	T	F	S
				1	2	3
4	5	6	7	8	9	10
11	12	13	14	15	16	17
18	19	20	21	22	23	24
25	26	27	28	29	30	31

June.

S	M	T	W	T	F	S
1	2	3	4	5	6	7
8	9	10	11	12	13	14
15	16	17	18	19	20	21
22	23	24	25	26	27	28
29	30					

July.

S	M	T	W	T	F	S
		1	2	3	4	5
6	7	8	9	10	11	12
13	14	15	16	17	18	19
20	21	22	23	24	25	26
27	28	29	30	31		

August.

S	M	T	W	T	F	S
					1	2
3	4	5	6	7	8	9
10	11	12	13	14	15	16
17	18	19	20	21	22	23
24	25	26	27	28	29	30
31						

September.

S	M	T	W	T	F	S
	1	2	3	4	5	6
7	8	9	10	11	12	13
14	15	16	17	18	19	20
21	22	23	24	25	26	27
28	29	30				

October.

S	M	T	W	T	F	S
			1	2	3	4
5	6	7	8	9	10	11
12	13	14	15	16	17	18
19	20	21	22	23	24	25
26	27	28	29	30	31	

November.

S	M	T	W	T	F	S
						1
2	3	4	5	6	7	8
9	10	11	12	13	14	15
16	17	18	19	20	21	22
23	24	25	26	27	28	29
30						

December.

S	M	T	W	T	F	S
	1	2	3	4	5	6
7	8	9	10	11	12	13
14	15	16	17	18	19	20
21	22	23	24	25	26	27
28	29	30	31			

DREADFUL ENCOUNTER.

It is hard for people who are not superstitious—or who think they are not—to understand the mental condition of persons who believe in ghosts, and are continually in fear because of some ridiculous "sign." In Yorkshire, England, according to the Rev. S. Baring-Gould, there is much dread of the Kirk-Grim, so called, an imaginary evil spirit in the shape of a huge black dog with eyes like saucers. He is said to haunt church lanes, and according to the popular belief, whoever sees him must die within the year.

On a stormy night in November Mr. Baring-Gould was out, holding over his head a big umbrella that had a handle of white bone. A sudden gust whisked the umbrella out of his hand, and away it went out of sight in the thick darkness and the storm.

That same evening a friend of the clergyman was walking down a lonely church lane, between hedges and fields, with no house near. Suddenly his feet and even his very breath were arrested by the sight of a great black creature which occupied the middle of the way directly before him, shaking itself impatiently, moving forward with a start, then bounding to one side, then running to the other.

No saucer eyes could be seen, but the creature had a white nose which, to the horrified traveller, seemed lit up with a supernatural radiance. Being a man of intelligence, however, he would not admit to himself that he was confronted by the Kirk-Grim. It must be a huge Newfoundland dog, he said to himself. So he addressed it in broad Yorkshire:

"Sith'ere, lass, don't be troublesome. There's a bonny dog, let me pass. I've no stick. I win't hurt thee. Come, lass, let me by."

At that moment a blast swept up the lane. The dog, monster, Kirk-Grim, whatever it was, made a leap upon the man, who screamed with terror. He felt the creature's claws in him, and he grasped—an umbrella!

Wednesday.
June 26th
"Last dance."
Bideford.
Eyes looked love
to eyes that
spake again!

515 C.M.
516 C.M.
467 L.M.

Bideford Breathings.

The farmers in this vicinity are busy at present getting out their years supply of wood. Messrs. John Williams & Sons have taken a contract of repairing the public wharf. As they are experienced hands we anticipate a speedy and substantial work. This place is soon to be sup- with a long felt want in the way of a new public hall. The shareholders held a meeting in the office of Mr. J. W. Richards on the 27 ult., and decided to erect it at once. There is already almost $300 subscribed. Our debating society is still in a prosperous condition.

BLUFF & Co.

PAGE 40: Unseen beneath the unfolded schedule is Eugene Field's short story "Conky Stiles," about a young man who quoted the Bible on every occasion. Perhaps Montgomery thought the story appropriate to mark the end of her days boarding at the Methodist parsonage in Bideford. On May 10, 1895, Maud and Mrs. Estey strolled to and from the post office. Maud would board at the "P.O." after her return from spring vacation in Cavendish. An ambitious and dedicated teacher, Montgomery created a complex teaching schedule for the many grades and dozens of children at the Bideford school.

PAGE 41: Lou Dystant proposed to Maud on June 30, 1895. Maud was disgusted by the fuss he made when she refused him and perhaps this is why she repeated here, somewhat dismissively, the very same lines from Whittier's "Maud Muller" she had used in 1894 to mark her refusal of Lem McLeod (Blue Scrapbook, p. 33). Three love stories make an ironic setting for Dystant's proposal. A celebrated beauty, Lady Hamilton was the devoted mistress of Lord Nelson. Two poems tell vastly different stories of love. The Procter poem (bottom left) tells of a man's shallow love, too quickly forgotten; the Longfellow poem (bottom right), of a man's steadfast love that lasts through life and beyond.

PAGE 42: At the top is a folded "Programme Examination" from the Bideford school, June 28, 1895. Following performances by twenty-one pupils, an address by the students, and appropriate thanks from school trustees and officials, they all sang "God Save the Queen." The Address continues inside with "our present or future welfare. Please except [sic] this as a feeble token of our regard. From your scholars of Bideford School." Interesting that Montgomery placed word of the graduation of Nate Lockhart, a childhood sweetheart, on this page (at bottom right) with her own "graduation" as Bideford's teacher. Emily Donelson for a time performed the duties of First Lady for her widower uncle, seventh U.S. president Andrew Jackson.

PAGE 43: The cartoon on "the Higher Education of Women" is a comment on Maud's next venture – to Dalhousie. The card commemorates Maud's last meeting of a group of young people who gathered in Mr. Hayes's "cosy little square hall." The "second degree" was "lunch after the newer members leave," according to Montgomery's unpublished diaries.

PAGE 44: A real-life drama was written as a note in the margin. On June 6, 1895, Maud attended a meal at the home of one of her Bideford pupils. She painted the scene vividly in her journal – inedible food and all. She proved her scholarship to the head of the family by telling him that *papyrus* was Latin for *newspaper*!

Time-Table.

[From Jan. 1st. 1895 to May 3rd 1895]. Bideford School. No 6.

L. M. Montgomery Teacher

Hour.	Monday + Wednesday.	Hour.	Tuesday + Thursday.
10–10.10	Bible reading Roll Call	10.–10.10	Bible reading. Roll-Call
10.10–10.20	First-Primer Class	10.10–10.20	First-Primer Class.
10.20–10.30	First-Grammar Class.	10.20–10.30	First-History Class.
10.30–10.45	Second Gram. Class.	10.30–10.45	Second History Class
10.45–11	Second Class.	10.45–11	Third Geog. Class. Second Class
11–11.30	Arithmetic 2nd Prim.	11–11.10	First-Primer Class.
11.30–11.40	Arithmetic Classes.	11.10–11.30	Dictation for VI. V + IV.
11.40–12.	Junior Latin Class.	11.30–11.40	Arithmetic and Algebra
12.–12.45	Dinner Hour.	11.40–12	Junior French.
12.45–1	First-Primer Class	12.–12.45	Dinner Hour.
1–1.15	Fifth Class.	12.45–1	First-Primer Class.
1.15–1.30	Fourth Class.	1–1.15	Sixth Class.
1.30–1.45	Third + Second Classes	1.15–1.30	Second Geography class.
1.45–1.55	Writing class.	1.30–1.40	First Geography class
[illegible]–2.15	Music + Sec. Primer	1.4[illegible]–2	Third + Second Primer
2.15–2.30	Arithmetic.	2.10–2.30	Junior Geometry Class.
2.30–2.40	Arithmetic Classes.	2.30–2.40	Arithmetic Classes Tables.
2.40–3	Writing. Roll Call	2.40–3	Writing. Roll Call
3.–3.30			
3.–3.30	Senior Latin + Caesar.	3.–3.30	Senior Geometry
3.30–3.45	Senior English	3.30–4	Senior French
3.45–4	Senior Can. History		
	Wednesday.		**Thursday**
11–11.10	Second Primer	11–11.10	Second Primer
11.10–11.30	Canadian History	11.10–11.30	Arithmetic and Algebra
3.45–4	Senior Hygiene	11.30–11.40	Arithmetic Classes.
	Friday.		
1.55–2.05	Junior Agriculture		1st. Monday. Bring Composition
2.05–2.15	Unit-Drill		2nd. Week Bring drawn Map
2.40–3	Recitations.		
[illegible]–3.40	Senior Latin + Caesar		All lessons must be prepared at Home.
3.40–4	Senior Agriculture.		Lucy. M. Montgomery. Teach.

heap more dignified than S…
My father always insisted that Conky…
his start in the Scriptures in…

…priceless virtues which ma…
career of h's Grandmother Cowles, a lady esteemed not more by the elders for her piety than by the younger folks for her cookies and squash pies.
When Conky was eight years old he got …our Sunday school for …

going to capture … the minister, was one of them. Deacon Cooley was another. There was talk at one…

We heard Conky's voice once and only once again. For when, just at the last he opened his eyes and saw that we were there, he smiled feeble-like, and the grace of the Book triumphed once more within him and he says—it seemed almost like a whisper, he spoke so faint and low: "Good-bye, boys; Second Timothy iv. 7."

And then, though his light went out, the sublime truth of his last words shone from his white, peaceful face.

"I have fought a good fight, I have finished my course, I have kept the faith!"—
Eugene Field in Chicago Record.

MY GRANDFATHER'S BARN.

Oh, my grandfather's barn was a jolly old barn
There the swallows used to build their nest up high
On the rafters in the peak, while we played at hide and seek.
Yet it didn't seem to make 'em very shy;
But they'd blink their little eyes,
As they'd listen to our cries
Like as though they did surmise that our fun
Was the most "rambunctious" kind
That was ever called to mind
Since the raising of young swallows was begun.

Oh, my grandfather's barn was a jolly old barn,
When the sun shed its autumn rays abroad;
When we picked the apple crop and the nuts began to drop,
And the jay in the crimson maple cawed.
Then we used to stow away
Yellow apples in the hay,
And we'd watch 'em day by day till they grew
So delicious that a bite
In their cheeks was rare delight,
And their taste beat sugared roses dipped in dew.

Oh, my grandfather's barn was a jolly old barn,
In the days of the long time ago.
With its big sliding door, and its roomy oaken floor.
Where our games set our spirits all aglow,
'Neath the rafters in the hay,
How we used to romp and play
In our childhood's happy day, full of glee;
How our laughter and our din
Made the merry moments spin—
Ne'er again such jolly, happy days for me!

PORTRAITS OF WOMEN. II

From a reproduction in carbon, by James L. Breece.
PORTRAIT OF LADY HAMILTON, BY ROMNEY.

THE STORY OF THE FAITHFUL SOUL.

FOUNDED ON AN OLD FRENCH LEGEND.

THE fettered Spirits linger
 In purgatorial pain,
With penal fires effacing
 Their last faint earthly stain,
Which Life's imperfect sorrow
 Had tried to cleanse in vain.

Yet, on each feast of Mary
 Their sorrow finds release,
For the Great Archangel Michael
 Comes down and bids it cease;
And the name of these brief respites
 Is called "Our Lady's Peace."

Yet once—so runs the Legend—
 When the Archangel came
And all these holy spirits
 Rejoiced at Mary's name;
One voice alone was wailing,
 Still wailing on the same.

And though a great Te Deum
 The happy echoes woke,
This one discordant wailing
 Through the sweet voices broke;
So when St. Michael questioned
 Thus the poor spirit spoke:—

"I am not cold or thankless,
 Although I still complain;
I prize our Lady's blessing
 Although it comes in vain
To still my bitter anguish,
 Or quench my ceaseless pain.

"On earth a heart that loved me,
 Still lives and mourns me there,
And the shadow of his anguish
 Is more than I can bear;
All the torment that I suffer
 Is the thought of his despair.

"The evening of my bridal
 Death took my Life away;
Not all Love's passionate pleading
 Could gain an hour's delay.
And he I left has suffered
 A whole year since that day.

"If I could only see him,—
 If I could only go
And speak one word of comfort
 And solace,—then, I know
He would endure with patience,
 And strive against his woe."

Thus the Archangel answered:—
 "Your time of pain is brief,
And soon the peace of Heaven
 Will give you full relief;
Yet if his earthly comfort
 So much outweighs your grief,

"Then through a special mercy
 I offer you this grace,—
You may seek him who mourns you
 And look upon his face,
And speak to him of comfort
 For one short minute's space.

"But when that time is ended,
 Return here, and remain
A thousand years in torment,
 A thousand years in pain:
Thus dearly must you purchase
 The comfort he will gain."

The Lime-trees' shade at evening
 Is spreading broad and wide;
Beneath their fragrant arches,
 Pace slowly, side by side,
In low and tender converse,
 A Bridegroom and his Bride.

The night is calm and stilly,
 No other sound is there
Except their happy voices:
 What is that cold bleak air
That passes through the Lime-trees,
 And stirs the Bridegroom's hair?

While one low cry of anguish,
 Like the last dying wail
Of some dumb, hunted creature,
 Is borne upon the gale:—
Why does the Bridegroom shudder
 And turn so deathly pale?

* * * * *

Near Purgatory's entrance
 The radiant Angels wait;
It was the great St. Michael
 Who closed that gloomy gate
When the poor wandering spirit
 Came back to meet her fate.

"Pass on," thus spoke the Angel:
 "Heaven's joy is deep and vast;
Pass on, pass on, poor Spirit,
 For Heaven is yours at last;
In that one minute's anguish
 Your thousand years have passed."

[ADE]LAIDE ANNE PROCTER.

Sunday.
June 30th
1885-
"Of all sad
words of tongue
or pen.
the saddest
are it might have been"

a bitter farewell!

"And thus we part to meet
no more.
As we have met so oft &
Jove!: Forget-me-not

Hall.
Ellen

L. Dystant

REPRESENTING
The Halifax Confectionery and
Baking Co. (Ltd.)
HALIFAX, N. S.

J. A. M. wrote me a few weeks ag[o]
concerning a poem by Longfellow that wa[s]
not published until after his death, with th[e]
request that I publish the lines. Here i[s]
the poem referred to:

Alone I walk the peopled city,
 Where each seems happy with his own;
Oh! friends, I ask not for your pity—
  I walk alone.

No more for me yon lake rejoices,
 Though moved by loving airs of June'
Oh! birds, your sweet and piping voices
  Are out of tune.

In vain for me the elm tree arches
 Its plumes in many a feathery spray;
In vain the evening's starry marches
  And sunlit day.

In vain your beauty, summer flowers;
 Ye cannot greet these cordial eyes;
They gaze on other fields than ours—
  On other skies.

The gold is rifled from the coffer,
 The blade is stolen from the sheath;
Life has but one more boon to offer,
  And that is Death.

Yet well I know the voice of duty,
 And, therefore, life and health must crave,
Though she who gave the world its beauty
  Is in her grave.

I live, O lost one! for the living
 Who drew their earliest life from thee,
And wait until with glad thansgiving
  I shall be free.

For life to me is as a station
 Wherein apart a traveller stands—
One absent long from home and nation,
  In other lands;

And I, as he who stands and listens,
 Amid the twilight's chill and gloom,
To hear, approaching in the distance,
  The train for home.

For death shall bring another mating
 Beyond the shadows of the tomb,
On yonder shore a bride is waiting
  Until I come.

In yonder field are children playing,
 And there—oh! vision of delight!—
I see the child and mother straying
  In robes of white.

Thou, then, the longing heart that breakest,
 Stealing the treasures one by one,
I'll call Thee blessed when thou makest
  The parted—one.

12. Dialogue "The Grown Ups Land". W. Cannon & M. McKenzie
14 Reading "Summer" Master Frank Grant
15. Speech Master Amos McKay.
16. Recitation "Little Christel". Miss Bertie Hayes.
17 Recitation "What A Boy Can Do" Master Claud Williams
18 Reading "Ellerslie" Master Clifford Hayes.
19. Recitation "Willies Breeches" Master Ray Sorrill
20 Recitation "How to Lighten Troubles" Miss Bebie Williams"
21 Closing Speech. Miss Bertie Ellis

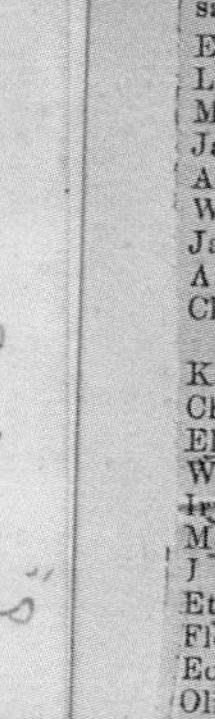

License Examinations.

FIRST CLASS (1895.)

Total number of marks 1400—necessary to obtain a license, 840.

Edith Anderson, Summerside, 1054.
Lillian Robertson, Ch'town, 1048.
Maggie James, Ch'town, 1036.
James Ramsay, Hamilton, 1032.
Ada McLeod, Eldon, 1029.
William Robertson, Marshfield, 1027.
James Stewart, L. Montague, 1025.
Amy McGregor, Ch'town, 1023.
Charles McCallum, Brackley Point, 992.
Katie Shaw, Murray Harbor, 989.
Charles Hardy, Alberton, 983.
Ella Stevenson, North River, 974.
Walter Curtis, Milton, 969.
Irving Howatt, French River, 964.
Mary Jost, Charlottetown, 959.
J A Seller, Union Road, 946.
Ethel B Connors, Bedeque North, 913.
Flora McKenzie, Charlottetown, 913.
Edison Stavert, Clarke's Mills, 902.
Oliver Lawson, Charlottetown, 873.
George McLeod, Milton, 869.
Minnie Kelly, Charlottetown, 866.
Katie McPhail, Orwell, 855.
Alberta Huestis, Charlottetown, 836.

Candidates for first class license, who have obtained second class:

Daniel McLeod, Stanley, 822.
Mary L Murphy, Summerside, 821.
Henry Phillips, Murray Harbor, 821.
Hensley Stavert, Clarke's Mills, 820.
Winfield Matheson, Charlottetown, 813.
James Campbell, Montague, 799.
William Bradley, Charlottetown, 789.
Enoch Mugford, Murray H South, 777.
George Purdy, Charlottetown, 751.
Maggie Thompson, Charlottetown, 719.

Note.--No. 25 first class English was not received by the examiner.

SECOND CLASS (REGULAR.)

Total number of marks 1400, necessary to obtain a license, 840.

John H McFadyen, Spring Park, 1248.
Alfred C Lawson, Stanhope, 1178.
Edward Laverty, Glenfinnan, 1163.
Emmet Mullaly, Souris, 1135.
Duncan McArthur, West River, 1134.
James Williams, Mount Pleasant, 1112.
Arthur B Campbell, Souris, 1105.
Stewart McNeill, Rocky Point, 1066.
Maggie Ross, Stanley, 1062.
Lizzie Dickieson, New Dominion, 1056.
Roderick McKenzie, Canoe Cove, 1955.
Ethel Henry, Malpeque, 1052.
D S Edmunds, St Dunstan's, 1044.
Emily F Ayers, Union Road, 1040.
Clara McDonald, Vernon River, 1035.
Charles Lannon, Summerside, 1035.
Thomas Trainor, Kensington, 1032.
Charles E McDuff, Brookfield, 1024.
Peter S Duffy, Emerald, 1020.
Wm McKie, Charlottetown, 1013.
Caleb Lane, New Perth, 1002.
Stella Campbell, Park Corner, 995.
Norman Campbell, Darlington, 987.
Annie Rodd, Brackley Point, 984.
Amos Monaghan, Kelly's Cross, 971.
Urban Christopher, Tignish, 970.
Ernest Collings, Albany Plains, 954.
Maurice Macdonald, Kelly's Cross, 947.
Annie Ramsay, Malpeque, 938.
Lizzie McRae, Bonshaw, 933.
Patrick Campbell, Rollo Bay, 932.
Vina Orr, French River, 919.
Alice Kelly, Kinkora, 917.
Wm E Campbell, Victoria Cross, 917.
Olivia Nicholson, Cardigan Head, 913.
John A Murphy, Murray River, 903.
Debbie Lowther, North Carleton, 900.
Euphemia Macdonald, DeSable, 893.
Nellie McNeill, Cavendish, 863.
Martin Gallant, [illegible]tico, 863.
Katie Monagha[illegible] Cr[illegible], 854.

Address

Dear and Respected Teacher
Having heard of your intention of leaving us we as scholars cannot allow this opportunity to pass without expressing to you how deeply we regret to hear of your departure.
We heartily thank you for the justice you have given to us, You have left nothing undone that would tend in any way to expan

"THE BEAUTIFUL MRS. DONELSON"

LEGEND OF THE ORANGE BLOSSOM

Like all familiar customs whose origin is lost in antiquity, the wearing of orange blossoms at a wedding is accounted for in various ways. Among other stories is the following pretty legend from Spain:

An African prince presented a Spanish king with a magnificent orange tree, whose creamy waxy blossoms and wonderful fragrance excited the admiration of the whole court. Many begged in vain for a branch of the plant, but a foreign ambassador was tormented by the desire to introduce so great a curiosity to his native land. He used every possible means, fair or foul, to accomplish his purpose, but all his efforts coming to naught, he gave up in despair.

The fair daughter of the court gardener was loved by a young artisan, but lacked the dot which the family considered necessary in a bride. One day chancing to break off a spray of orange blossoms, the gardener thoughtlessly gave it to his daughter.

Seeing the coveted prize in the girl's hair, the wily ambassador offered her a sum sufficient for the desired dowry, provided she gave him the branch and said nothing about it. Her marriage was soon celebrated, an[d] on her way to the altar, in grateful remem[brance] of the source of all her happiness she secretly broke off another bit of th[e] lucky tree to adorn her hair.

Whether the poor court gardener lost his head in consequence of the daughter's treachery the legend does not state, but many lands now know the wonderful tree, and ever since that wedding day orange blossoms have been considered a fitting adornment for a bride.

Two Cavendish Graduates at Wolfville.

WOLFVILLE, N. S., June 5.—[Special]—Two Islanders graduated from Acadia today with honors. They were Nathan J. Lockhart of Cavendish, honors in English and Malcolm W. A. McLean, Cavendish, honors in Classics,

Page 42 from the Blue Scrapbook

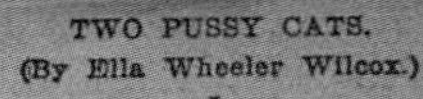

WHAT THE HIGHER EDUCATION OF WOMEN IS COMING TO.

Miss Brentwood (*Vassar '94, at home on vacation*)—"Don't wait breakfast for us, auntie. We'll be down as soon as we're through the morning calisthenics."

TWO PUSSY CATS.

(By Ella Wheeler Wilcox.)

I.

THE PET CAT.

Dainty little ball of fur, sleek and round and fat,
Yawning through the lazy hours, someone's household cat,
Lying on a bed of down, decked in ribbons gay;
What a pleasant life you lead, whether night or day.

Dining like an epicure, from a costly dish,
Served with what you like the best, chicken, meat or fish,
Purring at an outstretched hand, knowing but caresses;
Half the comforts of your life, pussy, no one guesses.

Romping through the house at will, racing down the hall,
Full of pretty, playful pranks, loved and praised by all,
Wandering from room to room to find the choicest spot;
Favored little household puss, happy is your lot.

Sleeping on my lady's lap, or dozing by the grate,
Fed with catnip tea if ill, what a lucky fate!
Loved in life and mourned in death, and stuffed may be at that,
And kept up on the mantelshelf—dear pet cat.

II.

THE TRAMP CAT.

Poor little beggar cat, hollow-eyed and gaunt,
Creeping down the alleyway like a ghost of want,
Kicked and beat by thoughtless boys, bent on cruel play;
What a sorry life you lead, whether night or day.

Hunting after crusts and crumbs, gnawing meatless bones,
Trembling at a human step, fearing bricks and stones,
Shrinking at an outstretched hand, knowing only blows;
Wretched little beggar cat, born to suffer woes.

Stealing to an open door, craving food and heat,
Frightened off with angry cries and broomed into the street;
Tortured, teased and chased by dogs, through the lonely night;
Homeless little beggar cat, sorry is your plight.

Sleeping anywhere you can, in the rain and snow,
Waking in the cold, gray dawn, wondering where to go;
Dying in the street at last, starved to death at that;
Picked up by the scavenger—poor tramp cat.

—'The Independent.'

WHY SANTA CLAUS' BEARD IS WHITE

A Legend: By M. A. Bird

DURING the babyhood of Santa Claus—long, long ago—while still many good and worthy folk believed wood-sprites lived in the holes of trees, witches in caves, and dwarfs deep down under earth, there lived in far Germany, on one of the lesser mountains of the Harz, a miner, with his wife and seven children.

Deep down in the bosom of the mountains was the mine. Here the father had worked each day from morn to night to feed, even scantily, his wife and children. At last came a season of great dearth. The miner fell sick. Sadly his wife hung out of sight his leather work-suit.

The cold winter with its cruel grasp stole down from the mountain-tops; still the miner lay sick; still the dearth of food throughout the little town; nowhere a mouthful to spare. The birds in the trees lived and were merry. Must the little children starve? Who had done it? "I tell you, it's the Gübich, king of dwarfs, who spoiled the crops last year. I know his pranks, curse him," said the oldest of the miners. "Who in summer steals all the raspberries and strawberries? He never eats aught else, and has lived like a prince, in his rocky cavern up there among the holy firs, ever since the old giant threw these mountains out of his shoe because the bit of sand hurt him. I tell you, the Gübich can make us sick with a glance, touch or breath. Save me from going near his home! Yet they say the cones off his trees are good to eat, and can be made into wondrous pretty things which sell well in the town below us. Starve or touch them? Starve, I say!"

"Dear husband," said the patient wife, "thou knowest the holy firs; I go to gather their cones. I will sell them and buy thee food which will make thee well. Children, care for thy father while I am gone."

Quickly throwing a shawl over her head and taking a basket on her arm, out into the gathering coldness of the coming night stepped the mother. The wind shook the alders at the cottage door until they nodded and peeped at the windows. It roughly rattled the dried foliage of the stately oaks, whose sacredness to the gods the elements were thought to respect, and then died away among the pines in a soft, sad music, that brought tears to the mother's eyes. It was like the moan the bairns made for bread. The tears broke into a sob; half-blinded, with bent head, she reached the edge of the holy forest.

Pityingly, out from his bed of clouds, the setting sun glanced warm and tender. He shot his parting rays among the firs, and filled their deep shadows with a cheerful glow. Suddenly, into the marked pathway of his light, stepped a little man with snowy beard, who gravely doffed his leathern cap and waited for the sad mother to reach him.

"Good woman, what ail'st thou? Why so sad?" broke upon her startled ear.

"Oh, sir, I mean no harm. My children starve; my husband never again will be well. I cannot see them ask each day for bread and give them none. I go to gather cones. Do let me pass and fill my basket."

"I would harm thee not, my friend," said the little man. "And knowest thou where the best cones can be found? Follow this path a hundred feet, and there they can be gathered with"—but the mother was on her way. A knowing look, a caress of his white beard, a sniff of the perfumed forest air, and the little man had vanished.

With glad feet the mother hurried on. Not a sound but the dropping of the cones broke the stillness of the forest. Faster and thicker they seemed to fall at each onward step. A perfect storm of cones. They dropped upon her head; they fell at her feet; they pelted her shoulders; they filled her basket. Frightened, the poor woman turned and fled, glancing neither to the right or left. Heavier and heavier the basket grew. Breathless and exhausted she reached her cottage door.

The mother entered and quickly barred the door. "Husband, husband, think what has happened! On the edge of the holy forest I met a little man with snowy beard, who told me where to gather the best cones. I hurried to find them, but the farther I went the faster the cones fell from the firs. They came about my head as thick as snow-flakes in mid-winter, yet the trees shook not. I was afraid and did not stop to pick up one; but some fell in my basket, and here they are."

"Hist, wife! Look, look thou! They are pure silver. It's the Gübich thou hast met."

Down the basket dropped. Around it grouped the mother and children. True, there lay the cones, silver every one, gleaming in the fire-light as had the beard of the little man in the golden glow of the sun.

The morrow's sun had tipped the graceful firs with gold, when again the mother stood at the edge of the forest. In a moment the Gübich was before her. "Good-morrow, good soul! Found'st thou not beautiful cones yester-eve?" And a laugh rang through the forest. The mother struggled to speak. "Keep thy thanks, I wish them not" continued the Gübich. "Be thou only faithful to thy husband's words, and each cold December give to me and my dear firs a loving thought to keep our hearts warm. Now hie thee home."

Not more quickly speeds the wind than the mother home again; not more happy are the birds than were the hearts in the miner's home that day. By night, nowhere a hungry soul on the "beautiful Hirbichenstein."

Dear Santa Claus—ever since, thy beard's been white as snow!

Dear Christmas joy—ever since, madly the Harz maidens dance around the graceful firs.

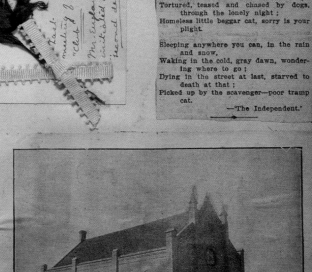

PRESBYTERIAN CHURCH.

Ba[illegible] Hits.

If one takes a[illegible]nterest in a paper is it necessary to *cleav*[illegible] to the Business Manager?

Was the Sophy scared of the Dog or did he merely want to see what was on the other side of the fence?

Mr. J. H. S. has been removed to more commodious quarters three doors west of his old stand, where he is now prepared to welcome his friends.

FOUND—On Friday, April 6th, near Prince Street School, a beautiful *Pearl* probably purchased at Taylor's Jewelry Store. Owner can have the same by shooting the finder. Apply to H. L., P. W. C.

The three essentials to human happiness are said to be—Something to do, something to love, and something to hope for. If this be so we know some P. W. C. students who ought to be happy. (A sort of grim humor pervades the above remark).

We notice that a society whose initials are N. M. A. H. S. has been formed among the young Ladies for the purpose of encouraging Spring Poets. It is said that at the end of the term they will award a medal to the composer of the best poem on "The Absent One".

In the Barn.

O Jack, are you up in the hay-loft?
  I'm coming up there, too.
I'm tired of being a lady,
  I'd rather have fun with you.
There's company in the parlor,
  And mamma whispered to me,
"Now do be a lady, Pussie,
  And see how good you can be."

But, Jack, it was really dreadful!
  I couldn't sit still, you know,
And most likely the company wondered
  To see me fidgeting so.
But I heard you laughing and shouting,
  And I knew you were having fun,
And I looked at the clock and wondered
  How soon her call would be done.

But when they were busy talking,
  And didn't remember me,
I just slipped out as softly!
  And here I am, you see.
O Jack! it is awfully jolly
  Not to be grown-up folks;
They never have fun in the hay-loft,
  Laughing and telling jokes.

They can't go hunting for hen's eggs,
  Or swing on the old barn-door,
Or climp this steep old ladder,
  And jump, like us, to the floor.
To sit in a chair is horrid.
  To sit on a beam is fun,
And we don't care if we're sunburned,
  We aren't afraid of the sun.

Just fancy mamma or sister
  Rolling about in the hay!
It makes me laugh—because surely
  Their "trains" would be in the way.
I heard papa call me a "Tom-boy;"
  I'd rather be that, I declare,
Than to sit for another hour
  So still in a parlor chair.

Just think of the time I wasted,
  When I might have been here with you!
And it may have been another half hour
  Before her visit is through.
I'm sorry for mamma and sister,
  Long dresses, long manners and all!
And Jack, I'll be sorrier still, dear
  When you and "Pussie" grow tall.

Page 44 from the Blue Scrapbook

After her happy year at Bideford, Montgomery attended Dalhousie and lived at Halifax Ladies' College on Barrington Street. The many small cards, with pressed flowers and quotations from Prince of Wales and Bideford days, seem to be replaced with colourful cut-outs and numerous clippings of poems, jokes, and events.

PAGE 49: Montgomery possibly conflated her Ladies' College experiences with her *Daily Echo* staff days in Halifax (1901–02) when she put the word *measles* from November 13, 1895, on a small card together with *Morris Street*; she lived on Church Street and then on Morris Street when she worked at the *Echo.* She contracted measles in late October 1895 and was finally released from the infirmary on November 17. In the central image – surrounded by a brilliant tulip cut-out, dried flowers, and an image of a Japanese maple leaf – the child looks wistfully out the window, perhaps reference to the fact that Montgomery did not get to go home for Christmas that year. One of Henriette Ronner-Knip's cats (Red Scrapbook, p. 35) is pasted beneath a poem about a little dog that waits loyally in vain for his child master, who has died. The other four clippings are comic, but the "Plaint of the Heroine of Fiction" suggests Montgomery the would-be novelist surveying modern writing and making a choice to tell a more conventional story, full of the very wistfulness, pathos, and humour evident on this page.

PAGE 50: A bit of McGill University ribbon is pasted beside a poem, "The Ideal," which offers a serious statement about the call Anne Shirley felt each time she beheld beauty and that Emily Starr would acknowledge as the inspiration along her "alpine path" (the latter from the poem "The Fringed Gentian"; Red Scrapbook, p. 23). Above the ribbon, the 1896 clipping draws attention because of two names, Norman Campbell (mentioned in one of the clippings on the previous page and good-natured brother of PWC friend Mary Campbell) and Edwin Simpson, who was soon to become a source of so much embarrassment and pain for Montgomery when she broke their secret engagement. "Thy Will be Done" was sent to Maud by the recently refused Lou Dystant. Montgomery's ironic comment on herself as a "wee, pure bud" may well be found in the cartoon next to the poem.

PAGE 51: Ann S. Stephen's "The Polish Boy" was a popular recitation piece. Meant to depict a rousing scene of patriotism and self-sacrifice, this is exactly the kind of poem Anne Shirley would have loved. Purple and gold were the colours of the Halifax Ladies' College and have been adopted by its successor, Armbrae Academy (primary to grade twelve).

PLAINT OF THE HEROINE OF FICTION.

I once had lovely golden hair,
  Or raven hair—no matter which—
I was as good and sweet and fair
  As any angel in a niche.
Or, if I did a little wrong,
  It was to prove me human still;
My feelings were extremely strong,
  But I disciplined my will.

A change has come—and what a change!
  With awful problems I am vexed,
From crime to crime I reckless range,
  I know not what will happen next.
From Frantic woe to frantic bliss,
  From frantic wrath to frantic glee—
I never wished to be like this!
  I can't make out what's come to me!

Gone are my gayety and cheer,
  Gone is my hero bold and true;
In my hysterical career
  I very often long for you!
Now me, all other woes above,
  My bitter destiny compels
To wed a man I do not love,
  Then fall in love with some one else.

Yet me how would you recognize,
  O Hero, if you met me now?
What scorn would lighten from your eyes
  And corrugate your manly brow!
The modern hero I have found,
  Upon the whole, I do not like;
He's either stupid or unsound,
  And if I were not worse I'd strike.

But I am worse—I never guessed
  How bad I could be till I tried,
Compelled too often to arrest
  My headlong course by suicide;
And though I cease from guilt and slang,
  A fresh reprieve I fain would beg—
For other authors seem to hang
  Theories on me like a peg.

Ah, yet I long a little share
  Of happiness and love to find;
Again I would be gay and fair,
  Loyal, and chivalrous, and kind!
Ah! do not bid me rant and rave
  Ah! do not bid me preach and bore;
Give back my Hero, true and brave,
  Whom I shall love forever more.

—*May Kendall, in Longman's Magazine.*

THE LITTLE BROWN DOG AT THE DOOR.

Early and late you watch and wait,
  Little brown dog at the door,
For a quick footfall and a boyish call,
  For your master to come once more.
    Eager to follow, through field and hollow,
      Wherever his feet may roam,
    Content to stray, if he leads the way,
      Wherever he is, is home.

But you never hear the whistle clear,
  Nor the sound of the boyish call,
Nor the scamper of feet all bare and fleet
  Down through the shadowy hall;
    Though long you wait at door and gate
      For your playfellow of old,
    With his eyes so blue and his heart so true,
      And his hair like the sunshine's gold.

'Tis a year and a day since he went away
  To a country beyond our ken,
And those who go that way, we know,
  Never come back again.
    Still early and late you watch and wait,
      Little brown dog at the door,
    But the voice is still, and watch as you will,
      Your master comes no more.

DOROTHY DEANE.

"Mearles"
Morris Street
Halifax
N.S.
November 18th
1895

NORMAN CAMPBELL, President of our Debating Society, comes from Darlington. We cannot say of him that "he toiled not, neither did he spin," for he has been successful in securing first class honors. His "length" of admiration for the frailer sex has often been commented on, but it never interfered with his working hours! Norman was a regular attendant at the evening services at the Kiak.

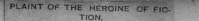

MUTUAL CONFIDENCES: [...]L FRIENDS.

BY MARY CLARK HUNT[...]N.

Said Miss Malvina Trotter to her neighbor Mrs. Potter,
  Together sitting on the porch one pleasant summer day,
"There's quite a startling story about young Mrs. Corey—
  Don't tell that I repeated it—or that's what people say.

"They quarreled with each other over one thing and another,
  Till her husband threw a cup of tea full in her face one day;
And vowing she would grieve him she now declares she'll leave him,
  Intends to sue for a divorce—or that's what people say."

"Do tell!" cried Mrs. Potter. "But I'm not surprised, Miss Trotter,
  I've thought they weren't quite happy. Now, don't you breathe a word
From *me*: but Deacon Draskitt stole a neighbor's bushel basket,
  And sold it for a quarter—or that is what I've heard.

"And his wife she is *so* cruel to that poor Pepita Buel,
  Whom she took from out the orphan's home! It actually occurred
That she called her 'lazy sinner,' made her go without her dinner,
  And whipped her, whipped dreadfully—or that's what I have heard."

Thus Miss Malvina Trotter and her neighbor Mrs. Porter
  That livelong summer afternoon with converse sweet beguiled,
Till no matter what their station, not a shred of reputation
  Was left in all that goodly town to woman, man or child.

"Dear me," mused Mrs. Potter when Mrs. Malvina Trotter
  With many a lingering last "good-night" had homeward turned her way,
"It's positively inhuman for any decent woman
  To be forever talking about 'what people say.'

Thought Miss Malvina Trotter as she left the house of Potter,
  "It's sad how many dreadful things have in this town occurred;
But worse than all together it puts in such high feather
  That gossip, Mrs. Potter, to tell "what she has heard."

An Exchange of Syllables.

The Atlantic monthly tells of a young lady who, to her intense mortification, often reverses her vowels all unconscious of it even after speaking.

One summer evening she was sauntering with a friend towards the village post-office of the little town where they were staying. On the way they encountered an acquaintance with a handful of letters.

"Ah, good evening," she said in her peculiarly gracious, suave manner. "Are you strailing out for your mole!"

The mystified young woman made some inarticulate reply and passed on. As soon as the friend could recover her gravity, she gasped, "I suppose you intended to ask Miss May if she was strolling out for her mail?"

The same young lady was relating a sad story of various misfortunes which had overwhelmed a dear friend.

"Think," she concluded pathetically, "of losing husband, children, property, and home at one swell foop!" and a howl of laughter rent the roof.

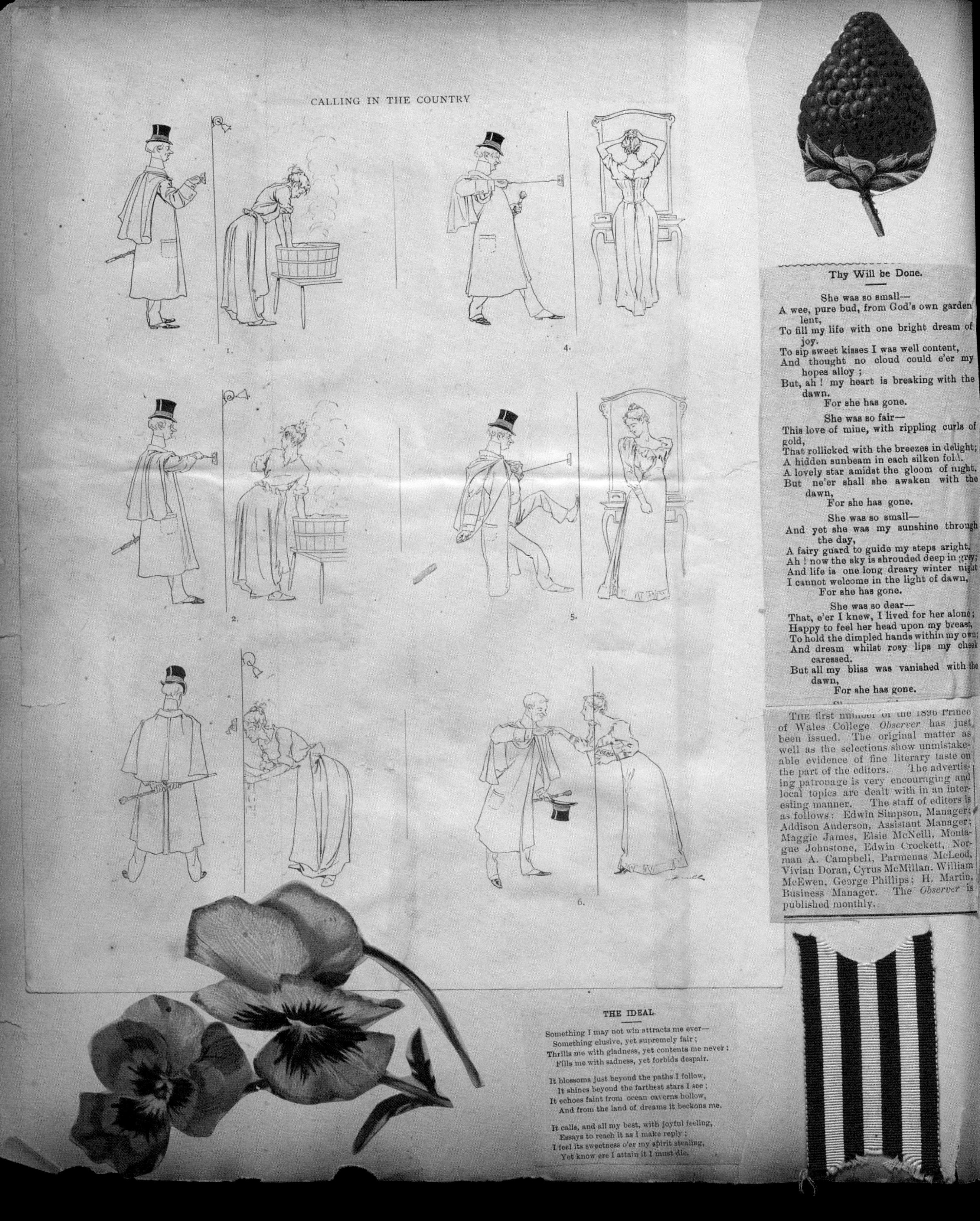

CALLING IN THE COUNTRY

1.

4.

2.

5.

6.

Thy Will be Done.

She was so small—
A wee, pure bud, from God's own garden lent,
To fill my life with one bright dream of joy.
To sip sweet kisses I was well content,
And thought no cloud could e'er my hopes alloy;
But, ah! my heart is breaking with the dawn.
For she has gone.

She was so fair—
This love of mine, with rippling curls of gold,
That rollicked with the breezes in delight;
A hidden sunbeam in each silken fold.
A lovely star amidst the gloom of night.
But ne'er shall she awaken with the dawn,
For she has gone.

She was so small—
And yet she was my sunshine through the day,
A fairy guard to guide my steps aright.
Ah! now the sky is shrouded deep in grey;
And life is one long dreary winter night
I cannot welcome in the light of dawn,
For she has gone.

She was so dear—
That, e'er I knew, I lived for her alone;
Happy to feel her head upon my breast,
To hold the dimpled hands within my own;
And dream whilst rosy lips my cheek caressed.
But all my bliss was vanished with the dawn,
For she has gone.

THE first number of the 1896 Prince of Wales College *Observer* has just been issued. The original matter as well as the selections show unmistakeable evidence of fine literary taste on the part of the editors. The advertising patronage is very encouraging and local topics are dealt with in an interesting manner. The staff of editors is as follows: Edwin Simpson, Manager; Addison Anderson, Assistant Manager; Maggie James, Elsie McNeill, Montague Johnstone, Edwin Crockett, Norman A. Campbell, Parmenas McLeod, Vivian Doran, Cyrus McMillan. William McEwen, George Phillips; H. Martin, Business Manager. The *Observer* is published monthly.

THE IDEAL.

Something I may not win attracts me ever—
Something elusive, yet supremely fair;
Thrills me with gladness, yet contents me never:
Fills me with sadness, yet forbids despair.

It blossoms just beyond the paths I follow,
It shines beyond the farthest stars I see;
It echoes faint from ocean caverns hollow,
And from the land of dreams it beckons me.

It calls, and all my best, with joyful feeling,
Essays to reach it as I make reply;
I feel its sweetness o'er my spirit stealing,
Yet know ere I attain it I must die.

THE POLISH BOY.

WHENCE come those shrieks so wild and shrill,
That cut, like blades of steel, the air,
Causing the creeping blood to chill
With the sharp cadence of despair?

Again they come, as if a heart
Were cleft in twain by one quick blow,
And every string had voice apart
To utter its peculiar woe.

Whence came they? from yon temple, where
An altar, raised for private prayer,
Now forms the warriors, marble bed
Who Warsaw's gallant armies led.

The dim funereal tapers throw
A holy luster o'er his brow,
And burnish with their rays of light
The mass of curls that gather bright,
Above the haughty brow and eye
Of a young boy that's kneeling by.

What hand is that, whose icy press
Clings to the dead with Death's own grasp,
But meets no answering caress?
No thrilling fingers seek its clasp.
It is the hand of her whose cry
Rang wildly, late, upon the air,
When the dead warrior met her eye
Outstretched upon the altar there.

With pallid lip and stony brow
She murmurs forth her anguish now.
But hark! the tramp of heavy feet
Is heard along the bloody street;
Nearer and nearer yet they come,
With clanking eyes and noiseless drum.
Now whispered curses, low and deep
Around the holy temple creep;
The gate is burst, a ruffian band
Rush in and savagely demand,
With brutal voice and oath profane,
The startled boy for exile's chain.
The mother sprang with gesture wild,
And to her bosom clasped her child;
Then, with pale cheek and flashing eye,
Shouted with fearful energy,
"Back, ruffians, back! nor dare to tread
Too near the body of my dead;
Nor touch the living boy; I stand
Between him and your lawless band.
Take *me*, and bind these arms, these hands,
With Russia's heaviest iron bands,
And drag me to Siberia's wild
To perish, if 'twill save my child!"
"Peace, woman, peace!" the leader cried,
Tearing the pale boy from her side,
And in his ruffian grasp he bore
His victim to the temple door.
"One moment!" shrieked the mother; "one!
Will land or gold redeem my son?
Take heritage, take name, take all,
But leave him free from Russian thrall!
Take these!" and her white arms and hands
She stripped of rings and diamond bands,
And tore from braids of long black hair
The gems that gleamed like starlight there;
Her cross of blazing rubies, last,
Down at the Russian's feet she cast.
He stooped to seize the glittering store;
Up springing from the marble floor,
The mother, with a cry of joy,
Snatched to her leaping heart the boy.
But no! the Russian's iron grasp
Again undid the mother's clasp.
Forward she fell, with one long cry
Of more than mortal agony.

But the brave child is roused at length,
And breaking from the Russian's hold,
He stands, a giant in the strength
Of his young spirit, fierce and bold.
Proudly he towers; his flashing eye,
So blue, and yet so bright,
Seems kindled from the eternal sky,
So brilliant is its light.
His curling lips and crimson cheeks
Foretell the thought before he speaks;
With a full voice of proud command
He turned upon the wondering band:
"Ye hold me not! no! no, nor can; 
This hour has made the boy a man.
I knelt before my slaughtered sire,
Nor felt one throb of vengeful ire;
I wept upon his marble brow,
Yes, wept! I was a child; but now
My noble mother, on her knee,
Hath done the work of years for me!"

He drew aside his broidered vest,
And there, like slumbering serpent's crest,
The jeweled haft of poniard bright
Glittered a moment on the sight.
"Ha! start ye back? Fool! coward! knave!
Think ye my noble father's glaive
Would drink the life blood of a slave?
The pearls that on the handle flame
Would blush to rubies in their shame;
The blade would quiver in thy breast
Ashamed of such ignoble rest.
No! thus I rend the tyrant's chain,
And fling him back a boy's disdain!"

A moment, and the funeral light
Flashed on the jeweled weapon bright;
Another, and his young heart's blood
Leaped to the floor, a crimson flood.
Quick to his mother's side he sprang,
And on the air his clear voice rang:
"Up, mother, up! I'm free! I'm free!
The choice was death or slavery.
Up, mother, up! Look on thy son!
His freedom is forever won;
And now he waits one holy kiss
To bear his father home in bliss,
One last embrace, one blessing—one!
To prove thou knowest, approvest thy
What! silent yet? Canst thou not fee
My warm blood o'er my heart congeal
Speak, mother, speak! lift up thy hea
What! silent still? Then art thou de
——Great God, I thank thee! Mother,
Rejoice with thee,—and thus— to die.
One long, deep breath, and his pale l
Lay on his mother's bosom—dead.

—*Ann S. Stephen*

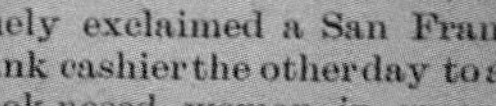

She Identified Herself.

"You must be identified," brusquely exclaimed a San Francisco bank cashier the other day to a tall, hook-nosed woman in green, red and blue, who brought in a check at a time his window was crowded.

"Well, I—I—why—I—no, it can't be! Yes, it is, too. Ain't you Henry Smith?"

"That's my name, madam," he replied, coldly.

"And you don't know me, Hen? I've changed some, and so air you; but I jist knowed I'd seen ye. You've got that same old cast in your left eye, your nose crooks a little to the left, an' you're a Smith all over. An' you don't know me? Don't know Salinda Spratt that you uster coax to become Salinda Smith? 'Member how you uster haul me to school on your sled and kiss me in the lane an' call me your little true love? 'Member how you cut up 'cause I give ye the mitten? Land! Hen, I could stand here all day talkin' over them old times! You kin identify me now, can't ye, Hen?"

"Hen" did so, but in a mood that almost produced apoplexy.—*Wasp.*

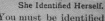

Halifax and Dalhousie are the focus of these pages but Cavendish and Bideford play parts.

PAGE 52: A large clipping or image was clearly removed from this page and replaced with the photograph at the top left. Inside the Halifax Ladies' College program, we find that Miss Mabel Dixon recited "The Polish Boy," from the scrapbook's previous page, page 51. No jolly "rackets" were marked on this 1890 calendar, which seems to have been kept for its flowers. Montgomery collected a few of these Scottish, Irish, and English jokes in the scrapbook; perhaps the study of Celtic literature gave them special charm for her. The Reverend Archibald mentioned in the central clipping, who had been minister in Cavendish for eighteen years, left for Nova Scotia in late 1895. The clipping "To Semiramis" was probably from Lou Dystant, since Montgomery commented disparagingly, in her journal in 1905, on his habit of underlining: "Lou's taste in verse was fearfully sentimental and he underlined like a school miss.... How Bertha Clark and I used to scream over those frantic clippings!"

PAGE 53: In August 1895, while Montgomery was getting ready to go to Dalhousie, Selena Robinson, her former Cavendish teacher and friend, came for a visit. They spent the days enjoying picnics and concerts, and stayed up half the night talking, hence the burnt match and the jokes referring to Maud's impending departure for school. The clipping at the bottom centre of the page describes the January 31, 1896, Dalhousie party given by the women for the men. Montgomery included a handwritten program from this party on page 58 of the scrapbook. In an unpublished diary entry, she said, "We have been thinking and talking of nothing else for a fortnight and it has been a brilliant success."

PAGE 55: The poem "You" may interest Montgomery readers because of the words "A flash!" Here *flash* refers to the dramatic appearance of an inspirational soul. In the Emily books, Montgomery would use the flash as an important metaphor for inspiration and for the fleeting glimpse of a perfect world beyond this earthly one. Montgomery expected to have a sad Christmas, since she was away from home, but was pleasantly surprised. The card on the right commemorates a New Year's Day party at 387 Brunswick Street in Halifax. "Rusty" became a feisty cat in Montgomery's Halifax novel about Anne's Redmond College days, *Anne of the Island* (1915). The list of grades belonged to Maud's Prince of Wales, not Dalhousie, days. Frank Allison Currier was one of the speakers at a Philomathic Society (an intellectual society also reproduced in *Anne of the Island*) meeting. Montgomery was also invited to give a paper to the Philomathic Society (Blue Scrapbook, p. 66).

An Englishman once boasted that he had been mistaken for a member of the Royal Family. A Scotchman, hearing this, replied that he had been addressed as the Duke of Argyle. Whereupon an Irishman said that he had been taken for a far greater person than either; for as he was walking along the street one day, a friend came up to him, exclaiming, "Holy Moses! is that you?"

HALIFAX LADIES' COLLEGE.

Elocution Recital

BY

MISS WHITESIDES' PUPILS,

TUESDAY, MARCH 24TH, 1896,

at 8 o'clock.

ACCOMPANIST. MISS TILSLEY.

BOASTING.

Three tailors were once boasting which could make the best suit for a man, one of the tailors being an Englishman, one a Scotchman, and the other an Irishman. The Englishman said, 'I could make a suit for a man if I only just looked at him as he was going round a corner.' The Scotchman said, 'And I could make a suit for a man if I only saw his coat tails as he was going round the corner.' 'Faith,' said Pat, 'and I could make a suit for a man if I only saw the corner he went round.'

Rev. W. P. Archibald, of Cavendish, leaves Monday for his future home in Sunny Brae, N. S. At a meeting of the Cavendish Literary Society, a few evenings ago, Mr. Archibald was presented with an address, expressive of deep gratitude to him for the service he has so earnestly rendered in connection with that Society. It was signed by Messrs Walter Simpson, George R. McNeill and John Laird, in behalf of the Society, who wished to convey to Mrs. Archibald and family their kind regards and good wishes for their happiness and prosperity. Mr. Archibald replied in an address replete with good advice to the young, emphasizing the necessity of their storing their minds with the best literature and the best only.

To Semiramis—"Some Day!"

BY CATHERINE ELLIOT.

I dreamed so dear a dream of you last night!
I thought I went to you and stood beside
Your chair. You took my hand in yours; looking
Up into my eyes you said: "There lies deep
Within stern Fate's decree, a bond called
Love; 'tis marked 'A Whim.' There is within
That bond a living Light, called Hope. You
Understand?"—I thought your hand had wandered
To my arm, and, burning with this mild caress
Unmeant, I bent above your head, my face
To make the softest pillow of your hair.
You moved not, nor one word spoke to break
The silent tumult in my heart, save
"Some day!"—half in earnest, half in jest.
My cheek touched yours, and, resting so, my
Wild and fervid happiness, no chains could
Chain. "And then, of course, your lips mine met?"
Ah, no! for I awoke, and knew I was
Not standing there. Beyond the stillness of
The night, I heard a voice in sadness say:
"She will not remember—you cannot forget."

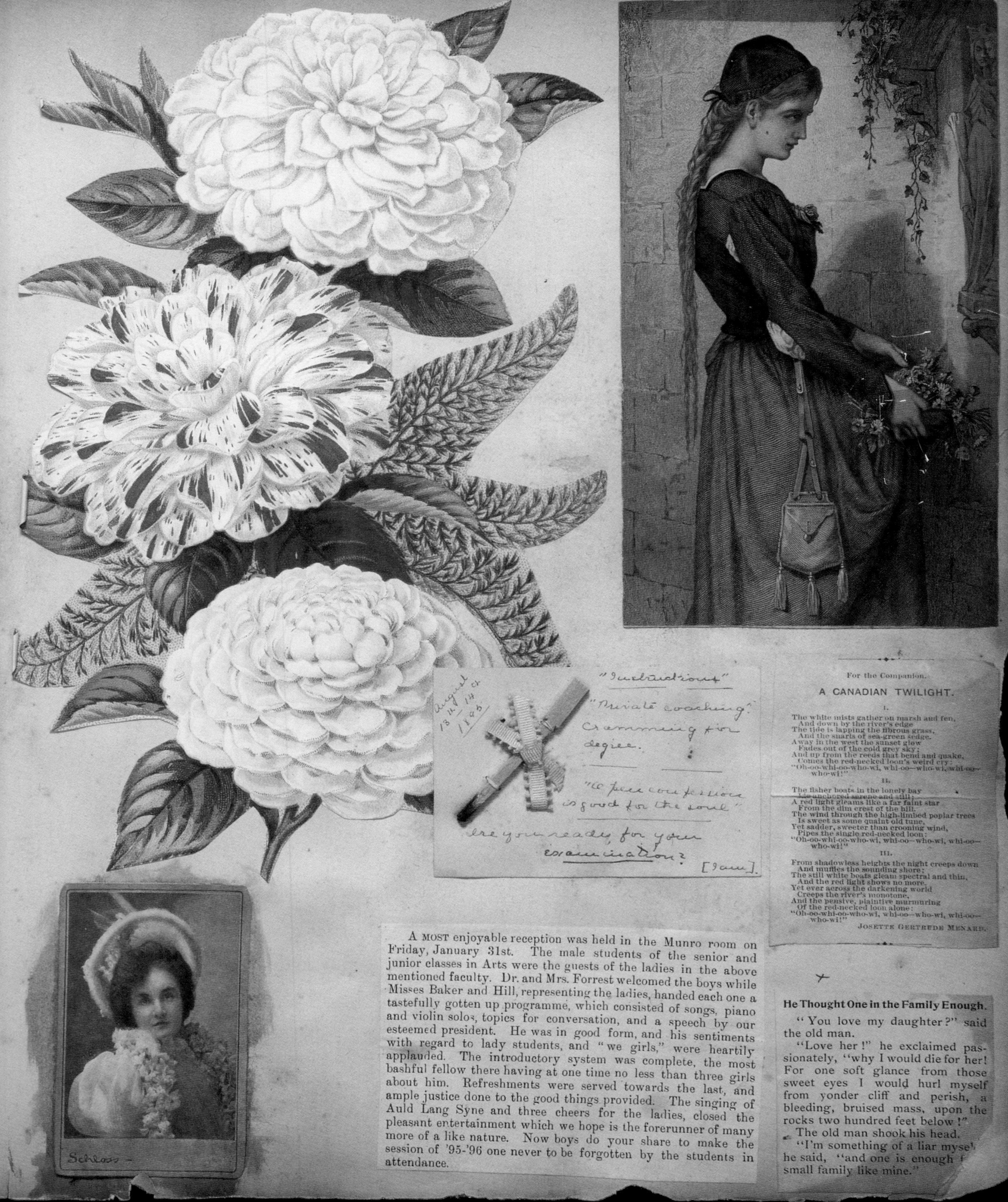
"Instructions"
"Private coaching"
Cramming for degree.
"A free confession is good for the soul"
Are you ready for your examination?
[9am].
August 13th/14th 1895
Schloss

For the Companion.

A CANADIAN TWILIGHT.

I.

The white mists gather on marsh and fen,
  And down by the river's edge
The tide is lapping the fibrous grass,
  And the snarls of sea-green sedge.
Away in the west the sunset glow
  Fades out of the cold grey sky;
And up from the reeds that bend and quake,
  Comes the red-necked loon's weird cry:
"Oh-oo-whi-oo-who-wi, whi-oo—who-wi, whi-oo—
    who-wi!"

II.

The fisher boats in the lonely bay
  Lie anchored serene and still;
A red light gleams like a far faint star
  From the dim crest of the hill.
The wind through the high-limbed poplar trees
  Is sweet as some quaint old tune,
Yet sadder, sweeter than crooning wind,
  Pipes the single red-necked loon:
"Oh-oo-whi-oo-who-wi, whi-oo—who-wi, whi-oo—
    who-wi!"

III.

From shadowless heights the night creeps down
  And muffles the sounding shore;
The still white boats gleam spectral and thin,
  And the red light shows no more.
Yet ever across the darkening world
  Creeps the river's monotone,
And the pensive, plaintive murmuring
  Of the red-necked loon alone:
"Oh-oo-whi-oo-who-wi, whi-oo—who-wi, whi-oo—
    who-wi!"

JOSETTE GERTRUDE MENARD.

A MOST enjoyable reception was held in the Munro room on Friday, January 31st. The male students of the senior and junior classes in Arts were the guests of the ladies in the above mentioned faculty. Dr. and Mrs. Forrest welcomed the boys while Misses Baker and Hill, representing the ladies, handed each one a tastefully gotten up programme, which consisted of songs, piano and violin solos, topics for conversation, and a speech by our esteemed president. He was in good form, and his sentiments with regard to lady students, and "we girls," were heartily applauded. The introductory system was complete, the most bashful fellow there having at one time no less than three girls about him. Refreshments were served towards the last, and ample justice done to the good things provided. The singing of Auld Lang Syne and three cheers for the ladies, closed the pleasant entertainment which we hope is the forerunner of many more of a like nature. Now boys do your share to make the session of '95-'96 one never to be forgotten by the students in attendance.

He Thought One in the Family Enough.

"You love my daughter?" said the old man.

"Love her!" he exclaimed passionately, "why I would die for her! For one soft glance from those sweet eyes I would hurl myself from yonder cliff and perish, a bleeding, bruised mass, upon the rocks two hundred feet below!"

The old man shook his head.

"I'm something of a liar mysel[f]," he said, "and one is enough [for a] small family like mine."

Page 53 from the Blue Scrapbook

A Woodland Song.

Clear and sweet and full of wierd, wild cadence
The rich notes rose and fell,
And now it was a plaintive song of story
Rang sobbing through the dell,
And now the glad trills of a nation's triumph
That warriors love to tell.

And someone from a far-off country listening
Thought of a sea-kissed shore,
Beyond whose stretch the swaying palm trees softly
Echo the billows roar.
That night a white-winged vessel southward sailing
Both bird and listener bore.

*   *   *   *   *   *

A silvery note! Oh! never such glorious music
As thrills the strange bird's song!
And eagerly a crowd of wondering people
To the dim shadows throng.
They do not know of *home* that bird is singing
Through hours sad and long.

L. R. Baker.

YOU.

The chief want in life is somebody who shall make us do the best we can.—Emerson.

A flash! You came into my life,
And lo, adown the years,
Rainbows of promise stretched across
The sky grown gray with tears;
By day you were my sun of gold,
By night, my silver moon,
I could not from the Father's hands
Have asked a greater boon.

Life's turbid stream grew calm and clear,
The cold winds sank to rest,
Hand-clasped with you, no bitter pain
Found dwelling in my breast;
I did not dread life's care and toil,
Your love dispelled all gloom,
And now on graves of buried hopes
The sweetest violets bloom.

My every breath and every thought
Were pure because of you,
I had not dreamed that Heaven could be
So close to mortal view;
My hands and feet were swift to do
The good that near them lay,
And in my heart throughout the year
The joy-bird sang each day.

A flash! You passed out of my life—
No, no! Your spirit still
Is sun and moon and guiding star
Through every cloud and ill;
As down the rain-bowed years I go
You still are at my side,
And some day I shall stand with you
Among the glorified.

—Clarence Urmey

Frank Allison Currier, or as the local papers used to put it "The Rev. F. A Currier," was one of the few theologues who were generally popular and could enjoy a joke as well as anyone. Currier was a popular pulpit preacher, his eloquent sermons drawing his fellow students from other churches. Possessed of a striking presence, he was unusually popular among his fair parishoners and others, and only a strong will like his could have withstood Cupids' darts. As a sportsman he excels, many a good fish story comes from his lips, and one of the articles he exhibits with pride is an old blunder buss with which he shot "many a moose." At present he is Arts' Librarian, and studies for M. A.

Page 55 from the Blue Scrapbook

Rose Hartwick Thorpe's poem "Curfew Must Not Ring To-Night" was a favourite recitation piece. In Chapter 19 of *Anne of Green Gables,* Anne pleads with Marilla to let her go to a concert where fellow student Prissy Andrews will be reciting the thrilling poem. Two largish items on this page have been removed and replaced with pictures cut from magazines. Perhaps Montgomery's *College Observer* poem "The Land of Some Day" was inspired by the "Land of 'Pretty Soon.'" Montgomery placed a write-up about former Pine Hill Divinity Hall seminarian and Cavendish minister Reverend Archibald immediately beneath an invitation to Pine Hill. She must have wondered at this page later when she became engaged to former Pine Hill seminarian and Cavendish minister Ewan Macdonald.

Early Literary Successes

Montgomery did not use her personal scrapbooks to celebrate literary triumphs. She preserved her published poems, short stories, and essays (and, later, reviews) in a separate series of scrapbooks, starting with her earliest poem, "Cape Leforce," in 1890. Literarily, her Halifax student days were very successful. She was invited by ambitious fellow students to share papers and ideas. The new PWC *College Observer* published a poem. Studying intently, she made time to write and send out pieces, and poems and short stories were accepted by popular magazines and newspapers such as *Golden Days,* the Chicago *Inter-Ocean, Youth's Companion,* the *Ladies' Journal,* and *American Agriculturist.* The editor of the Halifax *Herald* invited her to write "The Experience of a Girl Student at Dalhousie" for a special college edition of the paper. Montgomery recorded in her diary that the Halifax newspaper the *Evening Mail* ran a contest, and she won the first prize of five dollars, creating a witty poem in response to the contest topic "Which has the more patience under the ordinary cares and trials of life – man or woman?"

CURFEW MUST NOT RING TO-NIGHT.

I.

Slowly England's sun was setting o'er the hill-tops far away,
Filling all the land with beauty at the close of one sad day;
And the last rays kissed the forehead of a man and maiden fair,
He with footsteps slow and weary, she with sunny, floating hair;
He with bowed head, sad and thoughtful, she with lips all cold and white,
Struggling to keep back the murmur, "Curfew must not ring to-night!"

II.

"Sexton," Bessie's white lips faltered, pointing to the prison old,
With its turrets tall and gloomy, with its walls dark, damp, and cold—
"I've a lover in that prison, doomed this very night to die
At the ringing of the Curfew, and no earthly help is nigh.
Cromwell will not come till sunset;" and her face grew strangely white
As she breathed the husky whisper, "Curfew must not ring to-night!"

III.

"Bessie," calmly spoke the sexton—and his accents pierced her heart
Like the piercing of an arrow, like a deadly poisoned dart—
"Long, long years I've rung the Curfew from that gloomy shadowed tower;
Every evening, just at sunset, it has told the twilight hour;
I have done my duty ever, tried to do it just and right,
Now I'm old, I still must do it; Curfew, girl, must ring to-night!"

IV.

Wild her eyes and pale her features, stern and white her thoughtful brow,
And within her secret bosom Bessie made a solemn vow.
She had listened while the judges read, without a tear or sigh,
"At the ringing of the Curfew, Basil Underwood must die."
And her breath came fast and faster, and her eyes grew large and bright,
As in undertone she murmured, "Curfew must not ring to-night!"

V.

With quick step she bounded forward, sprang within the old church-door,
Left the old man threading slowly paths he'd trod so oft before;
Not one moment paused the maiden, but with eye and cheek aglow
Mounted up the gloomy tower, where the bell swung to and fro:
As she climbed the dusty ladder, on which fell no ray of light,
Up and up, her white lips saying, "Curfew shall not ring to-night.

VI.

She has reached the topmost ladder, o'er her hangs the great dark bell,
Awful is the gloom beneath her, like the pathway down to hell;
Lo, the ponderous tongue is swinging, 'tis the hour of Curfew now,
And the sight has chilled her bosom, stopped her breath and paled her brow.
Shall she let it ring? No, never! Flash her eyes with sudden light,
And she springs and grasps it firmly: "Curfew shall not ring to-night!"

VII.

Out she swung, far out; the city seemed a speck of light below;
She 'twixt heaven and earth suspended as the bell swung to and fro;
And the sexton at the bell-rope, old and deaf, heard not the bell,
But he thought it still was ringing fair young Basil's funeral knell.
Still the maiden clung more firmly, and, with trembling lips and white,
Said, to hush her heart's wild beating, "Curfew shall not ring to-night!"

VIII.

It was o'er; the bell ceased swaying, and the maiden stepped once more
Firmly on the dark old ladder, where for hundred years before
Human foot had not been planted; but the brave deed she had done
Should be told long ages after;—often as the setting sun
Should illume the sky with beauty, aged sires, with heads of white,
Long should tell the little children, "Curfew did not ring that night."

IX.

O'er the distant hills came Cromwell; Bessie sees him, and her brow,
Full of hope and full of gladness, has no anxious traces now.
At his feet she tells her story, shows her hands all bruised and torn;
And her face so sweet and pleading, yet with sorrow pale and worn,
Touched his heart with sudden pity—lit his eye with misty light;
"Go, your lover lives!" said Cromwell; "Curfew shall not ring to-night!"

ROSE HARTWICK THORPE.

Miss Montgomery

The Principal, Professors and Students of the Presbyterian College request the pleasure of your company at a

Conversazione,

in the College, on Friday evening, 27th March,

from 8.30 to 11.

An answer is requested to the Secretary.

Pine Hill, Halifax.

WE come now to a famous, and to their time the largest class. ARCHIBALD, WILLIAM P., divided with Scott the class prizes throughout their course, only once, it was in their Junior year, did they share honors with a third. With four others of his classmates, Archibald went into the ministry, and after a course at Pine Hill was in 1875 settled in Cavendish, P. E. I. There he remained till called to Sunny Brae, Pictou Co., during the past autumn. His studies did not end with his leaving College. He is still a student as was shown by his taking his B. D. from his Alma Mater in Theology in 1887, and by the fact that his name was mentioned for one of the recent vacancies on the staff of that Alma Mater. Said one of his Island brethren to the writer only a few days ago: "When Archibald came to the Island he was our worst preacher; when he left it he was our best." Thus P. E. I. finds its noblest use, —as a training school for Pictou County.

LAND OF 'PRETTY SOON.'

I know of a land where the streets are paved
With the things which we meant to achieve,
It is walled with the money we meant to have saved,
And the pleasures for which we grieve.
The kind words unspoken, the promises broken,
And many a coveted boon
Are stowed away there in that land somewhere—
The land of 'Pretty Soon.'

There are uncut jewels of possible fame
Lying about in the dust,
And many a noble and lofty aim
Covered with mould and rust;
And Oh! this place, while it seems so near,
Is farther away than the moon,
Though our purpose is fair, yet we never get there—
The land of 'Pretty Soon.'

The road that leads to that mystic land
Is strewed with pitiful wrecks
And the ships that have sailed for its shining strand
Bear skeletons on their decks.
It is farther at noon than it was at dawn,
And farther at night than at noon;
Oh, let us beware of that land down there—
The land of 'Pretty Soon.'

—Exchange.

Page 57 from the Blue Scrapbook

1 Chorus ---- Students
2 Address ---- President
3 Piano solo S C McL Miss Leichti
4 Your Favorite Hero - [illegible]
5 Violin Solo ---- Miss Hobrecker
6 " — ships ---- [illegible]
7 Chorus ---- Students
8 Social Amusements D J Burchell
9 Piano Solo --- Miss Hetherington
10. Bellers ---- [illegible]
Auld Lang Syne

PAGE 58: The programs for the January 31, 1896, party (shown opened above) put on by Dalhousie women for Dalhousie men were written by hand. Could "Just You, Dear" be another offering from Lou Dystant, rather heartlessly placed beside the proposal cartoon? The most important thing about the December 12, 1895, party (invitation at bottom right) was the outfit Montgomery wore; according to her journal, Ladies' College girls told her she looked "out of sight."

PAGE 60: Eugene Field (1850–95), famous for his nostalgia, appears several times in the Blue Scrapbook; "My Playmates" seems an apt reflection of Montgomery's own yearning for older days while homesick in Halifax. This magazine illustration seems to be a sadder version of the one on page 27 of the scrapbook. J.A.C. Rodgerson, from Pisquid, P.E.I., was in the Dalhousie 1896 graduating class. Montgomery may have met him through her cousin Murray Macneill of the same class.

PAGE 61: Prints of Edwin Landseer's 1851 painting *Monarch of the Glen* were commonly found in Victorian homes, the Campbell home in Park Corner among them. Dalhousie University (whose charter, unlike that of many similar institutions, had never excluded women) now has more than fifteen thousand students.

"BEHOLD WHAT CHANGES TIME CAN BRING!"

1795.

STUYVESANT LIVINGSTON'S GREAT-GRANDFATHER.— Be assured, Madame, that did language afford words to express my happiness, this poor English of ours would glow for a moment with the fires of ancient Greece. But I can only thank you for your favorable reply, and kissing your hand, remain your most obedient servant!

1895.

STUYVY *(who understands more English than Greek)*.— You WILL? O Emily! *darling!*

JUST YOU, DEAR!

If I could have my dearest wish fulfilled,
And take my choice of all earth's treasures, too,
And ask from heaven whatso'er I willed
I'd ask for you.

No man I'd envy, neither low nor high,
Nor king in castle old or palace new;
I'd hold Golconda's mines less rich than I,
If I had you.

Trial and privation, poverty and care,
Undaunted I'd defy, nor future woo;
Having my wife, no jewels else I'd wear,
If she were you.

Little I'd care how lovely she might be,
How graced with every charm, how fond, how true;
E'en though perfection, she'd be naught to me
Were she not you.

There is more charm for my true, loving heart
In everything you think, or say, or do,
Than all the joys of heaven could e'er impart,
Because it's you.

-St. Paul Pioneer Press.

Miss ... Montgomery.

The Officers and Members of the
Social Committee
of
Fort Massey Society of Christian Endeavor
invite you to a
Social Reception to be held at the Residence
of the Pastor, 97 Pleasant Street,
Thursday evening, at 8 o'clock.

MY PLAYMATES.

The wind comes whispering to me of the country green and cool,
Of redwing blackbirds chattering beside a reedy pool;
It brings me soothing fancies of the homestead on the hill,
And I hear the thrush's evening song and the robin's morning thrill;
So I fall to thinking tenderly of those I used to know
Where the sassafras and snakeroot and checkerberries grow.

What has become of Ezra Marsh who lived on Baker's hill?
And what's become of Noble Pratt whose father kept the mill?
And what's become of Lizzie Crum and Anastasia Snell,
And of Roxie Root who tended school in Boston for a spell?
They were the boys and they the girls who shared my youthful play;
They do not answer to my call! My playmates, where are they?

What has become of Levi and his little brother Joe,
Who lived next door to where we lived some forty years ago?
I'd like to see the Newton boys and Quincy Adams Brown,
And Hepsy Hall and Ella Cowles who spelled the whole school down!
And Gracie Smith, the Cutler boys, Leander Snow and all
Who I am sure would answer if they only hear my call!

I'd like to see Bill Warner and the Conkey boys again,
And talk about the times we used to wish that we were men!
And one, I shall not name her, could I see her gentle face
And hear her girlish treble in this distant, lonely place!
The flowers and hopes of springtime, they perished long ago,
And the garden where they blossomed is white with winter snow.

O cottage 'neath the maples, have you seen those girls and boys
That but a little while ago made, oh! such pleasant noise?
O trees, and hills, and brooks, and lanes, and meadows, do you know
Where I shall find my little friends of forty years ago?
You see I'm old and weary, and I've traveled long and far;
I am looking for my playmates, I wonder where they are!

Eugene Field.

Page 60 from the Blue Scrapbook

THE GLEN."—AFTE

DALHOUSIE COLLEGE, HALIFAX, THE DOORS OF WHICH ARE WIDE OPEN TO WOMEN.

PAGE 63: One wonders whom Montgomery was imagining in the earnest love poem "Until Death" as she pasted it into her scrapbook. "A Floral Love-Story" seems a playful commentary on her own extensive use of flowers in the whole of this first scrapbook. She pasted the flower poem onto another of Henriette Ronner-Knip's cat images, thus bringing together prominently, on one page, four abiding loves: fashion, flowers, poetry, and cats.

Fashion and Flowers

Montgomery's lifelong interests in fashion and flowers are connected through her love of colour. She told Scottish pen pal George Boyd MacMillan in 1905 (when she was writing *Anne of Green Gables*): "*Color* is to me what *music* is to some. Everybody *likes* color; with me it is a passion." Her diaries, letters, poems, and fiction are filled with descriptions vibrant with colour.

When Montgomery looked back at this scrapbook while writing *Anne of Green Gables,* she was reminded of the large puffed sleeves of 1895, which had come into fashion again in 1905. One of readers' favourite moments in *Anne of Green Gables* describes Anne's first Christmas at Green Gables, when Matthew gives her the perfect gift – a dress with puffed sleeves:

Oh, how pretty it was – a lovely soft brown gloria with all the gloss of silk; a skirt with dainty frills and shirrings; a waist elaborately pintucked in the most fashionable way, with a little ruffle of filmy lace at the neck. But the sleeves – they were the crowning glory! Long elbow cuffs, and above them two beautiful puffs divided by rows of shirring and bows of brown silk ribbon.

In explaining her love of colour to MacMillan, Montgomery said, "On my table is a color effect of yellow California poppies that makes me dizzy with delight every time I look at it"; similarly, a month before, in her journal, she had enthused over her garden, from which she had picked "the sweetest of sweet peas and yellow poppies, and nasturtiums like breaths of flame." Montgomery also knew something of the language of flowers – the meanings certain flowers were to suggest and the basis for the art of giving messages through bouquets. We find so many pansies, for example, in the scrapbooks because they suggest memory and remembrance. An avid gardener, Montgomery described in a 1901 diary entry the ideal garden, sequestered and old, bordered with clam shells or ribbon grass, and rich with crimson, luscious pinks, purples, oranges, yellows, whites – "all growing in orderly confusion."

UNTIL DEATH.

Make me no vows of constancy, my friend,
To love me, though I die, the whole lifelong,
And love no other till thy days shall end—
Nay, it were rash and wrong.

It would not make me sleep more peacefully
That thou wert wasting all thy life in woe
For my poor sake. What love thou hast for me
Bestow it ere I go!

Carve not upon a stone when I am dead
The praises which remorseful mourners give
To women's graves—a tardy recompense—
But speak them while I live.

Heap not the heavy marble on my head
To shut away the sunshine and the dew.
Let small blooms grow there, and let grasses wave,
And raindrops filter through.

Thou wilt meet many fairer and more gay
Than I; but, trust me, thou canst never find
One who will love and serve thee night and day
With a more single mind.

Forget me when I die! The violet
Above my rest will blossom just as blue,
Nor miss thy tears—e'en Nature's self forgets,
But while I live be true!

A FLORAL LOVE-STORY

Fair (Marigold) a maiden was, (Sweet William) was her lover;
Their path was twined with (Bittersweet), it did not run through (Clover).
The (Ladies' Tresses) raven were, her cheeks a lovely (Rose),
She wore fine (Lady's Slippers) to warm her small (Pink) toes.
Her (Poppy) was an (Elder), who had a (Mint) of gold,
An awful old (Snapdragon), to make one's blood run cold!
His temper was like (Sour Grass), his daughter's heart he wrung
With words both fierce and bitter—he had an (Adder's Tongue)!
The lover's hair was like the (Flax), of pure Germanic type;
He wore a (Dutchman's Breeches), he smoked a (Dutchman's Pipe).
He sent (Marshmallows) by the pound, and choicest (Wintergreen);
She painted him (Forget-me-nots), the bluest ever seen!
He couldn't serenade her within the (Nightshade) dark,
For every (Thyme) he tried it her father's (Dogwood) bark!
And so he set a certain day to meet at (Four-o'clock),—
Her face was pale as (Snowdrops), e'en whiter than her frock.
The lover vowed he'd (Pine) and die if she should say him no,
And then he up and kissed her beneath the (Mistletoe).
"My love will (Live-for-ever), my sweet, will you be true?
Give me a little (Heartsease), say only 'I love (Yew)!'"
She faltered that for him alone she'd (Orange Blossoms) wear,—
Then swayed like supple (Willow), and tore her (Maidenhair)!
For (Madder) than a hornet before them stood her Pop,
Who swore he'd (Cane) the fellow until he made him (Hop)!
Oh, quickly up (Rosemary)! She cried, "You'll (Rue) the day,
Most cruel father! Haste, my dear, and (Lettuce) flee away!"
But that inhuman parent so plied his (Birch) rod there
He settled all flirtation between that hapless (Pear).
The youth a monastery sought, and donned a black (Monkshood)!
The maid ate (Poison Ivy), and died within a wood.

PAGE 65: Perhaps Montgomery used Bayard Taylor's "John Reed's Thoughts" to help her brood up the characters of Matthew and Marilla. Though more self-aware and melancholy than Matthew, the speaker describes a staid life similar to the one Matthew and Marilla experienced before Anne arrived:

And sister Jane and myself, we have
learned to claim and yield;
She rules in the house at will, and I in
the barn and field;
So, nigh upon thirty years! – as if
written and signed and sealed.

In the 1905 journal entry about this scrapbook, Montgomery said it amused her to see in images such as this illustration how the skirt had to be held up when one walked, a gesture that became second nature over time. Under the fancy tab is Montgomery's cousin's name, Clara E. Campbell, or "Cade," who went to Boston to work when she was young (as did so many Maritimers) and settled in the United States.

E SLEEPING OF THE WIND

By Charles B. Going

great red moon was swinging
low in the purple east;
bins had ceased from singing;
noise of the day had ceased;
lden sunset islands
faded into the sky,
rm from the seas of silence
nd of sleep came by.

so balmy and resting
the treetop breathed a kiss,
lrowsy wood-bird, nesting,
ped a wee note of bliss;
over fragrant thickets
ft as an owl could fly,
ispered to tiny crickets
vords of a lullaby.

owly the purple darkened,
vhispering trees were still,
hush of the woodland harkened
crying whip-poor-will;
moon grew whiter, and by it
adows lay dark and deep;
fields were empty and quiet,
wind had fallen asleep.

JOHN REED'S THOUGHTS.

THERE'S a mist on the meadow below; the berring-frogs chirp and cry;
It's chill when the sun is down, and the sod is not yet dry;
The world is a lonely place, it seems, and I don't know why.

I see, as I lean on the fence, how wearily trudges Dan,
With the feel of the spring in his bones, like a weak and elderly man;
I've had it a many a time; but we must work when we can.

But day after day to toil, and ever from sun to sun,
Though up to the season's front and nothing be left undone,
Is ending at twelve, like a clock, and beginning again at one.

The frogs make a sorrowful noise, and yet it's the time they mate,
There's something comes with the spring, a lightness or else a weight;
There's something comes with the spring, and it seems to me it's fate.

It's the hankering after a life that you never have learned to know;
It's the discontent with a life that is always thus and so;
It's the wondering what we are, and where we are going to go.

My life is lucky enough, I fancy, to most men's eyes;
For the more a family grows, the oftener some one dies,
And it's now run on so long, it couldn't be otherwise.

And sister Jane and myself, we have learned to claim and yield;
She rules in the house at will, and I in the barn and field;
So, nigh upon thirty years!—as if written and signed and sealed.

I couldn't change if I would; I've lost the how and when;
One day my time will be up, and Jane be the mistress then;
For single women are tough, and live down the single men.

She kept me so to herself, she was always the stronger hand,
And my lot showed well enough when I looked around in the land;
But I'm tired and sore at heart, and I don't quite understand.

I wonder how it had been if I'd taken what others need,
The plague, they say, of a wife, the care of a younger breed?
If Edith Pleasanton now were near me as Edith Reed!

Suppose that a son well grown were there in the place of Dan,
And I felt myself in him as I was when my work began?
I should feel no older, sure, and certainly more a man!

A daughter, besides, in the house; nay, let there be two or three!
We never can overdo the luck that can never be,
And what has come to the most might also have come to me.

I've thought, when a neighbor's wife or his child was carried away,
That to have no loss was a gain; but now—I can hardly say;
He seems to possess them still, under the ridges of clay.

And share and share in a life is, somehow, a different thing
From property held by deed, and the riches that oft take wing.
I feel so close in the breast—I think it must be the spring.

I'm drying up like a brook when the woods have been cleared around;
You're sure it must always run, you are used to the sight and sound,
But it shrinks till there's only left a stony rut in the ground.

There's nothing to do but to take the days as they come and go,
And not to worry with thoughts that nobody likes to show;
For people so seldom talk of the things they want to know.

There's times when the way is plain and everything nearly right,
And then of a sudden you stand like a man with a clouded sight—
A bush seems often a beast in the dusk of a falling night.

I must move; my joints are stiff, the weather is breeding rain,
And Dan is hurrying on with his plow-team up the lane.
I'll go to the village store, I'd rather not talk with Jane.

—Bayard Taylor.

Acting and performance link these Dalhousie pages.

PAGE 66: Acting president Macdonald presided over the convocation, which was held privately out of respect for the death of George Munro, a chief Dalhousie donor. Montgomery's cousin Murray Macneill received many honours. Montgomery put the Dalhousie materials next to four other suggested performances: She made a woman emerge from the heart of a rose, she glued in a picture of a woman dressed for a part in a play, she commemorated the fall night at the Philomathic Society in 1895 when she presented her paper, and she remembered a comic adventure (June 6–7, 1895) from the summer before her Dalhousie days. Montgomery and Lucie Macneill drove to Darlington on June 6 to spend a couple of days with Mary Campbell: "Mary and Lu and I slept together and we laughed ourselves sick to hear Mary mimicking old Gaelic women talking. She can do it to perfection," Maud commented in her unpublished diaries. Montgomery was pleased to be invited to speak at the Philomathic. Ian Maclaren was the pen name of Dr. John Watson (1850–1907), whose 1894 bestselling book of sketches of Scottish life, *Beside the Bonnie Brier Bush,* was likely admired by Montgomery.

PAGE 67: On the top of the Dalhousie examination paper (shown opened here) Montgomery glued PWC colours and noted inside gleefully that she had taken her last examination ever. The dates 1884–96 mark the first time a Cavendish schoolteacher (Mr. Fraser) gave strict examinations and the last Dalhousie ones. Hedley Buntain, who took Maud to her first opera in Charlottetown when she was a student at Prince of Wales (Blue Scrapbook, p. 4), got married and next to the notice, perhaps ironically, Montgomery placed the program for *The Beggar Student.* Montgomery saw *Billee Taylor* with Halifax Ladies' College friend Lottie Shatford and did not care for the play itself. "But the 'living pictures' at the close were beautiful and well worth seeing," according to Montgomery's unpublished diaries.

PAGE 68: The performance of *Faust* made a huge impression on Montgomery (see also Red Scrapbook, p. 53): "It was grand. The fourth act in especial – the revel of demons and witches . . . was grandly horrible. I only wish I could see it all again. I never enjoyed anything so much" reads her unpublished diary entry for November 22, 1895. Ellen Beach Yaw, also known as "Lark Ellen," debuted on the New York stage in 1894. She was said to be able to sustain D above high D. How interesting to see cousin Bertie McIntyre praised beside Edwin Simpson in this PWC notice. When Montgomery became engaged to Simpson in 1897, she believed, as this article suggests, that he was going to be a lawyer (he became a Baptist minister).

CONVOCATION

OF

DALHOUSIE UNIVERSITY,

HALIFAX, N. S.

TO BE HELD ON

TUESDAY, 28th April, 1896.

PROF. C. MACDONALD, M. A., Acting President, in the Chair.

CHARLES MACDONALD, M.A.

PROFESSOR OF MATHEMATICS, DALHOUSIE UNIVERSITY,

The Society met again on Nov. 29th. "Scotch Authors" wa topic of the evening. The first paper was on "Crockett," and was by R. E. Crockett. He did full justice to himself and to his nam His character sketch was good, his history light and racy, his de tions vivid and his quotations apt.

Miss Montgomery followed with a paper on "Ian McLaren. was very well written, and was read with the enthusiasm the su demanded. The writings of this author draw forth eulogy rather criticism. Miss Montgomery's paper proved to be no exception t rule, and many fine points were brought out.

Mr. F. S. Simpson, B. A., discussed "Barrie," and succeede sustaining his former reputation as an essayist. He depicted Barri his works both in his beauty and his weaknesses in language, tha clear, forcible and sometimes humorous.

Messrs. Putnam, McKay, Milligan and Davidson took part discussion which followed. After thanking the writers the S adjourned.

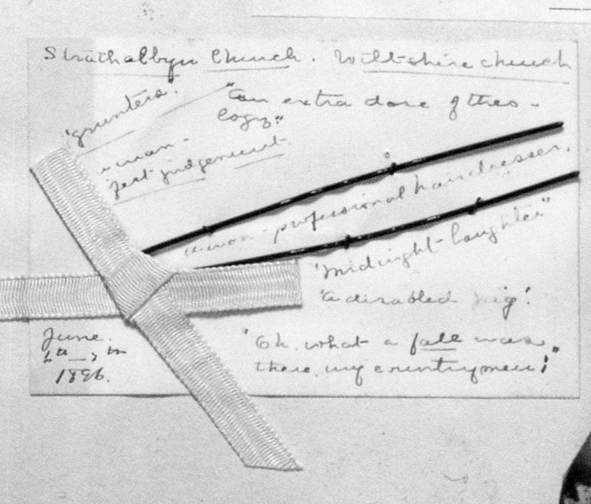

1884 — 1896

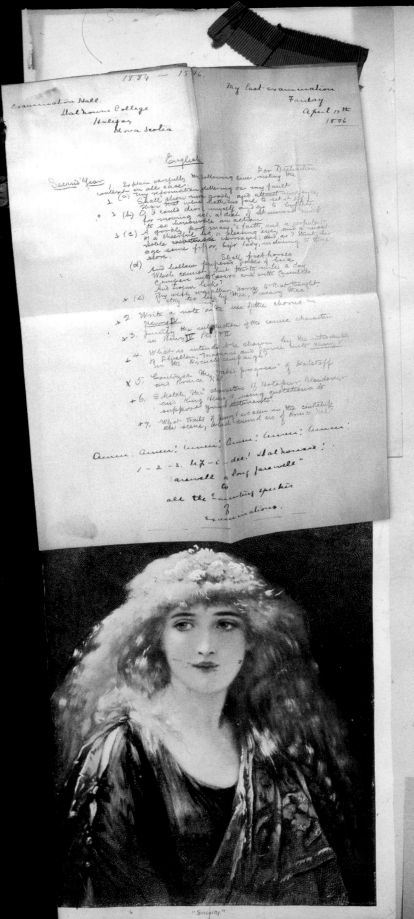

My last examination.
Friday
April 17th
1896

Examination Hall.
Dalhousie College
Halifax
Nova Scotia

English

Second Year — For Distinction

1. Explain carefully the following lines, noting the context in all cases:

(a) My reformation, glittering o'er my fault
Shall show more goodly and attract more eyes,
Than that which hath no foil to set it off.

(b) O, I could divide myself and go to buffets,
for moving such a dish of skimmed milk
to so honourable an action

(c) A goodly portly man, i' faith, and a corpulent,
of a cheerful look, a pleasing eye, and a most
noble carriage; and, as I think, his
age some fifty, or, by'r lady, inclining to three
score.

(d) Shall pack horses
And hollow pampered jades of Asia
Which cannot go but thirty miles a day
Compare with Caesars and with Cannibals
And Trojan Greeks?

(e) Thy wish was father, Harry, to that thought,
I stay too long by thee, I weary thee.

2. Write a note on the use of the chorus in Henry V.

3. Justify the introduction of the comic characters in Henry IV Pts I & II

4. What is intended to be shown by the introduction of Fluellen, Macmorris and Jamie into Henry V in the [illegible] campaign?

5. Contrast the "rake's progress" of Falstaff and Prince Hal.

6. Sketch the characters of Hotspur, Glendower and King Henry IV, using quotations to support your statements.

7. What traits of Henry V are seen in the courtship scene, which remind us of Prince Hal.

Ameen. Ameen! Ameen! Ameen! Ameen! Ameen!

1 - 2 - 3. Uz-i-dee! Dalhousie!

"Farewell a long farewell"
to
all the examining speakers
of
examinations.

"Sincerity."

From a photograph by Ad. Braun & Co. (Braun, Clément & Co., Successors) after the painting by Joseph [illegible]

Orange Blossoms.

(Friday, Nov. 22.)

"Two hearts that beat as one" were united in the holy bonds of matrimony Wednesday night at the residence of Mrs. (Rev.) James Allan, Prince street. It was the marriage of her neice, Miss Mamie McDonald, daughter of James McDonald, Esq., of Chatham, N. B., to Mr. Hedley V. Buntain head book-keeper of the firm of Messrs. Peake Bros & Co. Next in importance in this event were the groom's sister, Miss Ella Buntain, who acted as bridesmaid, and Mr. James B. Allan who supported the groom. Rev. T. F. Fullerton solemnized the marriage vows.

The bride, who also wore a gorgeous bridal veil, was beautifully attired in an elegant suit of cream cashmere, daintily trimmed with lace and ribbons to match; while the bridesmaid's dress of cream crepon also trimmed with lace and ribbon made up a very pretty costume. Both the bride and the bridesmaid carried tasteful bouquets of beautiful flowers.

After the ceremony the guests repaired to the dining room, where stood a spacious table laden with the choicest viands. While the happy company still lingered around the festival board a number of toasts were drunk and were responded to by several gentlemen present, all of whom eulogized very highly the youthful couple who had just joined heart and hand.

After supper the wedding party repaired to Mr. Buntain's residence on Prince street where the festivities continued until a late hour. The time, however, passed all too quickly enlivened as it was by genialty, music and happy chat.

The popularity of the bride and groom was fully shown by the choice variety of magnificent presents which they received, among them being a beautiful marble clock from the groom's employer Mr. Handrahan, an elegant cake from Mrs. Handrahan and some handsome gifts from his fellow employes. The GUARDIAN joins with their many friends in wishing Mr. and Mrs. Buntain many years of wedded bliss.

Be joy for ever near thee!

I've allus notissed fellers,
Hit's a risky thing to do
To kalkalate accordin'
To how things look to you.

The man 'at talks the nicest
Don't help you up the hill
The one 'at prays the loudest
Don't allus pay his bill.

Sometimes the biggest fishes
Bite the smallest kind o' baits;
An' mighty ugly wimmin
Can make the best o' mates.

The smartest lookin' feller
May be a reg'lar fool;
You're allus kicked the highest
By the meekest lookin' mule.

Academy of Music.

HALIFAX, N. S.

H. B. CLARKE, ... Lessee and Manager

Monday and Tuesday Evenings, April 6th and 7th, 1896.

THE

HUBERT WILKE COMIC OPERA COMPANY

Management, ... W. S. HARKINS

The Beggar Student.

Comic Opera in three acts and four scenes, by Millocker.

Stage Director .... Mr. Kirtland Calhoun

DISTRIBUTION OF CHARACTERS.

Symon, a Beggar Student .... Mr. Hubert Wilke
Janitzky, a Polish Nobleman .... Mr. Phillips Tomes
Gen. Ollendorf, Governor of Cracow .... Mr. Douglas Flint
Lieut. Poppenbring .... Miss Laura Pardee
Major Holtz .... Mr. Alex. Thompson
Capt. Schwantz .... Mr. Robt. Blake
Enterick, a Jailer .... Mr. Kirtland Calhoun
Puffke, his assistant .... Mr. E. G. Schaffer
Onifra, servant to the Countess .... Mr. Jas H. Jones
Zitka, an Innkeeper .... Mr. Wm. Pullman
Burgomaster .... Mr. Bergh Morrison
Countess Palmettica .... Miss Sylvester Cornish
Laura } her daughters. { Miss Josephine Knapp
Bronistava } { Miss Celie Ellis
Bogemcil, a cousin .... Mr. A. E. Arnold
Eva, his wife .... Miss Flo Echardt

SEE THIRD PAGE.

SYNOPSIS OF SCENES.

ACT I.—Scene 1. Courtyard of the Jail. Scene 2. The Fair at Cracow.
ACT II.—The Palace of the Countess Palmettica.
ACT III.—Gardens of the Palace.

Academy of Music.

HALIFAX, N. S.

H. B. CLARKE, ... Lessee and Manager

MONDAY EVENING, OCTOBER 21st, 1895.

Gilbert Opera Co.

Presenting Stephen's and Solomon's Nautical Comic Opera,

BILLEE TAYLOR,

OR, THE REWARD OF VIRTUE.

IN TWO ACTS.

Produced under the Personal Direction of JAMES GILBERT

CAST OF CHARACTERS:

Captain, the Hon. Felix Flapper, R. N., of H. M. S. "Thunderbomb," .... Hubert Dodd
Sir Mincing Lane, a self-made knight .... Elbert C. Cough
Billee Taylor, a virtuous gardener .... Harry Nelson
Ben Barnacle, Bo'sn of H. M. S. Thunderbomb .... Thos. Callahan
Christopher Crab, an unfortunate villian .... Frank Edwards
Felix Gilhooley .... Frank Ranney
Phoebe Farleigh, a Southampton Maiden .... Miss Ethel Balch
Susan .... Miss Marie Zahn
Eliza Dabsey .... Miss Katherin Power
Arabella Lane, Sir Mincing Lane's daughter .... Miss Florence Gilbert
Charity Girls, Soldiers and Sailors of H. M. S. Thunderbomb by the Grand Chorus.

SYNOPSIS.

ACT I.—The Village Green of the village of Southampton.
ACT II.—Portsmouth Harbor.

SEE THIRD PAGE.

Ellen Beach Yaw.

SUMMER'S DONE.

Along the wayside and up the hill,
 The golden rod flames in the sun ;
The blue-eyed gentian nods good-bye
 To the sad little brooks that run.
And so the summer's done, said I,
 Summer's done !

In the yellowing woods the chesnut drop ;
 The squirrel gets galore ;
Though bright eyed lads and little maids,
 Rob him of half his store,
And so the summer's done, said I,
 Summer's done !

The maple in the swamp begins
 To flaunt in gold and red,
And in the elm the fire-bird's nest
 Swings empty overhead ;
And so the summer's done, said I,
 Summer's done !

The barberry hands her jewels out,
 And guards them with a thorn ;
The merry farmer boys cut down
 The poor old dried-up corn ;
And so the summer's done, said I,
 Summer's done !

The swallows and the bobolink,
 Are gone this many a day ;
But in the morning still you here
 The scolding swaggering jay !
And so the summer's done, said I,
 Summer's done !

A wonderful glory fills the air,
 And big and bright is the sun ;
A loving hand for the whole brown earth,
 A garment of beauty has spun ;
But for all that, summer's done, said I,
 Summer's done !

Academy of Music.

HALIFAX, N. S.,

H. B. CLARKE, ... Lessee and Manager

Thursday and Friday Evenings and Saturday Matinee, November 21st, 22nd and 23rd, 1895.

ENGAGEMENT OF THE EMINENT ACTOR,

LEWIS MORRISON,

SUPPORTED BY

FLORENCE ROBERTS, Edward Elsner and White Whittlesey and his Carefully Selected Company,

In his Sublime Scenic and Dramatic Production of Goethe's Immortal

"FAUST."

Under the Management of EDW. J. ABRAM.

Rewritten and adapted for Mr. Lewis Morrison. Costumes by Gilbert, Dazian and Jahn. Electrical and Calcium effects by J. Frank Eline. Mechanisms by Michael and Sauter. Properties and Accessories designed by LaMartine. The Music selected from Gounod, Rossini and Meyerbeer, and arranged for this production by Jay Nova. The entire production painted by Noxon & Toomey.

CAST OF CHARACTERS.

SPIRITS.

MEPHISTO (his original creation) .... MR. LEWIS MORRISON
Sycorax } Witches. .... Miss Emma Mardoe
Zendoe } Witches. .... Miss Marie Thall

MORTALS.

Faust .... Mr. Edward Elsner
Valentine (Marguerite's brother) .... Mr. White Whittlesey
Siebel .... Mr. Edmund Elton
Wagner } Students. .... Mr. A. D. Foudray
Brander } Students. .... Mr. Charles Taylor
Frosch } Students. .... Mr. Fred. Salcombe
Altmeyer } Students. .... Mr. Scarle Dawley
Mathias } Students. .... Mr. Louis Gilbert
Martha .... Mrs. Nelson Kneass
Liza .... Miss Aileen Bertelle
Elsie .... Miss Lillian Armsby
Catharine .... Miss Florence Brooks

AND

Marquerite .... Florence Roberts

Peasant, Soldiers, Demons, Witches, etc.

SEE THIRD PAGE

ACT 1. Scene 1—Faust's Laboratory, overlooking the Grand Plaza. Scene 2.—The Grand Plaza of Nuremburg.
ACT 2. Marguerite's Cottage and Garden.
ACT 3. Square of the Fountains—Shrine of the Virgin.
ACT 4. The svmmit of the Brocken—Revels of the Demons on Walpurgis Night.
ACT 5. Scene 1—Nuremburg Prison. Scene 2—The Apotheosis.

ACT I.—Easter Eve. Faust in his study. Appearance of Mephisto, the Spirit of Evil. The Compact. Mephist offers to restore to Faust his youth, and undertakes to satisfy his cravings to knowledge and his impatience of limit tion with which that knowledge is bound. Faust defies him to fulfil his promise. Mephisto, showing Faust the visio of Marguerite, accepts the challenge, and gives Faust the draught of youth. They depart to the public square of Nuremburg, where Marguerite, returning from the Cathedral, is accosted by Faust. Mephisto is triumphant.

ACT II.—Faust is introduced into Marguerite's garden by Mephisto, who leaves a casket of jewels before her spinning wheel. Marguerite shows the jewels to Martha, her neighbor. Mephisto, who has followed, slyly plans with Martha that in the evening in the garden, Faust and Marguerite shall again meet. Faust, for refuge against himself then flies from Marguerite. Mephisto induces him to return, and the night witnesses the success of Mephisto's plan for the meeting of Faust and Marguerite.

ACT III.—Faust coming by night through the square of the Fountains on his way to Marguerite's house, encounter Valentine, her brother, who has just returned from the wars, and tempted by Mephisto, kills him in a duel. Mephist is again triumphant. Marguerite's story, for the present, ends as it began, at the Cathedral, where the "Judgment Chant" is being sung for the souls of the dead.

ACT IV.—The Witches' Carnival on the Brocken inaugarates the career of dissipation on which Faust is launched by Mephisto in order to make him forget the past, by the appearance of Marguerite's grief prepares for the catastrophe which ensues.

ACT V.—The scene in the dungeon ends the tragedy, with Marguerite's death and her final salvation. SCENE 2 **"The Apotheosis,"** "THE MOST BEAUTIFUL STAGE PICTURE EVER PRODUCED.

The entire production under the personal direction of MR. LEWIS MORRISON.

EXECUTIVE STAFF:

MANAGER .... MR. EDW. J. ABRAM
Business Manager .... Mr. Frank L. Bixby | Electrician .... Mr. Chas. Sauter
Treasurer .... Mr. Frank P. Wilkins | Stage Machinist .... Mr. Joseph Michaels
Stage Manager .... Mr. Edmund Elton | Property Master .... Mr. Harry Clayton

Between the second and third acts the orchestra will play the new and popular "Madison Square" March, by Edw. J. Abram. Published for piano by W. Witmark & Sons, 51 W. 28th St., N. Y.

A Song of the Camp-Fire.

Oh, the sparkle of the camp-fire on the sheltered woodland shore,
With the forest for a background, and the lake spread out before ;
While the frail canoes come tossing home to harbor in the bay,
And the star above the sunset marks the passing of the day !

As the summer night grows deeper, how the flame illumes the pines,
And its wavering reflection on the starlit water shines !
We have drawn a ring of magic in the wilderness and gloom,
And the darkness looms beyond it like the walls of some vast room.

Gathers now the twilight circle, each bronzed camper in his place,
While the laughter of the firelight meets the laughter on his face ;
And we sing the good old ballads, and the rolling college glees,
Till the owl, far up the mountain, hoots defiance in the trees.

Then the story and the laughter pass the merry circle round,
And the intervening silence thrills with many a woodland sound,—
Now the weird and ghostly challenge of the solitary loon,
Now the whistle of a plover, journeying southward 'neath the moon.

Ah ! the charm that hangs forever round the campfire's ruddy glow,
For the sage and for the savage, for the high and for the low !
There is something grand and godlike, being roofed with stars and skies,
And lulled solemnly to slumber by primeval lullabies.

JAMES BUCKHAM.

MISS BEATRICE MCINTYRE is a Charlottetown lady, and is a brilliant student. In all her classes she has acquitted herself with credit.

EDWIN SIMPSON, from Belmont, the Editor-in-Chief of the College OBSERVER, has been a prominent factor in eve-ything that tended to promote the interests of P. W. C. In debate he was a Hercules. Notwithstanding his many scruples, Ed. will, without doubt, be a star in the legal professio... He preferred spending his Sundays in the country.

SCENE, Church Social—Mr. D-k-y having asked for more pie.
Young Lady—" Mr. D-k-y, you have eaten more pie than I have."
Mr. D.—" Well, what of that. You must remember you were eating pie before I was born. You might give a fellow a fair start."

The last pages of the Blue Scrapbook abandon ordinary chronology almost entirely, revealing Montgomery reshaping events over many years.

PAGE 69: Dalhousie is recalled with an 1896 missionary program and her Dalhousie English professor Archibald MacMechan's poem. The daring, young, theatrical woman looks very much like Evelyn Nesbit (Introduction, p. 6), the model whose anonymous photograph Montgomery kept by her side while she wrote *Anne of Green Gables*. During Nesbit's husband's trial for murder in 1906, it was alleged that Stanford White's sexual assault of Nesbit took place after she lost consciousness from drinking champagne and swinging dizzily high on a red velvet swing (at White's urging). Nesbit herself served as special advisor for the 1955 movie about her life entitled *The Girl in the Red Velvet Swing*, starring Joan Collins. Did the brocaded bar here have any connection with the red velvet swing that was later to become a symbol of Nesbit?

PAGE 70: The fancy dresses that dominate this page and the next belong to the mid- to late 1890s. The Port Hill clipping suggests Bideford days, while the date on the elocution ticket marks it for 1891 Cavendish when Maud first met Lem McLeod at a social evening at her Uncle John Macneill's. The two singing robins seem to belong to stories from the Red Scrapbook with Nora Lefurgey, in 1903, and their secret-diary talk of "jays" and a "Rob-in" (Red Scrapbook, pp. 2–3).

PAGE 71: A Dalhousie ribbon is caught between the pages. The enormous puffed sleeves on the dress would make Montgomery recall, in her journal of 1905, how Dalhousie girls in the 1890s had to have others "stuff" their enormous sleeves into their coats for them. Alexena McGregor, a Prince Albert friend of Laura and Maud whom Montgomery also visited in 1930, married Fred Wright, perhaps providing the name Montgomery would give Diana's husband in the Anne series. The clipping describes Laura Pritchard's wedding to Andrew Agnew on June 3, 1896. After Laura's death in 1932, Montgomery transferred to her handwritten journals, for safekeeping, some of the memorabilia Laura had sent her from her wedding. Those items may have been here. The cluster of dried geraniums with the inscription "Malpeque March 28th 1897" is the only obvious memento from her months in Belmont. She and Alf Simpson drove on the ice over to Malpeque to her Aunt Emily's. Montgomery's unpublished diary entry reads happily, "Really, I don't think there is anything more delightful than a spin over good ice on a clear March evening under a sunset sky." The words to "In the Gloaming" could have been sent to her by Lem McLeod or Lou Dystant, but appearing as they do on the only page that has a direct reference to her time in Belmont, they may suggest instead a wish to leave Edwin Simpson or even a later lament at having left Herman Leard.

– Missionary Meeting –

(Jan 25th)

7. 30. P.M.

– "Four Phases of Missionary Work –

(a) Medical

R. Grierson. B.A

(b) Educational

Miss Montgomery

(c) Ladies' Work.

Miss Archibald

(d) Evangelical –

R. L. Coffin

All are welcome

"The Valley of Lost Sunsets."

Behind that misty ridge the suns of many yesterdays were lying in a valley that must be all golden with their shining.
—*From "Great-Grandmamma S...*

BEHIND the misty ridge of blue
The suns of all the yesterdays
Fill all the valley hid from view
With one transcendent golden blaze.
What other treasures harbour here,
—Lost treasures that the past have blest?—
Perchance "the snows of yesteryear;"
The birds that flew from last year's nest.

There where the gilded light is fed
By suns of all the yesterdays,
The roses of lost summers shed
Their scented petals o'er the ways,
'Mid sounds of all the brooks that purled,
And whispering trees, and songs of birds;
Lost myriad voices that the world
Made music to the heart's own words.

Here, too, their beauty re-illumed
By suns of all the yesterdays,
Our lost illusions lie entombed
In shimmering veils of sunset haze.
Those glints of Heaven that with us stayed
When thence to Earth we newly stepped,
But doomed—ah me!—to fail and fade
As slowly on through life we crept.

Here dallying in the golden beams
Of suns of all the yesterdays
Are dreams that once were only dreams,
And hopes fulfilled without delays.
Here life's lost morning breaks once more
With bloom of lovely youth eterne,
And Time, from out his garnered store,
Lets all our wasted hours return.

And here, maybe, we'll find erewhile,
With suns of all the yesterdays,
Lost voices speak, lost faces smile,
Lost eyes look back our loving gaze.
Old love will live, old hurts be healed,
Old ills forgot in new-found good;
And in that glorious light revealed
Old errors will be understood.

Farewell, oh, sun! that joins to-night
The suns of all the yesterdays,
Merging your solitary light
In their entirety. The days
Are shortening now; when done they be,
I'll climb the ridge—that lies so far
I cannot reach it now—and see
The "Valley where Lost Sunsets are."

H. M. WAITHMAN.

MY LADY OF DREAMS.

LAST Sabbath morn, I listen'd in the church;
The organ whisper'd music soft and low,
Pierced thro' with half-hush'd wailings. And I seem'd
To hear silk draperies lightly near me sweep,
And feel the breath of some one moving by.
But vain in shadow and half gloom the search
For shape or vision. Veil'd to outward eye,
Soft as the sighings of a babe in sleep,
The gracious Presence came of one I know,
And long have lov'd. My lover's dream I dream'd,
With eyes wide open, in my carven stall.

Wavering the dim air down, the sweet sounds fell,
Gathering body of an airy form,
That to my side, a living likeness, stole,
And nestled in my arm, against my heart,
With tender trust a-tremble, shy and warm.
That moment's sweetness, tongue can never tell.

* * * * * * *

Thus, Best-Belovéd, Love is all in all,
And Love, the perfect music of thy soul,
And thy life, my life, tho' we breathe apart.

Saint's Day, '95. ARCHIBALD MACMECHAN.

WHERE was he of the *Strong-Arm* when the doctor called to see him.

WHAT was the matter with the P. E. I. girl when she *chased* her room-mate through the window?

Just the Thing.

An English journal tells of an amusing rebuke administered to a sharp bargainer, one of those persons who always wish to get more than their money's worth. The offender in the present instance was a woman, who sent the following advertisement to a London paper:

"A lady in delicate health wishes to meet with a useful companion. She must be domestic, musical, an early riser, amiable, of good appearance, and have some experience in nursing. A total abstainer preferred. Comfortable home. No salary."

A few days afterward the advertiser received by express a basket labelled: "This side up—with care—perishable." On opening it she found a tabby cat, with a letter tied to its tail. It ran thus:

"MADAM,—In response to your advertisement, I am happy to furnish you with a very useful companion, which you will find exactly suited to your requirements. She is domestic, a good vocalist, an early riser, possesses an amiable disposition, and is considered handsome. She has had a great experience as a nurse, having brought up a large family. I need scarcely add that she is a total abstainer. As salary is no object to her, she will serve you faithfully in return for a comfortable home."

From Port Hill.

A session of the Grand Division, Sons of Temperance, was held in Port Hill Hall on the 26th ult., and as a report of which will, no doubt, be received from the usual quarter in due season, I will content myself at the present time by sending you an account of a public meeting held in the evening at which a programme, arranged by a committee appointed for that purpose, was creditably carried out. The meeting came to order, Bro. Anderson, G.W.P., in the chair, and he delivered the opening speech in his usual eloquent and pleasing style. He was followed by Bro. W. J. Montgomery who gave the address of Welcome, and the able manner in which he delivered it far exceeded the expectations of his fellow-members who selected him to perform that duty. Bro. Jas. Carruthers responded in a style characteristic of that gentleman, wit, humor, pathos and eloquence carefully arranged and resorted to in his speech with telling effect. "Sound the battle cry," was then rendered by the choir, Miss Katie Stewart, presiding at the organ, after which Bro. Wm. McNeil Simpson gave a very enthusiastic and effective temperance speech. Able and forceable addresses, in which those present were reminded of their duty to the present and future generations in regard to the plebiscite vote, were delivered in turn by Bros. Wright, A. Simpson and Arbing which were interspersed by choice selections from the choir, vis., "True hearted, whole hearted," "Marching on," "Good-bye, sweet day," "Evening bells," after which Bro. Arthur Simpson moved a vote of thanks be extended to the choir which was responded on their behalf by Bro. J. K. Ramsay. The thanks of the members of the Grand Division to the people of Port Hill for their kindness and hospitality was presented them by Bro. Jas. Carruthers. Bro. H. D. Dobie responded. The members of Port Hill Division who were identified with the musical part of the programme were assisted by Mr. Alfred Philips and Miss Annie Philips whose musical talents are of a high order, and noticeable among the queens of song who represented our sister divisions were Miss Nettie Miller of "Welcome" and Miss Matilda Boates and Miss Ella May McDonald of "Burns," who voices harmoniously mingled with the other voices of the choir. The meeting was concluded by the rendering of a praise anthem by the choir. —[Com.

AN EGYPTIAN ADVERTISEMENT.

The story of the proposed trolley line from Cairo to the Pyramids, recalls another instance of modern enterprise. A certain tract society commissioned a painter to place religious texts on all available objects in Egypt.

He traced this question on one of the pyramids:

"Do you want to be saved?"

Another painter, in the interest of a quack medicine concern, came along and added beneath:

"If you do, take Blank's pills."

"If bards of old the truth have told
The sirens have raven hair.
But o'er the earth since art had birth
They paint the angels fair."

ELOCUTION
RECITAL
ADMIT ONE.

Page 70 from the Blue Scrapbook

Agnew-Pritchard.

On Wednesday evening, June 3rd, the residence of Mr. and Mrs. R. J. Pritchard was the scene of a very pretty wedding, when their daughter Laura was united in the holy bonds of matrimony with Mr. Andrew Agnew. The bride was becomingly attired in a very handsome gown of heavy ivory gros grain silk, and carried a beautiful bouquet of Easter lillies and bridal roses. The bride was assisted by her two little sisters, Evelyn and Elma, prettily dressed in cream and heliotrope, while the groom was ably supported by Mr. W. G. Pritchard, brother of the bride. The ceremony, performed by the Rev. Mr. Lee, was witnessed by the members and immediate friends of the family, and after enjoying a most pleasant evening, the young couple departed for their cosy home on the corner of King Street and Saskatchewan Avenue, amidst showers of rice and good wishes. Although only a family wedding, the bride and groom were the recipients of many handsome and valuable presents.

In the Gloaming.

The interesting story of how the song "In the Gloaming" came to be written by Annie F. Harrison, now Lady Hill, was told in last week's Family Herald, on page 6. The words of the song are:

In the gloaming, oh, my darling! when the lights are dim and low,
And the quiet shadows falling, softly come and softly go,
When the winds are sobbing faintly with a gentle unknown woe,
Will you think of me and love me as you did once long ago?

In the gloaming, oh, my darling! think not bitterly of me!
Though I passed away in silence, left you lonely, set you free,
For my heart was crushed with longing; what had been could never be.
It was best to leave you thus, dear, best for you and best for me.

FRED. W. WRIGHT,

SWEETBRIER LANE.

Dearest of all are the sweet spring flowers
That come with the sun and rain.
I was stirred to the depth of my soul to-day
By the sight of the primrose again.
It was held in the grasp of a childish hand,
And its odors, subtle and sweet,
Were borne on the wings of the gentle wind
Through the city's unlovely street;
And in thought I was treading the turf again
In Sweetbrier Lane.

And the sweet pure air, a vigorous breath,
Swept down from the green hillside,
And rustled the myriad leaves of the trees
That o'ershadow the footpath wide—
The path that leads to the pasture-gate,
Where the cattle stand sleek and strong,
Where the blackbird whistles a low sweet note,
And the thrush pipes loud and long;
And my light heart echoed the glad refrain
In Sweetbrier Lane.

Miss Alexena MacGregor.

Mr. & Mrs. F. W. Wright.

Page 71 from the Blue Scrapbook

PAGE 72: The images of three women of such different moods and times stand out on this page. They surround a card from Laura Pritchard's home in Prince Albert, Laurel Hill Farm. The card was dated May 17, 1896, and the now faint inscription reads: "'Ah, memories of sweet summer eves / Of moonlit wave and willowy way / Of stars and flowers and dewy leaves / And smiles and tones more dear than they' 'The charm with Eden never lost.'" A notice at the bottom of the page says that Jack Sutherland, whose picture featured in Montgomery's Belmont bedroom, had gone to Ottawa to work. Are Eden and Mary Magdalen connected, wistfully and playfully, with the loss of handsome Jack?

Inside back cover:

Another Pritchard-Agnew wedding notice ties this page back to Laura and Will. "I Was a Bride in 1903" does not obviously belong to this page or to the scrapbook. In 1903 Ewan Macdonald was invested as a Presbyterian minister and was installed as Cavendish's minister. The three Canadian National Railway photographs belong to Montgomery's 1930 trip to visit Laura. When Montgomery left Prince Albert in 1891, she and Laura exchanged bouquets containing sweet peas (Blue Scrapbook, p. 18), and perhaps these magazine cut-out sweet peas were meant to recall that earlier exchange. The face in the flower lasso belongs to the 1920s or 1930s and not to the 1890s but may playfully suggest how the future is captured by the past. After her joyous reunion with Laura, following a thirty-nine-year separation, Montgomery wrote in her journal, on October 2, 1930, "I knew then that love was immortal."

The opening and closing scrapbook pages tell a happy story of friendship sustained and renewed. Willie Pritchard's calendar opened the scrapbook and his sister's wedding closes it. In 1930, Montgomery revisited her past in more ways than one when she travelled to Saskatchewan to see Laura Pritchard Agnew.

Determined to make this scrapbook end as it had begun, featuring sparkling moments or gently nostalgic ones, Montgomery preserved almost nothing from her miserable year of teaching in Belmont (1896–97). In April 1897 she grieved when she heard that Willie had died, and she became utterly wretched in June after accepting Edwin Simpson's marriage proposal. Neither the Blue nor the Red Scrapbook would chronicle Willie's death or her father's (in 1900), nor would either scrapbook picture obviously and unmistakably her agony over the broken engagement with Edwin Simpson, though the Red Scrapbook would hint more openly at such sorrows (Red Scrapbook, pp. 11–14).

The Blue Scrapbook was shaped to celebrate a happy girlhood and young womanhood – the background she would give Anne Shirley in Avonlea.

A Woman's Hour.

"Please state to the court exactly what you did between 8 and 9 o'clock on Wednesday morning," said a lawyer to a delicate looking little woman on the witness stand.

"Well," she said after a moment's reflection, "I washed my two children and sewed a button on Johnny's coat and mended a rent in Nellie's dress. Then I tidied up my sitting-room and made two beds and watered my house plants and glanced over the morning paper. Then I dusted my parlor and set things to rights in it and washed some lamp chimneys and combed my baby's hair and sewed a button on one of her little shoes, and then I swept out my front entry and brushed and put away the children's Sunday clothes and wrote a note to Johnny's teacher asking her to excuse him for not being at school on Friday. Then I fed my canary bird and cleared off the breakfast table and gave the grocery man an order and swept off the back porch and then I sat down and rested for a few minutes before the clock struck nine. That's all."

"All!" said the dazed lawyer. "Excuse me, judge; I must get my breath before I call the next witness."

Didn't Think it Was His Fault.

It is thought by some that eloquence is going out of fashion; that it is becoming, as all ambitious newspapers say, a less "important factor" in human life than formerly it was, when people read less, and depended more upon lectures and speeches. There may be a modicum of truth in this theory, but a smooth tongue and a logical faculty are still persuasive, as is happily illustrated by the following dialogue between a young man and a real estate agent, which we find reported in the Chicago *Post*:

The young man admitted that he had children, and the real estate man frowned and shook his head.

"We are very particular in regard to that building," he said at last, "and if you have children I am afraid I cannot let you have the flat."

"I am very sorry," returned the young man, meekly. "It seems rather hard that a man should be made to suffer for what is no fault of his own; but I suppose it can't be helped."

The real estate man looked surprised.

"You see," explained the young man, "I wasn't given a fair chance, for I never was told in my younger days that it was wrong to have children, or that there was any penalty attached. I supposed it was all perfectly natural and proper, but I presume the enormity of the offence is fully explained in all the schools now."

"Really, I —"

"Then I had a very bad example set me right in the family," interrupted the young man, "for my parents had children. It seems remarkable, doesn't it? But it's a fact; and they were held to be very estimable people, too. I was taught to revere them, and naturally I fell into the error of supposing that there was nothing unlawful or opposed to public policy about it, and so I married, and now I find myself in such disrepute that I can't get the kind of flat I want.

"I suppose it's all right," he continued, "but you must admit that it seems rather hard on a man who has always aimed to be a good citizen."

"My dear sir, you —"

"Now I think of it," broke in the young man again, "I suppose your parents were guilty of the same offence. I do not see how you can successfully deny it. Now, sir, I would like to ask you if you think it is fair for a man to expect his tenants to be more acceptable than his parents?"

"I was about to say, when you interrupted me," returned the agent, "that under the circumstances I am prepared to suspend the rule regarding children, and let you have the flat."

Rely not on another for what you can do yourself

"Ah, memories of sweet summer eves
Of moonlit wave and willowy way
Of stars and flowers and dewy leaves
And smiles and tones more dear than they".

"The charm with Eden never lost".

Saskatchewan
May 17th

"The Weeping Magdalen."

From a photograph by the Berlin Photographic Company after the painting by Murillo.

THE Patriot says that Mr. John D. Sutherland, son of Robert Sutherland, Esq., Seaview, and until recently accountant with A. B. Warburton, Esq., M. P. P., left Wednesday morning by the steamer Stanley, on his way to Ottawa, to assume the duties of the position to which he has been appointed in the Marine and Fisheries Department. Mr. Sutherland has just passed a very satisfactory examination for the civil service.

MARRIED.

AGNEW—PRITCHARD—At the residence of the bride's father, on Wednesday, June 3rd, by Rev. Mr. Lee, Laura, eldest daughter of R. J Pritchard, to Andrew Agnew, of Prince Albert.

Winnipeg papers please copy.

The Red Scrapbook

1890s to mid-1910

The image of a telephone on the cover of the Red Scrapbook suggests communication with the wide world beyond and at the same time intimacy and personal conversations. The Telephone Company of P.E.I. was formed in 1885, and Montgomery first mentioned the new invention in 1892 in her journals. Cavendish would not publicly debate the benefits of the telephone until 1910, two years after the publication of *Anne of Green Gables.*

After the unhappy year of teaching in Belmont (1896–97) and the galling engagement with Edwin Simpson, Montgomery taught in Lower Bedeque, P.E.I., and secretly fell in love with Herman Leard. When her grandfather died in 1898, she left teaching forever and returned to Cavendish. From March 1898 until March 1911, Montgomery lived in Cavendish and took care of her grandmother, wrote, supported community and church activities, and served as assistant post-mistress. She communicated with a wider world largely through reading, publishing, and letter writing. Many of her friends had left Cavendish or had married. She made only one extended trip away from home, going to Halifax for ten months in 1901–02 to work on *The Daily Echo* newspaper. Occasional hilarity counterbalanced a more sober life – in 1903 Maud and Cavendish schoolteacher Nora Lefurgey kept a comic joint diary of their escapades, and Maud stored corresponding souvenirs in her scrapbook.

In keeping with the Blue Scrapbook pattern of commemorating only selected events, making references in code, and ignoring strict chronology, Montgomery made almost no direct allusion in the Red Scrapbook to the two sea changes in her life: She became secretly engaged to the Presbyterian minister Ewan Macdonald (secretly, perhaps so that she could avoid the pressure to marry and therefore not have to leave her aging grandmother), and she published the wildly successful *Anne of Green Gables.* She followed her first novel immediately with a sequel, *Anne of Avonlea* (1909), and then *Kilmeny of the Orchard* (1910). She was writing her fourth novel, *The Story Girl* (1911), when she finished the Red Scrapbook. References to Ewan Macdonald were confined to a few printed newspaper notices of his activities, but she may have written some of these anonymously. Only one small clipping mentions *Anne of Green Gables.*

This is a writer's scrapbook, storing anecdotes and pictures and constructed to suggest miniature dramas and dialogues among the images. Montgomery used images and clippings to create a kind of audience and community for her own interior life, giving herself a visual outlet beyond words.

On the inside front cover, the picture of Sally Ward (1827–96), Kentucky belle, suggests several themes: prominent women of fashion, the successful "bad girl" (wealthy, divorced Sally Ward Lawrence Hunt Armstrong Downs was lionized), selective current events, and the pleasing power of a pretty face.

Her Plea.—A priest asked a young man who had come to confess how he earned his living.

"I'm an acrowbat, your riverence."

The priest was nonplussed.

"I'll show ye what I mean in a brace of shakes," said the penitent, and in a moment was turning himself inside out in the approved acrobatic fashion.

An old woman, who had followed him to confession, looked on horrified.

"When it comes my turn father," she gasped, "for the love of heaven don't put a penance on me like that; it 'ud be the death of me!"

GOOD NIGHT.

GOOD MORNING.

SALLY WARD, THE KENTUCKY BELLE

PREFERRED THE OLD WAY.

Mrs. Bradbury was instructing the new cook, who was not only new, but as green as her own Emerald Isle. One morning the mistress went into the kitchen and found Katie weeping over a pan of onions.

"Oh, you're having a harder time than you need to have, Katie," said she. "Always peel onions under water."

"Indade, ma'am," said Katie, "I'm the last one to do that, askin' yer pardon. Me brother Mick was always divin' and pickin' up stones from the bottom. It's little he couldn't do under wather, if 'twas tyin' his shoes or writin' a letther; but me, I'm that unaisy in it I'd be gettin' me mouth full and drownin' entirely. So if ye plaze, ma'am, I'll pale thim the same ould way I've always been accustomed to, and dhry me tears afterwards."

He—"They say he flung himself at her feet."

She—"I heard she threw herself at his head."

A CRISIS IN THE SCHOOLROOM.

The inspector of schools in a country district, being in a hurry to catch a train, stood in the doorway and endeavored to give out dictation to Standard II. in the main room, and at the same time to give a sum to Standard V. in the schoolroom, jerking out the words a few at a time alternately.

This was the sum: "If a couple of fat ducks cost four dollars and a half, how many can be got for twenty-one dollars and thirty-five cents?"

And this was the other dictation: "Now as a lion prowling about in search," and so forth.

Naturally enough the poor children, unaccustomed to such hurried dictation, heard both, and were sadly mixed. One girl's dictation began: "Now a couple of ducks, prowling about in search of a lion who had lost four dollars and fifty cents."

And a small boy in the schoolroom vainly endeavored to solve the mysteries of this extraordinary sum:

"If seventy-two couples of fat lions cost four dollars and a half, how much prowling could be got for twenty-one dollars and thirty-five cents?"

Inside front cover from the Red Scrapbook

L.M. Montgomery as Kodak Girl

Montgomery had a copy of the Kodak Girl hanging in her Cavendish bedroom beside her dressing table. Earning an income, fascinated by pictures, sending manuscripts into the wide world, Montgomery may have seen herself as a Kodak Girl. The Kodak Girl was part of a successful advertising campaign George Eastman launched in the early 1890s to make photography attractive to young women with money of their own to spend. Tucked casually under an arm, the Kodak camera became a fashion accessory that belonged with stylish clothes and leisurely movements. The Kodak Girl was depicted as independent and confident, effortlessly pursuing a hobby of her own.

A highly visual person who was attracted by pictures in magazines and books, Montgomery bought her first camera in the 1890s. Hers was probably a four-by-five-inch bellows camera that used a sensitized plate rather than film and took one image per plate. She created a darkroom in the Macneill homestead and delighted in developing her own photographs. Since photographers were uncommon in rural Cavendish, she took pictures for both public and private events. She often made inexpensive contact prints on specially treated paper, creating cyanotypes, or blue prints. The blue prints in the Red Scrapbook capture a few places and people in Cavendish and Park Corner. By the time Montgomery had begun to write *Anne of Green Gables,* in 1905, she was a successful composer of images, both written and photographic.

In 1911, when Montgomery was preparing to marry and go on a lifetime dream trip to visit literary scenes in Scotland and England, she treated herself to a new Kodak so she could take dozens of rolls of snaps. All the rest of her life she filled albums and boxes with pictures and eventually illustrated her handwritten journals. Montgomery's cyanotype, entitled "Hole in the Wall," has been added here from a later scrapbook page (not included in this book). When Montgomery died, she left behind some two thousand photographs, and evidence in all twenty of her novels of a good photographer's eye for shapes, light, and suggested story.

BOARDING HOUSE GEOMETRY.

(1) All boarding houses are the same boarding house.

(2) Boarders in the same boarding house and on the same flat are equal to one another.

(3) A single room is that which has no parts and no magnitude.

(4) The landlady of a boarding house is a parallelogram; that is, an oblong, angular figure which cannot be described, but which is equal to any thing.

(5) A wrangle is the disinclination of two boarders to each other that meet together but are not on the same flat.

(6) All the other rooms being taken, a single room is said to be a double room.

POSTULATES AND PROPOSITIONS.

(1) A pie may be produced any number of times.

(2) The landlady may be reduced to her lowest terms by a series of propositions.

(3) A bee line may be made from any one boarding house to any other boarding house.

(4) The clothes of a boarding house bed, though produced ever so far both ways, will not meet.

(5) Any two meals at a boarding house are together less than one square meal.

(6) On the same bill and on the same side of it there shall be two charges for the same thing.

(7) If there be two boarders on the same flat, and the amount of side of the one be equal to the amount of side of the other, each to each, and the wrangle between one boarder and the land-lady be equal to the wrangle between the landlady and the other, then shall the weekly bills of the two boarders be equal also, each to each. For if not let one bill be the greater—then the other bill is less than it might have been—which is absurd.

** ** **

PRIMA FACIE EVIDENCE.

An English lord of the manor was returning home one night, when he found a country bumpkin standing by the kitchen door with a lantern in his hand.

"What are you doing here?" the lord asked, roughly.

"I've come a-coortin', sir," was the reply.

"A-courting? What do you mean by that?"

"I'm a follower o' Mary, the kitchen maid."

"Is it your habit to carry a lantern when you are on such errands?"

"Yes, sir."

"Nonsense!" retorted the master, angrily. "Don't talk such stuff to me! Be off with yourself! Courting with a lantern! When I was young I never used such a thing."

"No, sir," said the yokel, moving rapidly away. "Judgin' by the missus, I shouldn't think ye did."

THE KODAK GIRL

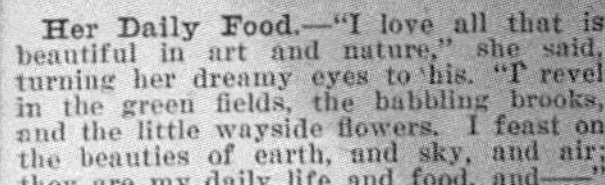

Her Daily Food.—"I love all that is beautiful in art and nature," she said, turning her dreamy eyes to his. "I revel in the green fields, the babbling brooks, and the little wayside flowers. I feast on the beauties of earth, and sky, and air; they are my daily life and food, and——"

"Maudie!" cried out the mother from the kitchen, not knowing that her daughter's beau was in the drawing room, "Maudie, whatever made you go and gobble up that big dish of mashed potatoes that was left over from dinner? I told you we wanted them warmed up for supper. If your appetite isn't enough to bankrupt your poor pa!"

A Puzzled Boy

A little boy was reading the story of a missionary having been eaten by cannibals.

"Papa," he asked, will the missionary go to Heaven?"

"Yes, my son," replied the father.

"And will the cannibals go there, too?"

"No," was the reply.

After thinking the matter over for some time the little fellow exclaimed :—

"Well, I don't see how the missionary can go to Heaven if the cannibals don't, when he's inside the cannibals."

A FATHER, fearing an earthquake in the region of his home, sent his two boys to a distant friend until the peril should be over. A few weeks after the father received this line from his friend: "Please take your boys home and send down the earthquake."

HE: "I saw our old neighbor, Mr. Skinner, to-day." She: "Did you? What is he doing now?" He: "He is interested in one of these wild-cat mining companies." She: "The idea! I never knew you had to mine for wild cats."—Exchange.

"You can say what you please, but it's a lucky thing for me that there are poets."

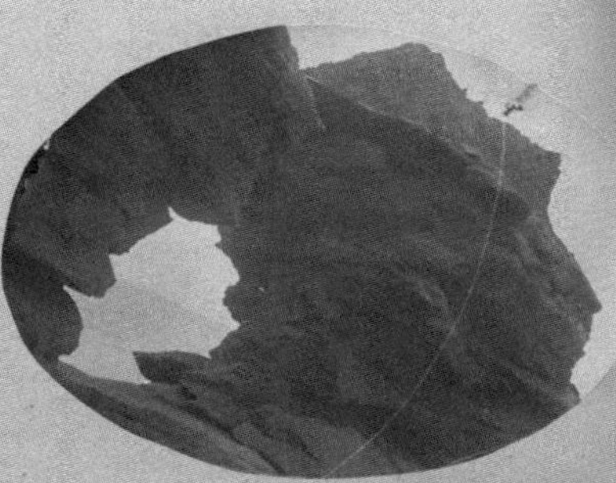

Montgomery's own cyanotype, "Hole in the Wall," added here from a later deleted page.

Montgomery's friendship with schoolteacher Nora Lefurgey was one of the bright spots in her many years of living with Grandmother Macneill in Cavendish, from 1898 to 1911. When twenty-eight-year-old Montgomery returned from working on the Halifax newspaper *The Daily Echo* in 1902, she found a kindred spirit in twenty-two-year-old Nora. For the first six months of 1903 they lived together at the Macneill homestead, sharing hilarity as they created a joint comic diary. Both women loved poetry and fiction and had impressive memories; Nora was daring and urged Montgomery to break out of the staid role a mature, unmarried woman was expected to play in the early 1900s in rural Canada.

The Cavendish Literary Society, begun in Cavendish in 1886, provided high-quality debates, lectures, and readings. Meetings were held in the Cavendish community hall, pictured here in Montgomery's cyanotype (top right). Montgomery first recited in public there in 1889, when Hattie Gordon was her teacher. Montgomery was the first woman to be elected to the executive and, after 1902, was frequently a member of the committee that set the programs. Ewan Macdonald was active in the Literary for the three years he was minister in Cavendish (mid-1903 to 1906), and he and Maud both gave programs on literature and ideas. In the fall of 1902 and the winter of 1903, Maud's experience of the Literary was through the laughing mock rivalries and dramas with Nora, involving the young men they inveigled into driving them over snowy or muddy roads.

In the fall of 1902, Maud served on the Entertainment Committee with Jeremiah S. Clark, George W. Simpson, Nora Lefurgey, and Rev. C.P. Wilson, and they came up with the typed program on this page. Maud's irreverent minutes of the Entertainment Committee meeting at the bottom of the page turn antics into story chapters. On February 6, the guest speaker did not arrive, and so members chose speaking topics from those placed in a hat. "Pa" was Arthur Simpson, whom Montgomery detested. The "jays" were code names for James Alexander Stewart and Joe Stewart, and the "robbin(g)" took place when James invited one of the two women into his sleigh, leaving Joe with only one. Shy James was the principal object of mock duels in the diary.

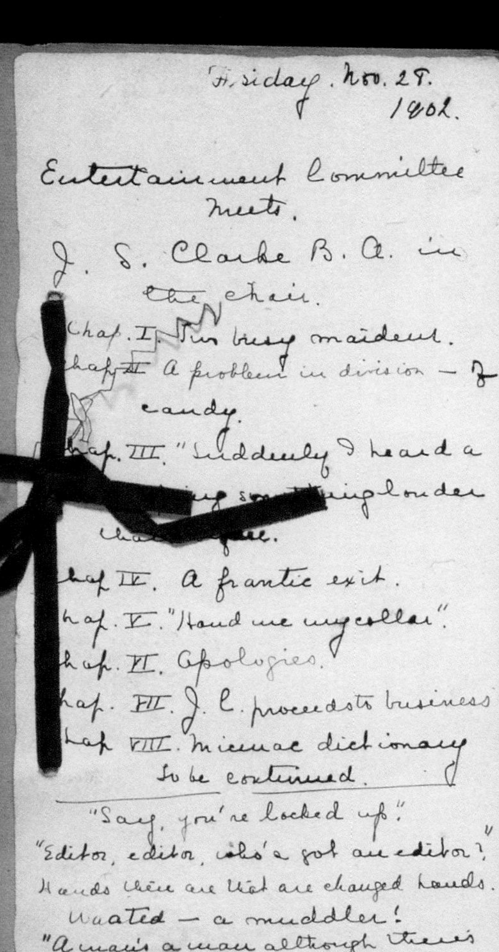

Friday. Nov. 28.
1902.

Entertainment Committee meets.

J. S. Clarke B. A. in the chair.

Chap. I. The busy maiden.
Chap. II. A problem in division — of candy.
Chap. III. "Suddenly I heard a [illegible] something louder than [illegible]."
Chap. IV. A frantic exit.
Chap. V. "Hand me my collar".
Chap. VI. Apologies.
Chap. VII. J. C. proceeds to business
Chap. VIII. Micmac dictionary
To be continued.

"Say, you're locked up".
"Editor, editor, who's got an editor?"
Hands there are that are changed hands.
Wanted — a muddler!
"A man's a man although there's nothing in him".

PROGRAMME

CAVENDISH LITERARY SOCIETY.

1902 -- 3.

Dec. 5th -- "The Indians of Canada." J. S. Clark.

Dec. 19th -- ....Christmas Entertainment.

Jan. 2nd -- Review of 1902 and outlook for 1903.
Arthur Simpson, Opener.

Jan. 16th -- Lecture ....Rev. E. P. Calder.

Jan. 30th -- Debate -- "Trusts Are Justifiable."
Geo. Simpson Vs. Walter Simpson.

Feb. 6th -- "The Making of a Newspaper."
L. M. Montgomery.

Feb. 20th -- Newspaper Night. J. S. Clark, Editor.
L. M. Montgomery, Associate Editor.

Mar. 6th -- Lecture .... Rev. J. W. McConnell.

Mar. 20th -- "The Poets." .... N. Lefurgey

April 3rd -- "Chinese Gordon." ... Rev. E.P. Wilson.

Friday
Dec 19.
1902

"Blessed are the disappointed — for their turn will come.

Rev. C. P. Wilson in the chair.

"Lo, the poor Indians!"
"Whispering angels".
"Gentle applause".
"Good long steps!"
"The interpretation thereof"
"One of the aborigines"
"A new departure".

Friday
Jan 2.
1903.

Rev. C. P. Wilson in chair.
No minutes read and approved.

Rev. Mr. Calder lectures on the Five Pillars of civilization".
There are lots of the fourth class.
The president takes a pain.
"First come, first served".
A chaperone.

Friday. Feb. 6.

Rev. C. P. Wilson in chair.
Lecturer does not come.
Jerry passes round the hat.
Freddie prefers "Forty fives".
Howard stands "straight up".
Jerry discusses "pork".
"Pa" gets personal on "Prohibition".
Two jays put their heads together and make a sobtin(?).
A horse in the sleigh is worth ten in conversation.

The secret diary Maud and Nora kept is the key to the February and March 1903 comic minutes. Those of March 20, 1903, note the absence of all three "jays" (James, Joe, and also Jerry Clark) and the presence of a "Rob-in" (Robert A. MacKenzie).

Months of drama underpin the page 3 collage: The "Cavendish School" clipping marks a farewell to Nora, meaning that Maud would again be without a close friend in Cavendish. The cedar may have come from teacher Hattie Gordon, long gone from Cavendish, or possibly from Gertie Moore, recently married in Portland (Red Scrapbook, p. 5, clipping below the leaf).

A magazine photograph of Cape Leforce shows it as it would have appeared in Montgomery's childhood. The code name "Night's Eye" (pasted on top of the flowers) was used by Daisy Williams, from Maud's Bideford teaching days, when the two of them sent their handwriting away for analysis (see Maud's "Psyche," Red Scrapbook, p. 15). A clipping announces that Mable Simpson would no longer be organist for the Presbyterian church in Cavendish; Maud filled the position and was thrown into frequent contact with Ewan Macdonald, her future husband, when he became minister.

Friends and Kindred Spirits

Friendly and sociable, with a knack for making others feel they had formed friendships with her, Maud Montgomery reserved her deepest affections for a few. She would have counted her two male penfriends, George Boyd MacMillan of Scotland and Ephraim Weber of Alberta, as kindred spirits (see page 104); interestingly, her strongest bonds (apart from those with her children) all seem to have been formed when she was young and before the publication of *Anne of Green Gables* had made her famous.

These two Island scrapbooks and her early Cavendish journals and letters suggest how readily a young Maud found jolly companionship whether she was in Prince Albert, Saskatchewan, or in Halifax at Dalhousie and at the *Echo* newspaper office, or on Prince Edward Island with schoolmates and community members. For forty-four years, Laura Pritchard Agnew was a dear friend. Maud also maintained a lifelong friendship with Myrtle Macneill Webb of Cavendish, whose children called her "Aunt Maud" (an account of the Webbs' garden party is found on page 52 of the Red Scrapbook), and she reconnected joyfully in Ontario with Nora Lefurgey after twenty-four years of separation. She was strongly tied to her Island cousins Frederica Campbell and Bertie McIntyre. It was from Frede that Maud borrowed the expression she used in later Anne books to define a kindred spirit: One who is of "the race that knows Joseph."

Somewhere between Anne Shirley and Emily Starr in her own ease with others, Montgomery had a genius for depicting friendships in her fiction.

February 27. 1903.

Rev. C. P. Wilson in chair

Two (jays) get home from funeral.

"Hold on" going up Davids hill.

The beloved disciple from New Glasgow appears.

"A Day in A Newspaper Office."

A quick despatch and now for the ball.

March 6. 1903.

Father Pierce in the chair, By Creon.

J. comes down like the wolf on the fold.

And the headache evaporates quickly and bold.

Theological ghosts & Telephone souls

Who-a, Olive.

The voice(s) of the Press.

Three "J's" are too many for one alphabet.

We "talk it over".

March 20th 1903.

Father Pierce in chair.

Muddy knees.

A paper on Byron.

"My native land, good-night."

"His favorite poet."

The absence of all three (blue)-jays.

Never mind, we have a Rob-in.

A good pung sleigh.

Tennis wants to race.

Finis of Literary 1902nd—1903.

Night's Eve—Strength and firmness of will is depicted in your writing. You are energetic, even inclined to be domineering. You are shy, unassuming and easily embarrassed. You are constant and steady and a very reliable character.

Cedar Portland Oregon

Mr Eliss Bishop of this town was married on Wednesday to Miss Fay McKenzie of Cavendish by Rev. A. D. Stirling of Cavendish at the bride's home. In the evening a recep ion was held at their home in Summerside.

Miss Mable Simpson the popular teacher of Hope River is resigning to take a course in the Halifax Ladies College. She will probably be succeeded in the school by A. C. Cullen of Bay View. Miss Simpson will be much missed in social circles and in the Presbyterian Church where she has been organist for some time past.

CAPE LEFORCE

CAVENDISH SCHOOL

On Friday, June 21st the semi-annual examinations of Cavendish school was held very successfully in the presence of a number of visitors. The children acquitted themselves with honor and the condition of the school reflects great credit on the energetic and popular teacher, Miss Nora LeFurgey.

At the close of the examination a beautiful dressing case was presented to Miss LeFurgey by her pupils, accompanied by the following address:—

DEAR AND RESPECTED TEACHER:

Having heard of your intention of leaving us, we as scholars cannot allow this opportunity to pass without expressing to you how deeply we regret to hear of your departure.

During the two years in which you have taught us you have labored most earnestly and diligently for our welfare and your kindness to and interest in us have endeared you both to pupils in the school and friends in the district. For all that you have done for us we thank you heartily and sincerely.

Our best-wishes will go forth with you in whatever new sphere of labor your lot will be cast. We hope that all the blessings of success, health and happiness may be yours.

In conclusion we ask you to accept the accompanying token of love and regard of your affectionate pupils signed on behalf of the school.

ANNIE P. MACNEILL,
PEARL SIMPSON,
ERNEST CLARK,
AILEEN LAIRD,
LOTTIE MACNEILL,
CHARLIE M. MACKENZIE,
FAYE MACKENZIE,
JEAN LAIRD.

A POOR ILLUSTRATION.

"I don't want to wear my old hat to church," said eight-year-old Gladys, "not even if it does rain. The trimming on that hat is all worn out, mother."

"It's the best thing for you to wear on a day like this," said her mother firmly. "And you must remember that it's the inside and not the outside—what is unseen, not what is seen—that God looks at, my little girl."

"Yes'm," said Gladys eagerly, "I do remember; but the lining of that hat is worn even worse than the trimming is!"

The marriage of J. D. A. MacIntyre at one time a resident of Sydney, to a P. E. Island young lady, takes place at Winnipeg next month. Mr. MacIntyre is in the real estate business in Edmonton.—Edmonton Ex.

"THE evidence," said the judge, "shows that you threw a stone at this man."
"Sure," replied Mrs. O'Hoolihan; "an' the looks av the man shows more than thot, yer honor. It shows thot Oi hit him."—*Chicago News.*

Page 3 from the Red Scrapbook

The home of Maud's Campbell cousins in Park Corner was always a refuge for her. Frede Campbell (1883–1919) was the dearest of all Maud's friends and relatives. Pages 4 and 5 are dominated by the Campbells and their home.

PAGE 4: Central to this page is a piece of black netting with the date November 29, 1902. Nora spent the night with Maud on November 28, 1902, following the Literary Society Entertainment Committee meeting noted on page 2; the next night, Frede arrived and stayed over. Maud's diary entry says they "conferred on sundry subjects very near to our hearts." The cyanotype at the top of the page is of the Campbell home in Park Corner, a second home to Montgomery and the place where she was married in 1911. Aunt Annie and Uncle John Campbell were famous for their hospitality, and the pantry was the scene of many of the merry cousins' escapades: Clara, Stella, George, and Frede Campbell were vital parts of Montgomery's life. Montgomery deliberately placed her Aunt Mary McIntyre's 1909 death notice in the midst of mementoes of the Park Corner Campbells. Aunt Mary belonged to the Park Corner Montgomery side of the family. Montgomery was close friends with Bertie McIntyre especially. Under the fancy name covers are Stella Campbell, Clara Campbell, Edith J. Pillman, and Mr. and Mrs. James Hiltz – all Park Corner people mentioned in Montgomery's journals.

PAGE 5: The Cavendish Baptist Church pictured in the cyanotype links to Maud's painful memory of her rejection of Edwin Simpson. She placed George Campbell's October 7, 1903, wedding invitation (inside the larger envelope; the envelope above it is empty) and write-up close to memorabilia associated with Ed, perhaps trying to neutralize the sting. Possibly Frede or Bertie put the **notice** in the newspaper about Montgomery's story, "Tannis of the Flats," which was first published in April 1904, and the similar one on page 4 about "Emily's Husband," published in the November 1903 edition of *Canadian Magazine*. The joke in the top left corner appeared in Montgomery's October 12, 1901, "Cynthia" column in the Halifax *Daily Echo*.

PAGE 6: This page reflects Maud's wide range of friends and acquaintances. Ephraim Weber, author of the poem "Lullaby," was a new pen pal from 1902, and Alma S. McNeill was a childhood friend and cousin. Lucy Lincoln Montgomery was a penfriend whose pieces are scattered through the early scrapbooks. Adelaide Johnson (1859–1955) later became world-famous for her sculptures of feminist icons Susan B. Anthony, Elizabeth Cady Stanton, and Lucretia Mott. Was Johnson, perhaps, a fan of *Anne of Green Gables*? Charles Marcil was a Liberal, Quebec journalist who sat in Parliament from 1900 to 1937 and served as Speaker of the House from 1909 to 1911.

Miss Lucy M Montgomery has a cleverly written story in the Canadian Magazine for November. We congratulate this talented Island writer on the quality and quantity of the work she is doing with her pen.

The early hours of New Year's Day were saddened for many relatives and warm friends by the death of Mrs. McIntyre, of Brighton, who passed away at four o'clock, after a short illness. Mrs. McIntyre was a daughter of the late Hon. Senator Montgomery, a sister of the late Hugh John Montgomery of Prince Albert, Sask., and an aunt of Miss L. M. Montgomery, the Canadian author and poet. She leaves a bereaved husband and five young men and women. James McIntyre and Miss Laura McIntyre left distant Edmonton Friday and are now on their way home to pay the last tribute of filial love and duty. Miss Bertie McIntyre of the Model School and Mr. C. McIntyre of the Bank of Nova Scotia, in this city, were with their mother in her last hours here.

Harry McIntyre of the Bank of Nova Scotia, Toronto, arrived home yesterday.

LAIRD—STEWART—At Cavendish, on April 5th, by Rev. John Murray, Edwin Everett Laird to Elizabeth Cranston Stewart.

The Sanctity of Cats

A Sunday-school teacher in Carthage, Ill., has a class of little girls, and it is her custom to tell them each Sunday of one little incident that has happened in the week and request the children to quote a verse of scripture to illustrate the story. In this way she hopes to impress the usefulness of Biblical knowledge upon the little ones. One Sunday she told her class of a cruel boy who would catch cats and cut off their tails. "Now, can any little girl tell me of an appropriate verse?" she asked. There was a pause for a few moments, when one little girl arose and in a solemn voice said: "Whatsoever God has joined together let no man put asunder."—New York *Tribune*.

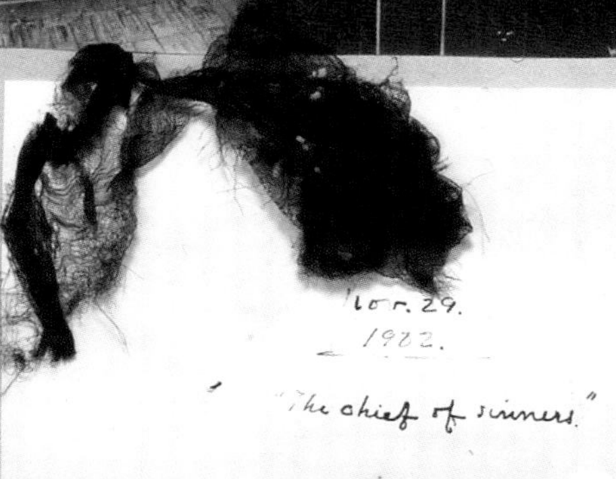

Accommodating

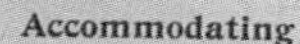

In one of Frank Sanborn's stories a gentleman requests release from his engagement. "I have been concealing something," he says to his *fiancée*. "The truth is, I am a somnambulist." "Oh, that needn't interfere," exclaimed the young woman. "I'm not particular. I was brought up a Baptist, but I'd just as soon change over to accommodate you."

A Memento of our Friend.

A SIMPLE CHANGE.

The little daughter of the house watched the minister who was making a visit very closely, and finally sat down beside him and began to draw on her slate.

"What are you doing?" asked the clergym[illegible]

[illegible] making your picture," said the child.

The minister sat very still and the child worked away earnestly. Then she stopped and compared her work with the original, and shook her head.

"I don't like it much," she said. "'Tain't a great deal like you. I guess I'll put a tail to it and call it a dog."—[Philadelphia Times.

Page 4 from the Red Scrapbook

A boy was asked to paraphrase the latter part of the Ballad of Lochinvar, which runs as follows:

"They'll have fleet steeds that follow," quoth young Lochinvar;
There was mounting 'mong Graemes of the Netherby clan,
Fosters, Fenwicks, and Musgraves, they rode and they ran,
There was racing and chasing on Canobie lea.

The unimaginative youth reflected awhile, and then wrote: "Loch left, followed by the whole gang."

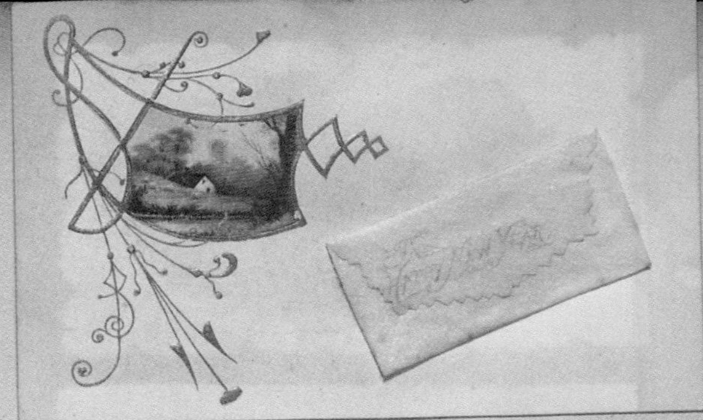

WEDDING BELLS

The home of Mr and Mrs John R Hooper, North Milton, was the scene of a very pretty wedding on Wednesday evening, 29th ult., when their only daughter, Miss Mary Elizabeth, was united in marriage to Mr Alexander C MacNeill of Cavendish. The nuptial knot was tied by the Venerable Archdeacon Reagh in the presence of the immediate friends of the contracting [illegible]

The bride who was given away by her father, was attended by her cousin Miss Hattie Rodd of Winsloe, as bridesmaid and little Miss Verna Hooper of Ch'town, as flower girl, while the groom was supported by Mr Ernest Bulman of South Rustico. The bridal gown was of grey broadcloth trimmed with white silk, while the bridesmaids were attired in figured muslin over white.

The bride was the recipient of many beautiful and costly presents. After the ceremony the company sat down to a bountiful wedding repast. The happy couple left for their future home at Cavendish on the following day with the best wishes of all who knew them.—Cor.

On the evening of Wednesday, October 7th the home of D. M. Johnstone of Long River was the scene of an extremely pretty wedding, when his sister Ella, was united in marriage to George L. Campbell of Park Corner. The rooms and stair case were lavishly decorated with ferns cut flowers and potted plants. At eight o'clock the strains of the wedding march played by Miss Stella Campbell, preceded the entrance of the bridal party. The Rev. Mr. Rattee of Malpeque performed the marriage ceremony in the presence of over one hundred guests. The bride was charmingly gowned in white silk, with trimmings of chiffon, applique and lace, with the bridal accessories of orange blossoms, veil and train, and carried a beautiful bouquet of roses and maiden hair fern. Miss Clara Campbell of Chestnut Hill, Mass., the sister of the groom, was bridesmaid and wore an extremely dainty dress of white point d'esprit with ornamentation of lace medallions. She carried a bouquet of lilies. Helen and Jean Johnstone, the little nieces of the bride made very charming flower girls, gowned in white organdy and lace, and carrying bouquets of chrysanthe mums and carnations. Mr George McKay of Clifton supported the groom. After the newly-married pair had received the congratulations of their friends an elaborate supper was served. The next feature of the evening was the arrival of the charivariers who turned out from all quarters in striking costumes to do honor to the event. After their departure a pleasant evening of music and dancing was spent. The bride and goom received a large number of very beautiful presents among which may be mentioned a handsome set of sable furs, the groom's gift to the bride, and a substantial check from the bride's brother. The groom's gift to the bridesmaid was a very pretty crescent of pearls. On the following evening a reception was held at the home of the groom's parents, Mr and Mrs John Campbell of Park Corner. The spacious rooms of the old homestead were beautified by flowers and autumn leaves and thronged with guests the younger element of which kept time to the violin in the good old fashioned way. Supper was served in Mrs Campbell's well known bountiful style and at a late hour the guests wended their homeward way with hearty wishes for the welfare and happiness of the young couple through their whole future life.

Announcements have been received of the marriage of Miss Gertrude A. Moore to John D. Sheel of Portland, Oregon. The ceremony took place at Portland on April 4th. Miss Moore formerly belonged to Crapaud, but has been in the west for several years. Mrs. H. J. Wright, Searletown, is a sister.

In the New York Criterion for August appears a very thrilling, illustrated story by L M Montgomery entitled "Tannis of the Flats." The PATRIOT hopes to be able to place it before its readers at an early date. By her talent as a poetess, and her ability as a prose writer, Miss Montgomery has made the productions of her pen welcome to the highest class publications both in Canada and the United States. We hope and believe that she is within reach of fame as a writer.

THE marriage of Miss Margaret James daughter of Mr. T. C. James of this city, to Rev. George Millar of Alberton, takes place tomorrow morning at seven o'clock at the bride's home. Rev. T. F. Fullerton will officiate. After the ceremony Mr. and Mrs. Millar will leave by the 7.45 train for New Brunswick.

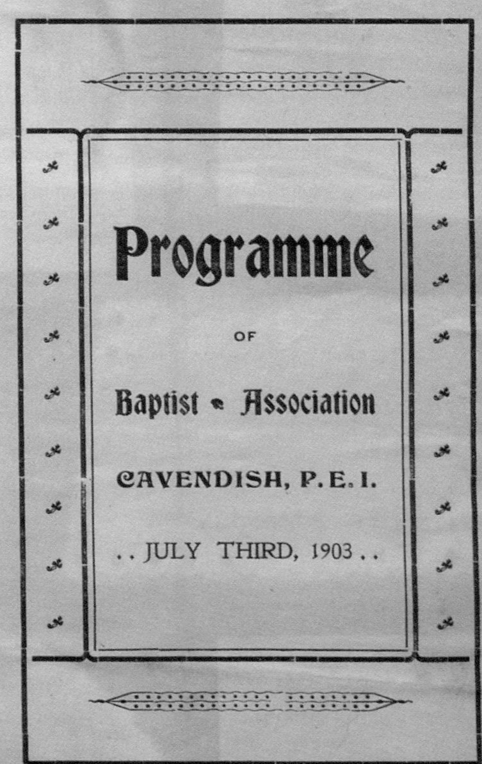

Programme

OF

Baptist Association

CAVENDISH, P. E. I.

.. JULY THIRD, 1903 ..

Adelaide Johnson requests the honour of your presence at an exhibition of her Portrait-busts and Medallions between the hours of noon and six p.m., from the eighth to tenth, January, nineteen nine. Studio and galleries, Five East Thirty-Sixth Street.

THE Presbyterian Church at Cavendish, tastefully decorated with flowers and ferns and autumn leaves, and filled with interested spectators, was the scene on Wednesday, September 23rd, 1903, at 10 a. m., of the marriage of Miss Mabel Simpson, of Mayfield, to Rev. Major H McIntosh, pastor of the Presbyterian Churches of West and Clyde Rivers The bride and bridesmaid, Miss Nora Lefurgey of Summerside, were becomingly dressed in white. The groom was ably supported by Rev R J Douglas of Little Harbour, Nova Scotia. The ceremony was performed by Rev Ewen McDonald assisted by Rev D B McLeod of Charlottetown. Mrs Cummings of Westville, N. S., sister of the bride, rendered appropriate music as the bridal party entered the church, and also on their retiring. Among the numerous and handsome presents was a gold watch from the bridegroom to the bride. The groom's gift to the bridesmaid was a beautiful pearl ring. After luncheon at the bride's mother's residence, the happy couple started on their wedding trip to Montreal and other Canadian cities.

A pleasing event took place yesterday afternoon at two o'clock at the residence of Rev. R. W. Stevenson, Kent Street, when Miss Maggie Warren daughter of T. A. Warren, North Rustico, was united in marriage to Russel McNeill of Cavendish. The ceremony was performed by Rev. W. R. Motley of Montague. The bride, who was unattended was becomingly attired in a suit of navy blue broadcloth with Persian velours trimmings and hat to match. After the ceremony the happy couple drove to their future home in Cavendish. The PATRIOT joins with their many friends in wishing them a long and happy journey through life.

THE LATE WILLIAM MONTGOMERY.

The recent death of William Montgomery removes one of Wakefield's oldest and most respected citizens. As briefly recorded in the ITEM, Mr. Montgomery died last Friday at the advanced age of 85 years. The funeral took place Monday at the late home of the deceased on Jordan avenue, Rev. Hugh A. Heath, pastor of the Baptist church, officiating. The pall bearers were Everett W. Eaton, Chester W. Eaton, Augustus D. Dimick and George H. Scovell. Undertaker Oliver Walton had charge. A profusion of floral offerings, sent by relatives and friends testified to the worthy character and esteem of the deceased. The burial was at Lakeside cemetery, in the family lot. George West of Byron st. sang "Pilgrims of the Night" at the services.

Mr. Montgomery was born in Scotland and came to America when 17 years of age with his father who was a cotton manufacturer. For many years Mr. Montgomery was engaged in the manufacturing of cotton in Biddeford, Me. and New York state. Later on, for a number of years be manufactured iron having foundries at Halifax, N. S. In 1880 Mr. Montgomery and family returned to the United States.

For some years Mr. Montgomery was in the employ of the Equitable Life Assurance society, but in recent years has lived in retirement, enjoying the blessings of a well spent and active life.

Mr. Montgomery's wife died in 1884. Three daughters and two sons survive the deceased. The daughters are Mrs. Mary G. Slocum, wife of President W. F. Slocum of Colorado college, Colorado Springs; Mrs. Margaret Goodale, wife of Gen Greenleaf A. Goodale of Wakefield. and Miss Lucy L. Montgomery of Wakefield. One of the sons is in northern Maine and the other resides in New York.

Mr. Montgomery was a Mason, having united with a Halifax lodge when a young man. He was a consistent member of the Congregational church and was a man of strict integrity and upright character.

HON. CHARLES MARCIL, M.P., THE NEW SPEAKER OF THE HOUSE OF COMMONS

OLD PRINCE OF WALES COLLEGR

—Many will be grieved to hear of [th]e death of Mrs. Rev. John Murray, [...]iton, which occurred on Wednesday [ni]ght last, at the age of 63 years. [Mr]s Murray had been in delicate [he]alth for the past year but no fear [w]as entertained of her death till a[b]out 24 hours before the call came. [M]rs Murray was a native of Halifax, [N]ova Scotia, and leaves to mourn [b]esides her husband, one daughter at [h]ome and one son at Sydney.

Alma S. McNeill

Lullaby

"ROCK-A-BY, hush-a-by, baby, my sweet,
Pink little fingers and pink little feet;
Soft is your pillow, your cradle is white—
Rock-a-by, hush-a-by, baby, good-night."

Pure are your eyes as the dew on the gra[...]
Close them in slumber your spirit will pa[...]
O'er bridges of clouds like a pilgrim of lig[...]
And journey to Elfland in silken-winged f[...]

Go, soar to God's bosom, whence lately [...]
came,
And tell him I love you, and bless his [...]
name;
Dumb are your lips, but your spirit is fre[...]
So, thank him for sending an angel to me.

Rock-a-by, hush-a-by, baby, my love,
My darling, my fairy, my heavenly dove;
Dream till the dawn brings the glow of the
light—
Rock-a-by, hush-a-by, baby, good-night.
—*Ephraim Weber.*

Rev. J. E. Menançon,
Presby. Church Agent.
Pointe-aux-Trembles Mission Schools. *(Near Montreal.)*

Page 6 from the Red Scrapbook

Literary Penfriends

Literary pursuits connected Montgomery to many people. She put part of a Cavendish Literary Society magazine together with the names of penfriends from a broader world, as though to suggest how wide her literary circle was becoming.

After the publication of *Anne of Green Gables,* Montgomery received letters from around the world, including from such illustrious writers as Samuel Clemens (Mark Twain). The imagination she celebrated and exercised in her scrapbooks, diaries, and photography – and gave to Anne Shirley and later heroines – eventually widened her literary community.

In her early Cavendish days, Montgomery was hungry for literary talk and entered into several pen relationships hoping to broaden her vistas and her circle. Lucy Lincoln Montgomery, an older woman writer from Wakefield, Massachusetts, was in frequent touch with her and sent along pieces. Montgomery made a point of visiting her when she went to Boston in the fall of 1910 to meet her publisher, L.C. Page. In 1900 she tried a pen friendship with Frank Monroe Beverly of Virginia, who wrote to her after admiring her magazine poem "Rain in the Woods." Their correspondence was not a success, but he put her in touch with Miriam Zieber of Philadelphia, who in turn introduced her, in 1902, to Ephraim Weber, a teacher from Alberta, and, in 1903, to George Boyd MacMillan, a journalist from Scotland. Weber loved to debate ideas and he and Montgomery argued; their friendship weathered the First World War though he was a pacifist and she was not. MacMillan loved cats and gardening, and he and Montgomery shared personal stories. For almost forty years she corresponded with these two men, writing farewell notes to each of them a few months before she died in 1942.

There must have been many other early literary correspondents about whom we now know nothing. Montgomery mentioned Gerald Carlton, the Irish American writer, to Weber and included his calling card and an article on him in the Red Scrapbook. She spoke little in her diary of Edith Russell, with whom she worked on the *Echo* in Halifax, but she included several of her verses in this scrapbook and Edith visited her in 1926 in Ontario, which suggests they had kept up a correspondence.

PAGES 8–9: Montgomery was a capable needlewoman. She preserved sample fabrics and also pieces of favourite outfits. Like Anne Shirley, she was fond of fashion and enjoyed new clothes.

The Cavendish Literary Magazine

Published at Cavendish, Prince Edward Island

March. Nineteen Hundred and Three.

—x—

L. M. Montgomery.

Miss Miriam Zieber

Geo. B. MacMillan.

34 Castle Street,
Alloa, N. B.

Page 8 from the Red Scrapbook

Page 9 from the Red Scrapbook

More fun with schoolteacher Nora Lefurgey was preserved on this page, and teaching and school provided wider themes. Even the Canadian National Railway photograph is probably from Montgomery's 1930 visit out west with Laura Pritchard Agnew, kindred spirit from her 1890 school year in Saskatchewan.

Joke square: Maud and Nora were both fond of photography, literature, and scrapbooking. The elaborately folded "screwveneer" square uses Kipling and quips to frame a cyanotype of Nora.

Poems: "The Smack in School" describes a noisy kiss by a bashful, overgrown schoolboy in a classroom of sixty boys and girls. Montgomery had exactly this number of students on her school roster in her first teaching post, in Bideford, P.E.I. "Good-By, Sweet Day" was a popular song performed at school and community gatherings. The music for it, by Thomas O'Neill, was published in 1880; the lyrics were by Celia Thaxter.

Cards: In their secret diary, Maud and Nora compete to see who can be sillier concerning Cavendish swains. The writing inside this card suggests the tenor of their play: "A tall usher – two is company / three a crowd."

Pictures: This young stone cutter was probably Freddy Clark, good friend of Montgomery and one of the frequently mentioned names in the joint secret diary. On April 26, 1903, Maud and Nora went out walking with "some vague idea of hunting up Freddy's stone quarry" but stumbled into bogs and thought better of the venture. The new moon was always a favourite image (see also Blue Scrapbook, p. 3).

Flowers: In September 1896, PWC chum Fanny Wise took over the Cavendish school and boarded at Montgomery's Uncle John Macneill's; the incident commemorated here may have involved Fanny.

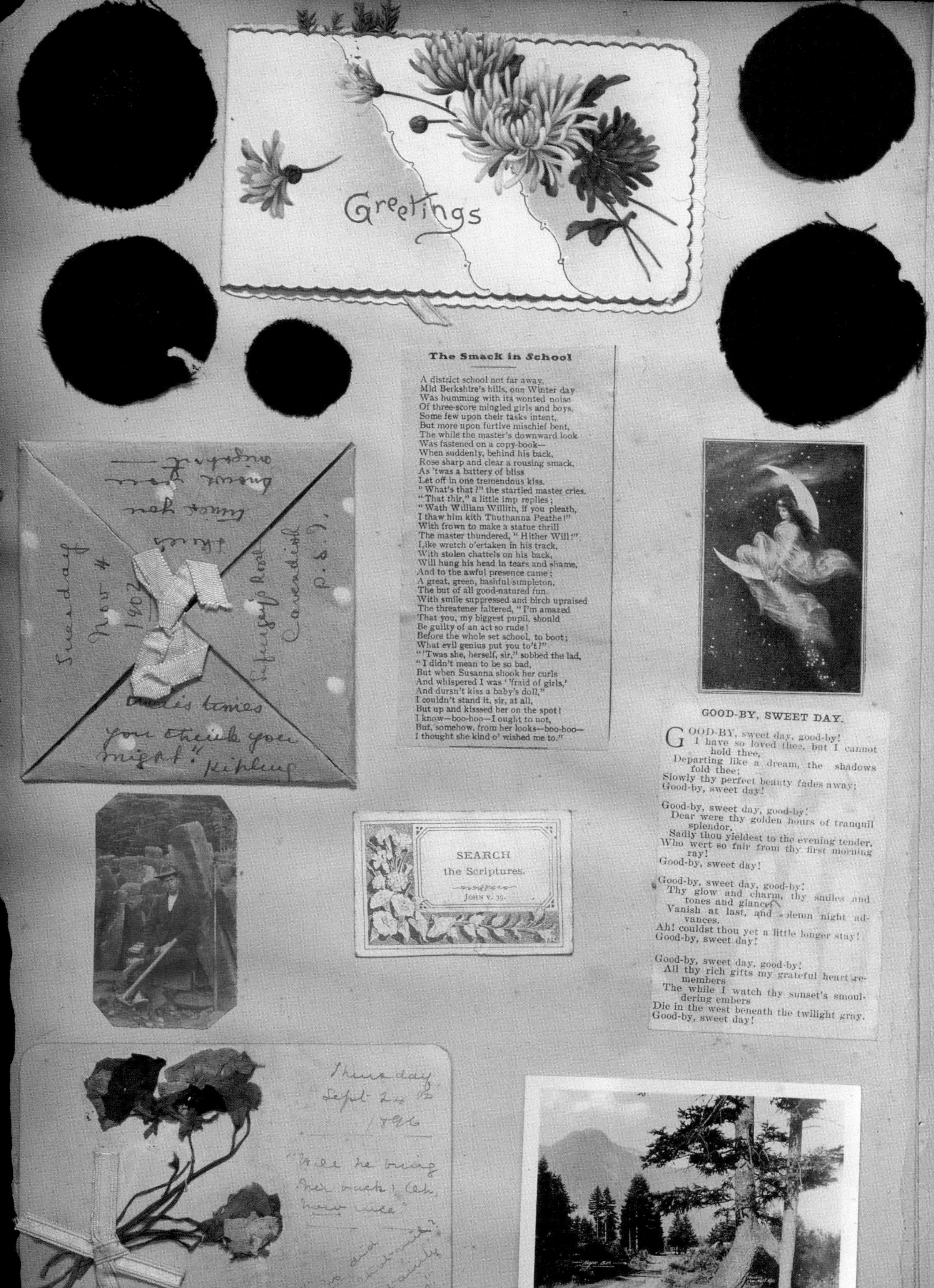

Page 10 from the Red Scrapbook

Running through the apparently jumbled dates and compressed layers of these three pages are two painful stories: one about Edwin Simpson; the other, about Herman Leard. Regretfully engaged to Simpson when she taught in Lower Bedeque and boarded with the Cornelius Leard family (1897–98), Maud fell passionately in love with the handsome young Herman. Back home in Cavendish, she broke the engagement to Simpson and was determined to conquer her feelings for Leard. In the summer of 1898, Maud made a trip to Bideford and, in the setting of her former carefree teaching days, realized how much her unhappiness over Ed and Herman had changed her. She then travelled from Bideford to Lower Bedeque to test how thoroughly she had suppressed her passion for Herman. Herman asked her to take a walk alone with him – perhaps on August 26, 1898 – and she refused, later wondering in her journal, on October 8, 1898, what would have happened if she had gone. "To the end of my life I shall go on wondering," she concluded. As it turned out, Herman died unexpectedly in 1899. Maud went on tormenting herself over Edwin Simpson – with his encouragement – until 1906, when she became engaged to Ewan Macdonald.

PAGE 11: The "High Court" headline sits like judgment itself beside the cut-out Mount of Venus that appears directly above Edwin Simpson's name. More than twenty years later, in her journal of November 22, 1926, she commented on the tiny clipping about Simpson: "A very harmless, commonplace note. Yet there was much behind it for me of unpleasant emotions." The end of the "High Court" clipping and the grim joke at the top left corner refer to the Boer War (1899–1902), in which Canada lost 277 soldiers, many of them in Bloody Sunday, the Battle of Paardeberg (1900).

PAGE 13: Other people's weddings: The December 13, 1899, wedding picture was taken by Maud at her Uncle John Macneill's home. Years later, Montgomery remarked on the unhappiness of Nettie Millar; the notice of her as bride is at the top left. What anguish is compassed in the wedding notice (bottom centre) of Herman's sister Helen? The 1903 Thompson wedding (invitation inside the envelope) was probably connected with the New York calling card of Miss Thompson on page 11 – an *Echo* contact?

PAGE 14: A burnt match, the fateful date, and the Latin "*vanitas vanitatum*" (vanity of vanities), all reminding Maud of lost love, head a page of weddings. After her PWC friend Mary Campbell married, in 1900, and the wedding party danced until dawn, Montgomery took the photograph top left. Lottie Shatford, a Halifax Ladies' College friend, recommended Montgomery for the *Echo* job; Montgomery got half a day off for Lottie's sister's wedding (invitation inside the envelope) on November 6, 1901, and probably wrote the article pasted beneath the invitation.

* * * * *

When the Transvaal war was at its height, Paul Kruger sent a commissioner to England to find out if there were any more men left there. The commissioner wired from London to say that there were four million men and women "knocking about the town," that there was no excitement, and that men were begging to be sent to fight the Boers. Kruger wired back, "Go north." The commissioner found himself in Newcastle eventually and wired to Kruger: "For God's sake stop that war! England is bringing up men from hell, eight at a time in cages!" He had seen a coal-mine.

* * * * *

NIGHT IS MY FRIEND

By Lucy Lincoln Montgomery

Long, long ago
Night was my Foe.
Through each slow and sleepless hour
Ghosts of the Past would creep and lower,
Terrors from the Future loom,
Magnified tenfold by gloom,
The weight of present care and pain
Pressed hopelessly on heart and brain.
Long, long ago
Night was my Foe.

Now to the end
Night is my Friend.
'Tis strange that years must come and go
E'er the blessedness we know—
Such a simple thing and sweet—
'Tis to leave all else complete,
Resting in enfolding Love;
And, though watches wakeful prove,
Learn what strength and comfort lie
In star-set spaces of the sky.
Now to the end
Night is my Friend.

Miss Thompson

Miss Katherine Creighton Thompson

315 West 94th Street

A Riddle

"I came unto an apple tree,
And apples were upon it,
I took no apples off
And I left no apples on it."

The President's First Trousers

When President Taft was seven years old his mother bought him a pair of short duck trousers. The first time they were washed they shrank badly. The boy was fat, but his mother wedged him into the trousers against his protest. He went out to play, but in a few minutes returned.

"Mamma," he said, "I can't wear these pants; they are too tight. Why, Mamma, they are tighter than my skin."

"Oh, no, they're not, Billy," replied his mother. "Nothing could be tighter than your skin."

"Well, all the same, these pants are. I can sit down in my skin, but I can't in these pants."

BORN

STIRLING.—At the Manse, Cavendish, May 25th, to Rev. and Mrs John Stirling, a daughter.

MARRIED

Rev. R. H. Stavert, returned today from a trip to Halifax, where he was attending the Post Graduate School at Pine Hill College. Mr. Stavert crosses this afternoon to P. E. Island to spend a few days at his old home in Wilmot Valley. —Moncton Times, May 3.

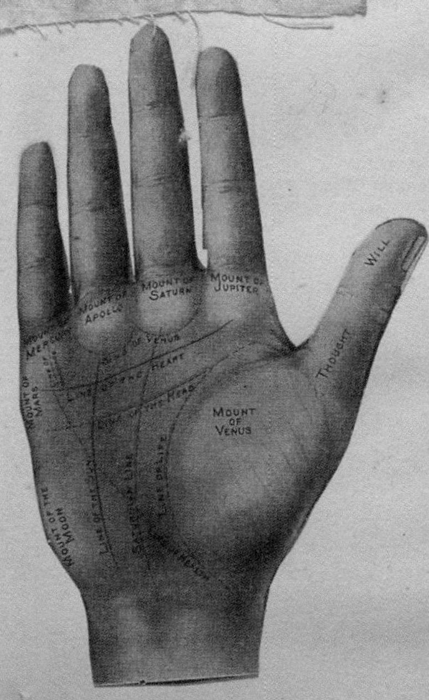

Rev Edwin Simpson of Illinois, and Burton Simpson of Acadia College are visiting in Bay View. The former occupied the pulpit of the Cavendish Baptist Church on Sunday evening.

HIGH COURT OF FORESTERS AT TIGNISH

An Interesting Session Closed

AND ADDRESSES DELIVERED

By Dr. Oronhyatekah and Others —A Successful Public Meeting.

PUBLIC MEETING.

The programme was opened by a selection from the 82nd Battalion Band of Charlottetown. This was followed by an address of welcome by Hon Edward Hackett, M P. He briefly reviewed and eulogized the great work that had been accomplished by Dr Oronhyatekah, and concluded his pointed remarks with a reassurance of welcome to the visitors. The next number was a well rendered solo by Miss Comstock, who had to respond to an encore. Capt Jos Read, M L A, the oldest Forester on P E Island, on behalf of the High Court thanked the citizens of Tignish for the splendid entertainment they had given. He illustrated the superiority of the I O F over other societies, by a comparison of the modes of travelling now with the stage coach of former days; the latter represented other societies, while the Foresters are emblematic of the Pulman Palace cars drawn by one of the greatest engines that was ever at the head of any train. (Applause)

Miss Lucy Lefurgey read "The Hose Race" in an admirable manner. She responded to a hearty encore with equal acceptance.

Dr Oronhyatekah next addressed the meeting. He was in good form and after telling a few anecdotes, he began the review of the I O F, following its history particularly since the year 1874, showing

the many obstacles which had been met and successfully combated.

He referred to the repeated attacks of the press on the Order and explained how, that instead of being an injury they had been a benefit and the most bitter attacks were always followed by large increase in membership. So much was this so that he had on one occasion written a note to the editor of an attacking paper, who had ceased his criticisms, to begin attacking again.

He referred to the publicly expressed opinion of the actuaries of London who had through their own medium, stated that the O F was organized on a sound financial basis. The Order now extends all over the United Kingdom, United States, France, Belgium, and Australia, carrying with it great possibilities of doing good, such as the sustenance and education of families, enabling them to reach a higher physical, mental and spiritual sphere in life, than they would otherwise. After a well told, well pointed story, he concluded by enumerating some of the benefits to be derived by being Foresters, urging all brethren to stand together in promoting the best interests of the order. The remaining numbers of the splendid programme were a Scotch solo by Dr McDougall, who was encored; a band selection, two readings by Mr Chas Clark, of Ottawa (a returned soldier who figured in the battle of Paardeburg) and a duet by Misses Comstock and Larkin, all of which were exceedingly well rendered and were well received. The meeting closed with the National Anthem.

MR. R. H. MONTGOMERY.

An interesting but quiet [illegible] place on Wednesday afternoon, May 3rd, at the home of Mr. and Mrs. Peter Millar, Bideford, P. E. I., it being the occasion of the marriage of their eldest daughter, Nettie, to Austin Ramsay of Freeland, Lot 11. Rev. Mr. Murdock tied the nuptial knot. Jas. Millar, brother of the bride, attended the groom, while Miss Alice Ramsay, sister of the groom, assisted the bride. Miss Maud Hayes played the wedding march.

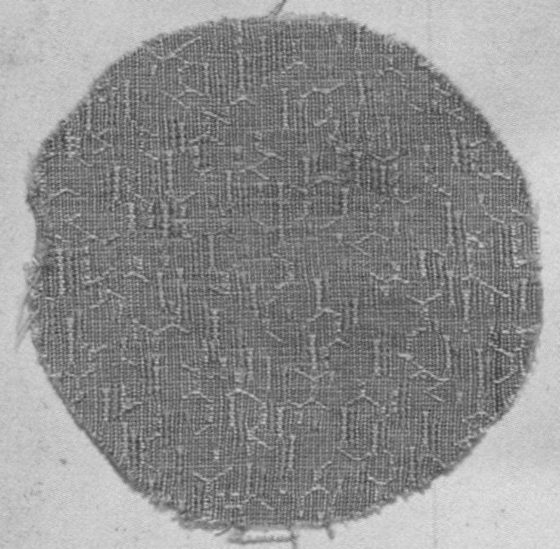

WEDDING BELLS.—On the evening of Wednesday, Dec. 13th, the residence of Mr. John F. McNeill, Cavendish, was the scene of a very pretty wedding, briefly referred to in yesterday's PATRIOT, when his niece, Miss Maggie McLeod, of Kensington, was married to Mr. Alvin Glover, of the same place. At the appointed hour the bridal party entered the parlor to the music of the wedding march played by Miss Fannie Wise, and took their stand under a beautiful arch of evergreens. The bride was simply but beautifully attired, being dressed in white sevis muslin with veil and wreath. She carried an exquisite bouquet of chrysanthemums. She was attended by her cousin, Miss Lucy McNeill, who wore navy blue serge with vest of white satin. The groom was ably supported by his brother, Mr. Robert Glover, teacher, of Carleton. The ceremony was performed by Rev. Chas. McKay, New London, assisted by Rev. Mr. McIntosh, of Cavendish. After a bountiful repast, usual on such occasions, a very enjoyable evening followed. In due time a party of chivariers arrived, and treated the assembled guests to an orderly serenade. Their costumes were particularly good. The many gifts were beautiful and useful; that of the groom to the bride may be specially mentioned—a pair of Persian Lamb gloves. On the following morning the happy couple departed, amid showers of rice and old shoes, for their future home in Kensington. Their many friends cordially wish them a happy wedded life.

DECEMBER
Sun Mon. Tue. Wed. Thu. Fri. Sat.
1 2 3 4 5 6 7
8 9 10 11 12 13 14
15 16 17 18 19 20 21
22 23 24 25 26 27 28
29 30 31 - - - -
RAPHAEL TUCK & SONS, LONDON, PARIS
COPYRIGHT

Mr. Arthur G. Harmon,
Miss Olive DeVore Eby,
Married
Wednesday, July twenty-fifth,
nineteen hundred,
St. Joseph, Michigan.

Miss Montgomery.

WEDDING WEDNESDAY.

The marriage of A. G. Thompson, a well known New York business man and Miss Jean Lyall, daughter of the late Professor Lyall, of Dalhousie College, took place at Miss Tremaine's residence, No. 31 Tower Road. The ceremony was a very quiet one and was performed by Prof. Falconer, assisted by Prof. Forrest. In the afternoon Mr. and Mrs. Thompson left for the United States on their wedding trip. They were recipients of very many wedding presents from friends in Halifax and New York.

Mr. Thompson is a member of the lumber dealing firm of James Thompson and Son whose business is located at Staten Island. Mr. Thompson's [illegible] is on Staton Island.

A very pretty wedding took place at the home of Mr. and Mrs. Cornelius Leard, Lower Bedeque, on Tuesday, March 26th, when their daughter, Miss Helen, was united in marriage to Mr Howard McFarlane of Sea Cow Head. The ceremony was performed by the Rev. E P Calven. The bride was becomingly dressed in a suit of pearl gray with white trimmings. After the ceremony a few of the most intimate friends partook of a repast, such as can only be prepared by women like Mrs. Leard. Their many friends join in wishing Mr and Mrs McFarlane a happy journey through life.

AT 8 o'clock this evening the residence of Mr. John McLure, North Rustico, will be the scene of a happy gathering to witness the nuptials of Mr. McLure's daughter, Miss Lavinia, to Mr. John A. MacMillan, Brackley Point. Rev. G. C. Robertson will be the officiating clergyman, and about sixty couples will join in the festivities of the occasion. The groom will be supported by Mr. Chester McLure, teacher, Alexandria, and Miss Celia MacMillan, Prince Street, sister of the groom, will act as bride's maid. The costume of the bride will be tastefully trimmed cream silk, and that of the bridesmaid a pretty lavender, both carrying bouquets to match. The wedding gifts are a large and choice variety of the useful and ornamental. After spending the evening in mirthful festivities the bridal party will drive to the groom's home at Brackley Point. Mr. and Mrs. MacMillan have the best wishes of a large circle of friends and in adding congratulations THE GUARDIAN heartily joins.

Page 12 from the Red Scrapbook

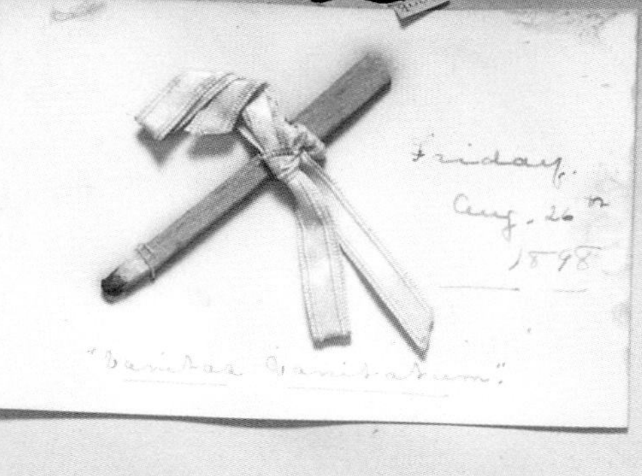

THE subjoined additional particulars of the following marriage have been received. On the evening of Wednesday, the 26th of June, the beautiful residence of Mr. Donald E. Campbell of Darlington was the scene of an exceedingly pretty wedding, when his daughter Mary was united in marriage to Mr. Archibald Beaton of O'Leary Station. At eight o'clock the wedding guests assembled on the lawn, the members of the bridal party took their stand under the arching trees and the Rev. Geo. Millar of Brookfield, assisted by Rev. Malcolm Campbell of 'trathalbyn, tied the nuptial knot. The bride was attired in a dress of steel-blue ady's cloth, with trimming of pearl applique and white satin and wore the dal veil and orange blossoms. She was nded by Miss Euphemia Beaton of eary Station, who wore a pretty gown lowered muslin, and by Miss Charlotte pbell, who made a dear little maid onor in dotted Swiss muslin with a uet of white carnations. Mr. Norman pbell, brother of the bride, supported groom. After the ceremony the bountiful wedding supper was served, which the evening passed pleasantly rious amusements while the younger sts danced in the wee sma' hours. y and beautiful presents testified to steem and affection of a large circle iends. On Thursday morning the married pair departed for an ex- wedding tour to the principal of Canada and the New England . Their many friends heartily con- wishing Mr. and Mrs. Beaton a happy, and prosperous wedded life.

SHATFORD-FRASER.

Interesting Event at St. Paul's at Noon To-day.

At noon today St. Paul's Church was the scene of an extremely pretty wedding, when Miss Edna E. Shatford was married to Mr. Edwin Fraser, C. E.

The bride was charmingly gowned in white voile over white taffeta, en traine, with lace trimming and with bridal veil, and carried a shower bouquet of white roses and maidenhair fern. She walked up the aisle alone, to the music of the wedding march from "Lohengrin" and was met at the head of the church by her father, Mr. John E. Shatford, who gave her away.

The service was choral and the ceremony was performed by Rev. W. J. Armitage.

Miss Lottie Shatford was the bridesmaid and wore cream broadcloth trimmed with point d' Ireland lace, with a white picture hat and bouquet of white and yellow chrysanthemums. The groom was supported by Mr. Stonewall Jackson, of New Glasgow. Messrs. Geo. W. and Robert H. Murray and John N. Creed were the ushers.

After the ceremony the bridal party repaired to the residence of the bride's brother, Mr. J. Franklyn Shatford, at 101 Pleasant Street, where a reception was held and luncheon served to about sixty guests.

Many of the groom's old friends from New Glasgow were present, among them being Robert M. McGregor, George Fraser and Frank Macneill.

The rooms were decorated with palms and smilax and streamers of white satin ribbon. Many beautiful gifts were received, including cheques from parents and immediate relatives. The groom's gift to the bride was a pearl pendant and to the bridesmaid a necklace.

Mr. and Mrs. Fraser left on the Maritime Express for their future home in Minneapolis. They will visit several Canadian cities en route. The bride's going-away gown was of ott[illegible] cloth, with hat to [illegible] sable furs. Their

The marriage of Miss Edith England, daughter of Mrs Edward England, of Bideford, to Mr E Bayfield Williams, of the law firm of McKinnon & Williams, Charlottetown, took place at the home of the bride's mother this morning. The ceremony was performed by Rev W E Johnson, B A, of Elgin, N B, in the presence of the immediate relatives and friends. The bride was becomingly attired in white brocaded silk and wore a travelling suit of steel grey broadcloth. The large number of elegant presents testified to the high regard in which the young couple are held. After a wedding breakfast Mr and Mrs Williams boarded the train at Ellerslie for Summerside, and took passage by the Northumberland on a honeymoon trip to Quebec, Montreal, Ottawa and other Canadian cities. They will return about July 1st, and reside in the handsome cottage lately occupied by Mr Benj. Davies, Charlottetown. The PATRIOT joins with hosts of friends in extending congratulations.

he meeting of Cavendish Literary last Friday evening, Miss Lucy tgomery read a very interesting n Tenneyson. In the course of the many choice selections were quoted the different poems. The paper scussed by Messrs. J. S. Clark, Walter n, Geo. W. Simpson, Geo. R. Mc- d others.

Professor William Archibald Spooner, of Oxford University, has become famous as a ludicrous word twister. Once, at a special service, seeing some women standing at the back of the church waiting to be seated, he rushed down the aisle and addressed the ushers as follows: "Gentlemen, gentlemen, sew these ladies into their sheets." Being asked at dinner what fruit he would have, he promptly replied: "Pigs, fleas." This is the way in which Dr. Spooner proposed to his wife: Being one afternoon at the home of her father, Bishop Harvey Goodwin, of Carlisle, Mrs. Goodwin said: "Mr. Spooner, will you please go out into the garden and ask Miss Goodwin if she will come in and make tea?" The professor, on finding the [illegible] said: "Miss Goodwin, your [illegible] to ask [illegible] if you would

Page 14 from the Red Scrapbook

Photograph: Maud's photograph of the birch tree, the "White Lady" from the Macneill property, may have been placed here to companion the birch bark at the bottom, on which she inscribed "Twas a goodly tree I ween," "the Monarch of the Forest," and "Haunted Wood." These three lines appeared in nine-year-old Maud's tribute to a birch tree, a poem entitled "The Monarch of the Forest."

Clippings: The "Cavendish Notes" and "Back Shore Notes" may have been written by Montgomery and refer to her trip to and from Park Corner to visit the Campbells. A wedding clipping noted that Frederica Campbell of Park Corner attended the bride. The "Psyche" clipping (top right), the companion to Daisy Williams's "Night's Eye" piece on page 3 of the scrapbook, interpreted Montgomery's handwriting and her ability to "appear utterly different from what you really are." Tucked into the bottom left corner, a tiny clipping marks the first of many scattered notes concerning Ewan Macdonald (variously spelled).

Card: Inside (see below), Maud commemorated a snowy Sunday outing with Nora Lefurgey, described in their secret diary. After evening church service, Jerry Clark (driving his horse, Olive) offered Nora a lift home and Maud was taken by Freddy Clark. The "*mean* trick" may refer to the fact that Jerry had apparently abandoned Nora at an earlier outing and offered her the drive this night to make amends.

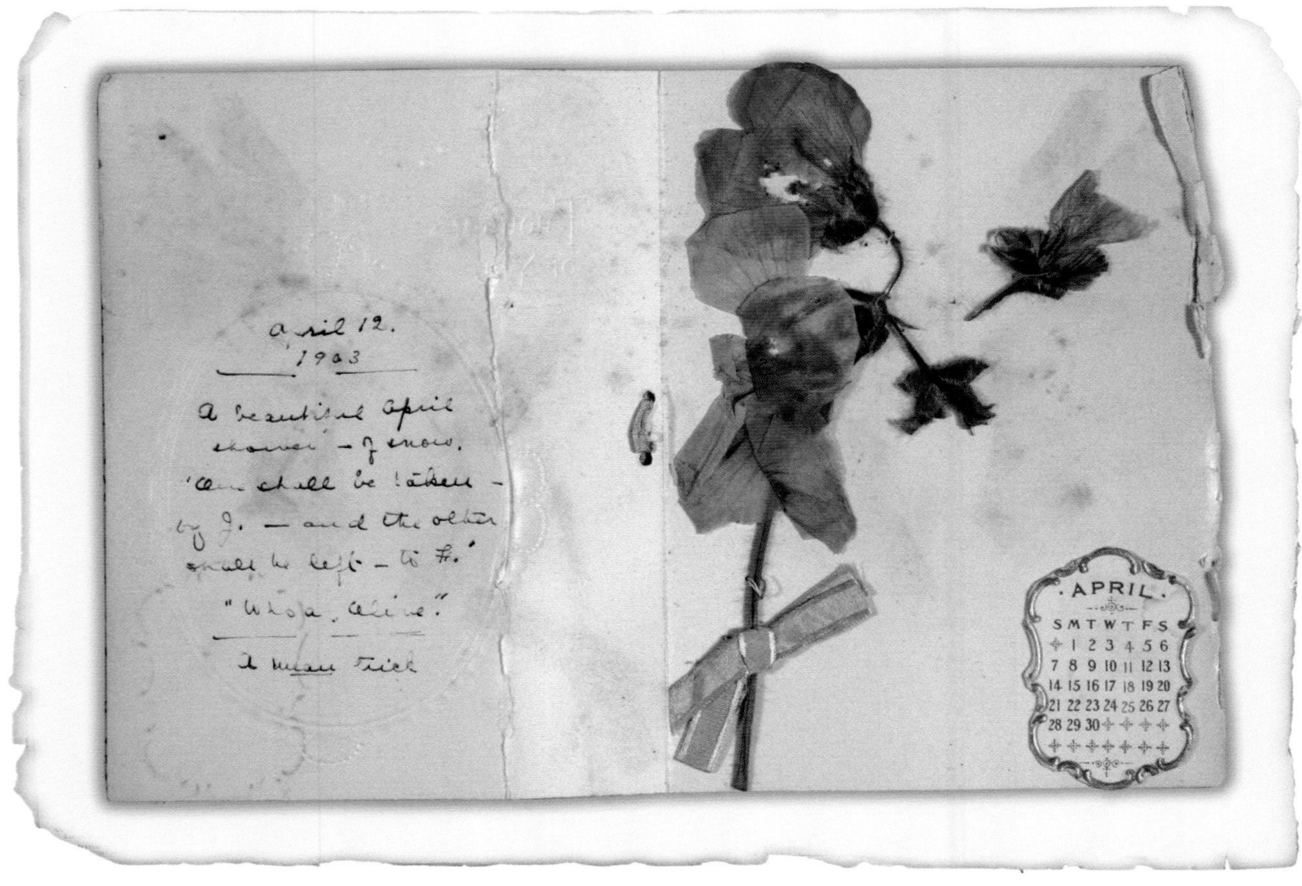

CAVENDISH NOTES.— The season for self-binders to begin their hum, is at hand. Quite a quantity of oats and wheat has seccumbed to the sickle, the former crop is very much broken down, but the wheat crop shows quite a lot of rust and wevil, despite all the fine, pure wheat which was sown last spring. —Cavendish is becoming a place of great attractions, particularly in regard to pleasure seekers.—A tea of grand success was held early in July, and picnics galore since then. —The old Presbyterian church, purchased by Geo. Bowness, of Stanley, is now a dilapitated mass of lumber.—The new society at their last meeting succeeded in securing a suitable site for the new church, and hope to see before long a very fine edifice.—Our school is rapidly regaining its former reputation, under the careful, skiful and energetic management of Miss Nellie McNeill.—We are pleased to see Mr. James A. Stewart home again. He has been absent for twelve years in the West and gives our young men great encouragements to go West.—Mrs. C. F. Simpson returned home from Nova Scotia, where she has been visiting her relatives. She was absent two weeks.—Mr. C. W. Jackson accompanied by his mother and sister left last week for their future home in Connecticut. We wish Mr. Jackson every success in his studies. —Miss Lucy Maud Montgomery is visiting friends at Park Corner. She is the guest of Mr. and Mrs. John Campbell.

BACK SHORE NOTES.—The managers of the several factories along the shore are:—Pineo Bros., McLeod & Rattray, LePage & Peters, Thomas Doyle, Moses Gallant, David Marks, James and Albert Graham. Report has it that some of the cleverest of those managers have secured their fishing ground already, by putting out their back lines. —Milk tendering for the drawing to the Stanley Bridge Cheese Factory seems the order of the day, between the farmers. Judging from the number of tenders sent in, the work will be performed at a cheap rate.—Mr. Thomas Doyle, Rustico, has recently disposed of his handsome gelding, Black Sporter, for a handsome sum. We understand Mr. H. S. McLure, teacher at Hope River, was the purchaser. This gelding is sired by the celebrated trotting stallion Bronze Chief, dam Hernando, granddam Morgan. Although young this colt has the breed and actions for being very speedy.—Miss Bertha McKenzie, of Cavendish, who spent the winter at Brackley Point, returned home a few days ago.—The industrious ladies of the C. T. Society still continue to meet at the home of one of the members on Wednesday afternoons of each week the Presbyterian congregations of Rustico, Cavendish and Stanley will miss with regret the aid of their pastor, Rev. G. C. Robertson, who has accepted the call to Bonshaw and adjoining sections. We wish him and his partner in life every success in their new field of labor.—We ergret to learn that Miss Katie McPhail has not completely recovered from her sickness of quinsy, but under the careful tre tment of Dr. Houston, of New Glasgow, we hope to see her around in a short time.—Cavendish school is greatly progressing under Mr. E Brown's guidance.— COM.

Rev. Mr. McDonald who preached in St. Andrew's congregation on Sunday, made a good impression. He has a fine strong face and his sermons were strong and well reasoned. He preaches again to-morrow.

CANENDISH NOTES.—Last week's storm of wind and rain did quite a lot of damage to the grain crops, the greater part of that which was standing is now almost totally ruined.—Mr. Chas. E. MacKenzie of South Granville spent Sunday at his home at Cavendish.—Miss L. M. Montgomery is home again after her week's visit to Park Corner.—We feel sorry for your correspondent of 7 h inst and he must certainly be in the ages of man viz dotage when he calls the Presbyterian church a "New Society" perhaps we have a modern Methuselah amongst us when he likens the Presbyterian Church established early in the sixteenth century unto a "new society."—Milk isdecreasing at present but the output from Cavendish for this seasen far exceeds that of any previous year. Cavendish supplies over 6 000 lbs milk daily to Stanley cheese factory more than double the quantity sent three years ago. — Mrs. Seth MacKenzie of Lowell, Mass., who has been visiting her former home here left for home on 8th inst, she was accompanied by Miss Annie McLure who goes on a two months visit to friends in Lowell, Chelsea, Wakefield, etc.— Miss Lucy MacNeill left on 9th for St. John N. B. to attend the exhibition.—It is understood that the mass meeting of the C. G. Club spoken of a few weeks ago has been postponed until after harvest.—The fishermen are slowly gathering their scanty harvest from the sea: very few mackerel have been taken on the North side this year and owing to the scarcity of bait very few cod or hake have been caught and but for the lobster catch which was about the average our fishermen would fare slimly enough. This fact brings vividly to our minds the lines of the poet.

"Companions of the sea and silent air
The lonely fisher thus must ever fare
Without the comfort, hope, with scarce
a friend
He looks through life and only sees
its end."

AN interesting event took place at the home of Mrs Jeremiah Smith, Orwell, on Wednesday afternoon, Aug 22, when her daughter, Bessie, was united in marriage to Charles H Robertson, of Marshfield. The ceremony was performed by Rev Robt Sinclair assisted by Rev D B MacLeod. The bride, beautifully gowned and carrying a handsome bouquet, entered the room on the arm of her uncle, Mr D McLeod. She was attended by Miss Frederica Campbell Park Corner, and the groom was supported by his cousin N Bannerman Robertson. The ceremony being over, a dainty supper was served, after which the bridal party drove away in the midst of showers of rice to the home of the groom in Marshfield where a reception was held and a very pleasant evening spent. The valuable wedding gifts attested the good will and esteem in which the contracting parties are held by their friends.

"HERBIE, it says here that another octogenarian's dead. What's an octogenarian?"

"Well, I don't quite know what they are, but they must be very sickly creatures. You never hear of them but they're dying."

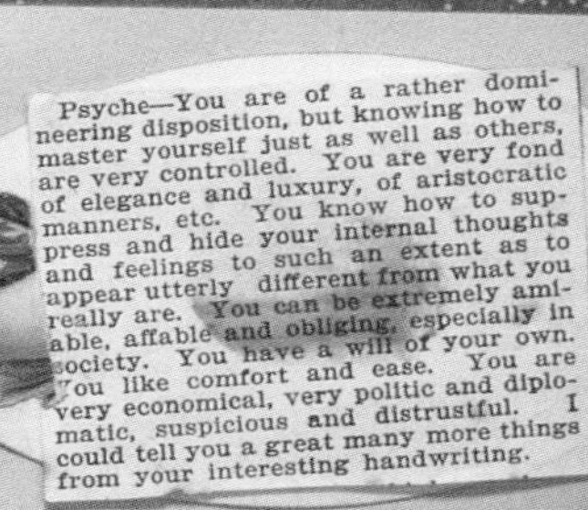

Psyche—You are of a rather domineering disposition, but knowing how to master yourself just as well as others, are very controlled. You are very fond of elegance and luxury, of aristocratic manners, etc. You know how to suppress and hide your internal thoughts and feelings to such an extent as to appear utterly different from what you really are. You can be extremely amiable, affable and obliging, especially in society. You have a will of your own. You like comfort and ease. You are very economical, very politic and diplomatic, suspicious and distrustful. I could tell you a great many more things from your interesting handwriting.

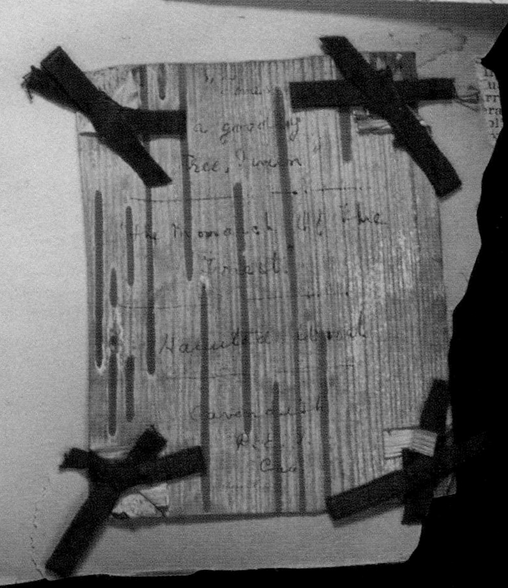

Poems: The odd wistfulness of "The Petrified Fern" and the sorrow of "Dreamers of Dreams" are offset by the American folk-song "Katie Lee and Willie Gray" and jokes.

Birch bark: This probably belonged to another of Montgomery's outings with Nora. The date reads November 6, 1902, and the heading reads "To each man his work." Perhaps they attended together one of the revival meetings of Sam MacDougall, who created a stir when his background was exposed. Montgomery's diary documented the scandal on November 30, 1902:

November has really been quite an exciting month. Early in it the Baptists started up a series of revival meetings. They got an "evangelist" to help them called MacDougall – Christian name, Sam.

Really, he was delicious! He was good-looking – if you happened to fancy his style – and had such melting dark eyes. The fifteen-year-olds went down before those eyes like ninepins. And he could groan so heart-rendingly! Also he could sing! For the rest, he was illiterate, sensational and so vulgar that he set the teeth of my spirit on edge. But I went – bless you, yes. It was fine fun. I was sorry when I had to miss a night!

This went on for about three weeks – and then came the expose. Cavendish hasn't enjoyed such a scandal for a decade. The Rev. Sam turned out to be, not only a fake – that might have been endured – but a Presbyterian – or, as he pronounced it, Presbytarian. The Baptist blood curdled with horror. Poor Sammy was hustled out of the place and since then peace and dullness have resumed their reign.

[KA]TIE LEE AND WILLIE GRAY.

—A good many years ago a little song [was p]opular, which sung the affection of a boy for a small girl. He offers to [carry] her basket but she will only let him 'carry half,' and it is the same in later years when he offers to carry life's burdens for her. Their names were Katie Lee and Willie Gray. Ans.—The following verses are probably what you are in search of. We do not know who was the author.

Two brown heads, with tossing curls,
Red lips shutting over pearls,
Bare feet white and red with dew,
Two eyes black and two eyes blue—
Little boy and girl were they,
Katie Lee and Willie Gray.

They were standing where a brook,
Bending like a shepherd's crook,
Flashed its silver, and thick ranks
Of green willows fringed the banks;
Half in thought and half in play
Katie Lee and Willie Gray.

They had cheeks like cherries red;
He was taller—'most a head;
She, with arms like wreaths of snow,
Swings a basket to and fro,
As she loiters, half in play,
Chatting there with Willie Gray.

'Pretty Katie,' Willie said,
And there came a dash of red
Through the brownness of his cheek,
'Boys are strong and girls are weak,
And I'll carry, so I will,
Katie's basket up the hill.'

Katie answered with a laugh:
'You shall only carry half.'
And then, tossing back her curls,
'Boys are weak as well as girls.'
Do you think that Katie guessed
Half the wisdom she expressed?

Men are only boys grown tall;
Hearts don't change much, after all:
And when, long years from that day,
Katie Lee and Willie Gray
Stood again beside the brook,
Bending like a shepherd's crook,

Is it strange that Willie said,
While again a dash of red
Crossed the brownness of his cheek:
'I am strong, and you are weak,
Life is but a slippery steep,
Hung with shadows, cold and deep.

'Will you trust me, Katie dear,
Walk beside me without fear?
May I carry—and I will—
All your burdens up the hill?'
And she answered with a laugh,
'No—but you may carry half.'

Close beside the little brook,
Bending like a shepherd's crook,
Washing with its silver bands,
[L]ate and early at the sands,
[Is] a cottage where, to-day,
Katie lives with Willie Gray.

In the porch she sits, and lo!
Swings a basket to and fro—
Vastly different from the one
That she swung in years agone:
This is long, and deep, and wide,
And—has rockers at the side.

7

DREAMERS OF DREAMS.

We are all of us dreamers of dreams ;
On visions our childhood is fed ;
And the heart of the child is unhaunted, it seems,
By the ghosts of dreams that are dead.

From childhood to youth's but a span,
And the years of our youth are soon sped ;
Yet the youth is no longer a youth, but a man,
When the first of his dreams is dead.

There's no sadder sight this side the grave
Than the shroud o'er a fond dream spread,
And the heart should be stern and the eyes be brave
To gaze on a dream that is dead.

'Tis as a cup of wormwood and gall
When the doom of a great dream is said,
And the best of a man is under the pall
When the best of his dreams is dead.

He may live on by compact and plan
When the fine bloom of living is shed,
But God pity the little that's left of a man
When the last of his dreams is dead.

Let him show a brave face if he can,
Let him woo fame or fortune instead,
Yet there's not much to do but bury a man
When the last of his dreams is dead.

—William Herbert Carruth.

The Petrified Fern.

In a valley, centuries ago,
Grew a little fern leaf, green and slender,
Veining delicate and fibres tender,
Waving, when the wind crept down so low;
Rushes tall and moss and grass grew round it,
Playful sunbeams darted in and found it,
Drops of dew stole in by night and crowned it,
But no foot of man e'er trod that way—
Earth was young and keeping holiday;

Monster fishes swam the silent main,
Stately forests waved their giant branches,
Mountains hurled their snowy avalanches,
Mammoth creatures stalked across the plain;
Nature reveled in grand mysteries,
But the little fern was not of these,
Did not number with the hills and trees;
Only grew and waved, its sweet wild way—
No one came to note it day by day.

Earth one time put on a frolic mood,
Heaved the rocks and changed the mighty motion
Of the deep, strong currents of the ocean;
Moved the plain and shook the haughty wood,
Crushed the little fern in soft, moist clay,
Covered it and hid it safe away;
Oh! the long, long, long centuries since that day!
Oh! the agony! Oh! life's bitter cost,
Since that useless little fern was lost!

Useless? Lost? There came a thoughtful man,
Searching nature's secrets, far and deep;
From a fissure in a rocky steep
He withdrew a stone, o'er which there ran
Fairy pencilings, a quaint design,
Veinings, leafage, fibres clear and fine,
And the fern's life lay in every line!
So, I think, God hides some souls away,
Sweetly to surprise us the last day.

—By Mary Lydia Bolles Branch.

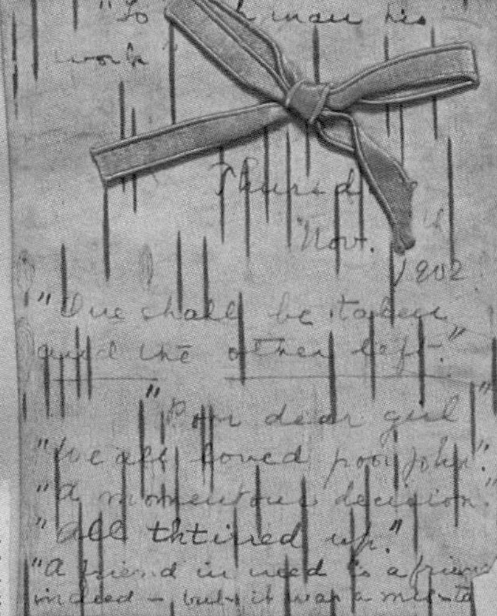

"Who-o?" "You!"

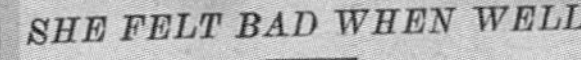

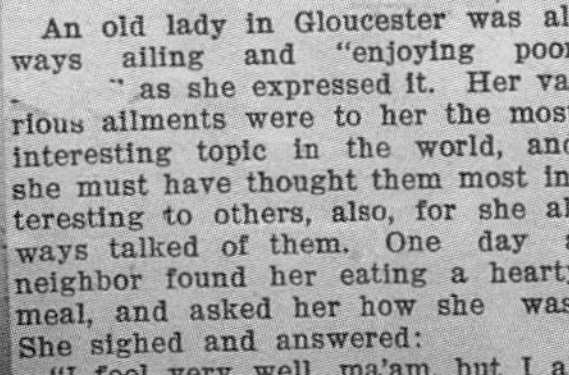

SHE FELT BAD WHEN WELL.

An old lady in Gloucester was always ailing and "enjoying poor [health]" as she expressed it. Her various ailments were to her the most interesting topic in the world, and she must have thought them most interesting to others, also, for she always talked of them. One day a neighbor found her eating a hearty meal, and asked her how she was. She sighed and answered:

"I feel very well, ma'am, but I always feel bad when I feel well be[cause] I know I am goin[g] to feel worse

After the rector had announced that the new hymn books were ready, the curate announced the time for the baptism of infants. The rector, being deaf, followed immediately with the surprising statement: "They can be had at the rectory for sixpence each; with stiff backs for one shilling."

Page 16 from the Red Scrapbook

Envelope, clipping, and program: On March 4, 1901, Montgomery recorded in her unpublished diary:

Two of my letters were quite nice. One was from a certain Alfred Mason, who, it seems, is an organist of Pittsfield, Mass., and who says he has taken a great fancy to those verses of mine "A Pair of Slippers" and wants my permission to publish them as a song with the music he had written for them. Oddly enough, the other letter was similar in kind, being from a Miss Chadkins in Boston who wants to set "When the Fishing Boats Come In" to music. Of course I am pleasantly tickled.

Similar requests are still made of the heirs of L.M. Montgomery.

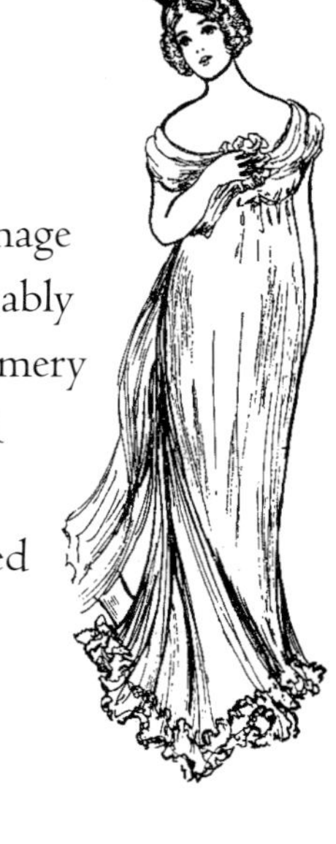

Photograph: The image of Mount Robson (probably from 1930, when Montgomery collected the other CNR photographs on her trip to Saskatchewan) replaced something, and the tear along the bottom of the page suggests another alteration.

113 South St
Pittsfield
Mass
Feb 16/01

Miss Montgomery
I have taken a great fancy to your poem "A pair of Slippers"

Alfred T. Mason

A pair of slippers worn, you know,
By grandmamma in the long ago;
Fashioned from satin of ivory hue,
Just the size of a fairy's shoe,
Silver buckles, rosettes and all,
Worn for the first at her birthnight ball.

Somebody thought her sweet and fair,
Somebody praised her golden hair.
Straight into somebody's heart danced she
While the violins tinkled so merrily.
In her dainty slippers and gown of white
Grandpapa found his bride that night.

Long are the years that have passed away,
But hearts of love keep their youth for aye.
Grandmamma's golden hair is white,
But her smile is as sweet as it was the night
She danced, the queen of the maidens all,
With grandpapa at her birthnight ball.

L. M. Montgomery

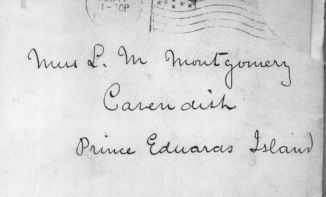

Miss L. M. Montgomery
Cavendish
Prince Edward Island

PITTSFIELD FEB 17 1-30P

RECENT MUSICAL EVENTS

IN PITTSFIELD.

MUSICAL CLUB.

The thirty-fourth concert of the Musical Club was given and the last meeting of the season held, at Mrs. J. D. Coit's residence Monday evening. It was well attended and proved a most enjoyable concert. The star of the evening was Mr. Leo Liebermann, of New York City. He was in good voice, and if he had been willing it is probable he would be singing there yet, as his encores were—well, he had to encore everything. Perhaps the response to the song by our own composer was as hearty as any to which he and singer bowed their acknowledgements together. Mr. Liebermann is an artist, one of those big chested tenor robustos that carry you along with them in their crescendos to such an extent you are musically mesmerised, and when he has finished ordinary talking seems gibberish. Mr. Escher did some very clever work with his violin, especially in the softer parts of his numbers. He was ably assisted by Mrs. Stevenson and Miss Bissell. Mr. Mason played all of Mr. Libermann's accompaniments and evidently is a great favorite with the Musical Club for he is always there Appended is the program.

Suite for Piano and Organ. — Op. 11 Goldmash
Allegro,
Andente sostenuto,
Allegretto Moderato.
Mrs. W. C Stevenson and Mr. Escher.

Whether we die, or we live, — Frances Allitsen
Mr Francis.

Aria,—La Gioconda, — Ponchielli.
Mr. Liebermann,

a. Herbstlied, — O. Weil.
b. Fruhlingslied.
Violin obligato,
Mr Liebermann and Mr. Escher.

a. I Cannot help loving thee, — Clayton Johns.
b. A Resolve, — H. de Fontenailles
Mr. Francis.

Rondo Capriccioso, — Saint Saens.
Piano and Violin.
Miss M. A Bissell and Mr Escher.

a. I wait for thee, — C. B Hawley
b. A pair of slippers, — A. T. Mason
c. O come with me, — F. Vanden Stucken
Mr. Liebermann.

Thirty-Fourth Concert

of the

Musical Club

Entertained by Mrs. James D. Colt,

Monday, March Fourth,

1901

Pittsfield Massachusetts

Mr. Leo Liebermann
Tenor

Mr. Carl Escher
Violin

Mr. Alfred T. Mason
Accompanist

It is with regret that the PATRIOT is called upon to chronicle the death of Marie V. Munroe, aged 26, wife of Mr. Fred Compton, St. Eleanors. The sad event took place on Sunday, June 30th. Mrs. Compton had been ill for some time and death was not unexpected. The deceased formerly taught school in Prince County and was a very popular young lady. The funeral which took place yesterday was largely attended.

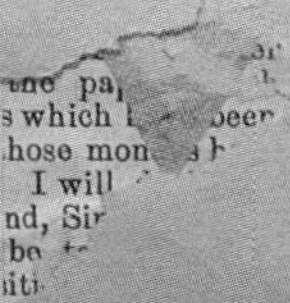

the pa...
s which ... been
hose mon...
I will
nd, Sir
bo...
iti...

Mamma—If you eat any more of that pudding, Tommy, you will see the bogie man to-night.

Tommy (after a moment's thought) —Well, give me some more. I might as well settle my mind about the truth of the story once for all.

Page 17 from the Red Scrapbook

The immediacy, suggested fun, and nostalgia of the next two pages together were freshly re-created when Montgomery imagined *Anne.* Montgomery's teacher, Hattie Gordon, inspired the character of Anne's beloved Miss Stacey, and escapades with Nora kept memories and daring alive.

This page preserves genuine souvenirs from Maud's teens, while the next page records episodes with Nora keyed to their joint secret diary. In her own journal entry of April 12, 1903, written in a far different vein, Montgomery marvelled at that diary: "If a stranger were to read that record he would be sure to think that it was written by a couple of harum-scarum girls in their frivolous teens."

Photograph: The photograph of the Cavendish school pasted onto the calendar is Montgomery's own.

Clippings: Hattie Gordon features in both articles: "Cavendish School" (left) comes from the 1889–90 school year when Maud was still a full-time pupil under Miss Gordon; "Entertainment at Cavendish School" describes the Christmas concert of 1891 when Maud had returned from a year out west with her father and stepmother and agreed to help her former teacher decorate the school and fill the program. Commenting on her nostalgia in preserving the articles, Maud included the sentimental poem "Twenty Years Ago" and also the school joke about a short tale, placed carefully beneath a snippet of squirrel's tail.

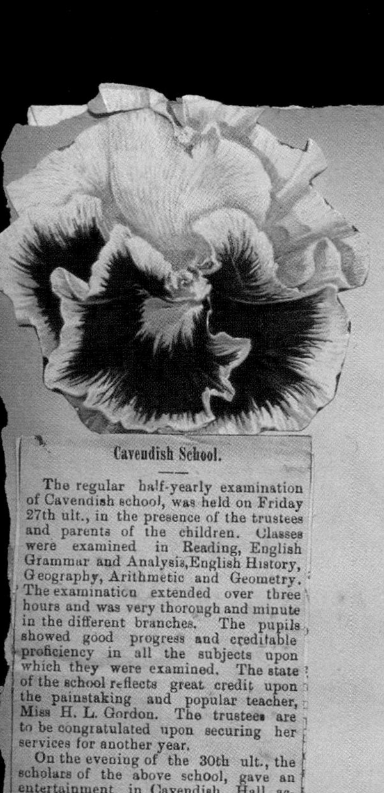

Cavendish School.

The regular half-yearly examination of Cavendish school, was held on Friday 27th ult., in the presence of the trustees and parents of the children. Classes were examined in Reading, English Grammar and Analysis, English History, Geography, Arithmetic and Geometry. The examination extended over three hours and was very thorough and minute in the different branches. The pupils showed good progress and creditable proficiency in all the subjects upon which they were examined. The state of the school reflects great credit upon the painstaking and popular teacher, Miss H. L. Gordon. The trustees are to be congratulated upon securing her services for another year.

On the evening of the 30th ult., the scholars of the above school, gave an entertainment in Cavendish Hall, according to the following programme:

Opening Speech—Master John Laird.

Welcome Song—Choir.

Recitation—"Aunt Keziah," Miss Mamie Simpson,

Recitation—"Brave Atta Wayne," Miss Maggie Clark.

Reading—"Burdock's Music Box," Master Neil Simpson.

Instrumental music—"Swedish Wedding March," Miss Maud Montgomery.

Dialogue—"Rival Orators," N J Lockhart and Chesley Clark.

Recitation—"The Arsenal at Springfield," Master John Laird.

Reading Speech—'Buckwood's Wedding,' Miss Maud Montgomery, Master Garfield Stewart.

Music—'Music Everywhere,' Choir.

Recitation—'Little Christel,' Miss Artie McNeill.

Reading—'If I were a Girl,' Master Archie McNeill.

Recitation—'The Last Hymn,' Miss Clara McKenzie.

Instrumental Music—'Medley,' Miss Maud Montgomery.

Recitation—'Neddie's Thanksgiving Visit,' Master Garfield Stewart.

Dialogue, Society for Suppression of Gossip—'Eight Girls.

Recitation—'How to Lighten Troubles,' Miss Lottie Simpson.

Music—'Life is what we Make it,' Choir.

Reading—'Miss Witchhazel and Mr Thistlepod,' Master Chesley Clark.

Speech—Master Frank McNeill.

Recitation—'Katie's Letter,' Charles McKenzie.

Recitation—'A peck of Troubles,' Miss Edith Spurr.

Recitation—'The best Beauty,' Miss Helen Archibald.

Solo—'The Cows are in the Corn,' Miss Maggie Clark.

Recitation—'The Old Farmer's Legacy,' Miss Annie Stewart.

Reading—'The Magic Lantern,' Master Austin Laird.

Recitation—'The Boy's Complaint,' Fred Clark.

Music—'Social Song,' Two Girls and a Boy.

Recitation—'Over the hills to the Poor House,' Miss Maud Montgomery.

Dialogue—'The Census Taker,' Three [illegible]nd Two Boys.

[illegible]on—'Eddie's Treasures,' Miss [illegible]ird.

[illegible]—'Hiawatha's Departure,' N [illegible]t.

[illegible]nental Music—'Battle of Water-[illegible] Emma Simpson.

[illegible]tion—'The Scholmaster's Guests' [illegible]ontgomery.

[illegible]ion—'Ship on Fire,' School.

[illegible]—'Along the River,' Choir.

[illegible]g Speech,—Miss Mamie Simp-[illegible]

[illegible] bye Song—Choir.

[illegible]oove lengthy and varied pro-[illegible]was rendered with great spirit [illegible]s by the scholars. All, from [illegible]st to the oldest acquitted [illegible] the satisfaction and delight [illegible] At the close, compli-

The summer's flower is to the summer sweet, Though to itself it only live and die.

Hourly joys be still upon you!

Tempest

RAPHAEL TUCK & SONS, LONDON, PARIS

COPYRIGHT

J. C. Spurr, Mr. Walter Simpson and the chairman of the evening, Rev. Wm. P. Archibald. On motion, a vote of thanks to the teacher and scholars, for the excellent entertainment which they had given, was passed unanimously. The unanimous verdict of the audience was that a more enjoyable evening had not been spent for a long time.

Twenty Years Ago.

(Published by request.)

I've wandered to the village, Tom, I've sat beneath the tree,
Upon the schoolhouse playing ground, that sheltered you and me;
But none were left to greet me, Tom, and few were left to know,
Who played with us upon the green, some twenty years ago.

The grass is just as green, Tom; barefooted boys at play
Were sporting just as we did then, with spirits just as gay.
But the "master" sleeps upon the hill, which, coated o'er with snow,
Affording us a sliding-place, some twenty years ago.

The old school house is altered now: the benches are replaced
By new ones, very like the same our penknives once defaced;
But the same old bricks are in the wall, the bell swings to and fro;
It's music just the same, dear Tom, 'twas twenty years ago.

The river's running just as still; the willows on its side
Are larger than they were, Tom; the stream appears less wide;
But the grape-vine swing is ruined now, where once we played the beau,
And swung our sweethearts—pretty girls—just twenty years ago.

The spring that bubbled 'neath the hill, close by the spreading beech,
Is very low—'twas then so high that we could scarcely reach;
And, kneeling down to get a drink, dear Tom, I started so,
To see how sadly I am changed, since twenty years ago.

Near by that spring, upon an elm, you know I cut your name,
Your sweetheart's just beneath it, Tom, and you did mine the same;
Some heartless wretch has peeled the bark' 'twas dying sure, but slow,
Just as she died, whose name you cut, some twenty years ago.

My lids have long been dry, Tom, but tears came to my eyes,
I thought of her I loved so well, those early broken ties;
I visited the old church-yard, and took some flowers to strow
Upon the graves of those we loved, some twenty years ago.

Some are in the church-yard laid, some sleep beneath the sea;
But few are left of our old class, excepting you and me;
And when our time shall come, Tom, and we are called to go,
I hope they'll lay us where we played, just twenty years ago.

—Anonymous.

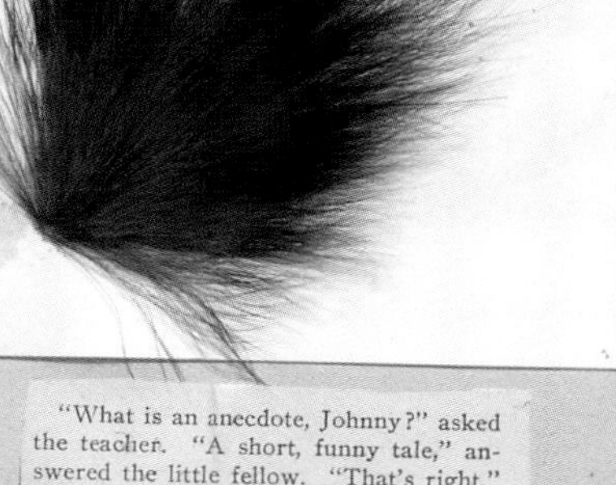

"What is an anecdote, Johnny?" asked the teacher. "A short, funny tale," answered the little fellow. "That's right," said the teacher. "Now, Johnny, you may write a sentence on the blackboard containing the word." Johnny hesitated a moment, and then wrote this: "A rabbit has four legs and one anecdote."—*Exchange.*

Entertainment at Cavendish School.

The pupils of the Cavendish School gave an entertainment consisting of music, vocal and instrumental, dialogues and recitations, on the 22d inst., in the Cavendish Hall. The hall was very tastefully decorated for the occasion with evergreen mottoes such as 'We Delight in Our School,' 'Welcome To All,' 'A Merry Christmas.' The pupils, with their teacher, Miss H. L. Gordon, were all seated on the platform, and all, from the youngest to the eldest, had some part to play in the programme. Miss L. M. Montgomery, a former scholar, rendered valuable assistance. A large and appreciative audience greeted the children, and followed the programme with evident pleasure. The rendering of the programme was carried out with great spirit; all the youthful performers acquitted themselves in a most creditable manner. The teacher deserves much praise for the time and trouble taken by her in preparing the school for this most successful entertainment. Rev W. P. Archibald occupied the chair. At the close a vote of thanks was moved in appropriate terms by the Rev. J. C. Spurr, which being seconded by Mr. Charles Simpson, was carried unanimously. The proceeds of the evening amounted to $15.

PROGRAMME:

Opening Speech.......Master Chesley Clark
Opening Song—Chorus ....
Rec—A Grievous Complaint....Freddie Clark
Rec—Little Kitty.......Miss Lottie Simpson
Rec—Daisy's story..... Miss Katie McNeill
Music—Inst.........Miss Maud Montgomery
Rec—The Independent Farmer. Austin Laird
Rec—Mrs Mary Jane....Miss Lyle Archibald
Rec—Willie's Breeches.....Master Garfield Stuart..........
Reading Brown's Good Boy.........Presco[illegible]
.................................McN[illegible]

Page 18 from the Red Scrapbook

By continuing the school program clipping from 1891, pasting in the Boston Comedy program, and including souvenirs from times with Nora, Maud brought her past and present into direct dialogue. A yellow garter, a cyanotype of a woman in snow, a Victorian coin, and a straw bow all belong to stories Maud and Nora wrote up in their joint diary.

Yellow garter: This story, for a while, dominated the secret diary. For days, Maud accused Nora of having stolen – even eaten! – her yellow garter, which was eventually discovered in their shared bedroom. Later diary entries concentrated on the competitive swiping of souvenirs and the tug-of-war for the attentions of "soulful" James Stewart. Montgomery turned banter into comic chapters here and preserved the garter itself on the card.

Cyanotype: Maud mentioned this image in the joint diary as something of a mystery. She took a photograph of gentlemen in a parlour, she said, and when she developed the plate, she discovered instead Nora standing in the snow.

Coin: Montgomery may have referred to this coin when she wrote in the secret diary that she "crept into the next room and looted a Victoria Regina." This one-cent coin, with Queen Victoria pictured on one side and the words *New Brunswick* on the other, was probably part of the Canadian Confederation coinage issued between 1873 and 1901.

Card: On February 20, Maud and Nora went to a dance at Alec Macneill's that went until five in the morning. While there, she and Nora flirted competitively with James and Joe Stewart.

Straw bow: On the night of January 25, Nora became ill (supposedly having swallowed the yellow garter) and, despite the help of Nora's friends, Drs. Simpson and Honeywell, she was not able to recover Maud's garter and could give her only this straw bow as a substitute for it.

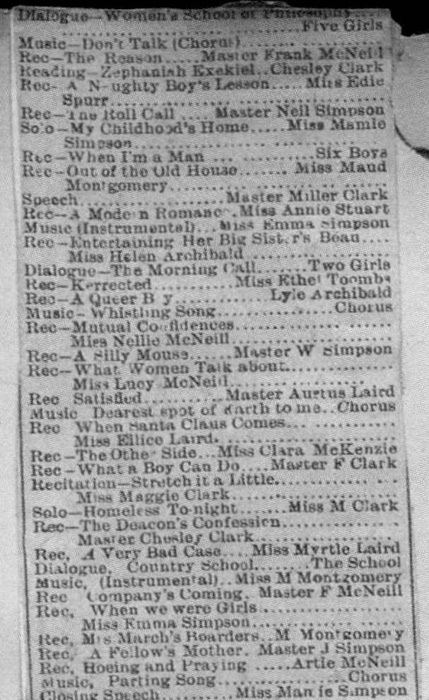

Dialogue—Women's School of Philosophy........ Five Girls
Music—Don't Talk (Chorus)..........
Rec—The Reason......Master Frank McNeill
Reading—Zephaniah Exekiel..Chesley Clark
Rec—A N-ughty Boy's Lesson......Miss Edie Spurr..........
Rec—The Roll Call ....Master Neil Simpson
Solo—My Childhood's Home......Miss Mamie Simpson..........
Rec—When I'm a Man ... .Six Boys
Rec—Out of the Old House.......Miss Maud Montgomery..........
Speech....................Master Miller Clark
Rec—A Modern Romance..Miss Annie Stuart
Music (Instrumental)...Miss Emma Simpson
Rec—Entertaining Her Big Sister's Beau.... Miss Helen Archibald ....
Dialogue—The Morning Call.......Two Girls
Rec—Kerrected............Miss Ethel Toombs
Rec—A Queer Boy..............Lyle Archibald
Music—Whistling Song..............Chorus
Rec—Mutual Confidences.............. Miss Nellie McNeill..........
Rec—A Silly Mouse.......Master W Simpson
Rec—What Women Talk about.............. Miss Lucy McNeill..........
Rec Satisfied...........Master Austus Laird
Music Dearest spot of earth to me..Chorus
Rec When Santa Claus Comes... .... Miss Ellice Laird. ....
Rec—The Other Side...Miss Clara McKenzie
Rec—What a Boy Can Do....Master F Clark
Recitation—Stretch it a Little.............. Miss Maggie Clark..........
Solo—Homeless To-night.......Miss M Clark
Rec—The Deacon's Confession.............. Master Chesley Clark..........
Rec, A Very Bad Case....Miss Myrtle Laird
Dialogue, Country School.......The School
Music, (Instrumental)..Miss M Montgomery
Rec Company's Coming. Master F McNeill
Rec, When we were Girls.............. Miss Emma Simpson..........
Rec, Mrs March's Boarders..M Montgomery
Rec, A Fellow's Mother. Master J Simpson
Rec, Hoeing and Praying .....Artie McNeill
Music, Parting Song..................Chorus
Closing Speech..........Miss Mamie Simpson

1903.
Lost, Stolen, or Strayed.
Chap I. A mysterious disappearance.
Chap II. A disconsolate girl.
Chap III. A long-suffering joke
Chap IV. The Lost is found

Friday. Feb. 20
1903

Last dance, before Lent.

A cosy corner on the stairs.

"The moon is in her last quarter" at five o'clock in the morning.

OPERA HOUSE

TO-NIGHT

Boston Comedy Co.

H. PRICE WEBBER, Manager.

The performance will consist of the great society drama entitled

EAST LYNNE

Or, The Elopement

LADY ISABEL }
MADAME VINE } ....EDWINA GREY
Archibald Carlyle ....George B. Bates
Sir Francis Levison..........................C. F. Whitman
Lord Mount Severn..........................B. F. Loring
Richard Hare..........................H. Andrew McKnight
Mr. Dill..........................W. H. Bedell
Joyce..........................Eula Whitman
Barbara Hare..........................Adelaide Roberts
Miss Cornelia Carlyle..........................H. Price Webber

---

Change of Programme Nightly

MURLEY & GARNHUM, Steam Printers, Charlottetown

PAGES 20–21: Montgomery brought together two Halifax experiences: as a Dalhousie student living at Halifax Ladies' College (1895–96) and as a newspaper woman with *The Daily Echo* (1901–02).

The black-and-white magazine photographs show the exterior and some interior rooms of the Ladies' College. The Halifax Hotel Christmas menu, listing such delicacies as fried smelts, sirloin of Christmas beef, and "calves head à la vinaigrette," was probably a souvenir from a meal with Bertha Clark, who had been the housekeeper at Halifax Ladies' College when Maud was a student and had then become the housekeeper at the Halifax Hotel. Maud visited Bertha when she was homesick and wanted to enjoy a good dinner.

Edith M. Russell, author of "A Century Greeting" as well as the poem "An Easter Lesson," was a fellow worker at the *Echo.* J.M. Baxter may have been the Baxter with whom Maud shared an office at the *Echo.*

The broken leaf has "Dalhousie College 1901" written on it in black ink. Montgomery was sent to cover Dalhousie events while on the newspaper staff.

One newspaper assignment Montgomery related with glee in her journal was the writing up of "Le Bon Marche." When she told the proprietor of the Bon Marché that she had been assigned to review his wares for the *Echo,* he promised her a new walking hat if she gave the store a good write-up. Montgomery thought he was joking, but when her highly favourable review appeared, she was delighted to find he did send along a new hat. The front and back views of a fashionable feathered hat may have been the very one she received from the upscale store.

Montgomery's cyanotype may show Stella Campbell with long-time suitor Life Howatt (who did not marry her). Below Stella in her large flowered hat is a small bouquet from a party in Stanley Bridge in 1896, when Montgomery had finished her year at Dalhousie and was preparing for her second (and unhappy) teaching post, in Belmont, P.E.I.

PAGE 23: The serene black-and-white magazine image of nearby Bay View Mills Farm creates a striking contrast with Montgomery's cyanotype of Cavendish shore. Seated sedately on the rough rocks of the shore, two friends of Maud – Emily Montgomery and Tillie McKenzie – enjoy a picnic. The torn envelope and card reading "Inquire within" are connected to one of Maud and Nora's escapades. Inside the envelope is an invitation to a Valentine's Day party (at John C. Clark's) on February 13, at which the two competed to swipe souvenirs. The napkin is probably part of the spoils and bears the blurred pencilled names of Jack Johnston, Effie Simpson, Nora Lefurgey, and the first names Everett (Laird) and Clemmie (Macneill). The poem "The Fringed Gentian" provided lifelong inspiration for Montgomery's writing.

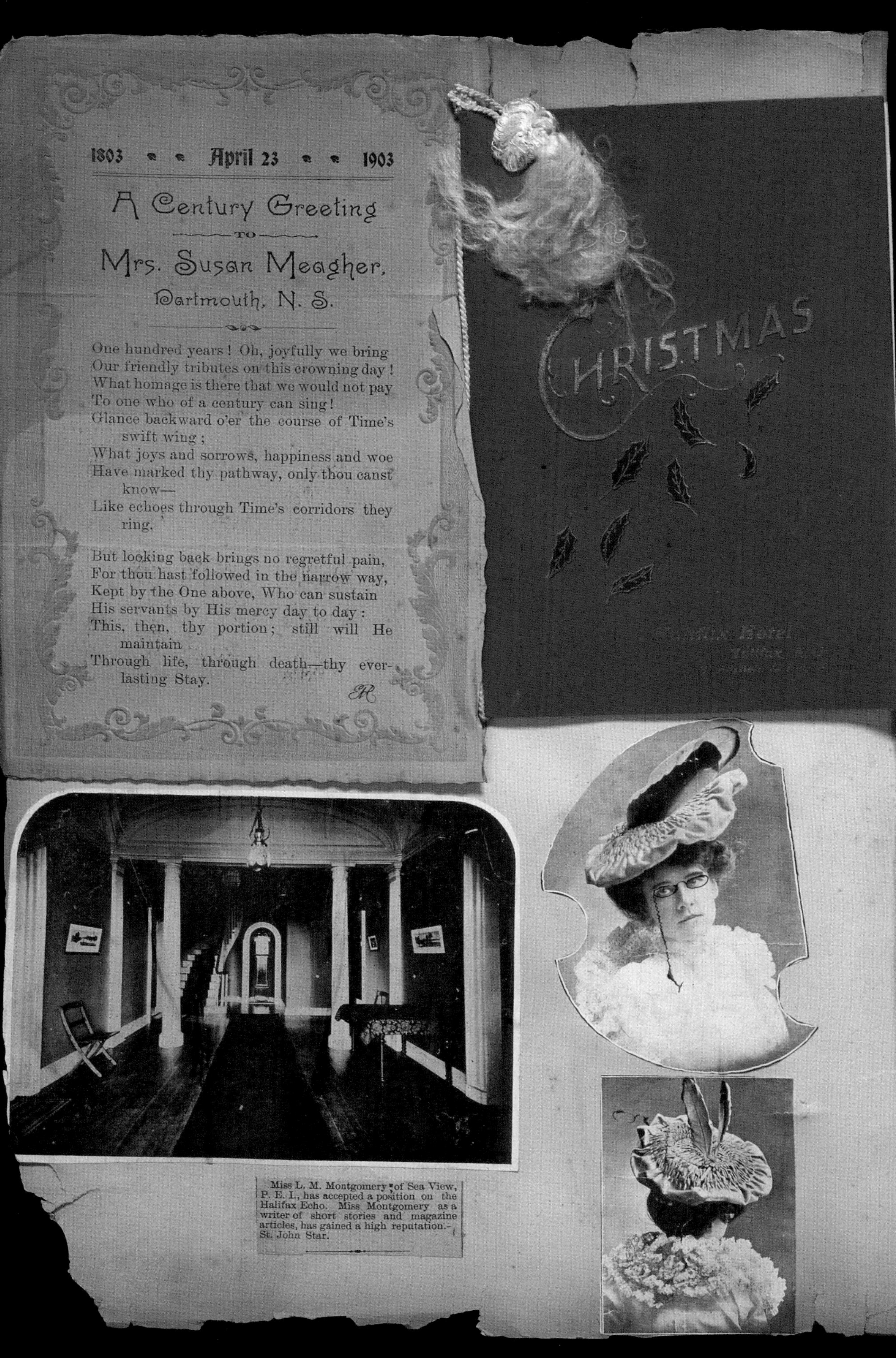

1803 April 23 1903

A Century Greeting

TO

Mrs. Susan Meagher,

Dartmouth, N. S.

One hundred years! Oh, joyfully we bring
Our friendly tributes on this crowning day!
What homage is there that we would not pay
To one who of a century can sing!
Glance backward o'er the course of Time's
swift wing;
What joys and sorrows, happiness and woe
Have marked thy pathway, only thou canst
know—
Like echoes through Time's corridors they
ring.

But looking back brings no regretful pain,
For thou hast followed in the narrow way,
Kept by the One above, Who can sustain
His servants by His mercy day to day:
This, then, thy portion; still will He
maintain
Through life, through death—thy ever-
lasting Stay.

R

Miss L. M. Montgomery, of Sea View, P. E. I., has accepted a position on the Halifax Echo. Miss Montgomery as a writer of short stories and magazine articles, has gained a high reputation.—St. John Star.

Page 20 from the Red Scrapbook

J. M. BAXTER,
Treasurer.

AN EASTER LESSON.

I'm glad that it rained at Easter
  To thwart the women that go
To church with no thought of Eastertide,
  But only their hats to show;
No Christ and his resurrection
  Appeals to them, for they care
For naught but the costly article
  That nestles above the hair.

I'm glad that it rained at Easter,
  I pity the poor tired men,
Who wish to worship with reverence,
  But are oft prevented when
They raise their eyes from their prayer-
        books
  To seek the clergyman's face,
And all they can see is a surging mass
  Of flowers and silks and lace.

I'm glad that it rained at Easter—
  It sounds like an unkind thought,
When all should be bright in memory
  Of Christ, from the dark grave brought;
But until the meaning of Easter
  Comes true to you and me,
The beautiful, holy Eastertide
  Is fraught with idolatry.

E.M.R.

March 31, 1902.

LE BON MARCHE.

Knowing fathers, husbands and brothers will go to the Bon Marche, at the corner of Sackville and Barrington streets, to select Christmas gifts this season for daughters, wives and sisters. Why? Because to any rightly constituted woman no gift is more acceptable than a pretty new hat. And at this establishment all tastes and purses may be suited, for the selections displayed range from the plain walking hats up to the most elaborate of imported confections for smart functions. This year a special effort has been made to prepare a large and varied assortment of trimmed hats, because the large sales of former Christmas seasons has led the proprietor to believe that hats make most useful and desirable Christmas presents. They show two windows filled with charming hats, both home-trimmed and imported. After night, especially, these windows are very attractive, owing to the electric illuminations which show up the millinery to the best advantage. A fine assortment of serviceable and natty "ready-to-wear" hats is a feature of the holiday stock. Neither are the small folks forgotten, for there are some exceedingly dainty bonnets for them, which need only a chubby face beneath them to set them off to the best advantage. One of these should be mother's present for the baby. A large assortment of ribbons and silks for fancy work is also shown, and all the latest novelties in veilings may be found at this enterprising and up-to-date millinery establishment.

RECEPTION ROOM.

"NON-SERVIAM."

O God who reign'st in realms above,
Look down in mercy and in love
Upon Thy children gathered here—
Fill Thou our hearts with holy fear.
The changing skies, the torrent's flow
Proclaim Thy power above, below,
And still resounds, O God Most High,
From ingrate hearts this deathless cry,
        "Non Serviam!"

The mountain tops and pine-clad hills,
The mighty seas and sparkling rills,
Thy temple groves and prairie home,
The brilliant studded azure dome,—
All—all with one accord declare
The Greatness that is everywhere,
And yet, a mortal dare defy
Thy sacred laws by ruthless cry,
        "Non Serviam!"

"Non Serviam!"—and this to Thee,
Thou God of boundless Majesty!
A marvel great 'twould be to us
Did slave address a master thus!
Can we, created by Thy hand,
Ere dare Thy mandate to withstand?
A "Fiat" still my prayer shall be,
And never more I'll say to Thee
        "Non Serviam!"

Halifax   L. C. in Catholic Record.

A Mathmetical Query.

Little six-year-old Harry, while reading a chapter of Genesis, paused and asked his mother if people in those days used to do sums on the ground. He had been reading the passage which says: "And the sons of men multiplied upon the face of the earth."

* * *

THE FRINGED GENTIAN.

Lift up thy dewy, fringed eyes,
  O little Alpiae flower!
The tear that trembling on them lies
  Has sympathetic power
To move my own; for I, too, dream
  With thee of distant heights,
Whose lofty peaks are all agleam
  With rosy, dazzling lights.

Where aspirations, hopes, desires,
  Combining, fondly dwell—
Where burn the nerer-dying fires
  Of genius' wondrous spell.
Such towering summits would I reach,
  Who climb and grope in vain:
O little flower! the secret teach—
  The weary way make plain.

Who dreams of wider spheres revealed
  Up higher, near the sky,
Within the valley's narrow field
  Cannot contented lie;
Who longs for mountain breezes rare,
  Is restless down below—
Like me, for stronger, purer air
  Thou pinest, too, I know.

Then whisper, blossom, in thy sleep,
  How may I upward climb
The Alpine path so hard, so steep,
  That leads to heights snblime?
How may I reach the far-off goal
  Of true and honored fame,
To write upon its shining scroll
  A woman's bumble name?

Page 23 from the Red Scrapbook

Favourite Poems

Many poems saved in these scrapbooks fired Montgomery's imagination, and their themes can be detected in her own works. "The Fringed Gentian" (Red Scrapbook, p. 23) inspired Montgomery's writing from the time she was a child. She discovered the poem, written by Ellen Rodham Church and Augusta DeBubna, in a copy of her grandmother's magazine *Godey's Lady's Book,* dating from the late 1880s. The metaphors of the "alpine path" and the "shining scroll" became parts of Montgomery's story of her career, published in a magazine in 1917, and underlay the three volumes of the autobiographical Emily series. Striving up the "alpine path," Montgomery had published more than eighty short stories and more than 120 poems by Valentine's Day in 1903.

The scrapbook poems, contemporary or popular in her times, were clipped from newspapers and magazines. They deal with tragic, comic, and sentimental romance; inspiration; human foibles (including vanity and gossip); the beauties of nature; heroism; nostalgia for childhood, school days, parents, and older times; good-humoured battles between the sexes; and beloved pets (most notably cats). The tragic valour of the young martyr in "The Polish Boy" (Blue Scrapbook, p. 51) would have wrung a tear from Anne Shirley, and the heroic "Curfew Must Not Ring To-Night" (Blue Scrapbook, p. 57) actually appears in *Anne of Green Gables.* "The Bend of the Road" (Red Scrapbook, p. 25) captured an image Montgomery had probably loved since childhood and which she transformed into Anne's "bend in the road" metaphor for life's surprises.

Montgomery was charmed by Eugene Field's nostalgia and by the light touch of Charles B. Going. In Going's comic poem about a train passenger's moment of love at first sight, "Dorothy: A Disappointment" (Blue Scrapbook, p. 13), Montgomery was likely struck by her own lifetime favourite expression of building "castles in the air." Going used the expression in gentle self-mockery, while Montgomery used it throughout her career, as she did in the 1904 poem "Air Castles" (which serves as an epigraph to this volume), to suggest the rapture and power of daydreaming.

"An Adventure with Wolves": Montgomery included this kind of story, by literary hopeful and penfriend Frank Monroe Beverly, in issues of the Cavendish Literary Society magazine (Red Scrapbook, p. 7).

"A Glimpse of 'Two Homes'": In another clipping, Frede Campbell created a lesson about discipline that suggests some of the insights she achieved in years as a rural schoolteacher. Frede and Maud were each other's great supporters and shared their trials as teachers and as professional women, each struggling on her own "alpine path" (a phrase from Maud's favourite poem, "The Fringed Gentian") to success.

A Glimpse of "Two Homes."

I am a "school marm," and while sitting at my desk or visiting about the district, have gleaned a certain amount of facts. "Ting, ling, ling," goes the school bell, and in troops the coming generation of Fairville. The teacher glances over the group, and smiles with satisfaction when she notices the "Punctual Four" taking their places, with the promptness for which they are noted. The "Punctual Four" consist of two boys and two girls. If you ever visit Fairville school you will quickly recognize them by their blooming faces, well brushed hair, and immaculate collars, boots, and nails. Their clothes are carefully put on, and neatly mended. The teacher has no need to call on them to "Look alive," every half-second. Oh! no; their mother taught them how to do that long ago, for they are the children of Mrs. Joe. Smart—illustrious for her cookery, thrift, tidiness—and sharp temper. About fifteen minutes after roll-call, two other children saunter in. The teacher frowns, and remarks severely, "Late again." They take their places, and create a clatter, searching for slates, pencils, etc. In appearance, they are the direct opposite of the "Punctual Four." The teacher notes that Jackey is out at the elbows, and that Mintas' boots are minus the required number of buttons. Jackey and Mintas' mother (Mrs. Josh Easy) belongs to the class of good-natured but untidy mothers. School is out. The teacher takes a stroll around the village. Mrs. Joe. Smart has been a trifle more ungracious than usual, therefore Joe Sighs, takes his hat from the peg, and calls on Mrs. Josh. Easy. Joe stays thirty minutes, and arrives at the following conclusions: "Josh is in need of 'mending up;' those children are 'sassy' brats. Josh Easy is going behind, and his temper ain't extry; Mrs. Easy may be good-natured, but she's no wife for a workingman. I guess I'll go home and spend the evening with Martha Sharp." When Joe went home he kissed Martha, and Martha said, "I wouldn't be sich an old fool, Joe Sharp," but somehow her voice did not sound as sharp as usual. 'Reader, which home do you prefer?'

F. E. Campbell,
Sea View,
P.E.I.

FRANK MONROE BEVERLY.

AN ADVENTURE WITH WOLVES.

A great change has taken place in this section of the Old Dominion during the last forty years. Back in the 60's the whole face of the country was almost one uninterrupted forest. Here and there little patches were cleared up, and rude log cabins, the homes of the pioneers, usually marked these "clearings." Game was then plentiful, and the inhabitants depended mostly upon wild meat for their use. Bear, deer and other game roamed the forests in great numbers. The wolf and the panther were frequently met with and were often a source of annoyance to the people.

But the situation has now changed. The forests primeval have given way to the broad fields, the days of log cabins have passed by, and neat cottages (and even more substantial buildings) are to be seen scattered over the country: and the big game has gone. But it is not so much of the present time I wish to write. My narrative has to do with the year of '61, and, having said enough by way of preface, I will now proceed.

On last New Year's night—that is to say, the beginning of the year 1900—I was returning home from a visit to friends over in Cumberland Mountain in company with a man of some 60 years of age, with whom I had fallen in on my way. We were afoot and night had overtaken us. It was not very dark; there was a snow on the ground; and so we had no trouble in finding our way. Along the base of the mountain there flows the Pound River. This stream was frozen over. Just about the time we reached the river the snow commenced falling—a driving snow that met us square in the face. We walked across the stream on the ice and when we reached the sho[re] my companion sa "Here I had quite a serious adventu once. When we get home I will relate it, if you care to hear it." Of course I would hear it; but I did not insist on his relating it then, for I was thinking more of the supper I knew my good dame would have awaiting my arrival and the snug warmth of our fireside than of hearing an adventure related. So I waited till we reached home. After supper I reminded him of his promise and he gave me the following narrative:

"On New Year's night, away back in '61—39 years ago and that's a long time—I was on my way home from the 'Mountain.' I then lived with my parents in a log cabin, a hundred yards perhaps from where this house sets. As I said before, I was coming from the 'Mountain'—the river being frozen over as it is to-night. About the time I reached this side of the river I heard some ugly growls proceeding from the laurel brush above me. I thought of running back across the river; but I hesitated for a few moments, trying to decide what was best to do, when I saw three or four dark looking objects bound out into a little opening near the bank of the stream. The vicious growling was kept up almost incessantly and the objects seemed to be coming towards me. I knew that I must do something: my indecision left me and I sprang to a beech tree up which I climbed, not an instant too soon; for, as I swung myself up by the branches of the tree something caught me by the coat-tail, and, had the cloth not given away, I should doubtless have been pulled down. But as it was I made my way up into the upper branches of the tree minus a coat-tail; but I did not consider it a great loss at that time.

"I was then out of reach of these wolves, as I found them to be; but my fears were that they would stay near the tree and watch for me all night. It was cold; pretty much such a night as this. It was only about half a mile from home; but I had my doubts as to my being able to make Father or the boys hear me, should I call to them. However, I would try. But, loud as I could halloo, I could get no response. Then my heart sank within me; for I felt sure that I should freeze before daylight should I have to stay up in the tree all night. I grew almost desperate and made another last desperate effort. This time I heard Father's voice in response. He had become uneasy and started out to see if any trouble had befallen me; for he looked for my return home by night. I called to him again upon his nearer approach and told him that I was treed by a pack of wolves. One of my brothers was with him. They both had guns, they said, and our faithful old dog was along. I told them where I was and they ventured up close enough to see the wolves beneath the tree. After assuring themselves that I was in the tree, they discharged their pieces into the pack. Then the old dog ran up, and began a vigorous barking. There was a wild commotion among the wolves, and I could tell from the noise that one of them was badly wounded. I was also sure that some of them were leaving. Then all became quiet beneath the tree. Father and brother then ventured up and found that one wolf lay dead on the ground, while the others had fled. Tha was the only adventure I ever had wi wolves in these here Virginia mountai but, somehow, I don't yet feel quite in passing that point after nightfall."

Freeling, Va. F. MONROE BEVERL

Page 24 from the Red Scrapbook

PAGES 25–27

Spanning more than ten years, these pages play with several themes: poetic imagery, romances, and the drama of the everyday.

Poetic imagery: "The bend in the road" is one of the most prominent and important metaphoric shapes in Montgomery's life and work. The poem "The Bend of the Road" on page 25 describes the irresistible allure of the unknown future, and the postcard above it and the magazine cut-out at the bottom left offer visual interpretations of the curve. Anne Shirley is stricken dumb by the sunset beauty of the White Way of Delight early in *Anne of Green Gables* when she and Matthew round a bend in a road on their way to Avonlea. By the end of the book, a mature Anne has made a metaphor out of that bend, seeing her life's journey as a road with surprising, enticing bends in it. The last chapter of *Anne* is entitled "The Bend in the Road" and the penultimate sentence of the novel reflects Anne's optimism: "There's always the bend in the road!" The magazine photograph (p. 25, bottom left) is of the Cavendish shore; interestingly, many of Montgomery's photographs were organized around a similar bend or curve: Montgomery's and Anne's beloved Lover's Lane is frequently photographed and described with that provocative bend.

Romances: The greeting card on page 25 and the white cards on pages 26 and 27 all detail more Nora-Maud escapades-turned-into-dramas, breathlessly explained in their secret diary. The mock romantic battles Maud and Nora enjoyed found full and frequent coverage in the scrapbooks while real secrets and heartaches were hidden in the pages or absent altogether. The calling card for Mr. and Mrs. J.D. Sutherland (p. 25) may touch on a real disappointment. Maud had kept Jack Sutherland's photograph in her bedroom in Belmont and his name appeared often, always positively, in the early diaries. The initials "L.D.," written on the bottom of the postcard on page 25 (top left), suggest Bideford suitor Lou Dystant. Maud's cyanotype, on page 26, of the then-new Cavendish Presbyterian Church captures the arched windows and doorway. This church would become an emblem for her romance with the new minister, though it may also have reminded her of the embarrassment and pain she suffered over rejecting the man who eventually became a Baptist minister, Edwin Simpson.

The drama of the everyday: Page 27 of the scrapbook preserves the first part of a long clipping from 1889 (bottom right), assessing prize winners for the *Montreal Witness* newspaper competition, where Montgomery's poem "Cape Leforce" received attention. In 1899 several Cavendish women formed the Sewing Circle to help raise money for the new Presbyterian church. The clipping about the fundraiser was centrally placed on page 26, and the photograph of the new church was glued above, proving success.

A JOB LOT OF JUMBLES.

WHEN one of Nature's lovers poetically wrote in his lady friend's autograph album the lines: "What is rarer than a day in June?" and the ever predatory small brother answered the query in a scrawly hand, "*A Chinaman with Whiskers,*" it would seem that the lad had dished up something that is rareness personified.

* * *

Little Elmer was playing out on the roof, when suddenly he lost his balance and began to slide. "Oh, God," he prayed, "please don't let me——" but his progress was suddenly stopped. "Never mind, God," he continued, "I've caught on a nail."

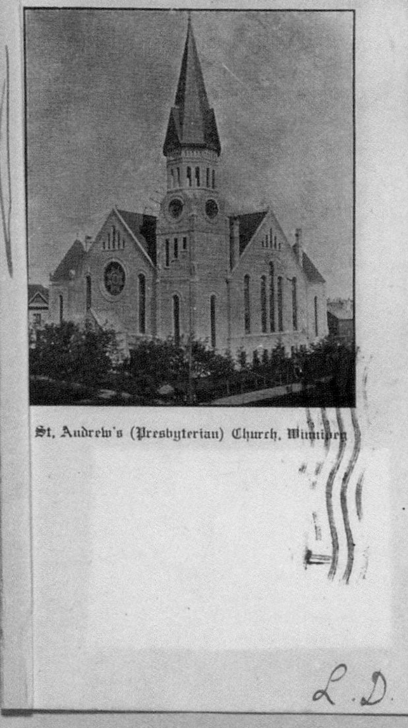

St. Andrew's (Presbyterian) Church, Winnipeg

L. D.

MR M J McLeod of Edmonton, Assistant Provincial Treasurer of Alberta, and a son of the late Norman McLeod, St Avard's has arrived in Charlottetown. On Tuesday, next he will be married, at Bideford, to Miss Daisy Williams, a popular young lady of that place Mr McLeod has been in the West for a number of years and for the past year has been a resident of Edmonton, the seat of government in the province of Alberta. After his marriage on Tuesday next Mr McLeod will return with his bride to the West. Miss Williams, who was formerly on the nursing staff of the Prince Edward Island hospital, is a sister of Mr A E Williams formerly manager of the Bank of New Brunswick and of Mr E Bayfield Williams formerly of this city.

OBITUARY.—The death took place at her home in Cavendish, on Monday, the 19th inst., of Hattie Myrtle, eldest daughter of William Laird, at the early age of twenty-four years. The deceased was a person of quiet and unassuming manner, and by her gentle and lovable disposition endeared herself to all who knew her. During her severe illness which lasted several months she was calm and resigned, and died trusting in the merits of a crucified Redeemer. The funeral service which was conducted by Rev E. Macdonald assisted by Rev A A Smith, of Coldstream, N S, took place on Wednesday, the 21st inst., and was very largely attended. To the bereaved family we extend our sincerest sympathy.

The Bend of the Road

Oh that bend of the road, how it baffles, yet beckons !
What lies there beyond—less or more than heart reckons ?
What ends, what begins, there where sight fails to follow ?
Does the road climb to heaven, or dip to the hollow ?
Oh what glory of greenness, what lights interlacing,
What softness of shadow, what bounty of spacing,
What refreshment of change—aye, what beauty Elysian
The sweep of that curve may deny to the vision !
Oh my soul yearns for sight ! Oh my feet long to follow,
Swift-winged with sweet hope as with wings of a swallow !
Though lonely the way, void of song, void of laughter,
—I must go to the end—I must know what comes after !

GRACE DENIO LICHFIELD, in the *Century*.

TINY SLIPPERS

(ON SEEING A PAIR OF EGYPTIAN SANDALS TWO THOUSAND YEARS OLD)

By Sir Edwin Arnold

TINY slippers of gold and green,
Tied with a moldering golden cord!
What pretty feet they must have been
When Cæsar Augustus was Egypt's lord!
Somebody graceful and fair you were!
Not many girls could dance in these:
Who was the shoemaker made you, dear,
Such a nice pair of Egyptian "threes?"

Where were you measured? In Saïs, or On,
Memphis, or Thebes, or Pelusium?
Fitting them featly your brown toes upon,
Lacing them deftly with finger and thumb,
I seem to see you—so long ago!
Twenty centuries, less or more,
And here are your sandals; but nobody knows
What face, or fortune, or name you bore.

Mr & Mrs J. D. Sutherland

"Where the coast alternates between bold cliffs and long reaches of sand dunes."

Men may rise on stepping-stones
Of their dead selves
to higher things.
In Mem.
JULY.
Sun 6 13 20 27
Mon 7 14 21 28
Tue 1 8 15 22 29
Wed 2 9 16 23 30
Thu 3 10 17 24 31
Fri 4 11 18 25
Sat 5 12 19 26
AUGUST.
Sun 3 10 17 24 31
Mon 4 11 18 25
Tue 5 12 19 26
Wed 6 13 20 27
Thu 7 14 21 28
Fri 1 8 15 22 29
Sat 2 9 16 23 30

Entertainment

....IN THE....

Town Hall, Prince Albert,

....ON....

Tuesday, October 3rd, 1899,

UNDER THE AUSPICES OF

Prince Albert Public School.

Miss Marietta La Dell, B.E.,

ASSISTED BY

REV. J. H. LAMBERT

and Leading Local Talent.

SOCIAL AT CAVENDISH.—A very pleasant social and entertainment was he d in the Presbyterian Church, Cavendish, on Monday evening, in honor of Rev. George Laird, who is at present on a visit to his native place after an absence in the North West of over twenty years. After a good programme had been rendered tea was served by the ladies. The tables were set in the class rooms and a couple of hours were pleasantly spent in social chat and amusement. Following is the programme:

Chorus, "Send out the Sunlight"—Choir.
Address by Chairman—Rev. M. H. McIntosh.
Solo—Rev. George Laird.
Recitation—Miss Ethel McKenzie.
Recitation—Miss Myrtle McNeil.
Solo—Mrs. Roger Simpson.
Recitation—Miss Bertha Hillman.
Speech—Rev. George Laird.
Recitation—Miss Nora Lefurgey.
Solo—Mr. E. J. McKenzie.
Recitation—Miss Elice Laird.
Recitation—Miss L. M. Montgomery.
Solo—Rev. George Laird.
Address—George Simpson, M. L. A.
Recitation—Miss Charlotte Simpscn.
Recitation—Miss Hazel McKenzie.
Recitation—Master Ernest Simp:on.
Music, "The Beautiful City"—Chon.

Monday, Jan 12.
1903.

"When minister meets minister there comes the tug of war".

"Love in the abstract".

"Sour apples – ecent aspece".
"no wonder they are sour; you know where she keeps them".

Three on the platform:- The "disciple" is horrified.
He's going to pray [illegible] with his father

THE entertainment held in the Cavendish hall on Tuesday evening, the 25th inst., under the management of the members of the Sewing Circle, was a grand success, notwithstanding the unfavorable weather and roads. Rev. M. H. McIntosh occupied the chair, and in a few well chosen remarks, given with his usual eloquence and humor, opened the meeting, and the following program was creditably rendered:

Instrumental Duet—Miss Eveline McLeod and Mr. McClure.
Reading—Selected, Mr. Neil Simpson.
Solo—"Just Break the News to Mother," Miss Ethel Hopgood.
Recitation—"Little Christel," Miss Myrtle McNeill.
Quartette—Dr. and Miss Houston and Mr. and Miss Stevenson.
Recitation—"The Organ Builder," Miss Katie McNeill.
Solo—"I Want My Presents Back," Mr. R. Stevenson.
Reading—"Selected" Mr. John F. McNeill.
Duet—Mr. and Miss McKenzie.
Recitation—"Selected" Mr. McCoubrey.
Solo—"Just to say Good Bye," Miss Janetta McLeod.
Dialogue—"Why we never married," seven maids and seven bacholars.
Solo—"Selected" Mr. R. Stevenson.
Recitation—"The Maiden's Sacrifice," Mr. A. E. McKenzie.
Recitation—"The sermon," Miss Eveline McLeod.
Instrumental Duet—Miss Eveline McLeod and Mr. McLure.
Recitation—"Sleepy," Miss Myrtle McNeill.
God Save The Queen.

At the close of the program the ladies of the "Sewing Circle" presented an autograph quilt, to be sold by auction. Mr. John Stewart was then called on and he did justice to the occasion. Mr. James Stewart was the purchaser at the sum of eight dollars. The "Autograph Quilt" contained some two hundred and fifty names from whom a contribution of eighty dollars was received. The proceeds go to the New Presbyterian Church building fund. After the close of the meeting, a supper was given at the home of Mr. and Mrs. John F. McNeill by the Ladies of the Sewing Circle to their friends and visitors who contributed to this entertainment. The party numbered in all about sixty guests.

I. O. F. at New Glasgow.

The claim made by the members of the Independent Order of Foresters that their Society is a social as well as a fraternal organization was fully proved at New Glasgow, on Thursday evening, 11th inst. The At Home given in the Hall by the members of Court Nonpariel was the most enjoyable affair ever held there.

The committee at first decided to sell only fifty tickets, but seventy-five had to be sold, or there would have been charges of partiality. Promptly at 7 30 p. m. the High Chief Ranger of Prince Edward Island, Dr. H. W. Robertson was introduced as the Chairman of the evening, and after delivering a neat and practical address, he stated that the first item on the program would be the public installation of the officers of Court Nonpariel. The important ceremony took place at once, High Secretary L. U. Fowler acting as Marshal. The following are the officers installed:—

Chief Ranger, Artemas Moffatt.
Vice Chief Ranger, Eddie Stevenson.
Rec. Sec'y., J. C. Houston, M. D.
Fin. Sec'y., B. B. Stevenson.
Treas., A. E. Douglas, M. D.,
Orator, James E. Moffatt.
Organist, R. W. Stevenson.
Sr. W., Nelson Orr.
Jr. W., Allan Moffatt.
Sr. Beadle, James Houston.
Jr. Beadle, Frank Andrew.
Past Chief Ranger, Jas. Bullman.
Court Deputy, Geo. Houston.
Physicians, Drs. Houston and Douglas

The balance of the program consisted of vocal and instrumental music, recitations, speeches and readings. Special mention should be made of the solo sung by Miss McLeod of Hunter River; the duett by R. W. Stevenson and his little niece; the recitation by J. Gordon McKay, Miss Montgomery, Miss Stevenson, and Rogers Fowler.

The supper had been arranged in the upper hall by the ladies and if Foresters anywhere are proud of their mothers, wives, sisters and daughters, the members of Court Nonpariel certainly should be, for the High Chief Ranger who is admitted to be a judge of such things, publicly stated that it was the best spread he had ever sat down to. That there was abundance

Page 26 from the Red Scrapbook

goes without saying seven large baskets were sent the next day to the poor of an adjoining settlement.

The tables in the supper room were not sufficiently large to accomodate at once the 150 couples, but while part were enjoying themselves up stairs, some in the lower hall were having a social chat, others explaining Forestry, while others listened to instrumental music given by Messrs. John Marks, Mott. Harding and P. H. Gallant. It is said that there was a dance and some officers of the high court took part, but for this your correspondent cannot vouch as he left the hall at eleven o'clock. H ping that every "at home" the Foresters have at New Glasgow will have the same success.

THE concert and basket social held in New Glasgow Hall last night was a decided success. Mr. Wm. Laird very ably performed the duties of chairman. The programme was excellent throughout. The recitations given by Miss Montgomery of Cavendish and Miss Ella Bagnall, also the duetts by Miss A. E. Harris and C. McDonald, of Ch'town are worthy of special mention, their renditions proving most pleasing to the audience who evidently appreciat a good thing. Mr. W. D. McCoubrey auctioned the baskets with his wonted ability. The prices obtained averaging 50c each. The proceeds amounted to $32, which sum will go towards the public library. While the entertainment and social were all that could be desired, the pleasure of the audience was considerably marred by four or five uncouth youths from a neighboring locality who evidently consider themselves smart as long as they conduct themselves in the most unmanly manner possible. As those youths are well known and have been repeatedly annoying meetings held by the people of Glasgow, they had better take warning in time, otherwise they will be prosecuted to the full extent of the law. A word to the wise is sufficient.

A correspondent writes: "Having occasion to travel many sections of the Island at different times, I notice some great improvements particularly in the buildings and cemeteries, etc. I see some very fine churches and schoolhouses, but one thing noticeable is the care and pains taken in fixing up some of the cemeteries. Worthy of note is the one at Belfast Church, Vernon River Chapel and some smaller ones of other denominations—not forgetting to make special mention of Cavendish which is tastefully arranged and a credit to the people. But moving a little further what is found. A large, well-finished church with a cemetery in a most disgraceful condition. No doubt there are some very fine monuments but what of that, when it's a very forest; in some places you have to turn up the branches to find the graves. Truly it's a disgrace to find this place made a dumping-ground for stones and sticks of all sorts, where old Scotch settlers who worked early and late to clear and till the soil, are lying in their graves forgotten to a certain extent. Why not appoint a man to clean up and look after this place? If they don't want to pay for it let each one clean of his or her own plot. Where is the clergy man in charge of this parish; can't he make a move in this matter? They want a Doyle or a Sinclair among them. I hope the next time I have to pass through this section there will be a change for the better."

CONVENT

—OF THE—

Faithful Companions of Jesus,

PRINCE ALBERT.

Distribution of Prizes

PRESIDED BY

His Honor Joseph Royal, Lieut.-Governor.

WEDNESDAY JUNE 17TH, 1891.

ANNUAL FORESTER BANQUET

—

Of Court Nonpareil at New Glasgow Thursday

—

OFFICERS ARE INSTALLED

—

Eloquent Speeches Delivered and a Pleasant Evening Spent by all Present,

—

The annual banquet giv n by the Foresters of Court Nonpar ll at New Glasgow on Thursday night 15th was an event of more than ordinary note. After the cere... [illegible] ...on of officers for the

Foresters and invited guests repa red to he dining hall where under the Forestic lecorated room gleamed crystal in nagnificent array and intermingled the necessaries to satisfy the most fastidious. At the head of the hall hung a majestic Union Jack and nicely worked were the letters I. O. F. To the left hung the beautiful charter of the Court and to the lower right hung an elaborate picture of Supreme Chief, Dr. Oronhyateka. After ample justice had been done at the table the following toasts were drunk in pure cold water:

The King.—The National Anthem.

Dr. Oronhyateka.—He's a Jolly Good Fellow.

Song.—Bro. R. W. Stevenson.

Forestry.—Responded to by Bro. L. U. Fowler.

Reading—Miss Lefurgey.

Canada—Bro. D. C. Lawlor.

Professions—Bro. W. Simpson, Bro. Dr. Douglas.

Reading—Miss May Macleod.

Island Industries—C. A. Stevenson William Moffatt.

Quartette—R. W. Stevenson, Laura Houston, Miss Reed, Mrs. W. W. Smith.

Sister Societies—Bro. Morley Seller, L. Clark, William Laird.

Recitation—Bro. C. E. Mackenzie.

Ladies—R. E. Bagnall and others.

Solo—E. E. Mackay.

Court Nonpariel—Bro. George Houston D. H. C. R.

Every address and number was fittingly neat and appropriate.

We must particularize the reading by Miss Lefurgey whose inimitable style and diction is a drawing card wherever her services are secured.

We could but note the pleasure stamped on all countenances during the evening and as all rose to sing God Save the King. They dispersed feeling repaid amply for their attendance.—COM

January 18. 1903.

"One shall be taken and the other left."

"He cometh not," she said.

She who will not go when she can, cannot when she would.

A sleigh at the door is worth two across the road.

Blessed are those who expect nothing for they shall not be disappointed

A Humane Pater.—One reads so frequently of the paternal boot as applied to the undesirable youthful suitor that it is a pleasure to chronicle the more humane method adopted by a wealthy Glasgow merchant for choking off a "follower" of his daughter. The girl was very young, so was the follower, but nevertheless he called formally on the object of his affections. The merchant and his wife entered the room, the latter bearing a glass of milk and a huge slice of bread spread with butter and jam.

"Now, dear, run away to bed," said the kindly mother to her daughter: "it's time that all good girls should be in bed."

Then the Glasgow merchant addressed the astonished young man.—

"Now, youngster, you drink that glass of milk, and take that slice of bread and jam to eat on the road home—and hurry, for your mother must be anxious about your being out so late by yourself."

The young man did not call again.

DOMINION PRIZE COMPETITION.

REPORT ON THE PRINCE EDWARD ISLAND STORIES.

JUDGE ALLEY'S CRITICISM—A NUMBER OF GOOD STORIES—THE PROVINCE PRIZE GOES TO PRINCE COUNTY.

Prince Edward Island is the banner province in respect to the number of stories sent for the *Witness* Dominion Prize Competition in comparison with the population. The number sent from this Island was seventy-two, which is one for every 621 of population. This is a remarkable showing and one we are very proud of. The report by Judge Alley is a very interesting

JUDGE ALLEY'S REPORT.

CHARLOTTETOWN, P.E.I.,
11TH MAY, 1889.

Messrs. John Dougall & Son,

DEAR SIRS,—I beg to return to you the papers—72 in number—written by competitors from this Province for the Dominion Prize Competitions, and to send you the following report regarding them:

QUEEN'S COUNTY.—The number of stories forwarded to me from competitors in this county, according to the endorsement on the wrapper enclosing them was 27, and the number from the city of Charlottetown was five. I found, however, that one of those enclosed in the parcel for Queen's County was from Prince street school, Charlottetown, thereby reducing the number from Queen's County to 26, and increasing that from Charlottetown to six.

The best essay, in my opinion, from Queen's county is from Uigg School, No. 14, and is marked by me Q. A. It is an authentic story, told in a racy and readable way, and though its subject may in one sense be said to be a local incident, it exemplifies a principle which is world wide and universal. Next in the order of merit among the contributions of this county may be ranked three stories, which I have marked Q. B., Q. C. and Q. D. respectively. The first is a well written narrative of an interesting historical incident in the county, and the second is a legend graphically told of a tragedy said to have occurred about the time of the establishment of British rule in the island or... spot which has perpetuated the memory of ... of the principal actors in the occurrence by ... riving from him its name. The third is a sto... of a destructive fire which swept over an exte... sive district in the county some fifty years ag... I would recommend the first two for publica... tion, and the last might also be published, bu... will require some revision in punctuation a... construction of its sentences before it appears ... the press. The story I have marked Q. E. is ... tragedy told in a tragic as well as in a turgi... style, and I am rather disposed to be sceptic... as to its authenticity. If true, the ex... perience of the writer was a remarka... one, and the story is worthy of rep... duction. The stories marked Q. F. and ... which relate ... [illegible]

Page 27 from the Red Scrapbook

Cyanotypes: Gesturing again to the"Bend of the Road" poem and image on page 25, Montgomery pasted on page 29 (bottom right) her photograph of the curve in the Macneill lane that led up to the side of the house where her "dear den" window was. At the top of the page, she pasted a photograph featuring the south-facing window (top right) she used to look out while she wrote.

Magazine photographs: Rounding out the drama she has created, over several pages, from common threads a total of fourteen years apart, are two hopeful images. The "Just Out" caption for the chicks seems a joyful commentary on the black-and-white magazine image of the woman emerging from the photographic paper. With the clipping about Ewan (top left), the prominence of the church in her activities, the bend in the road, and her own gable window (in the room she loved but knew she would be forced to leave when Grandmother Macneill died) surrounding this image, did Montgomery mean to suggest a possible transformation in her life?

Memorabilia: Montgomery placed a sentimental poem "Light Enough," which Lem McLeod gave her, immediately above a piece of paper bearing the date March 4, 1893, that commemorated a wild sleigh ride with Lem after an evening with Clara Campbell at Amanda Macneill's house. On this same page with Lem McLeod memorabilia, Maud pasted the Cavendish note (which she may have written; top left) announcing Ewan Macdonald's September 1903 ordination and installation. With these pieces she placed "At Grandmother's," which nostalgically describes a house, now empty, that had formerly been filled with life. Was Montgomery already, in constructing these pages, linking Ewan with her future years when her grandmother would die and her gable room would be empty – imagining a "bend in the road" she would have to face? In the secret-diary entry for June 21, 1903, Maud made it clear that she was impressed with Ewan Macdonald: "This morning we had a Highlander to preach for us and he was 'chust lofely' and all the girls got struck on him. My heart pitty-patted so that I could hardly play the hymns."

NOTES FROM CAVEND.SH AND VICINITY

The Presbyterian Church, Cavendish, was the scene of a large and interesting gathering on Tuesday, the 1st inst., on the occasion of the ordinati n and induction of Ewen McDonald as the minister of the congregation.

The church was filled to the doors with members of the congregation from different sections of the country. The ladies had the building beautifully decorated with cut flowers and potted p ants. After an able and appropriate sarmon from Rev. Edwin Smith, the moderator Rev. A. D. McDonald in a solemn service ordained Mr McDonald to the office of the holy ministry and formally induc ed him into the pastoral charge of the congregation. The new minister was then ad dressed by Rev Mr McLean on the duties of his office, while Rev. Mr Spencer reminded the congregation of their obligations to their pastor. Mr McDonald was then introduced to the members of the congregation, and received a most hearty welcome. The new pastor is commencing his work under favorable conditions among a people noted for loyalty to their church and pastor and from them he re ceived a most hearty and unanimous call. The PATRIOT wishes Mr. McDonald a pleasant and successful ministry in his first charge. Lieutenant D Stewart is spending a short vacation in Cavenoish and Bay View. Mr. and Mrs. James Williams of Fountain Mills were visiting friends in Bay View this week. J J McLeod, of Riverdale was attending the Presbytery meeting in Cavendish on Tuesday representing the Bonshaw and Hampton congregation. This congregation are calling Rev A D McDonald, of Montrose Mr and Mrs George Green, of St John are visiting in Bay View the guests of Mrs (Hon) George Simpson. Considerable harvest is cut in Bay View and Cavendish and promises to be a good crop. At present cutting is delayed by damp weather. Frank Andrew is discharging coal from his schooner at Bay View wharf. Charles Taylor, Esq., Malpeque, paid a flying visit to Bay View and Cavendish on Tuesday and attended the ordination service in the Presbyt rian Church.

The rose looks fair,
but fairer we it deem
For that sweet odour
which doth live
in it.
Sonnet
It is the mind
that makes the body rich.
Taming of the Shrew.
COPYRIGHT

SUN LIFE ASSURANCE COMPANY OF CANADA.

Head Office: MONTREAL.

Represented by

E. M. Russell
for Dartmouth

AT GRANDMOTHER'S.

Under the shade of the poplars still,
Lilacs and locusts and clumps between,
Roses over the window sill,
Is the dear old house with its door of green.

Never were seen such spotless floors,
Never such shining rows or tin,
While the rose-leaf odors that came thro' the doors,
Told of the peaceful life within.

Here is the room where the children slept,
Grandmamma's children, tired with play,
And the famous drawer where the cakes were kept,
Shrewsbury cookies and caraway.

The garden walks where the children ran,
Through the flowers and learn their names,
The children thought, since the world began,
Were never such garden walks for games.

There were tulips and asters in regular lines,
Sweet-Williams and marigolds on their stalks,
Bachelor's buttons and sweet pea vines,
And box that bordered the narrow walks.

Pure white lilies stood corner wise
From sunflowers yellow and poppies red
And the summer pinks looked up in surprise
At the kingly hollyhocks overhead.

Morning glories and larkspur stood
Close to the neighborly daffodil;
Cabbage roses and southernwood
Roamed thro' the beds at their own sweet will.

Many a year has passed since then,
Grandmama's house is empty and still
Grandmama's babies have grown to men
And the roses grow wild o'er the window sill.

Never again shall the children meet
Under the poplars gray and tall,
Never again shall the careless feet
Dance thro' the rose-leaf scented hall.

Grandmama's welcome is heard no more
And the children are scattered far and wide,
And the world is a larger place than of yore
But hallowed memories still abide.

And the children are better men to-day
For the cakes and rose-leaves and garden walks,
And grandmother's welcome so far away
And the old sweet Williams on their stalks.
—*Arthur Wentworth Eaton, in the Youth's Companion.*

LIGHT ENOUGH.

What need of light? By far too bright
  The fire your dark eyes show.
Mine must reveal the love I feel.
  So let the lamp burn low.

Leave me the dark! Too fair a mark
  For Cupid's cruel bow
And archer art is my fond heart.
  So let the light burn low.

For, if my love should hopeless prove,
  Then must I learn to know
Darkness alone till life be flown.
  So let the light burn low.

And—if you say the word I pray—
  That one sweet word would show
My fate to me so bright to see,
  'Twere best the lamp be low.
    —J. L. Heaton in "The Quilting Bee

JUST OUT
By W. E. Vilmer

Mar. 4th. 1893

Little Dot: "I know something my teacher doesn't know." Mamma: "Indeed! What is it?" "I know when the world is coming to an end, and she doesn't. I asked her, and she said she didn't know." "O, well, who told you?" "Uncle John. He said the world would come to an end when children stopped asking questions that nobody could answer."—*Exchange.*

Page 29 from the Red Scrapbook

Using her photographs to anchor the pages and their stories, Montgomery placed old and new items together, sometimes suggesting ironic parallels.

PAGE 32: Two cyanotypes depict the interior and exterior of the old Cavendish Presbyterian Church, which was torn down in 1899. L.M. Montgomery was buried in this church's graveyard in 1942. Montgomery's picture of Lover's Lane was affixed to a 1902 June calendar but the date written on it was September 16, 1902. No journal entry explains this date. Montgomery had become friends with Nora Lefurgey in the summer and fall of 1902 and she had also, in August 1902, deepened her friendship with first cousin Frede Campbell. The cartoon "A Swell Affair" (placed humorously next to a joke about royalty, or "swells") likely had real resonance for Maud, who frequently suffered from ulcerated teeth. As so often happened in Montgomery's creative arranging of clippings, a funeral and a wedding were placed next to each other.

PAGE 33: In keeping with the other entertainment pieces on this page, the full moon scene is a trick photograph. During the processing, Montgomery pasted the moon into the daytime photograph that also appears on page 48 of this scrapbook. The 1894 *College Record,* from Montgomery's year at Prince of Wales College, published her comic piece "Extracts from the Diary of a Second Class Mouse," recalling, among other episodes, the March 8, 1894, peanut party where students gleefully hurled at each other four pounds of peanuts during Professor Harcourt's class. She placed beside this remembered hilarity an **article** praising actress Sadie Calhoun in a production she saw in Charlottetown. The magazine picture of a bride was pasted in to cover the spot where something had been removed.

PAGE 34: Photographs of the old Baptist church and Amanda Macneill's house in Cavendish suggest related stories. Amanda was one of Maud's childhood best friends; the May 13, 1890, picnic, commemorated by the white card at the top of the page, included Amanda, Maud, schoolteacher Hattie Gordon, and others from school, and probably inspired the Golden Picnic in *Anne of Avonlea*. As though reliving schoolgirl fun from more than a decade earlier, Maud described on the May 1903 calendar an outing with Nora Lefurgey that happened to take place at the Baptist church. The mock romance involved Maud (L.M.M.), Robert A. MacKenzie, Nora Lefurgey, and Henry S. McLure, whose sister's death is the one noted on page 32. The Kamloops Bridge image, probably from Montgomery's 1930 visit out west, replaced an earlier item but may also have been a deliberate marker for revisited schoolgirl fun she enjoyed with Laura Pritchard Agnew. Perhaps including "The Literary Maid of All Work" was Montgomery's way of laughing at how she had come to see her weaving of tales after her life as a newspaper woman.

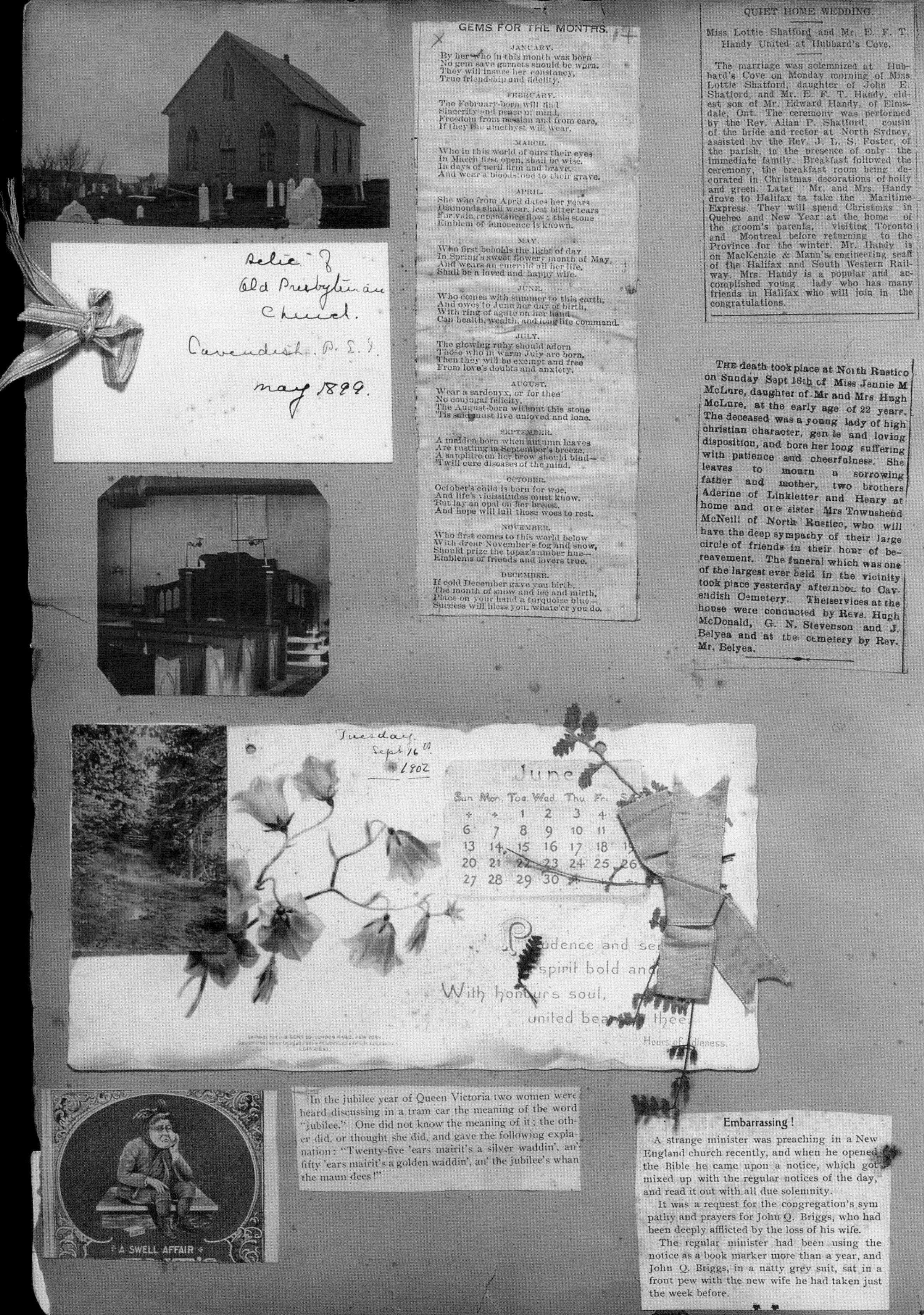

GEMS FOR THE MONTHS.

JANUARY.

By her who in this month was born
No gem save garnets should be worn.
They will insure her constancy,
True friendship and fidelity.

FEBRUARY.

The February-born will find
Sincerity and peace of mind,
Freedom from passion and from care,
If they the amethyst will wear.

MARCH.

Who in this world of ours their eyes
In March first open, shall be wise.
In days of peril firm and brave,
And wear a bloodstone to their grave.

APRIL.

She who from April dates her years
Diamonds shall wear, lest bitter tears
For vain repentance flow; this stone
Emblem of innocence is known.

MAY.

Who first beholds the light of day
In Spring's sweet flowery month of May,
And wears an emerald all her life,
Shall be a loved and happy wife.

JUNE.

Who comes with summer to this earth,
And owes to June her day of birth,
With ring of agate on her hand
Can health, wealth, and long life command.

JULY.

The glowing ruby should adorn
Those who in warm July are born.
Then they will be exempt and free
From love's doubts and anxiety.

AUGUST.

Wear a sardonyx, or for thee
No conjugal felicity.
The August-born without this stone
'Tis said must live unloved and lone.

SEPTEMBER.

A maiden born when autumn leaves
Are rustling in September's breeze,
A sapphire on her brow should bind—
'Twill cure diseases of the mind.

OCTOBER.

October's child is born for woe,
And life's vicissitudes must know.
But lay an opal on her breast,
And hope will lull those woes to rest.

NOVEMBER.

Who first comes to this world below
With drear November's fog and snow,
Should prize the topaz's amber hue—
Emblems of friends and lovers true.

DECEMBER.

If cold December gave you birth,
The month of snow and ice and mirth,
Place on your hand a turquoise blue—
Success will bless you, whate'er you do.

QUIET HOME WEDDING.

Miss Lottie Shatford and Mr. E. F. T. Handy United at Hubbard's Cove.

The marriage was solemnized at Hubbard's Cove on Monday morning of Miss Lottie Shatford, daughter of John E. Shatford, and Mr. E. F. T. Handy, eldest son of Mr. Edward Handy, of Elmsdale, Ont. The ceremony was performed by the Rev. Allan P. Shatford, cousin of the bride and rector at North Sydney, assisted by the Rev. J. L. S. Foster, of the parish, in the presence of only the immediate family. Breakfast followed the ceremony, the breakfast room being decorated in Christmas decorations of holly and green. Later Mr. and Mrs. Handy drove to Halifax ta take the Maritime Express. They will spend Christmas in Quebec and New Year at the home of the groom's parents, visiting Toronto and Montreal before returning to the Province for the winter. Mr. Handy is on MacKenzie & Mann's engineering seaff of the Halifax and South Western Railway. Mrs. Handy is a popular and accomplished young lady who has many friends in Halifax who will join in the congratulations.

THE death took place at North Rustico on Sunday Sept 16th of Miss Jennie M McLure, daughter of Mr and Mrs Hugh McLure, at the early age of 22 years. The deceased was a young lady of high christian character, gentle and loving disposition, and bore her long suffering with patience and cheerfulness. She leaves to mourn a sorrowing father and mother, two brothers Aderine of Linkletter and Henry at home and one sister Mrs Townshend McNeill of North Rustico, who will have the deep sympathy of their large circle of friends in their hour of bereavement. The funeral which was one of the largest ever held in the vicinity took place yesterday afternoon to Cavendish Cemetery. The services at the house were conducted by Revs. Hugh McDonald, G. N. Stevenson and J. Belyea and at the cemetery by Rev. Mr. Belyea.

In the jubilee year of Queen Victoria two women were heard discussing in a tram car the meaning of the word "jubilee." One did not know the meaning of it; the other did, or thought she did, and gave the following explanation: "Twenty-five 'ears mairit's a silver waddin', an' fifty 'ears mairit's a golden waddin', an' the jubilee's whan the maun dees!"

Embarrassing!

A strange minister was preaching in a New England church recently, and when he opened the Bible he came upon a notice, which got mixed up with the regular notices of the day, and read it out with all due solemnity.

It was a request for the congregation's sympathy and prayers for John Q. Briggs, who had been deeply afflicted by the loss of his wife.

The regular minister had been using the notice as a book marker more than a year, and John Q. Briggs, in a natty grey suit, sat in a front pew with the new wife he had taken just the week before.

Page 32 from the Red Scrapbook

Miss L. M. Montgomery

The College Record

Vol. I. Charlottetown, April, 1894. No. 3.

... House ... recognized favorite, Sadie C... appeared before a Charlottetown audience in which, it was easy to perceive, there were many of her admirers. The house was crowded and Miss Calhoun and her company of players should feel flattered by the attention and applause bestowed upon them—even if the same was richly marited as happened to be the case. In the dramatization of Mary J. Holmes' well-known novel "Lena Rivers" Miss Calhoun in the title role did some very effective work. She really is worthy of more than the usual application of complimentary terms handed out on occasions of this sort, for her talent is manifest to the senses, and her charm is more than ordinary. Her delineation of the part excited the liveliest sympathy and admiration and her success was testified by generous applause. Miss Calhoun received a handsome boquet as a tribute to her skill. The other members in the cast acted well their parts presenting the play in a manner that was well balanced—no one part detracting from the high quality marking the whole performance. It will be good news to theatre-goers to know that "Lena Rivers" is to be repeated on Friday night, the closing night of Miss Calhoun's engagement here. To-night the play will be "Miss Calvert of Louisiana." The Knickerbocker Quartette between the first and second acts sang some selections in good taste and their music was harmonious and pleasing.

Monday's Child is fair of face.
Tuesday's Child is full of grace.
Wednesday's Child has far to go.
Thursday's Child is full of woe.
Friday's Child is loving and giving.
Saturday's Child must work for her living.
But the Child who is born on the Sabbath Day
Is witty and wise and gentle and gay.

Mixed Up.—At a trial in a German court a man appeared as a witness. "Your name?" asked the judge.

"Vell, I calls myself Fritz, but may be I don't know if it is Henrich. You see, Judge, dat mine moder she haf two poys; one of them was me and one mine proder, and toder was myself; ...n't know which, and my moder, she ...t know, too; and one of us was named ...z, and toder Henrich, or one Henrich ... toder Fritz. I don't know which it ... and one of us got died, and my ...r she could never tell which it was, ...r mine broder, who got died. So you ...Mr. Judge, I don't know whether I ...ritz or Henrich, and my... ...poy."

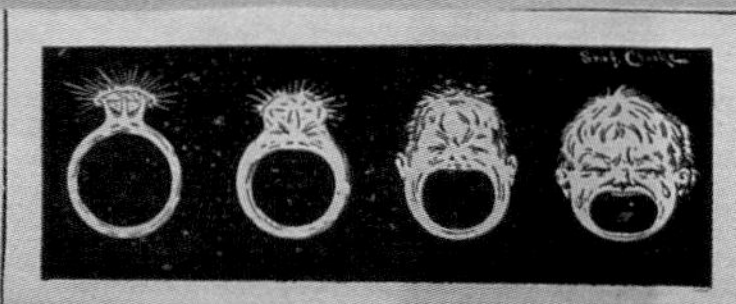

EVOLUTION OF THE ENGAGEMENT RING:

MARRIED

HOUSTON-FRASER—A... the Manse, Cavendish, April 1... the Rev. John Stirling, ... Houston and Ann... both of Mayfield.

Page 33 from the Red Scrapbook

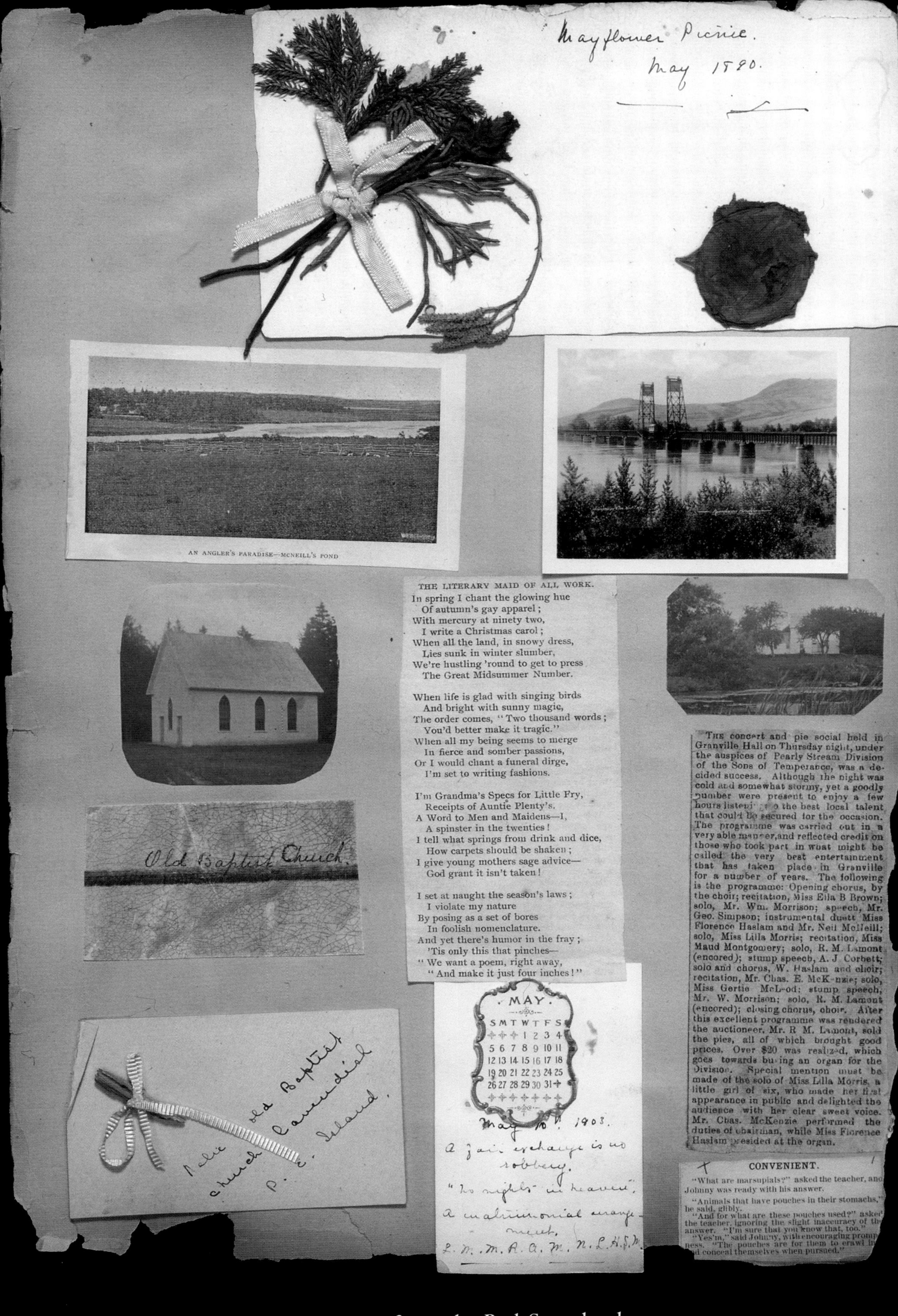

Mayflower Picnic.
May 1880.
AN ANGLER'S PARADISE—MCNEILL'S POND
Old Baptist Church.
Relic old Baptist church Cavendish P. E. Island.
MAY.
S M T W T F S
1 2 3 4
5 6 7 8 9 10 11
12 13 14 15 16 17 18
19 20 21 22 23 24 25
26 27 28 29 30 31
May 10th 1903.
A fair exchange is no robbery.
"No nights" in heaven.
A matrimonial arrangement.
L. M. M. A. A. M. N. L. H. S. M.

THE LITERARY MAID OF ALL WORK.

In spring I chant the glowing hue
  Of autumn's gay apparel;
With mercury at ninety two,
  I write a Christmas carol;
When all the land, in snowy dress,
  Lies sunk in winter slumber,
We're hustling 'round to get to press
  The Great Midsummer Number.

When life is glad with singing birds
  And bright with sunny magic,
The order comes, "Two thousand words;
  You'd better make it tragic."
When all my being seems to merge
  In fierce and somber passions,
Or I would chant a funeral dirge,
  I'm set to writing fashions.

I'm Grandma's Specs for Little Fry,
  Receipts of Auntie Plenty's.
A Word to Men and Maidens—I,
  A spinster in the twenties!
I tell what springs from drink and dice,
  How carpets should be shaken;
I give young mothers sage advice—
  God grant it isn't taken!

I set at naught the season's laws;
  I violate my nature
By posing as a set of bores
  In foolish nomenclature.
And yet there's humor in the fray;
  'Tis only this that pinches—
"We want a poem, right away,
  "And make it just four inches!"

THE concert and pie social held in Granville Hall on Thursday night, under the auspices of Pearly Stream Division of the Sons of Temperance, was a decided success. Although the night was cold and somewhat stormy, yet a goodly number were present to enjoy a few hours listening to the best local talent that could be secured for the occasion. The programme was carried out in a very able manner, and reflected credit on those who took part in what might be called the very best entertainment that has taken place in Granville for a number of years. The following is the programme: Opening chorus, by the choir; recitation, Miss Ella B Brown; solo, Mr. Wm. Morrison; speech, Mr. Geo. Simpson; instrumental duett Miss Florence Haslam and Mr. Neil McNeill; solo, Miss Lilla Morris; recitation, Miss Maud Montgomery; solo, R. M. Lamont (encored); stump speech, A. J Corbett; solo and chorus, W. Haslam and choir; recitation, Mr. Chas. E. McKenzie; solo, Miss Gertie McLeod; stump speech, Mr. W. Morrison; solo, R. M. Lamont (encored); closing chorus, choir. After this excellent programme was rendered the auctioneer, Mr. R M. Lamont, sold the pies, all of which brought good prices. Over $20 was realized, which goes towards buying an organ for the Division. Special mention must be made of the solo of Miss Lilla Morris, a little girl of six, who made her first appearance in public and delighted the audience with her clear sweet voice. Mr. Chas. McKenzie performed the duties of chairman, while Miss Florence Haslam presided at the organ.

CONVENIENT.

"What are marsupials?" asked the teacher, and Johnny was ready with his answer.

"Animals that have pouches in their stomachs," he said, glibly.

"And for what are these pouches used?" asked the teacher, ignoring the slight inaccuracy of the answer. "I'm sure that you know that, too."

"Yes'm," said Johnny, with encouraging promptness. "The pouches are for them to crawl in and conceal themselves when pursued."

Page 34 from the Red Scrapbook

This tribute to cats is largely drawn from magazine illustrations by Henriette Ronner-Knip (see also Blue Scrapbook, p. 22). Inside the card is Maud's cyanotype of her cousin Tottie (Annie) Macneill holding the cherished Bobs. Montgomery took this photograph of the Macneill farmyard from her grandmother's kitchen door: Is that Bobs at centre bottom? Bobs, originally called Coco, was renamed for Field Marshall Lord Roberts of Kandahar, British leader and hero in the Boer War, affectionately known as "Bobs." The "soulful" (noted on the white card) was Maud and Nora's secret-diary nickname for James Alexander Stewart. Nora had asked a riddle about why James was like Bobs, and this card (perhaps the whole page) represents Maud's mock indignant reply.

Cats

Montgomery was passionate about cats. Topsy's fur from 1887 and Maud's father's wedding invitation are the oldest dated souvenirs in the Blue and Red Scrapbooks. Other cat names, and fur, are preserved on other pages: Favourites include Carissima, Firefly, Max, Toms, Bobs, Laddie, Daffy I, and Daffy II. She had pictures of cats hanging on the wall of her Cavendish bedroom and later, in Ontario, she adopted an ink drawing of a black cat as part of her signature (see epigraph, p. iii). Ewan Macdonald shared her affection for cats, and Montgomery's two sons grew up loving them. Dozens of photographs of Montgomery's children and playmates include cats. She also took portraits of the cats alone. Her next to last published novel, *Jane of Lantern Hill* (1937), was dedicated to the memory of her beloved grey striped cat, Lucky – "the charming affectionate comrade of fourteen years."

Montgomery was never without at least one cat when she had a home of her own, arranging for Daffy (it's not clear from the journals if this was Daffy III) to be sent by crate to Ontario once she was settled there after her marriage in 1911. Frede Campbell shared her love for cats, as did Scottish pen pal George Boyd MacMillan. It is a puzzle that cats play so small a part in young Anne's life – though Marilla's probable disapproval of them would have been a direct reflection of Grandmother Macneill's notion that cats were barn animals, not indoor pets. In old age even Grandmother Macneill grew fond of the grey tabby, Daffy, and was comforted by him. Perhaps cats appear prominently in Anne's adult life because Grandmother Macneill was no longer alive to read the stories. Montgomery gave to Emily Byrd Starr her fascinated devotion to cats.

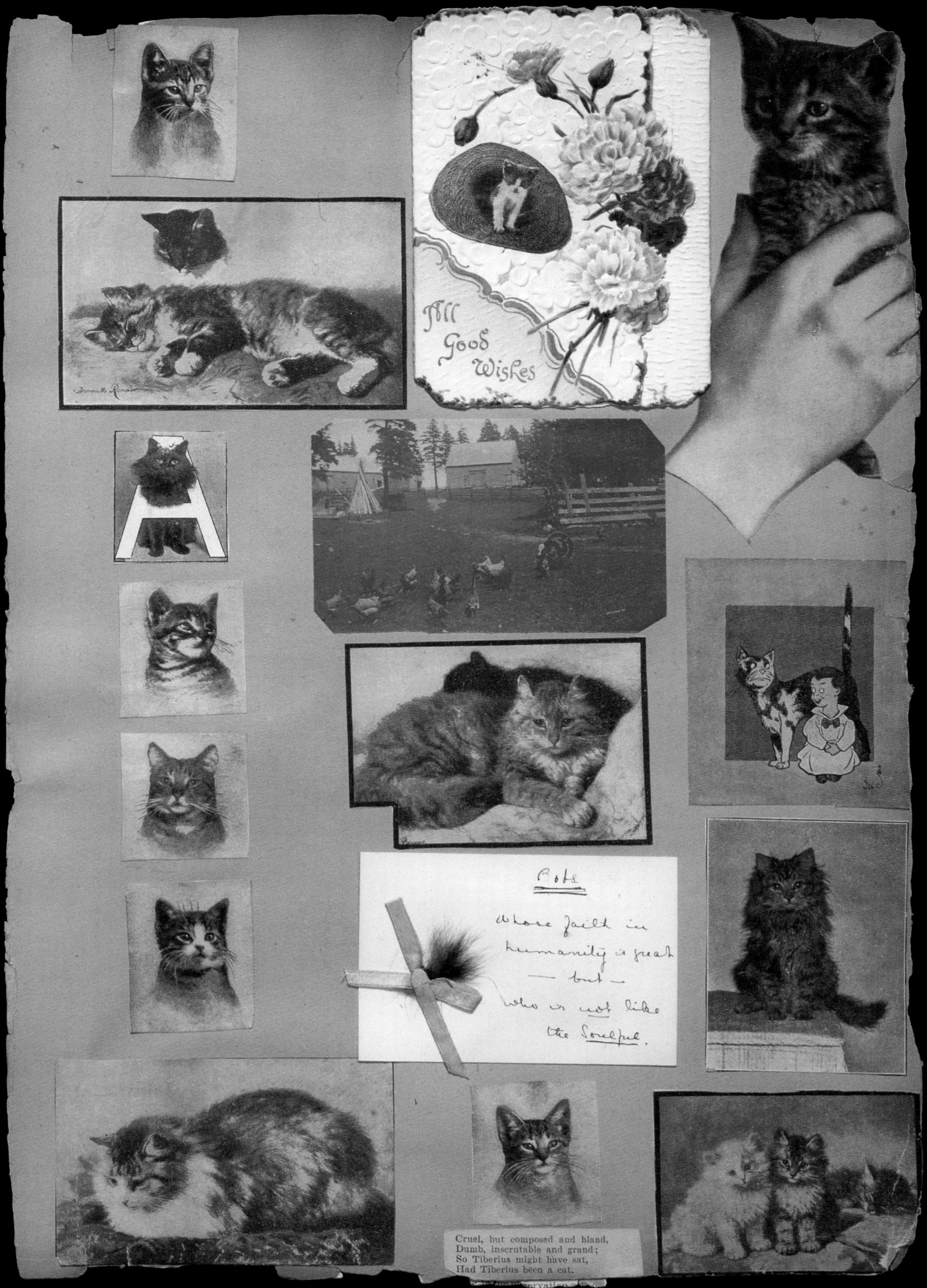

Page 35 from the Red Scrapbook

These pages tell stories – with other people's pictures as well as Montgomery's own – of favourite things.

PAGE 36: Montgomery pasted a notice of the birth of Laura Pritchard Agnew's son among a host of baby pictures. Many of Montgomery's schoolmates were marrying and having children. Is there special significance, given Rev. Ewan Macdonald's growing importance in her private life, of the increase in the number of ecclesiastical jokes that appear together with the familiar teaching ones? "When the Cows Come Home" may have been a piece she and Laura shared.

PAGE 37: Laura Pritchard Agnew's younger sister Evelyn married in 1903 (her wedding invitation is inside the envelope). More than seven years later, on July 5, 1911, Maud would have the same hymn played at Evelyn's wedding, "The Voice That Breathed O'er Eden," at her own wedding in the Campbell parlour in Park Corner. Pictured holly is paired with artificial holly, perhaps a souvenir Laura sent from her sister's wedding. The torn card may be from the old pack Maud and Nora refer to in their secret diary of 1903. The suggested harmony of "My Symphony" seems a kind of benediction on Evelyn's wedding despite the intervening cards.

PAGE 38: Montgomery glued her cyanotype of her adored Lover's Lane onto an old calendar. "A Woman's Last Word" is a joke about the pride of two estranged lovers; Anne Shirley's snubs of Gilbert are almost this pointed. One item in the play advertisement stands out. Under "Specialty Stars" one finds "The Girl with the Dog with the Auburn Hair." Was Montgomery reminded of how she had tormented red-headed Austin Laird in school days by her writing of the poem "The Boy with the Auburn Hair"? She and Austin refused to speak to each other for some time afterward. The picture of the sheep ranch may have triggered another memory: On September 4, 1893, according to her journal entry, Maud dreamt that an Australian girl had written to ask her to send "'one of those delightful little auburn *sheep.*' I think Austin must have been haunting my pillow." Reversing the situation, Montgomery had Anne Shirley crack her slate over Gilbert Blythe's head when he teased her about her red hair with "Carrots! Carrots!" in *Anne of Green Gables.*

Born.

AGNEW—On July 9th, 1902, the wife of A. Agnew, of a son.

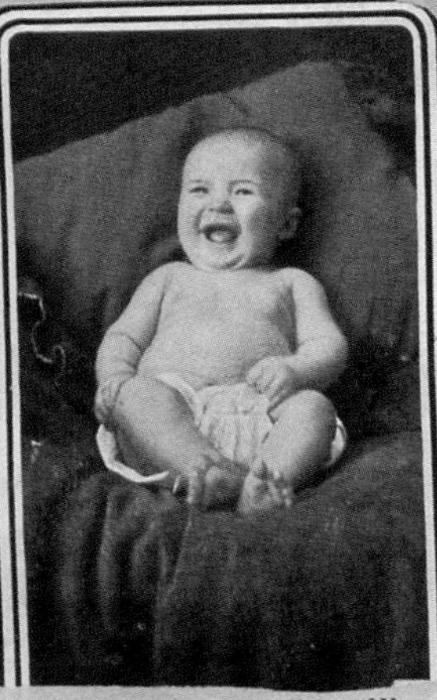

WHEN THE COWS COME HOME.

(Edith Hunter, St. Etienne De Beauharnois, very kindly sends the words of "When the cows come home' by Mrs. Agnes E. Mitchell, which was asked for by 'Prairie' in a recent issue of the 'Witness.')

With klingle, klangle, klingle,
Way down the dusty dingle,
The cows are coming home.
Now sweet and clear, and faint and low,
The airy tinklings come and go.
Like chimings from the far off tower,
Or patterings of an April shower
That makes the daisies grow;
Koling, koling, kolinglelingle,
Far down the darkening dingle,
The cows come slowly home.
And old-time friends, and twilight plays,
And starry nights, and sunny days,
Come trooping up the misty ways,
When the cows come home.

With jingle, jangle, jingle,
Soft tones that sweetly mingle,
The cows are coming home:
Malvine and Pearl, and Florimel,
DeKamp, Red Rose and Gretchen Schell,
Queen Bess and Sylph and Spangled Sue,
Across the fields I hear her 'loo-oo'
And clang her silver bell:
Goling, goling, golinglelingle,
With faint far sounds that mingle,
The cows come slowly home.
And mother songs of long-gone years,
And baby joys and childish fears,
And youthful hopes and youthful tears,
When the cows come home.

With ringle, rangle, ringle,
By twos and threes and single,
The cows are coming home,
Through violet air we see the town,
And the summer sun a-slipping down,
And the maple in the hazel glade
Throws down the path a longer shade
And the hills are growing brown
To-ring, to-rang toringleringle,
By threes and fours and single,
The cows come slowly home.
The same sweet sound of wordless psalm,
The same sweet June day rest and calm.
The same sweet scent of buds and balm,
When the cows come home.

With tinkle, tankle, tinkle,
Through ferns and periwinkle
The cows are coming home,
A-loitering in the checkered stream
Where the sun rays glance and gleam;
Clarine, Peachbloom and Phoebe, Phyllis,
Stand knee-deep in the creamy lilies,
In a drowsy dream;
To-link, to-lank, to-linklelinkle,
O'er banks with buttercups a-twinkle,
The cows come slowly home.
And up through memory's deep ravine
Come the brook's old song and its old-time sheen,
And the crescent of the silver queen,
When the cows come home.

With klingle, klangle, klingle,
With loo-oo, moo-oo, and jingle,
The cows are coming home,
And over there on Merlin Hill,
Sounds the plaintive cry of the whippoor-will
And the dew-drops lie on the tangled vines,
And over the poplars Venus shines,
And over the silent mill.
Ko-ling, ko-lang, kolinglelingle,
With a ting-a-ling and jingle,
When the cows come come slowly home.
Let down the bars; let in the train
Of long gone songs and flowers and rain,
For dear old times come back again,
When the cows come home,

Mrs. F. Bennett. Mrs. Garvock. H.C.,

One Thing Troubling Him

AN old Scotch fisherman was visited during his last illness by a clergyman, who wore a close-fitting clerical waistcoat, which buttoned behind. The clergyman asked the old man if his mind was perfectly at ease. "Oo, ay, I'm a' richt; but there's just ae thing that troubles me, and I dinna like to speak o't." "I am anxious to comfort you,' replied the clergyman. "Tell me what perplexes you." "Weel, sir, it's just like this," said the old man, eagerly. "I canna for the life o' me mak' oot hoo ye manage tae get intae that westkit." —*N. Y. Observer.*

Schoolmaster (turning round sharply): "Which of you is it that is daring to make faces at me?" Six Youngsters (in chorus): "Freddy Brown, sir." Schoolmaster: "Ah! Then you six boys stand up and be caned. If you saw Freddy Brown making faces, it shows that you were not attending to your lessons."

Page 36 from the Red Scrapbook

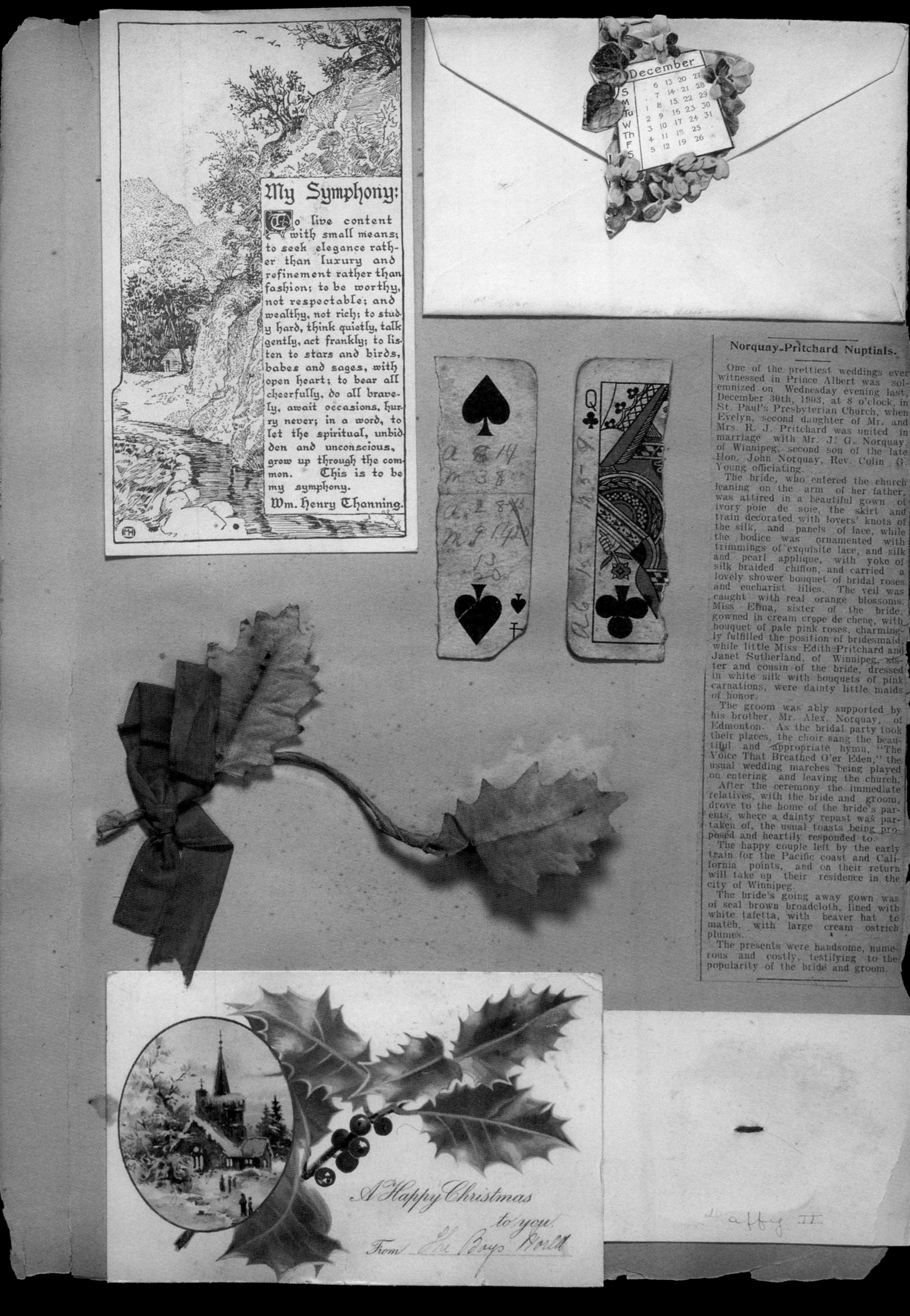

My Symphony:
To live content with small means; to seek elegance rather than luxury and refinement rather than fashion; to be worthy, not respectable; and wealthy, not rich; to study hard, think quietly, talk gently, act frankly; to listen to stars and birds, babes and sages, with open heart; to bear all cheerfully, do all bravely, await occasions, hurry never; in a word, to let the spiritual, unbidden and unconscious, grow up through the common. This is to be my symphony.
Wm. Henry Channing.
December
A Happy Christmas
to you.
From

Norquay-Pritchard Nuptials.

One of the prettiest weddings ever witnessed in Prince Albert was solemnized on Wednesday evening last, December 30th, 1903, at 8 o'clock, in St. Paul's Presbyterian Church, when Evelyn, second daughter of Mr. and Mrs. R. J. Pritchard was united in marriage with Mr. J. G. Norquay, of Winnipeg, second son of the late Hon. John Norquay, Rev. Colin G. Young officiating.

The bride, who entered the church leaning on the arm of her father, was attired in a beautiful gown of ivory poie de soie, the skirt and train decorated with lovers' knots of the silk, and panels of lace, while the bodice was ornamented with trimmings of exquisite lace, and silk and pearl applique, with yoke of silk braided chiffon, and carried a lovely shower bouquet of bridal roses and eucharist lilies. The veil was caught with real orange blossoms. Miss Ethna, sister of the bride, gowned in cream crepe de chene, with bouquet of pale pink roses, charmingly fulfilled the position of bridesmaid, while little Miss Edith Pritchard and Janet Sutherland, of Winnipeg, sister and cousin of the bride, dressed in white silk with bouquets of pink carnations, were dainty little maids of honor.

The groom was ably supported by his brother, Mr. Alex. Norquay, of Edmonton. As the bridal party took their places, the choir sang the beautiful and appropriate hymn, "The Voice That Breathed O'er Eden," the usual wedding marches being played on entering and leaving the church.

After the ceremony the immediate relatives, with the bride and groom, drove to the home of the bride's parents, where a dainty repast was partaken of, the usual toasts being proposed and heartily responded to.

The happy couple left by the early train for the Pacific coast and California points, and on their return will take up their residence in the city of Winnipeg.

The bride's going away gown was of seal brown broadcloth, lined with white tafetta, with beaver hat to match, with large cream ostrich plumes.

The presents were handsome, numerous and costly, testifying to the popularity of the bride and groom.

Page 37 from the Red Scrapbook

OPERA HOUSE

Four nights commencing Monday, September 24th

The Nineteenth Edition of CHARLES H. YALE'S Forever and Ever

DEVIL'S AUCTION

Re-written, re-arranged and staged under the personal direction of

CHAS. H. YALE

and produced with new scenery by John W. Wilkins and T. A. Manning

Costumes and Armour by Van Horn & Son, and Armour from designs of McIlvaine. Wig by A. M. Buch & Co. Shoes by Bertrand & Co. Tights by Nolan & Co. Mechanical Effects, A. J. Overpeck and Stephen MacNeill. Properties, William Ullrich. Light Effects, William P. Currans.

CAST

MORTALS

Carlos, a poor shepherd........Miss Beatrice Clements
Toby, a donkey, afterwards transformed into a man........R. T. Brown
Pere Andoche, an old Flemish Farmer........W. H. Lorella
Count Fortuno, created by Mephisto's art to resemble a mortal ....Miss Madge Torrence
Going Gone, an auctioneer........James A. Franks
Tresbem, a bailiff........George Cole
Madeline, Andoche's daughter........Miss Florence Clements
Janet, a milkmaid........Miss Annie Lloyd
Peasants, Villagers, etc.

MONGOLIANS

Kow Wow Chang, Grand Mandarin........W. H. Lorella
See Shing, his astrologer........Henri Earle
Hoang Kan, his doctor........Thomas Saelyr
Moon Show, Soothsayer........Wm. Speurl
Koket........Miss Julia Lake
Oriental attendants of the Mandarin

IMMORTALS

Crystalline, the fairy protectress........Miss Alice Stoddard

INFERNALS

Mephisto, the evil one........Henry P. Thomas
Chaos, an imp of darkness........Ben Leando
Witches, Gnomes, Goblins, Skeletons and Demons

PRINCIPAL DANCERS

Amelia Maveroffer........Premier Absolute
Hilda Maccari........Premier Characteristic

SPECIALTY STARS

Richard T. Brown........Comedian and Mimic
Annie Lloyd........The Vital Spark
The Three Brothers Leando........Comedy Acrobats
Irene and Zaza........The Girl with the Dog with the Auburn Hair
Sisters Clements........Descriptive Duetists

AND

THE SIDONIA TROUPE........of Eight English Singers and Dancers
Direction Alfred and Madame Phasey

Overture—Forever and Ever Devil's Auction........Perle
Leon M. Polachek and Orchestra

SYNOPSIS OF SCENERY, INCIDENTS, BALLETS AND FEATURES

ACT I.—Scene 1.—The Caverns of Gloom (new). Revolving Transformation to Andoche Valley (new).

THE SISTERS CLEMENTS, in their Singing and Dancing Specialties

First time of the new Comic Divertisement, arranged by Madame Phasey, entitled

LES DANSE GROTESQUE, introducing Entire Corps de Ballet and Principal Dancers, AMELIA MAVEROFFER and HILDA MACCARI, Grand Finale and Comic Tableau

ACT II.—Scene 1.—Flemish Landscape. MISS ANNIE LLOYD, THE VITAL SPARK, in Unique Specialties. Scene 2.—The New and Comical Trick Scene CASTLE INSOMNIA. Mechanical change to Scene 3. THE GARDENS OF THE MANIKINS. Brilliant Mongolian Ballet arranged by Madame Phasey.

THE FEAST OF THE DRAGON, introducing the Corps de Ballet and European Premieres, AMELIA MAVEROFFER and HILDA MACCARI

THE THREE BROTHERS LEANDO, Comedy Acrobats

RICHARD T. BROWN, Comedian and Mimic

The Laughable Manikin Scene—Imposing Tableau

ACT III.—Scene 1.—The New Electric Sensation. THE DANCE OF THE ELEMENTS, interpreted by Amelia Maveroffer and Hilda Maccari

THE MUSICAL DOLLS, Misses Wasserman, Lake, Young, Stoddard, Munn Sisters, Maccari and Troy. Scene 2.—The Palace of Flora. THE FAMOUS SIDONIA TROUPE, the English Singing and Dancing Octette Direction of Alfred and Madame Phasey

IRENE and ZAZA, the Girl with the Dog with the Auburn Hair

Scene 3.—The Realms of Despair. Scene 4.—A new magnificent transformation scene, entitled "The Flight of Time," concluding with the magnificent missen scene, "The Palace of Hours."

CANADIAN PACIFIC

Low rate Excursions to

MONTREAL

Rate for round trip from CHARLOTTETOWN $13.30. Tickets good going September 27th, 28th, 29th and October 1st, good to return until October 16th, 1900.

Ask for tickets via St. John and the C. P. R. Short Line. [C]lose connections to and from Prince Edward Island.

Sweet is it to have done the thing one ought.
The Princess
SEPTEMBER
Sun 7 14 21 28
Mon 1 8 15 22 29
Tue 2 9 16 23 30
Wed 3 10 17 24
Thu 4 11 18 25
Fri 5 12 19 26
Sat 6 13 20 27
OCTOBER
Sun 5 12 19 26
Mon 6 13 20 27
Tue 7 14 21 28
Wed 1 8 15 22 29
Thu 2 9 16 23 30
Fri 3 10 17 24 31
Sat 4 11 18 25
RAPHAEL TUCK & SONS LTD LONDON

SHEEP RANCH IN CALIFORNIA

By Nellie E. Stiffler

A WOMAN'S LAST WORD.

If the two young people of whom *Answers* tells this story were not reconciled by their own absurdity, they at least furnished amusement for others.

They had been engaged, but had quarreled, and were too proud to make up. Both were anxious to have people believe that they had entirely forgotten each other.

He called at her home one day to see her father—on business, of course. She answered the doorbell.

Said he: "Ah, Miss Jepkin, I believe. Is your father in?"

"No, sir," she replied, "father is not in at present. Do you wish to see him personally?"

"I do," he answered, feeling that she was yielding, "on very particular personal business," and he turned proudly to go away.

"I beg your pardon," she cried after him, as he reached the lowest step, "but who shall I say called?"

Poring over boxes of souvenirs and clippings, just as she pored over pages of notes and snippets of recorded dialogues and descriptions before she began writing her novels, Montgomery chose items for these pages from as early as 1889 and as late as 1906. Spots of paper-covered glue and partially covered ragged edges suggest she could have been altering stories or raiding the scrapbook for illustrations for her handwritten journals.

PAGE 39: The *Prince Edward Island Magazine* photograph of Simpson's Mill (a landmark in Montgomery's day; top left), a piece of poetry from the same magazine by her esteemed PWC Professor Caven, and Montgomery's cyanotype of Cape Leforce (a much earlier magazine photograph of this same place appears on page 48 of the Red Scrapbook) all demonstrate a love of home that breathes in every page of Montgomery's Anne series. The Lieutenant-Governor's calling card may belong to the fall of 1910 when she was invited to meet the Governor General of Canada, Earl Grey, because he loved *Anne of Green Gables.*

PAGE 40: The words *Lovers' Lane* in the poem's title (top left), like the title of the poem that appeared on page 25 of the Red Scrapbook – "The Bend of the Road" – is of immediate interest to fans of *Anne of Green Gables.* The reference to the four seasons – a fall leaf, the mention of "Winter in Lovers' Lane" and of spring and summer in "The Daisies' Song" (the metaphoric evergreens from pen pal Ephraim Weber's piece belong to all seasons) – might suggest that the place Lover's Lane was the theme for this page. Yet it may be lovers themselves who unite the items. In preserving Herman Leard's brother's wedding announcement beside the Clinton Scollard poem surely Montgomery was thinking of the late Herman. Handsome, married Edwin Smith, who appeared in Cavendish in 1901 and in 1903 gave the sermon at his friend Ewan Macdonald's induction service, would show up again prominently in the Macdonalds' Ontario life. Marks on this page suggest Montgomery used a cut-out of a fashion model to replace someone's picture.

PAGE 42: In the summer of 1904, Montgomery was reading her old journal of 1894 to assess how much she had changed. The 1894 Prince of Wales *College Record* published Montgomery's comic playlet "The Usual Way," in which Millicent and Rose convince themselves they are studying hard while actually eating chocolates, watching passersby, and gossiping. Montgomery preserved a concert program (featuring musical pieces and a two-act drama) held on the tenth anniversary of her PWC graduation. Point Pleasant Park, where Montgomery liked to walk when she lived in Halifax, featured in *Anne of the Island* (1915) as the spot where Anne went for walks during her college years at "Redmond" in "Kingsport." Perhaps the comic mule barometer referred ironically to her personal progress in ten years.

...n photo by A. W. Mitchell — SIMPSON'S MILLS, BAY VIEW — *See article on Cavendish in this number*

THE LOST ALPHABET.

('Daily Mail,' London.)

The Board of Education insists that scholars in the first and second year's course in higher elementary schools shall spend at least four hours per week in the study of science, half of which time must be devoted to practical work. The ages of these scholars will vary between ten and twelve. Half of them are girls. Touching this a Halifax correspondent, who signs himself 'W. D.,' sends us the following:—

Seated one day at my lessons,
  I was wearily trying to cram
A problem in hydrostatics—
  Something about a gramme.
I know not if I was dreaming,
  I fancy I wanted my tea;
But I heard a melodious murmur
  Like the sound of A, B, C.

It flooded the dreary class-room
  Like an echo from long ago,
It filled my soul with yearnings
  And my eyes with H_2O.
I couldn't think where I had heard it,
  My memory seemed to halt;
It brought back the days when children
  Called sodium chloride 'salt.'
It made me forget for a moment
  The smells and formulae,
And it trembled away into silence
  With a sound I thought was D.

I have sought, but I seek it vainly,
  That A, B, C, divine;
I heard it in my childhood,
  But now I am nearly nine.
I learn about nitric acid,
  I learn about NH_3;
Perhaps when I go to the Technical School
  I shall learn my A, B, C.

AT THE DUNK.

By John Caven.

...AUSE here,—and look upon a sight as fair
  As ever painter limned of poet's dreams:
...g the forest-tops the sun's last beams
...nger caressingly, while here and there
...purple patch drops through the heated air
...n Dunk's clear waters, as, with graceful sweep,
...hey lave the forest roots or noiseless creep
...eneath the flowers the meadow's margins bear.
...A thoughtful stillness reigns: on earth or sky.
...o sound to jar, no cloud the blue to dim:
...ith chirp and croak, the night-hawk hurries by,
...d high-perched robin chants his compline hymn;
... up, the rapids seem to heave a sigh,—
...nk, mourning meets the tide—a grave to him.

AN UNFORTUNATE PITCH

A MUSICAL ANECDOTE

Copyright 1888, by Ivers & Pond Piano Co.

Now it happened one morning, not a very 12/8 ago, that a farmer by the name of [music] set out for Boston to sell a load of [music] and to buy a new *p*. His horse had not been young very recently, and his [music] movement was about *largo tranquillo;* but when he had gone a little more than [music] of the distance, he unexpectedly took fright at a stranger who carried a large [music] in one hand and a [music] of ducks in the other, and rushing down a [music] where the road made a [music], he upset the load, throwing the farmer to the ground [music] on his [music]. At first he seemed a little dazed and somewhat off his [music]. He got a [music] into his head that an earthquake had made his load *tr* [music] so that he lost his [music] and that a great ground [music] made the road pitch and roll like a ship in a [music] However, in a [music] time he recovered his consciousness in a great [music] *poco a poco.* The stranger came up to help on a *Presto* [music] and said they would have things fixed in *tr*/2 It took them but a 2/4 to get some [music] from the fence, right up the wagon, put every [music] in place and [music] them on with a [music], making everything *Allegro.* The horse had ceased to [music] with fear, and they started again. Having reached Boston, the farmer sold his grain to a dealer in [music], then bought a new *p f* at the rooms of Ivers and Pond, who do business on a large [music]. He paid [music] of the price in cash and gave a [music] over his own [music] for the [music]. On the way back he did not [music] his morning experience, but safely reached his journey's [music].

Ben Marcato.

LITTLE BROWN HANDS.

(By Mary H. Krout.)

They drive home the cows from the pasture,
  Up through the long, shady lane,
Where the quail whistles loud in the wheat field,
  That is yellow with ripening grain.
They find, in the thick waving grasses,
  Where the scarlet-lipped strawberry grows,
They gather the earliest snowdrops,
  And the first crimson buds of the rose.

They toss the hay in the meadow,
  They gather the elder-bloom white,
They find when the dusky grapes purple
  In the soft-tinted October light.
They know where the apples hang ripest,
  And are sweeter than Italy's wines,
They know where the fruit hangs the thickest,
  On the long, thorny blackberry vines.

They gather the delicate seaweeds,
  And build tiny castles of sand;
They pick up the beautiful sea-shells,
  Fairy barks that have drifted to land.
They wave from the tall, rocking tree-tops,
  Where the oriole's hammock nest swings,
And at night-time are folded in slumber
  By a song that a fond mother sings.

Those who toil bravely are strongest;
  The humble and poor become great;
And from those brown-handed children
  Shall grow mighty rulers of State.
The pen of the author and statesman,
  The noble and wise of the land,
The sword and chisel and pallette,
  Shall be held in the little brown hand.

"Children," said the teacher, while instructing the class in composition, "you should not attempt any flights of fancy, but simply be yourselves, and write what is in you. Do not imitate any other person's writings or draw inspiration from outside sources." As a result of this advice, Johnny Wise turned in the following composition: "We should not attempt any flites of fancy, but rite what is in us. In me there is my stummick, lungs, hart, liver, two apples, one piece of pie, one stick of lemon candy, and my dinner."—*Selected.*

Ecclesiastical Humor.

Some stories about children collected by the late Bishop How of England are amusing.

A little cousin of his being asked who was the first man, promptly answered Adam. Asked next who was the first woman, he thought a little and then hesitatingly replied Madam.

A boy being asked the meaning of Archangel replied, "An angel who came out of the ark." Another derived Pontifex from Pons a bridge, adding, "It means the Chief Priest, just as we say Archbishop."

"John Wesley," wrote a boy in an examination paper, "invented Methodist chapels, and afterward became Duke of Wellington."

Unusually bright is this:—"A parable is a heavenly story with no earthly meaning."

The mother of a pupil in a school for physiology conducted by a country rector wrote to the latter, saying:—"Reverend sir,—Please not to teach our Susan any more about her inside; it makes her so proud."

Ignorance was quite as common among the oldsters as the youngsters. The Bishop tells of a parish school where the teacher giving an oral lesson on the English language pointed out that there are many words pronounced the same, but spelled quite different.

"Now," he said, "there's the word 'har.' There's the har you breathe and the har of your head and the har that runs in the 'ields and the har to an estate, all spelled quite different, but all pronounced the same."

Let Them Do It

A FARMER'S wife who had no very romantic ideas about the opposite sex, and who, hurrying from churn to sink, from sink to shed, and back to the kitchen stove, was asked if she wanted to vote.

"No, I certainly don't!" she said. "I say if there's one little thing that the men folks can do alone, for goodness' sake let 'em do it!"

The Lieutenant-Governor

Prince Edward Island

WINTER IN LOVERS' LANE

BY CLINTON SCOLLARD

IN LOVERS' LANE 'TIS WINTER NOW
 (WILL SPRINGTIDE NEVER COME AGAIN?),
AND NOT A BIRD FROM ANY BOUGH
 VOICES THE OLD DIVINE REFRAIN.

THE PATH THAT GLEAMED WITH GREEN AND GOLD
 SHOWS STAR ON EVANESCENT STAR—
PALE FRAGILE BLOSSOMS OF THE COLD
 WHITER THAN JUNE'S WHITE LILIES ARE.

AND NOT A FOOTFALL WAKES THE HUSH
 WHEN THE FAINT SILVER OF THE MOON
GLINTS O'ER THE COVERT WHENCE THE THRUSH
 SPILLED, SUMMER-LONG, ITS JOCUND TUNE.

THOSE TREMULOUS TRYSTINGS, ARE THEY DONE,—
 THE MEETING JOY, THE PARTING PAIN?
WILL HEARTS NO MORE BE WOOED AND WON
 IN MEMORY-HAUNTED LOVERS' LANE?

AH, WAIT TILL APRIL'S BUGLE-CALL
 RINGS, RICH WITH RAPTURE, UP THE GLEN,
TILL MAY ONCE MORE HER FLOWERY THRALL
 WEAVES AMOROUSLY—AND THEN—AND THEN!

THE home of John and Mrs Bowness, Bedeque will be the scene of a happy event this evening at seven o'clock when their daughter Carrie T. will be united in matrimony to W. Calvin Leard, son of Cornelius Leard of Lower Bedeque. The ceremony will be performed by Rev Neil McLauchlin in the presence of immediate relations and friends. The bride is to be attended by her sister Miss Lizzie Bowness and she will wear white organdie trimmed with lace and insertion, and white roses. The dress of the bridesmaid will be of white organdie, trimmed with lace, and pink roses. The groom will be supported by A. H Affleck of Searletown. The presents are very beautiful and testify of the popularity of the happy couple. After spending the evening at the bride's parents where music will be furnished by Miss Carrie Pridham and Mis May Leard, Mr and Mrs Leard leave for their future home in Lower Bedeque. The Guardian joins with other friends in extending sincere best wishes.

Cultivating Evergreens

By Ephraim Weber

LET us keep fresh. The mildew of egotism has a hundred subtle fungi, which are withering many nice people around the tips and edges. That central self-reference eats the chlorophyl out of a character, and leaves us pale mullein stalks by the wall, when we ought to be evergreens by the veranda. A man and his wife, having settled in a bleak country, drove twenty miles on a difficult trail for a few little spruces and jack-pines to plant by the door. Have we taken half that trouble to freshen our beings with a new taking to heart the lives of our fellows? Have we even gone as far as visiting a mission or a soap factory to sensitize our sympathy? Something of this kind might not be a bad way to begin the evergreen work.

REV. EDWIN SMITH, M. A.

THE DAISIES' SONG.

[For the Transcript.]

We had a peaceful sleep
All through the winter night,
But when winds of March were blowing,
And soft April rains were flowing,
We crept slowly toward the light.

"Come," said May, "my dear ones,
And put your green gowns on."
Then, cried June, "My darling daisies,
All around your yellow faces
Your white-frilled caps now don."

Then began the frolic,
The wild and merry fun,
The wind piped up a lively tune,
Our pulses throbbed with joy of June;
We laughed, we danced, we sang and pranced,
We swayed, we whirled, we sprang and twirled,
We bobbed to the ground in our glee;
No flowers so jolly as we
Under the smiling sun.

A dandelion near
In solemn tones cried out—
"Daisies, daisies, do be quiet,
You are making such a riot!
You disturb my meditations
With your comical gyrations;
You 're crazy without doubt."

"O moon-faced dandy, dear!
Half asleep 'mong the grasses,
Would n't you dance with legs like these,
And broad-frilled caps to catch each breeze,
That o'er the meadow passes?"

So again to the wind's gay tune,
We started in joyous motion;
Now with drooping heads and lazy,
And now in a circle mazy,
Each little white-capped daisy
Bobbed about as if crazy,
In mad and wild commotion.

LUCY LINCOLN MONTGOMERY.

Old Gentleman: "Do you mean to say that your teachers never thrash you?" Little Gentleman: "Never. We have moral suasion at our school." Old Gentleman: "What's that?" Little Boy: "O, we get kep' in, and stood up in corners, and locked out, and locked in, and made to write one word a thousand times, and scowled at, and jawed at, and that's all."

WHERE JONES WENT

A series of revival services was being held in a Western and placards giving notice of the services were posted in cons ous places. One day the following notice was posted: " Its Location and Absolute Certainty. Thomas Jones, bar soloist, will sing 'Tell Mother I'll Be There.'" L. M. Libb

Miss L M Montgomery

The College Record

"Non Collegio sed vitæ discimus."

VOL. I. P. W. COLLEGE, CHARLOTTETOWN. MARCH, 1894. NO. 2.

The College Record.

THE RECORD will be published monthly during the remainder of the term.

Subscription price 25 cents, in advance. Single copies 10 cents.

EDITORS—E. N. M. Hunter, H. McKinnon.

BUSINESS MANAGER—T. R. MacMillan.

Address all communications to

BUSINESS MANAGER,
P. W. College,
Charlottetown.

P. W. COLLEGE, MARCH, 1894.

The College Record.

This is the second number of The Record, and we have to thank the students and others for the generous manner in which they received the first, and for the mild criticism which was passed upon it. We are well aware of its many defects, but how to remedy them is much more difficult to perceive. Any suggestions that would tend to the improvement of the paper would be thankfilly received.

We would like to see more of the students contribute some articles,—not poetry(?) alone, but some good prose compositions or letters on any subject of general interest. Some of the poetical effusions which we have lately received are marked by the "prodigal exuberance of early genius," and give unmistakable evidence of the approach of Spring.

As time goes by, and the students increase in numbers, it becomes more apparent that the present College building is wholly inadequate to meet the demands made on it for accommodation. This year there are nearly 170 students, and as it is almost impossible to seat so many, the need of a new and larger building is felt to be urgent.

The system of ventilation—the windows—is bad, and, in cold weather, is injurious to the health. When we go home this summer, let us impress on our parents the necessity of a new building, that, when the time comes for footing the bills, they may know that the money is wisely expended

---

It is with pleasure that we see Prof. Earle engaged as Musical Director. The students take quite an interest in the music, and will, no doubt, profit much from the instruction. Let us all do our best, that we may have some good singing at commencement.

We are in receipt of a new publication,—"Prince Street School Times,"—which we welcome to our table. It is a bright and interesting journal, and we must congratulate the young ladies on their new departure, and wish it a successful future.

"Now, boys," said the Sunday school teacher, "surely some one of you can tell me who carried off the gates of Gaza. Speak up, William." "I never touched 'em!" said the indignant William, with a suspicion of tears in his youthful voice. "I don't see why folks always blame it on me when things get carried off."

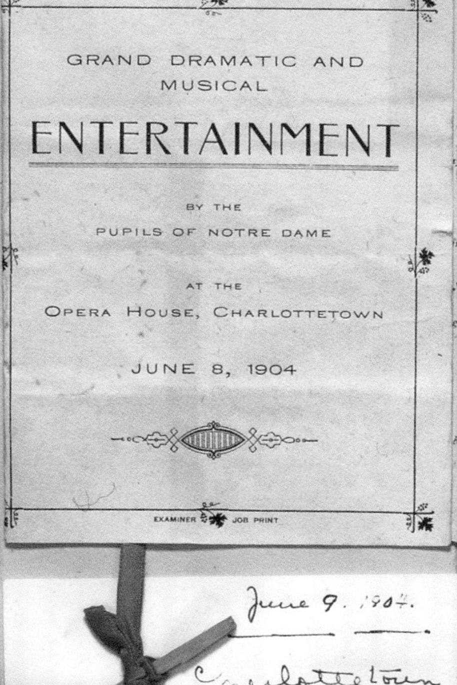

GRAND DRAMATIC AND MUSICAL

ENTERTAINMENT

BY THE

PUPILS OF NOTRE DAME

AT THE

OPERA HOUSE, CHARLOTTETOWN

JUNE 8, 1904

EXAMINER JOB PRINT

June 9. 1904.

Charlottetown P. E. I.

"Who can put up the biggest bluff?"

MULE BAROMETER
(HANG OUTSIDE)
DIRECTIONS.
If tail is dry FAIR
If tail is wet RAIN
If tail is swinging WINDY
If tail is wet and swinging STORMY
If tail is frozen COLD
"Page Fences wear best" under any weather conditions.
Get the Page WHITE BRAND
DON'T BE LIKE THE MULE'S TAIL--BEHIND--
The Page Wire Fence Co., Ltd
WALKERVILLE, TORONTO, MONTREAL, ST. JOHN

Notman Studio
12042
Road in Park

A PRETTY BIT OF SCENERY IN POINT PLEASANT PARK, HALIFAX.

Amid wedding notices, community clippings, and jokes, two stories burn with shame. The shame Maud suffered over her broken engagement with Edwin Simpson continued to haunt her whenever he visited the area or wrote to her. She was similarly distressed when she was physically attracted to Oliver Macneill (a distant cousin who was visiting from the United States) but not in love with him (and was, in fact, secretly engaged to Ewan Macdonald at the time). This situation may have opened an old wound in her similar feelings for Herman Leard.

PAGE 44: Here, Maud took a March calendar and affixed to it an August calendar for yet another year, writing beneath it "trial by fire" and the date that she received a painful letter from Edwin Simpson. Ed was visiting on the Island, and Maud had successfully avoided him in Cavendish. When she received his unwelcome letter, she knew her luck had finally run out. Her unpublished diary entry of August 12, 1903, recalls her torment: "I felt in my bones that all these respites were merely by way of enhancing the torture. I remember a schoolmaster who had a habit of making several feints with the ruler before he really brought it down on my outstretched palm. The experiences of life seem to repeat themselves." Pen pal Lucy Lincoln Montgomery's poem "Immortal Hope" becomes ambiguous when read beside the reference to Edwin Simpson. Could Maud hope that he would now leave her alone or would his hope flare again?

PAGE 46: The black-and-white group photograph pictures Scottish pen pal George Boyd MacMillan, in the back row at the far right. In the centre of the page is Maud's photograph of the altar of the Cavendish Presbyterian Church and below it a **notice** of a wedding in which "Rev. Ewen McDonald" assisted. Beside this notice are two 1909 announcements concerning Oliver Macneill of South Dakota, who fell quickly and passionately in love with Maud. On September 21, 1909, after only a few weeks of his visits, she realized, "I must walk no more in Lover's Lane with Oliver Macneill." He proposed to her and she refused, but she felt a keen attraction and confessed to her journal: "But tonight I found that I was again playing with fire." The "again" referred to the similar feelings she had had for Herman Leard. In Lower Bedeque, in 1897–98, she had been engaged to Simpson; here in 1909, she was engaged to Ewan Macdonald.

PAGE 47: The many flowers on this page, along with the surprised innocence of the kittens, create a celebratory mood. The dramatic bouquet could come from a time with Ewan or perhaps from a comic outing with Nora Lefurgey, who visited Cavendish for a couple of weeks in July 1904.

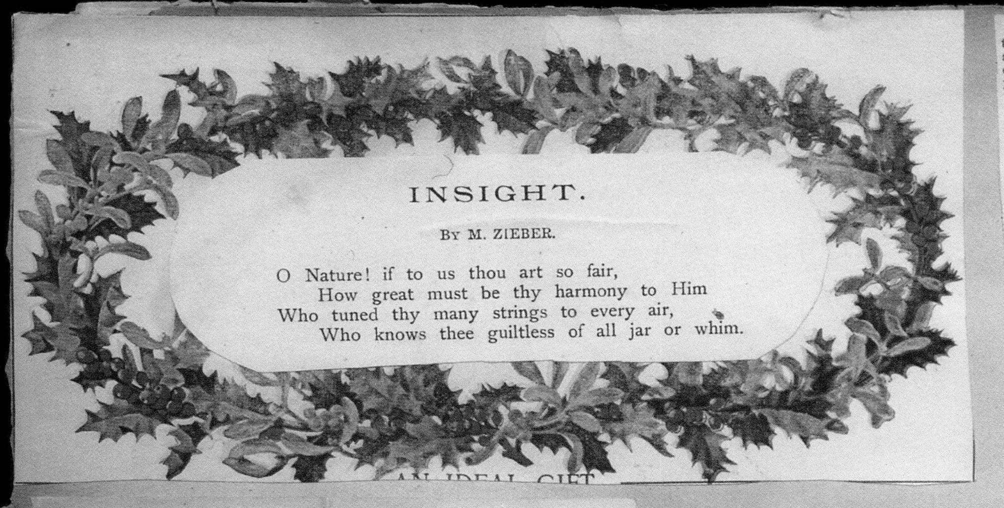

INSIGHT.
By M. Zieber.
O Nature! if to us thou art so fair,
How great must be thy harmony to Him
Who tuned thy many strings to every air,
Who knows thee guiltless of all jar or whim.

A Great Reward.—The following little story was sent to the Roller Monthly, and was written by a little boy in Denver, one of a class of children of six or eight years of age, who had been requested to write a story, they to select a subject, and their compositions not to be subject to revision by their teacher, but to be read before the children's parents exactly as written.

A poor young man fell in love with the daughter of a rich lady, who kept a candy shop.

The poor young man could not marry the rich candy lady's daughter because he had not enough money to buy any furniture.

A wicked man offered to give the young man twenty-five dollars if he would become a drunkard.

The young man wanted the money very much, so he could marry the rich candy lady's daughter, but when he got to the saloon he turned to the wicked man and said,—

"I will not become a drunkard, even for great riches. Get thee behind me Satan."

On his way home he found a pocketbook containing a Million dollars in gold; then the young lady consented to marry him. They had a beautiful wedding and the next day they had twins.

Thus, you see that Virtue has its own reward.

Announcement

A missionary Concert will be held here on thursday next at 7 Oclock Miss Martha M Clark returned missionary will be present a silver collection will be taken up for the mission band

The violets now,
that strew the gree
lap of the new-com

IMMORTAL HOPE.

Out to the starry night
I took my hope deferred,
My hope, that sought in vain for years,
Through troubled days and nights of tears,
One heart-inspiring word.

I chose a shining star
From hosts above my head,
And said, "I'll watch that through the night:
When its last gleam shall fade from sight
Then will my hope be dead."

So through the evening dim,
And midnight's chilling air,
My dying hope held to my heart,
I strove, in anguish, e'er we'd part,
To breathe a willing prayer.

O'er the horizon far,
And out of sight they swept;
Pleiades faded like a mist,
Orion, too, the boundary kissed,
And my star onward crept

Till, trembling on the verge
Of dawn, it passed away.
I kissed my dead hope on the eyes,
So still it lay in that pale guise,
Then turned to face the day.

In amber air there shone
The glorious star of morn.
My hope sprang up and oped its eyes,
I caught a glimpse of Paradise
In that first glow of dawn.

Lucy Lincoln Montgomery.
In the Waverley Magazine for October.

Page 44 from the Red Scrapbook

Hours splendid as the past may still be thine.
And bless thy future as thy former day.
Elegy on Newstead Abbey
November
Sun. Mon. Tue. Wed. Thu. Fri. Sat.
December
Sun. Mon. Tue. Wed. Thu. Fri. Sat.

Do You See the Point?

"Any idiot knows," said Rex the Riddler, "that the real reason the Boers sleep with their boots on is that they want to keep De Wet from defeat. But can you tell me this. Why cannot a deaf and dumb man tickle nine women? You'll never guess it. Give it up? Well, a deaf and dumb man can't tickle nine women because he can only gesticulate. See?"

A pretty home wedding will be solemnized in this city, at seven o'clock this morning at the home of T. C. and Mrs James, when their daughter, Miss Mary, will become the wife of Rev W. A. McKay of Wick, Ontario. The bride, who will be unattended, will wear an imported tailored suit of blue cloth, with black and white picture hat. Rev T. F. Fullerton performs the ceremony in the presence of the immediate friends of the family, after which the young couple will leave by the Northumberland for Nova Scotia, the groom's former home, and then proceed to New York. The happy couple will have the best wishes of a large circle of friends, the bride being a general favorite who will be greatly missed.

PROF. HOWARD MURRAY, LL D.

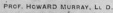

The home of W. A. and Mrs. Macneill, Cavendish, was the scene of a pleasant social event on the evening of Monday, September 6th, when several of their friends gathered in to meet Mrs Emma Wright of Oakland, Cal. and Oliver Macneill of Dakota. A delightful evening was spent in games, music and recreations, among which latter must be mentioned those of his own composition given by the genial host. At a late hour the guests seperated, unanimous in their expression of thanks for the kindness of host and hostess.

A VERY pleasing event took place on Tuesday evening, 25th inst, at 7 o'clock, at the residence of John T. and Mrs Hillman, Bay View, when their daughter, Miss Margaret M, was united in marriage to H L McReavy, senior member of the firm of H L McReavy & Co. of Boston, in the presence of sixty of their immediate friends and relatives. The ceremony was performed by the Rev J G Belyea, assisted by the Rev. Ewen McDonald. The bride looked charming in a dress of white crepe du chene over white satin. She wore a birdal veil and carried a bonquet of white American Beauty roses. She was attended by her sister, Miss Bertha M., who was gowned in pale blue silk and carried a bonquet of carnations. The groomsman was D. C. Harvey, of Cape Traverse, cousin of the bride. Immediately after the ceremony the company repaired to the dining room where they enjoyed the bounteous repast prepared for the occasion. Mr and Mrs McReavy left for a tour of the principal places of interest on the Island. They will leave for their future home in Boston on Saturday 29th inst. The groom's present to the bride was a gold bracelet and to the bridesmaid a gold signet ring. The numer us and costly presents from friends at home and abroad attest to the popularity of both bride and groom. The PATRIOT joins with many friends in extending hearty congratulations.

On Wednesday, September first, Mr and Mrs Laird of Cavendish gave a very enjoyable afternoon tea in honor of their sister, Mrs Emma Wright of Oakland, Cal., and their nephew Oliver McNeill, who are at present visiting them. After tea a very pleasant evening was spent, with an impromptu program of music, readings and speeches by the guests. Among the latter were the four sisters … and her mother, Mrs. W. … who has attained to the … ninety … years Com…

Page 46 from the Red Scrapbook

May
Christmas
be
a time
of rest
and
peace.

On the evening of Wednesday, June 22, the residence of Archie Best of Mount Royal was the scene of a very pretty wedding when his sister, Euphemia, was united in marriage to R. Bruce Hayes, of Ellerslie. At 7 o'clock the bridal party amid the company of about thirty guests assembled in the parlor and Rev. D. McLean of Springfield tied the nuptial knot. Miss Bertie Hayes of Ellerslie, cousin of the groom played the wedding march. The bride who was given away by her brother was attired in a suit of white silk, trimmed with over lace and white ribbon and wore the bridal veil and orange blossoms. She was attended by Miss Annie Campbell of Darlington who wore a pretty gown of white dimity, trimmed with valenciennes lace and white ribbon. The groom was ably supported by Dr. G. P. McDougall of O'Leary. After the ceremony the usual bountiful wedding supper was served after which the evening passed very pleasantly in various amusements. Many beautiful presents testified to the esteem and affection of a large circle of friends. The happy couple will start in a few days for Winnipeg where they intend to reside.

They're rather tiny, and rather afraid,
The world's such a wonderful place;
When told to look pretty, they all three obeyed
With the utmost politeness and grace!

The annual examination of Hope River school took place on Friday. There was a good attendance from the district and several visitors from Cavendish, including Rev Ewen McDonald, Miss L M Montgomery and Miss Brown teacher of Cavendish school. The various classes were examined by the teacher, Miss Brown, Rev Mr McDonald and Miss Montgomery and acquited themselves in such a way as to win the warmest encominms from the various examiners. After the examinations were over Master Ernest Simpson on behalf of the pupils presented the teacher Miss McKay with an address and dressing case. Rev Mr McDonald, Messrs George Simpson, Walter Simpson and Misses Brown and Montgomery congratulated the pupils and teacher on the efficiency of the school. Miss McKay who is leaving the school for a rest has endeared herself to the scholars in a marked degree during the three years she has been in the school, and her efficiency as a teacher won the confidence of the parents.
—Corr.

Friday. July 10
1904
The dawn of
Murphy.

Page 47 from the Red Scrapbook

In these pages, Montgomery wove together early preoccupations, matrimonial dreams, and a writer's life.

PAGE 48: Lady Sophia Montgomerie (1863–1942) was the daughter of the fourteenth Earl of Eglinton. Montgomery's father insisted on his family's clan link with the Earls of Eglinton, naming his Saskatchewan house Eglinton Villa. Marian Keith was the pseudonym of Canadian novelist Mary Esther Miller (1874–1961), who married Duncan MacGregor in 1909. The presence of Keith's photograph here suggests Montgomery's awareness of other Canadians in the writing market with whom she would be compared. Montgomery first met Keith in person in Toronto in December 1911 when the Canadian Women's Press Club held a reception for the two of them. Since Montgomery had read only *Duncan Polite* (1905) and had not liked it, she was embarrassed by Keith's enthusiasm for her work. "A Defeated Motion," a comic political poem, was written by *Echo* co-worker Edith Russell. The old magazine picture (bottom left, repeated from page 3) is Cape Leforce (subject of a first writing success) from her childhood. The archway of stone is Montgomery's own picture that she turned into a moonlit scene earlier in the scrapbook, on page 33. The lock of hair is from Maud Beaton, named for Montgomery, and the daughter of Mary Campbell Beaton, Maud's grand PWC chum.

PAGE 50: The shoestring bow suggests the neat tying together of stories. A clipping describes the August 1906 farewell picnic in Cavendish for Ewan Macdonald, who was leaving to study in Scotland. Montgomery herself may have written the highly flattering piece. On October 12, Maud recorded in her diary that he had left and that she was surprised to find herself engaged to him. Curiously, in the journal entry mentioning the picnic, Montgomery concentrated on her meeting with Edwin Simpson (rather than on Ewan) and was pleased to find that she was finally free – after more than seven years – of embarrassment or shame in talking with him. The envelope holds a 1905 wedding invitation from Bertha Clark (a Halifax Ladies' College friend); her groom was Mr. Black. Amid the male portraits for Sun Life of Canada is Edith Russell's picture.

PAGE 52: This page is the only place in the Island scrapbooks where *Anne of Green Gables* is directly acknowledged. By 1910, two years after its publication, the novel had already become a permanent part of the Cavendish landscape. The notice of a garden party at the Webb farm declared proudly that guests could see the Lake of Shining Waters from the Webb orchard and could then "walk through the beautiful path known as 'Lovers' Lane' now made famous by the author of 'Anne of Green Gables.'" Interestingly, the clipping is given no special prominence among other matters.

Lady Sophia Montgomerie

(Photo. by Lafayette)

By Marian Keith

His Last Request.

Pat was in the habit of going home drunk every night and beating his wife Biddy—not because he disliked her, but because he thought it was the thing to do. Finally Biddy lost patience and appealed to the priest. The priest called that evening, and Pat came home drunk as usual.

"Pat," said the priest, "you're drunk, and I'm going to make you stop this right here. If you ever get drunk again I'll turn you into a rat—do you mind that? If I don't see you I'll know about it just the same, and into a rat you go. Now you mind that."

Pat was very docile that night, but the next evening he came home even worse drunk than ever, kicked in the door, and Biddy dodged behind the table to defend herself.

"Don't be afraid, darlint," says Pat, as he steadied himself before dropping into a chair, "I'm not going to bate ye. I won't lay the weight of me finger on ye. I want ye to be kind to me tonight, darlint, and to remember the days when we was swatehearts and when ye loved me. You know his riverince said last night if I got dhrunk again he'd turn me into a rat. He didn't see me, but he knows I'm dhrunk and this night into a rat I go. But I want ye to be kind to me, darlint, and watch me, and when ye see me gettin' little, and the hair growin' out on me, and me whiskers gettin' long, if ye ever loved me, darlint, for God's sake, keep yer eye on the cat."—Selected from the Ladies' Home Journal by Miss L. M. Keller, Buffalo, N. Y.

Rev. R. H. Stavert, Grand Worthy Patriarch of the Sons of Temperance paid a visit to Carsonville yesterday and last evening gave an illustrious lecture on the subject of temperance. John Leiper occupied the chair and introduced the speaker. The hall was well filled and all went away feeling that they had had a pleasant and profitable evening. Mr. Stavert left this morning on return to Harcourt. —Exc. (Rev. Mr. Stavert is a native of this province.)

A DEFEATED MOTION.

The motion is that we resolve
  This parliament to now dissolve,
'Tis wrong our country's state affairs
  Be run by men of sixty years.
The seniors all are in the lead;
  'Tis plain this garden we must weed.

There's Member B—— from County Clare,
  Although he pompadours his hair
And sets his glasses on just so,
  And has what all the world calls "go,"
He's in his sixties, there's no doubt,
  So he is one to hustle out.

The honorable Mr. Jay——,
  Like Mr. B——, has had his day;
Though eloquent in a debate,
  We all lament he's out of date,
And so resign his stately form
  To perish 'neath the chloroform.

But what the need to thus compare?
  It drives us to a dull despair;
For each seems useful in his place,
  Performs his part with easy grace,
Takes active interest in each bill,
  Except this one, which strives to kill
The men of sixty years, because
  Doc. Osler adds it to our laws.

Now, gentlemen, shall we retire
  At this eccentric man's desire?
Or shall we stay alive and show
  That, though the years may come and go,
We're never older than we feel,
  And vastly wiser by a deal.

A sage at sixty and a fool
  At thirty is the common rule.
The question, then, for you and me,
  Is this: "To be, or not to be?"
I, for my part, am sixty-seven,
  But want more years this side of heaven.

And you, no doubt, all feel the same,
  For suicide's a crying shame.
Just then the ballots round were passed;
  Then scrutineers worked hard and fast.
The verdict was one mighty "Nay!"—
  The old men's parliament would stay.

EDITH M. RUSSELL.

Dartmouth, N. S.

A kindergarten teacher was explaining to the little ones what wool was. "Feel my dress," she said. "It is made of wool. Many of our winter clothes are woollen."

A little later, to refresh his memory, she asked, "John, of what are your trousers made?"

"Of papa's old ones," shouted Johnny.

Lucy Lincoln Montgomery.

A FEW OF NOVA SCOTIA'S REPRESENTATIVES.—SUN LIFE OF CANADA.

A. R. McQueen, New Glasgow, M. N. Davison, Windsor. A. H. Mackay, Salt Springs, Pictou Co.
B. W. Mosher, Spring Hill. Miss E. M. Russell, Women's Dept.
G. A. Gadbois, Supt. Thrift Dept. E. W. W. Sim, Cashier. W. J. Marquand, Manager for Nova Scotia, Halifax. Dr. A. F. Buckley, Med. Examiner, Halifax. R. D. Bell, Inspector for N.S., Halifax.
A. McArthur, Pictou. J. G. Worth, North Sydney
W. Woodhead, Halifax. J. W. Betcher, Sydney. J. Percy Miller, Halifax.

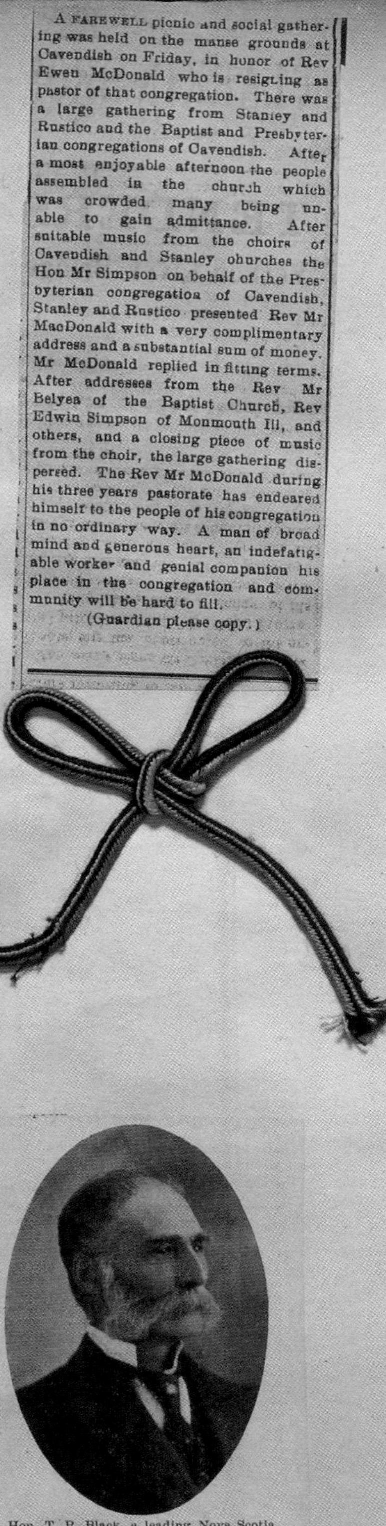

A FAREWELL picnic and social gathering was held on the manse grounds at Cavendish on Friday, in honor of Rev Ewen McDonald who is resigning as pastor of that congregation. There was a large gathering from Stanley and Rustico and the Baptist and Presbyterian congregations of Cavendish. After a most enjoyable afternoon the people assembled in the church which was crowded many being unable to gain admittance. After suitable music from the choirs of Cavendish and Stanley churches the Hon Mr Simpson on behalf of the Presbyterian congregation of Cavendish, Stanley and Rustico presented Rev Mr MacDonald with a very complimentary address and a substantial sum of money. Mr McDonald replied in fitting terms. After addresses from the Rev Mr Belyea of the Baptist Church, Rev Edwin Simpson of Monmouth Ill, and others, and a closing piece of music from the choir, the large gathering dispersed. The Rev Mr McDonald during his three years pastorate has endeared himself to the people of his congregation in no ordinary way. A man of broad mind and generous heart, an indefatigable worker and genial companion his place in the congregation and community will be hard to fill.

(Guardian please copy.)

Hon. T. R. Black, a leading Nova Scotia agriculturist, who is a strong supporter of the Maritime Winter Fair.

Perm. address Box 1254
Boston U.S.A.

Mrs. David Crownfield.

89 Mt. Vernon St.
Boston - U. S. A.

Page 50 from the Red Scrapbook

In Memory of

Mr. W. D. MacIntyre

Inspector of Schools

FOR PRINCE COUNTY

1899–1905

THE WEEK.

In response to our request for "something lighter," two valued contributors have done these verses :

Greek Versification is vexation ;
Spelling after the manner of President Roosevelt is a pernicious FAD.
Your Problems B are not for me ;
And the Problem Editor who sits down to read fifty-word rhyming philosophy suggests mottoes for a wastepaper-basket far more than for tea-caddy, sundial, or blotting-PAD !

IN LIGHTER VEIN (BY REQUEST).
The Muse Jocose at your behest
Descends to do her level best
To make your paper brighter.
The Poets' *Corner*, Muses' *Ring*
Joy to her heart, perpetual bring,
Men therefore call her "Leiter."

We thank them, but we award our Prize of *Half a Guinea* to Mr. GEORGE BOYD MACMILLAN, 34, Castle-street, Alloa, N.B., for a reflection which, whatever he thinks of it himself, is more amusing than anything else sent in this week :

Most of our creeds have become so petrified that we can grab them by the handle—"I believe"—and becudgel our ecclesiastical antagonists with them. Now, creeds are moral developers, and—like physical developers—should be used daily till they require readjustment to take more out of the user.

THE LATE HON. GEO. SIMPSON

THE funeral of the late Hon. George Simpson will take place tomorrow at 2 p m, to Cavendish Cemetery, about two miles from his home in Bay View. He was a member of Court New London, I. O. F, and that Order, including the Royal Foresters from Summerside will have charge of the funeral arrangements. Members of the Provincial Government, and other friends from this city will be present.

AN ENJOYABLE GARDEN PARTY HELD

A garden party was given on the 18th inst by Ernest and Mrs Webb of Cavendish in honor of George and Mrs Abbott of Lawrence, Mass, who have been spending a vacation at Bay View the guests of Walter and Mrs Simpson. A number of invited friends were preeent and among them was Miss Maggie G. McNeill who has lately returned to her native isle after sixteen years absence, eleven of which were spent in Klondike. The tables were spread under the shade of the apple trees in "Old Orchard" in full view of the Lake of shining water, and a bounteous repast was served by the hostess assisted by the ladies of the party. After ample justice had been done at the tables, some engaged in games while others enjoyed a walk through the beautiful path known as "Lovers' Lane" now made famous by the author of "Anne of Green Gables." After an afternoon of thorough enjoyment the party separated to their homes after expressing their hearty thanks to the host and hostess. Mrs (Rev) L. G. McNeill of St John was one of the guests ... enjoyed the ...

"A Sad Suicide," a diabolical temper, and a black cat prompt the visual drama created here.

Clipping: William C. Macneill was the father of Montgomery's childhood best friend and third cousin, Amanda. When W.C. Macneill killed himself, on May 3, 1907, Maud and Amanda had already grown far apart. In fact, Montgomery did not register the suicide in her journal until ten years later, after she had read a letter from unhappily married Amanda and was dismayed by Amanda's constant complaints about her husband. On September 27, 1917, Montgomery wrote:

If she would but control her own diabolical temper he would be good enough to her. If she does not control that same temper she will end up as her wretched old father did in insanity and suicide. Shall I ever forget that night after his death and the way Amanda behaved! It was enough to make one believe the old legends of devil possession.

Mephistopheles photograph: Montgomery had seen Lewis Morrison in *Faust* in Halifax when she was a Dalhousie student in 1895 and had put the play advertisement in the Blue Scrapbook (p. 68). She may have kept the Morrison publicity photograph among her souvenirs or a more recent one may have surfaced closer to the time of the suicide. In any case, the placement of the devil and the article side by side was a powerful wordless comment on the scene she wrote up ten years later. She may have looked at this very page after reading Amanda's distressing letter and have been freshly reminded of her own image of the diabolical. As a teenager in Saskatchewan, Montgomery briefly owned a black cat named Mephistopheles, who disappeared one day because Maud's stepmother (herself a woman Maud said threw tantrums) could no longer abide its fits. A tuft of Mephistopheles's fur was preserved on page 37 of the Blue Scrapbook (bottom left; only a shadowy trace of the fur remains).

River photograph: Montgomery probably revisited and edited this page in 1930 after her trip to Saskatchewan. On October 10, 1930, she noted in her journal that Prince Albert's River Street looked much as it had in 1890 except for the presence of a bridge that now spanned the river. Montgomery used white ink to erase the bridge so that the scene would look more like the Prince Albert she knew in her youth.

Wedding notice: In keeping with her frequent pairing of wedding and funeral notices, Montgomery placed a write-up of her cousin Laura McIntyre's 1909 wedding below the suicide article (the wedding invitation appears on page 59 of the Red Scrapbook).

A SAD SUICIDE

Victim Was William C. McNeill of Cavendish.

BODY WAS FOUND LAST NIGHT

Lying Face Downward in Clark's Pond, in a Foot and a Half of Water.

A sad suicide occurred yesterday in Cavendish, the victim being William C. McNeill, aged 77, a prominent, highly respected resident, with many relatives in that section of the country.

He left home in the afternoon and his friends becoming uneasy organized a searching party.

At seven o'clock they found Mr McNeill's body lying face downward in Clark's Pond in a foot and a half of water.

The unfortunate man although in good circumstances, and the owner of a farm of two hundred acres, had been in poor health recently and his mind had given away under the strain.

He leaves to mourn three sons and two daughters, some of whom had been residing with him at Cavendish. Ther is one son in Kensington.

AYLESWORTH—McINTYRE.

A pretty wedding took place at two o'clock yesterday afternoon at the home of E. M. Carpenter, Fourth street, when Mrs Carpenter's brother, R. B. Aylesworth, of Calgary, was united in marriage to Miss Laura McIntyre, of this city. The ceremony was performed by Rev C. A. Myers, pastor of Westminster Presbyterian Church, in the presence of a few immediate friends, including Mrs. (Dr.) Alesworth, Collingwood, Ontario, mother of the groom, and Miss Beatrice McIntyre, Charlottetown, P. E. I., sister of the bride. After the ceremony Mr and Mrs Aylesworth left on the afternoon train on a trip to the coast. They will make their residence in Calgary, where Mr Aylesworth conducts a drug business. — Edmonton Bulletin, Aug. 17.

Photograph by Marceau, Los Angeles, Cal.

LEWIS MORRISON, ONE OF THE OLDEST OF ROAD STARS, IN HIS FAMILIAR CHARACTER OF *MEPHISTOPHELES* IN "FAUST."

Page 53 from the Red Scrapbook

Coming to the end of the second scrapbook, Montgomery tied together old and new items as though she was preparing to leave her Cavendish home.

PAGE 55: In the envelope is an invitation to the 1904 wedding of her dear PWC and Cavendish friend Fanny Wise. Bideford days were recalled through the death notice of Bayfield Williams's sister. A wedding notice details how former Cavendish schoolteacher Wellington McCoubrey returned to Prince Edward Island for his honeymoon. Fabric swatches, perhaps having to do with Fanny Wise's wedding, were markers for Montgomery's lifelong interest in clothing and fashion. Verse (centre left) by former pen pal Frank Monroe Beverly appears beside a picture of two begging cats, presumably by Henriette Ronner-Knip. Maud put an ecclesiastical joke beside a teacup cut-out that bears the intriguing message: "Wanted: a Sherlock Holmes." The teacup is actually the front portion of the card that she pasted onto page 47 (top left), with a flower bearing Hattie Gordon's initials and the date 1895. Would a Sherlock Holmes have been needed in curious Cavendish to figure out Montgomery's relationship with Ewan Macdonald?

PAGE 57: Irish American author Gerald Carlton may have been one of Montgomery's penfriends whose correspondence is now lost. His success was just the kind to have attracted her admiration when she herself was struggling for a toehold in the literary world. The author of "To a Wounded Tern," Jeremiah S. Clarke, was the familiar Jerry – a "jay" – of the secret diary of Nora and Maud. His poem appeared in the March 1900 issue of the *Prince Edward Island Magazine*. Several of the magazine photographs and clippings Montgomery pasted into her scrapbook were from the early volumes of that journal.

PAGE 58: Miss Baker was a familiar figure when Montgomery visited Prince Albert in 1890–91. She lived just a "couple of doors from us," Montgomery said, and Maud used to have suppers with her – according to her October 11, 1930, journal entry, Miss Baker made grand chocolate cake. The story about the "champion of the Sioux" may have prompted Montgomery to include Jerry Clarke's poem on the previous page (or vice versa), since Jerry was himself an enthusiastic teacher of Native people. The Baptist program must have been a reminder that she would herself some time soon be serving as a minister's wife. Situated between the program and the poem "Departure," describing the farewell to a loved house, is a photograph of a swan and its cygnet. Was Montgomery obliquely gesturing to the child she hoped marriage would bring?

—The sudden death of Mrs. Rev. E. S. Weeks, Bideford has cast a gloom of sadness over many hearts. She was in her usual health up to a few days before her death, when she became suddenly ill of penitonitis and passed away on Wednesday last, at the early age of 28 years. Mrs. Weeks was a daughter of the late Albert Williams and leaves to mourn her husband, an infant five months old, her mother, who is now in Edmonton, Alberta, one sister, Mrs. Murdock McLeod, Edmonton, and five brothers, A. E. of Moncton, N. B., Clifford of Boston, E. Bayfield, Edmonton, Teacher and Claud, Bideford, besides many friends. The funeral will take place today at two p. m.

A TICKET FOR BONNYWICKET

By Frank Monroe Beverly

SHE looked somewhat dejected,
The girl at Coalbrook did;
The agent at the window
The surging crowd kept hid—
She wanted a ticket
For Bonnywicket.

Though hard she tried to see him,
The throng had kept her back;
The more she tried to enter,
The denser grew the pack—
She'd get no ticket
For Bonnywicket.

Then helpless and appealing,
Her eyes on me she cast;
She looked like one who passes
Through trouble sharp and vast—
"I want a ticket
For Bonnywicket."

"And thus comes your dejection,
My gentle lass," I said.
"Well, I will make an effort—
This throng seems quite ill-bred—
To get a ticket
For Bonnywicket."

I pressed on to the window,
By crowding through the pack,
And saw the busy agent,
Then forced my slow way back—
I had a ticket
For Bonnywicket.

But those sweet eyes, appealing,
I thought without design,
Had fled, and left me minus
Two dollars-forty-nine!
To sell: A ticket
For Bonnywicket.

Father and Son

The Sydney Post of Tuesday says: "At 6.15 this morning the wedding was solemnized at the residence, George St., of Miss B. Blanche Taylor, eldest daughter of the late George W. Taylor, formerly of De Bert, Colchester County, to H. A. Wellington McCoubrey, of New Glasgow, P. E. I., senior member of the firm of McCoubrey & Bulman, of this city. Rev. O. N. Chipman, pastor of Pitt St. Baptist Church, tied the nupital knot. The bride wore a charming going away gown of brown panama cloth, with hat to match, a costume that looked exceedingly becoming. Both the principals were unattended. The happy couple were the recipients of a large number of handsome souvenirs from their host of friends, suited to the occasion. Mr. McCoubrey's fellow guests of Alfonse Hotel tendered their departing bachelor friends a timely gift in the shape of a finely finished chocolate set. After the wedding breakfast, Mr. and Mrs. McCoubrey left by the early train on a month's visit to Prince Edward Island, and arrived in this City on Tuesday evening.

X The late Bishop Selwyn delighted to tell the following racy incident in his varied experience: While Bishop of Litchfield he was walking one day in the Black Country, and observing a group of colliers seated by the roadside in a semicircle, with a brass kettle in front of them, inquired what was going on. "Why, yer honor," replied a grave-looking member, "it's a sort of wager. Yon kettle is a prize for the fellow who can tell the biggest lie, and I am the umpire." Amazed and shocked, the good bishop said reprovingly, "Why, my friends, I have never told a lie that I know of since I was born." There was a dead silence, only broken by the voice of the umpire, who said in a deliberate tone, "Gie the bishop the kettle."

Page 55 from the Red Scrapbook

GERALD CARLTON

Of the many stars of Park Row, none is of greater magnitude than Gerald Carlton. Though this is the third generation in which he has lived and labored, he is as young and active as when he first won his spurs in the fields of literature and journalism.

The secret of his success as well as of his popularity is intense activity. No man has ever led a more strenuous life or has achieved more than has he. Within the compass of forty years, he has made his mark as a soldier, traveler and consul, as poet, playwright and novelist, as editor, staff writer and man of affairs.

GERALD CARLTON

No one among modern American writers better represents the genius of Ireland. Carlton was born in the Emerald Isle, educated and brought up under the best traditions of Irish social life. This chapter of his experience gives a delicious flavor to his speech, and is forever being betrayed by the keen wit and droll humor that mark the Milesian temperament.

It was long ago noticed by Voltaire that the highest wit went hand in hand with the deepest thought, and Carlton's case is no exception to this rule. In his advocacy of novel reforms and of lofty ideals, his best work has been marked by a brilliancy and hearty fun which made his scholarship all the more attractive and irresistible. Yet is must not be supposed that his genius is of a polemic or didactic character. He has always sought to please and make happy rather than to argue or to teach. But in his work he has so used all the powers of the human mind as to give his lightest utterances a more than ephemeral value.

He is probably best known through his poems, short stories and novels. The first are delightful bits of versification, such as might be expected from a compatriot of Moore and Yeats. In fiction, he has been indefatigable and has produced over two hundred novels and novelettes. Not one has sold less than 5,000 copies, and some have passed the 100,000 mark.

In his methods of work he belongs to past rather than present schools. He avoids the problem novel and all the sex questions about which so many volumes, bright and dull, have been written. His characters have always been taken from actual life, and in the last analysis are the very people whom the reader meets in New York, London, San Francisco and Hong-Kong. In the selection of characters he has always been guided by a fine sense of fitness. He eschews morbidity and monstrosity, preferring to sin, if possible, on the side of naturalness rather than that of eccentricity. For that reason his stories are clean and wholesome and are filled with fresh air, sunlight and good health.

As a member of the consular service, Carlton proved himself tactful, energetic and efficient. He was one of the big army of Government representatives who uphold the honor of the American flag abroad and who make the American gentleman loved and respected in other lands.

William E. S. Fales.

Edward F. Feist has assumed charge of the Cassville (Mo.) *Daily Herald*.

The marriage of Miss Janet Irene MacNeill, only daughter of Dr. R. and Mrs. MacNeill, of Charlottetown, to Mr. John K. Macdonald, merchant of Wycocomagh, Cape Breton, will take place at half past six this evening, at the nome of the bride, 135 Pownal Street. The ceremony will be performed by Rev. T. F. Fullerton, pastor of St. James Church, city, in the presence of near relatives and intimate friends of the bride and groom. The bride will be attended by Miss Mame Hughes, daughter of Hon. George Hughes, and the groom by Mr. Charles D. Herman, of Dartmouth, N. S. The bridal costume is of ivory silk eolienne. It is trimmed with ball fringe and handmade Irish crochet, the gift of tne bride's cousin, Mrs. A. E. Morrison of this city. The veil and orange blossoms and a bouquet of bride's roses and carnations complete the beautiful costume. The bridesmaid will wear pale green eolienne with lace trimming, and carry a bouquet of pink carnations. There are many beautiful wedding presents from friends in this province and in Cape Breton. The groom's gift to the bride will be an amethyst and pearl pendant, and to the bridesmaid a pearl pin. After the ceremony supper will be served, and Mr. and Mrs. MacDonald will leave by the evening express on a wedding trip to Albany, New York, Quebec, Toronto, Montreal, Niagara Falls, Buffalo, Halifax and other cities. The bride's travelling costume is a blue tailor-made suit with hat to match. She will wear a fur lined coat with mink trimmings, a gift from her parents. The enjoyable event is creating great interest in this city, where the bride, who is one of our most estimable and accomplished young ladies, has many warm friends. The groom who is well known in commercial circles in Cape Breton as a successful and enterprising business man is also widely popular. The Patriot joins with their acquaintances in THE Island and the other Island, in wishing Mr. and Mrs. MacDonald an overflowing measure of happiness and prosperity.

ABOUT CATS.

Prof. Wilder, of Cornell University, wrote a description of the cat some years ago, from which we take the following:—

'Its anatomical structure considered, the cat is more decidedly specialized and more finely differentiated than man, and is in some respects a finer creature. It is as nearly perfect as an animal can be in anatomical structure. The muscles are more delicate, they are prettier, and in some cases they are more complex. The eye is protected in a way ours is not, there being a third lid. The shape of the cat is beautiful. It uses all its force to advantage, and never wastes any. When it makes a leap, it will light in just the right place. It can turn in the air in a very slight space, and it always alights on its feet.

'The cat has extreme keeness of apprehension. It recognizes its friends, and its foes. A single spank will alienate the dearest pet of a cat for at least a month.

'If cleanliness is next to godliness, the cat is the most religious of animals. Cleanliness is not only a habit, but a fad with it.

'The affection of cats for human beings and for each other is remarkable. Their homing faculty is extraordinary.

'In Germany thirty-seven cats were carried in sacks twenty-four miles in various directions, and all of them were home within twenty-four hours.

'How a cat purrs nobody knows, and nobody is likely to find out, because the cat purrs only when it is happy, and it is not likely to be happy when an investigation is going on to discover how it purrs.'

To a Wounded Tern.

By Jeremiah S. Clarke.

I.

You beautiful bird, whose tapering wings
Bore to heaven your lithe, frail form
When, a messenger of the King of Kings,
And yourself the king of the storm,
You skimmed the white surf, where old ocean flings
With a passionate fiendish glee
His strength on the beach, that echoing rings
With a wonderful harmony;
While your mate's shrill screech to my warm heart brings
A melody pleasing to me;

II.

Your joy is no more, for a cruel ball
By a mischievous sportsman aimed
Has pierced your bosom, so shapely and small,
And left you—Oh fairest one—maimed.
Alone—on a stone—too feeble to call,
You are waiting for death's cold hand.
O, have I a heart in my bosom at all
If I pass you, or pitiless stand,—
Nor help you to bear, nor throw on the pall?
Ah! sad ending of life so grand!

III.

I clasp in my hand your fluttering breast,
Though I sigh as you struggle there.
I close—a moment—and you are at rest;
Then I almost breathe a prayer
For your mate and brood in the lonely nest
On the sand-dune over the bay,
As the wind blows cool, and the glowing west
Announces the close of the day.
[Must your feathers rest on a lady's crest
While your body moulders away?]

PROGRAMME

—OF—

N. W. Queen's Sunday School Convention

Cavendish Baptist Church

July 15, 1909

MORNING SESSION

10.00—Devotions led by Mr. Arthur Simpson
10.30—Revie[illegible] Year's Work, by the President
App[illegible] of Committees
11.00—Reports [illegible] District Superintendents of Departments
Discussion
12.00—Closing

AFTERNOON SESSION

2.30—Devotions, led by Rev. John Gillis
Minutes
3.00—Report of the District Secretary-Treasurer
Discussion
3.30—"How Did Jesus Teach?" By Rev. W. I. Green
"Teaching of the Sunday School Lesson." By Mr. A. Moffatt
"The Home Department." By Rev. J Stirling
Conference, led by the Field Secretary
Music. Offering
5.00—Closing

EVENING SESSION

7.45—Song Service, led by Mr. Theodore Pickering
8.15—Minutes
Reports of Committees
8.30—Address—"The Sunday School as an Educational Opportenity of the Church." By Rev. H. R. Bell
Music
9.15—Address, by the Field Secretary
Music. Offering
9.45—Closing

A MODERN HEROINE

The Funeral of Miss Baker Took Place at Dundee To-day.

STORY OF HER MISSION WORK AMONG THE SIOUX A THRILLING ONE.

The remains of the late Miss Lucy Margaret Baker, the pioneer lady missionary among the Sioux Indians, who died at the Royal Victoria Hospital on Sunday evening, were conveyed this morning on the 7.25 train from Bona-

THE LATE MISS LUCY BAKER.

venture station to her old home at Dundee, Quebec, where the funeral will take place this afternoon. The body was accompanied on its last journey by Mr. W. A. Baker and Mr. J. R. Baker, brothers of the deceased.

The nature of Miss Baker's life work was recently described in 'Collier's,' in an article on 'The Borderland Woman,' by Miss Agnes C. Laut. Miss Laut said in part:

'One day we went to call at a cottage in Prince Albert, where lived a little lady of the old school—the kind [illegible] lace and black silk—

to the West in the seventies to inaugurate some sort of academy for the frontier. Clergymen came out at the same time on the same errand; but they did not stay. The post was perilous and lonely, six weeks from the nearest town by fastest travel; and one after another—there was a twenty-year procession of them—the white-shirted gentlemen chucked their commissions (got a 'call' elsewhere) and withdrew; but Miss Baker, with blue blood in her veins and high living behind, stayed on. Then, when settlement came, the academy gave place to modern institutions; and the little lady seemed stranded high and dry, like other good things of the old school left behind by the tide of progress; but wait a bit. The borderland woman doesn't strand easily.

Across the river from the new town was a band of 'outcast dogs,' outlaw Sioux, driven from the United States after the massacres with prices of $1,000 reward on their heads and girdles round their waists, made of scalp locks from the murdered down in Minnesota. Canadian tribes would have nothing to do with the outlaws. They were a hunted, hounded, haunted band, living no one knew how, keeping to themselves, suspicious of all comers.

'The Canadian Government would, of course, do nothing for these American Indians; but to the little Christian lady of the old school this didn't seem a very Christian-like policy, and without any prospect of the salary which came from the church afterward, she told Commander Perry, of the Mounted Police, that if he would put up a tent for her over on the Sioux camping ground, she would see, what could be done for the outcasts.'

The Sioux resented any white coming among them. They thought she might be a spy, after that $1,000 reward; and they would not answer when she accosted them for passage across the river. Watching her chance, she followed a young hunter, who had been selling his game in the town, down to his dugout on the river, and when he jumped in to push himself off, she jumped in after him; that was the way she got her first passage across. Later an old dugout was procured, and in this she punted herself back and forth, through all kinds of weather and ice runs.

'How the little lady won the arab outcast youngsters to school, mastered the Sioux xtongue, pouring over the Riggs Missouri Dictionary till four in the morning, forgetting to eat; how she and Miss Cameron, a kindred spirit, who had joined her, with their own hands, taught the outlaws to make doors and windows and sashes for the houses are all stories in themselves.

To-day Miss Baker is worshipped by those Indians, who would have murdered her, and by their children's children. When a salary at last came from the church and the reserve was finally granted the outcasts by the Government, the old chief came to her. 'Miss Baker,' he said with puzzled look, drawing a circle on the new ground with his cane, 'if we build on the new reserve here,' pointing to the rim of the circle, 'will you build here in the centre? Will you stay in the centre if we go into houses?'

DEPARTURE

BY

CAMILLA L. KENYON

O LITTLE house, so plain and bare,
My slow feet linger on your stair
For the last time. I shall no more
Come hither. When I close the door
Upon you now, I shall be through
With all the dear, sad past, and you.

Dear house! And yet, I did not guess
Before there was this tenderness
Hid in a heart that often swelled
With angry yearning, and rebelled
At your low walls, the humble guise
You wore to careless stranger eyes.
I chafed so at the meager ways,
The narrow cares, the fretted days,
The life you were the shell of; yet
Now, for your sake, my cheeks are wet.

Oh, wild dark sea of change and chance!
Oh, varying winds of circumstance!
How kind, how sure, this haven seems,
How dear the past — its hopes, its dreams,
The old, old love, the toil, the care.
Forth to the future now I fare,
Yet still with backward gaze that clings
To the old, worn, familiar things;

With backward gaze that seems to see,
Bidding their still farewell to me,
Dim shapes, whose wistful eyes entreat
Remembrance. Ah, unechoing feet,
Ah, unheard voices, sad and kind,
These too, these too, I leave behind!
Here, with the old dead years, alone
I have you safe — you are mine own.

Farewell; my hand has left the door
That opens to me now no more.

The most interesting item on this late scrapbook page is the folded, typewritten horoscope page, which appears below in miniature. Note the warning about the "2d week in Cancer": Montgomery's wedding day was July 5. The writer, who identifies herself as an Aquarius woman, was probably Maud's cousin Bertie McIntyre, whose sister Laura's wedding was announced inside the Edmonton post-stamped envelope. Bertie's birthday was January 24, whereas the other possible writer of the horoscope, Frede Campbell, was a Pisces, born on February 22. George Boyd MacMillan, a great lover of flowers and postals, may have sent the tulip postcard. Edith Russell's "Two Pictures" suggests a contrastingly bleak image for the colourful postal. "The Valiant," a poem praising mothers, was placed between a clipping (left) about the Cape Traverse school farewell to Frede Campbell (mistakenly referred to as H.E. Campbell in the clipping) and a wedding notice (right) of Frede's and Maud's Stanley Bridge friend, Margaret Ross (Stirling; also spelled incorrectly in the clipping). With Montgomery's financial support, Frede, in 1910, entered the newly created two-year Household Science program at Montreal's Macdonald College. That year would bring huge changes in the lives of soulmates Maud and Frede, changes Montgomery featured in the opening pages of her Ontario scrapbooks.

SAGITTARIUS Nov. 22d to Dec. 21st.

Sagittarius people are the industrious ones of the earth. They work unceasingly and with the greatest zest. They are far seeing and possess quick thought, enterprise, and great perseverance. Sagittarius people are honorable, truthful, and safe guardians of a secret, but are apt to be too blunt of speech and too impetuous. Their ideals are high, and an appeal to their heart is alwya s sure of a response. These people give freely without thought of the morrow. Many great musicians and writers are born under this sign. The women are affectionate, and will deny themselves everything for the benefit of those they love. These people are bright and witty, and misfortunes are powerless to crush them. Sagittarius gives magnetism, talent, and ability. Those under its influence possess great occult power if developed and exercised. Rheumatism is the disease most likely to trouble these subjects. Sagittarius is a fortunate sign. All Sagittarius people are most likely to succeed while under the influence of their own sign. These subjects are warned that the 2d week in Cancer may prove unfortunate to them. (This will account for any rejected M.S.S. that you may have sent away or received from June 28th to July 5th.)

MARRIAGE-- A union will prove happiest with Aries, Aquarius, or Pisces people. (That would be Mar. 21st to Apl. 19th; Jan. 20th to Feb. 19th; Feb. 19th to Mar. 21st. I'm an Aquarius, so that with the above knowledge there would be danger of my proposing to you were I a man.)

GOVERNING PLANET-- Jupiter. (That may account for your admiring him so much. Did you recognize him as your boss when you were regaling me with an account of his beauty?)

ASTRAL COLORS-- Gold and green. (I have observed that people are usually fond of their astral colors. You certainly are. Trees, grass, daffodils, buttercups and goldenrod will bear me out in my assertion.)

BIRTH STONES-- Diamonds and Turquoise.

FLOWER-- Clover.

" I have shaken the dew in the meadows
From the clover's pale-hued gowns."

"And fleet winds steal from clover slopes
The fragrance of the new-mown hay.
. . . .
"And all the golden air is sweet
With incense rose-red clover yields."

I am glad to find you so loyal to the flower that destiny has decreed for you.

I wrote this in the twilight, hence many blunders.

$ $

TWO PICTURES.

(A Fresh Air Sermon by Edith M. Russell.)

Sturdy little bare legs wading in the surf—
"Gee! but ain't this bully! bestest fun on eurf!
Makes me awful hungry. Seems jes like a dream—
Buttermilk an' curd balls, strawberries an' cream!
Say! but won't to-morrer be the biggest day—
Me an' t'other fellers goin' ter help make hay!
Guess I won't git homesick; wusn't that way yet.
Like ter stay here allus—dandy place, you bet!"

Little tear-stained features pressed against the pane—
"Nothin' much a-doin' here is this ole lane.
Wished I wus a kiddie like them ones they say
Has a week o' picnic down there at Cow Bay.
Mother goes out washin', father's worse'n dead;
Much es we kin manage git a loaf er bread.
Wish that nice kind ECHO'd ketch a sight o' me—
Never seen no ocean; never climbed no tree."

Hear the children pleading—list their plaintive cry—
Give them aid refreshing lest they droop and die;
Give them one small pleasure far from city strife.
They are but existing—teach the joy of life.
Will you heed their pleading?—ye who hoard your tin.
Scripture says that rich men scarce' can enter in.
Would you seek the city that is paved with gold?
Practice then the motto: "Nothing I withhold."

$ $

Groeten uit het Bollenland

EDMONTON, ALTA
AUG 18
12 - M
190

Miss L. Maud Mon
Cavendish
P. E. Island

—The following address and presentation was made to Miss H. E. Campbell who is principal in Cape Traverse school. Miss Campbell's ability and popularity is very much in evidence. Miss Stella, her sister, who is in charge of the primary department was also remembered by the scholars in her room. The teachers in turn returned the compliment and the children arrived home to the bosom of their parents beaming with smiles. Cape Traverse has been favored with exceptionally good teachers of late years, and continue to feel that their happiness is complete in regard to school matters. The address was signed on behalf of the school by Annie C. Irving and Olga J. Crosby: "It is with feelings of deep appreciation and gratitude in recognition of your kindness to us since you have become our teacher that we humbly ask you to accept this small token at our hands. We are quite conscious of your untiring devotion to the arduous task you are engaged in and we have fully appreciated your lofty motives in trying to cultivate in each of us the attributes of a higher and grander life. But this small gift at our hands is not a measure of compensation. This debt we shall always owe you. It is only a mere symbol of how we admire your high aims, your moral and genial character, and your amiable and pleasant face. In after years in whatever part of the great field of life we may be called to labor, we shall look back with pleasure to our school days and cherish the remembrance of the happy hours which we spent at school while under your care.

THE VALIANT

Not for the star-crowned heroes, the men that conquer and slay,
But a song for those that bore them, the mothers braver than they!
With never a blare of trumpets, with never a surge of cheers,
They march to the unseen hazard—pale, patient volunteers;
No hate in their hearts to steel them,—with love for a circling shield,
To the mercy of merciless nature their fragile selves they yield.
Now God look down in pity, and temper thy sternest law;
From the field of dread and peril bid Pain his troops withdraw!
Then unto her peace triumphant let each spent victor win,
Tho' life be bruised and trembling,—yet, lit from a flame within
Is the wan sweet smile of conquest, gained without war's alarms,
The woman's smile of victory for the new life safe in her arms.
So not for the star-crowned heroes, the men that conquer and slay,
But a song for those that bore them, the mothers braver than they!

M. A. De WOLFE HOWE.

A very happy event, in which the communities of Stanley Bridge and Cavendish were much interested, was celebrated in the Presbyterian church at the former place yesterday, when Rev. John Sterling and Miss Margaret Ross were united in the Holy bonds of matrimony. The ceremony was a very joyous one and was performed by Rev. Mr. Strathie assisted by Rev. Mr. Sterling, brother of the groom. The bride was attended by her sister Miss Winnifred Ross and was given away by her brother J. Stanley Ross. The groom was supported by Rev. Mr. Miller of Hopewell, N. S. After the ceremony the bride and groom were driven to the station where they took passage for Summerside from whence they will proceed to Montreal, Toronto and other Canadian cities, being absent on their wedding tour for about a month. Mr. and Mrs. Sterling were departed on their journey by the best wishes of the large number of friends gathered to speed them off. One of those present said: "We gave them rice—not by the handful but by the bagful." Mr. Sterling will be much missed by his congregation during his absence, but all join in wishing him a very happy wedded life.

Page 59 from the Red Scrapbook

Dramatically, Montgomery ended the second volume of her scrapbooks with an image of Halley's comet, which she used to emphasize different themes on the same page. At the top half of the page, the comet belongs to timeless romance; at the bottom, it may suggest human frailty. In a larger context, it may be a mature artist's declaration of purpose and power.

Montgomery paired a picture of Halley's comet with Clinton Scollard's poem "The Comet," which describes it as a "torch in the hand of God." These splendidly romantic images are reinforced at the top of the page by "An Epitaph of Egypt," telling of a girl in the time of the pharaohs who was "sweet of heart" and had earned immortality: "The love that left thee with the stars / Still proves thee peerless in the dust."

The bottom part of the page shows Montgomery's wry humour. Halley's comet itself was a disappointment to her. An avid amateur astronomer, she had looked forward to seeing it; on May 23, 1910, she was sorry to find it so faint. A clipping and a wedding notice (in the envelope) tell of the marriage, on July 20, 1910, of Oliver Macneill, the man who had proposed so ardently to Montgomery less than a year before and who had caused her to feel a flicker of the shaming passion that had scorched her painfully with Herman Leard. Perhaps Montgomery used the comet to laugh at the transience of Oliver Macneill's passion and to reflect on her own. Close to these notices Montgomery placed a joke about a little girl who is unable to think of a way to draw marriage and so leaves the page blank. Facing marriage with a man she said she did not love passionately, did Montgomery fear that page herself?

The comet could also suggest steadfastness of purpose. The driving light pursues its own path. Montgomery pasted William Henley's famous poem "Invictus," minus its title, on the page facing this one (not reproduced here), amid invitations and notices. Henley's aggressive images invite a comparison with Montgomery's favourite inspiration piece, the gentle "The Fringed Gentian" (Red Scrapbook, p. 23). Images in Henley's poem also encourage a reading of Montgomery's comet as self-affirmation. The final stanza of his poem seems appropriate:

It matters not how strait the gate,
How charged with punishments the scroll,
I am the master of my fate:
I am the captain of my soul.

Over the years of collecting and arranging the items in the two scrapbooks, Montgomery had become a mature woman and an accomplished artist. With humour, irony, and sheer courage she determined to climb her "alpine path" to enduring fame.

An Epitaph of Egypt

BY ETHEL M. HEWITT

"Within the tomb of a young girl, probably a daughter of Mena, the founder of Memphis, was found the simple inscription that she was 'Sweet of heart.'"

HERE, in this weltering, western world,
The veil of sixty centuries lifts,
And strews a crowded London floor
With trove of Egypt's sandy drifts.
Here, among goblets kings have quaffed,
Love laughs to scorn the goldsmith's art,
Where one small stone in brief attests
Mena's young daughter "Sweet of heart."

Oh, surely, crowned with praise like this,
She found the gods' dread judgment kind;
The Secret Faces at the Gate
Smiled like the ones she left behind.
So long it has been well with thee,
Since love and sorrow sealed thy sleep,
That even Egypt fails to stir
Thy memory in its shrouded sleep.

So long upon thy happy brows
The Overcomers' Crown has pressed,
It cannot hurt that strangers' eyes
Break in upon thy quiet rest.
No space within the Fields of Peace,
Nor any earth-strayed winds recall
How the last lotus on life's brink
Flung the first whiteness on thy pall.

Yet well through all the changeful years
Thy tomb has kept its ancient trust!
The love that left thee with the stars
Still proves thee peerless in the dust;
More splendid than these gems which light
Death's way for kings with quenchless flame,
A chisel steeped in tears has traced
The legend of thy fragrant fame.

THE COMET.

(Clinton Scollard in The New York Sun.)

Fashioned of fire and flame,
Out of the dawn you came;
Now you have taken flight
Into the nether night.
Courier of the dark,
What is the word you bring,
Flashing across the sky's wide arc
In your ceaseless wandering?

Guest of the constant stars,
Aldebaran and Mars,
Worlds of the upper seas,
Orion, the Pleiades,
Have you for them a sign?
Symbol are you of the soul,
Of that inscrutable power divine
That moulded the cosmic whole!

Yesterday—to-day—
And never a sage can say,
Probing with mortal skill
To fathom immortal will!
And still as the ages steal
O'er us, who are kin to the sod,
Through the outer vast you will burn and wheel,
A torch in the hand of God!

Rev. H. R. Stavert, Harcourt, N. B., a native of this province, has returned after a visit to Portland, Boston and other American cities.

AS A SLIGHT diversion the teacher suggested that each child in the class draw a picture from which she could guess what the child wanted to be when grown. All sorts of articles were illustrated: books for bookkeepers, hats for milliners, etc. One little girl, however, had a blank sheet.

"Why, Doris, don't you want to be anything when you are grown?"

"Yessum," said Doris; "I want to be married, but I don't know how to draw it."

Married

Wednesday at the home of Mrs. Frank Campbell occurred the marriage of Mr Oliver McNeill, of Tulare and Miss Mabel Lee of Summerside, Prince Edward Island, Canada. Reverend Harkness officiated.

Miss Lee is the only daughter of R. C. Lee of Summerside. Miss Lee was born in Minneapolis but she has spent the greater part of her life in Summerside where her parents have resided for a number of years.

Mr. McNeill is well and favorably known in Tulare and Spink county. He is a native of Canada but has spent the past twenty-eight years of his life in Spink county. At the present time he is engaged in farming near Tulare where he has large land interests.

The many friends of Mr. McNeill join in wishing him the greatest of happiness in his new life.

Mr. and Mrs. McNeill will be at home to their friends on their farm near Tulare after the first of August

Northville Chapter O. E. S.

Inside back cover from the Red Scrapbook

Afterword

By Dr. Francis W.P. Bolger, CM

L.M. MONTGOMERY had a deep and passionate affection for Prince Edward Island, re-creating it as one of the best characters in *Anne of Green Gables.* The Island's rich colours and contours were parts of all her landscape descriptions and informed her characters' love of beauty and feeling of home. The Island scrapbooks, filled with colourful souvenirs, are themselves a tribute to the P.E.I. life that nurtured her seeing and imagining.

Montgomery's personal life changed dramatically on July 5, 1911, when she married Rev. Ewan Macdonald, who had moved from P.E.I. to a ministry in Leaskdale and Zephyr, Ontario. Never again would she live full time on Prince Edward Island. Instead, she visited it as often as her marriage, motherhood, and writing allowed. She also visited it in her dreams, in her diaries and scrapbooks, and in the stories she created to people it anew.

Montgomery captured something of her feelings about P.E.I. in her passages for *The Spirit of Canada,* a commemorative booklet prepared for the visit of King George VI and Queen Elizabeth in 1939. Montgomery wrote:

Peace! You never know what peace is until you walk on the shores or in the fields or along the winding red roads of Abegweit on a summer twilight when the dew is falling and the old, old stars are peeping out and the sea keeps its nightly tryst with the little land it loves. You find your soul then. You realize that youth is not a vanished thing but something that dwells forever in the heart. And you look around on the dimming landscape of haunted hill and long white-sand beach and murmuring ocean, on homestead lights and old fields tilled by dead and gone generations who loved them . . . even if you are not Abegweit born, you will say . . . "Why . . . I have come home."

Always, Prince Edward Island was L.M. Montgomery's home and her inspiration.

Selected References

Bolger, Francis W.P. *The Years before "Anne."* Charlottetown: Prince Edward Island Heritage Foundation, 1974.

Cavendish Literary Society Minute Book. Prince Edward Island Public Archives, Cavendish Literary Society Fonds (1886–1924), acc. 2412.

Epperly, Elizabeth R. "Approaching the Montgomery Manuscripts." In *Harvesting Thistles: The Textual Garden of L.M. Montgomery,* edited by Mary Henley Rubio, 74–83. Guelph, ON: Canadian Children's Press, 1994.

—. *The Fragrance of Sweet-Grass: L.M. Montgomery's Heroines and the Pursuit of Romance.* Toronto: University of Toronto Press, 1992.

—. *Through Lover's Lane: L.M. Montgomery's Photography and Visual Imagination.* Toronto: University of Toronto Press, 2007.

—. "Visual Drama: Capturing Life in Montgomery's Scrapbooks." In Gammel, *The Intimate Life of L.M. Montgomery,* 189–209.

—. "The Visual Imagination of L.M. Montgomery." In *Making Avonlea: L.M. Montgomery and Popular Culture,* edited by Irene Gammel, 84–98.

Gammel, Irene, ed. *The Intimate Life of L.M. Montgomery.* Toronto: University of Toronto Press, 2005.

—. *Making Avonlea: L.M. Montgomery and Popular Culture.* Toronto: University of Toronto Press, 2002.

—. "'... where has my yellow garter gone?' The Diary of L.M. Montgomery and Nora Lefurgey." In Gammel, *The Intimate Life of L.M. Montgomery,* 19–87.

Kouwenhoven, John A. *Half a Truth Is Better Than None: Some Unsystematic Conjectures about Art, Disorder, and American Experience.* Chicago: University of Chicago Press, 1982.

Kunard, Andrea. "Photography for Ladies: Women and Photography at the Turn of the Twentieth Century." *Picturing a Canadian Life: L.M. Montgomery's Personal Scrapbooks and Book Covers.* lmm.confederationcentre.com/english/collecting/collecting-3-1d.html.

L.M. Montgomery Institute. *The Bend in the Road: An Invitation to the World and Work of L.M. Montgomery.* CD-ROM. Charlottetown: L.M. Montgomery Institute, 2000.

McCabe, Kevin, comp., and Alexandra Heilbron, ed. *The Lucy Maud Montgomery Album.* Toronto: Fitzhenry and Whiteside, 1999.

Montgomery, Lucy Maud. *Anne of Green Gables.* 1908. Toronto: Penguin, 2006.

—. *Jane of Lantern Hill.* 1937. Toronto: McClelland and Stewart, 1989.

—. *My Dear Mr. M: Letters to G.B. MacMillan from L.M. Montgomery.* 1980. Edited by Francis W.P. Bolger and Elizabeth R. Epperly. Toronto: Oxford University Press, 1992.

—. "Prince Edward Island." In *The Spirit of Canada,* 16–19. Foreword by Sir Edward Beatty. n.p.: Canadian Pacific Railway, 1939.

—. *The Selected Journals of L.M. Montgomery.* 5 vols. Edited by Mary Rubio and Elizabeth Waterston. Toronto: Oxford University Press, 1985–2004.

—. *The Story Girl.* 1911. Toronto: McGraw-Hill Ryerson, 1944.

—. Unpublished diary entries, 1891–1929. L.M. Montgomery Papers, University of Guelph Archives.

—. Unpublished letters to G.B. MacMillan. National Archives of Canada.

Picturing a Canadian Life: L.M. Montgomery's Personal Scrapbooks and Book Covers. Virtual Museum of Canada. lmm.confederationcentre.com.

Rubio, Mary Henley, ed. *Harvesting Thistles: The Textual Garden of L.M. Montgomery.* Guelph, ON: Canadian Children's Press, 1994.

West, Nancy Martha. *Kodak and the Lens of Nostalgia.* Charlottesville: University of Virginia Press, 2000.

Acknowledgments

A partnership was formed among the Lucy Maud Montgomery Birthplace Trust; the Heirs of L.M. Montgomery, Inc.; the Confederation Centre Art Gallery and Museum (CCAGM); and the L.M. Montgomery Institute (LMMI) to make this annotated scrapbook possible. The Lucy Maud Montgomery Birthplace Trust is fortunate to have had the Island historian and Montgomery scholar Dr. Francis W.P. Bolger at its helm for more than two decades. The Trust wisely allowed the scrapbook pages to be digitized by the CCAGM in order to mount a Virtual Museum of Canada exhibition, *Picturing a Canadian Life: L.M. Montgomery's Personal Scrapbooks and Book Covers* (lmm.confederationcentre.com) in 2002; this important step also meant that the Trust could henceforth display digital images rather than fragile pages of the scrapbooks. The L.M. Montgomery Institute of the University of Prince Edward Island provided the Montgomery scholarship and research expertise for the Virtual Museum exhibition. Supporting the LMMI, the Virtual Museum, and all legitimate projects dealing with Montgomery and her works are the heirs of L.M. Montgomery – David Macdonald, Trustee, and Ruth Macdonald. Kate Macdonald Butler leads the family committee of the Anne of Green Gables Licensing Authority Board and is ably supported with the legal and literary advice of Marian Dingman Hebb and Sally Keefe Cohen.

As editor and annotator of the scrapbooks, I have had the privilege of working with the partners and also with the generous Island Montgomery relatives, John and Jennie Macneill of Cavendish and George and Maureen Campbell of Park Corner. Elizabeth DeBlois, director of the LMMI, a gifted scrapbooker herself as well as a passionate Montgomery fan, has helped throughout this project. Kevin Rice, registrar of the CCAGM, is always a delight to work with, and Jon Tupper, the CCAGM director, has been staunchly supportive. Simon Lloyd, archivist at the Robertson Library, University of Prince Edward Island, and chair of the LMMI committee, is an enthusiastic and sensitive sleuth. Among the numerous scholars who provided their expertise and findings, I mention most gratefully Irene Gammel, Mary Beth Cavert, Jennifer Litster, and Carolyn Collins. It would be impossible to complete any Montgomery project without relying on Mary Rubio and Elizabeth Waterston, the co-editors of Montgomery's *Selected Journals.* They have been unfailingly generous with all LMMI ventures. Thank you to Linda Amichand, University of Guelph Archives, for helping to solve numerous puzzles. A special thanks is reserved for Donna Jane Campbell, LL.D., research associate with the LMMI and Montgomery collector (and donor) extraordinaire. I am grateful to Budge Wilson, multiple award–winning author and brave creator of the authorized *Anne of Green Gables* prequel *Before Green Gables,* for sharing information about her time boarding at the Halifax Ladies' College. I thank Barbara Leighton of Armbrae Academy (successor of the Halifax Ladies' College) for helpful information, and I thank Richard Goodall for details about Frederick Goodall's portrait of Mrs. Devereux. For early support for a scrapbook project, I thank Jonathan Webb.

Helen Reeves of Penguin Group (Canada) is the editor of every writer's dream. Judy Phillips has been a most patient and helpful copy editor and I am grateful to her for her careful attention. Without Anne-Louise Brookes and her great questions and observations, where would I be? I want to thank my sister, artist Carolyn Epperly, and her daughters, Keely, Ciara, and Caitrin Robinson, for their lifetime love of Montgomery and their dear support of me.